Margaret Atwood's Fairy-Tale Sexual Politics

Margaret Atwood's Fairy-Tale Sexual Politics

Sharon Rose Wilson

University Press of Mississippi *Jackson*

Publication of this book
was made possible in part
with the assistance of the government of Canada.

The paper in this book meets the guidelines for permanence
and durability of the Committee on Production Guidelines
for Book Longevity of the Council on Library Resources.

Distributed in Canada by E C W P R E S S, Toronto

Library of Congress Cataloging-in-Publication Data

Wilson, Sharon Rose.
Margaret Atwood's fairy-tale sexual politics /
by Sharon Rose Wilson.
p.   cm.
Includes bibliographical references (p.) and index.
ISBN 0-87805-639-4 (alk. paper)
1. Atwood, Margaret Eleanor, 1939–   —Political and social
views.   2. Feminism and literature—Canada—History—
20th century.   3. Atwood, Margaret Eleanor, 1939–
—Knowledge—Folklore.   4. Fairy tales—History and
criticism.   5. Folklore in literature.   6. Sex role
in literature.   7. Myth in
literature.   8. Intertextuality.   I. Title.
PR9199.3.A8Z95   1993
818'.5409—dc20   93-30903
CIP
British Library Cataloging-in-Publication data available

Contents

To Roger and Stephen

Abbreviations

AC	*The Animals in That Country*	*LO*	*Lady Oracle*
BE	*Bluebeard's Egg*	*LBM*	*Life Before Man*
BH	*Bodily Harm*	*MD*	*Murder in the Dark*
CE	*Cat's Eye*	*PP*	*Power Politics*
CG	*The Circle Game*	*PU*	*Procedures for Underground*
DG	*Dancing Girls*	*RB*	*The Robber Bride*
DP	*Double Persephone*	*Surf*	*Surfacing*
EW	*The Edible Woman*	*Surv*	*Survival*
FB	*For the Birds*	*SP*	*Selected Poems*
GB	*Good Bones*	*SP II*	*Selected Poems II*
HT	*The Handmaid's Tale*	*SW*	*Second Words*
I	*Interlunar*	*TS*	*True Stories*
JSM	*The Journals of Susanna Moodie*	*THP*	*Two-Headed Poems*
		WT	*Wilderness Tips*
KB	*Kaleidoscopes Baroque*	*YAH*	*You Are Happy*

Introduction

Like Shakespeare, Margaret Atwood reuses the old, great stories, modifying and usually subverting them, hiding their traces in order to reveal contemporary landscapes, characters, and problems. On several occasions, Atwood has admitted that fairy tales, particularly those of the Grimm brothers and Hans Christian Andersen, have influenced her work, including *Power Politics, Surfacing, The Handmaid's Tale*, and her little-known watercolors (Atwood Tape and Telephone Call, December 1985). Several works (*Surv, SW*) make explicit fairy-tale references, and some offer self-reflexive fairy-tale commentary (*BE*). Atwood has also discussed fairy tales as an art form, referred to Bruno Bettelheim's well-known study of them,[1] and humorously compared her early writing self, in a world where "women were supposed to Be, not Do," to "the third son in a fairy tale: dumb but hopeful and, as a consequence, stupidly, but luckily, fearless" ("Where" 9). Even the poems she wrote as a child foreshadow her later interest in the "protean changes in shape" so characteristic of fairy tales. According to Atwood, when she saw *Snow White* for the first time at "some too-early age (5?) . . . . I was [riveted] with fear. The transformation of the evil queen into the witch did me in forever" (J. Rosenberg 2). But echoes of fairy tales or literary folktales constitute more than simple influence or allusion: they function as intertexts or texts within texts (Scholes 145).

Drawing on fairy-tale archetypes in reader's memories and imaginations, in other literature and in history, this book examines what fairy-tale patterns (including fairy-tale images, motifs, themes, and structures) mean within Atwood's texts; how these patterns change throughout Atwood's career (e.g., becoming more recognizably political); and how her handling of these inter-texts varies from Gothic and tragic to tragicomic, comic, satiric, and parodic. In speaking of fairy tales, I am referring to what folklorists call *Märchen* rather than folktales, literary tales, or fakelore even though the Grimms' tales are popularized rather than traditional *Märchen*.

As Chapter 1 details, this study is centered in the fact of gender: Atwood is a *woman* author, and she uses fairy tales dra-matizing cannibalism and dismemberment of *females*. Thus, one of Atwood's major themes is sexual politics; recent feminist theo-ry, both North American and French, is useful in interpreting her texts. A term first used in Kate Millett's germinal work of feminist literary criticism by that title (1970), *sexual politics* refers to the politics of sexual relationships, power structured in patri-archy so that one group—males—controls another—females. Part of what Margaret Atwood calls "power politics," sexual politics is a central concern in women's studies courses. Atwood often parodies the influence of popular culture and our expecta-tions of "plot" in sexual relationship—our simultaneous anticipa-tion of "true romance" and fear of self-amputation. Along with numerous other women artists, including Adrienne Rich, Anne Sexton, and Angela Carter, Atwood "re-visions"—resees or transforms—images that actually or seemingly constrict women and men's roles and lives. Beginning by dancing for others and becoming passively frozen, amputated, and cannibalized, At-wood's personae transform themselves, often through magical eating or touching or through ritual immersion in the natural world. Atwood's archetype,[2] or characteristic pattern, is a move-ment from fairy-tale dismemberment or cannibalism to meta-morphosis and healing.

Furthermore, because Atwood is active in Canadian politics (including its feminist movement and its branches of P.E.N. and Amnesty International), is one of Canada's best-known spokes-persons, and presents Canadian issues even in works without Canadian settings, this study treats Atwood and her work in a

Canadian context. As a literary critic partly responsible for Canadian studies becoming a legitimate academic focus in Canada
and around the world, Atwood is extraordinarily knowledgeable
about Canadian literature and criticism. Her *Survival: A Thematic Guide to Canadian Literature* (1972) is still controversial and
may even have helped precipitate a literary shift away from its
central premise. Nevertheless, in addition to providing useful
teaching and textual information, *Survival* still provides an excellent introduction to Canadian literature and reminds readers,
especially non-Canadians, of Atwood's relationship to other major Canadian authors, including Margaret Laurence, Alice
Munro, and Anne Hébert, and to such characteristically Canadian themes as the "Rapunzel syndrome" (209–10) and the
search for national and personal identity. Other Canadian writers allude to French-Canadian fairy tales and legends, including
loup garou or werewolf stories, or use motifs similar to some of
Atwood's: the colonized or silenced womb, silenced Mother
Goddess, and divided self; shape shifting; the necessity of naming; and the need to find a language oriented in the body and
nature—*l'écriture féminine*. A number of Canadian writers, such
as Nicole Brossard and Lola Lemire Tostevin, also deconstruct
or destructure confining patterns (see Neuman and Kamboureli).
Thus, in addition to other Atwood scholarship and general critical theories, both Anglophone-Canadian and Quebecois critical
theories, especially their feminist formulations, are important to
an understanding of Atwood's texts and influences.[3]

A careful study of Atwood's work must also include reference
to the visual art Atwood often designed as book illustrations or
covers. With the exception of my preliminary articles ("Camera"
29, "Bluebeard's" 385–86, "Sexual" 205–14, "A Note" 111–16),
previous work on Atwood has rarely discussed either her little-
known visual art or its relationship to Atwood's intertexts and to
the major images of her poetry, fiction, and criticism.

The treatment of fairy tales in literature is not only important
for Atwood studies, however: it has significant implications for

feminist theory and literary criticism, and I hope it will stimulate further interdisciplinary study. Too frequently, feminist critics look more at popular "diluted" stories, such as Walt Disney films, than to folktales in their many variants. Thus, they tend to assume that *all* fairy tales necessarily limit gender roles. For example, Mary Daly refers to fairy tales as poison apples and speaks of the "mind-dismembering myth" that, even in contemporary fairy tales, induces masochism in females, sadism in males; mother hating; and paralysis.[4] Psychologists, psychoanalysts, and folklorists sometimes overlook aesthetic and, assuming that the term is now applied to women, humanistic qualities of fairy tales. Viewing folktales primarily as agents of maturation (Bettelheim, Von Franz), psychologists and psychoanalysts may ignore gender or folklore issues. Recently, even folklorists have tended to focus on Wilhelm Grimm's modifications of oral tales, on the tales' sexism and racism, and on the use of folklore as an instrument of socialization (Zipes, *Fairy Tales* 46). As the well-known psychoanalytical folklorist, Alan Dundes, observes, folklorists have sometimes "gone astray" in their research on the Grimms, sometimes merely identifying tale type rather than interpreting tales or exploring their literary use.[5] Many other academics discuss fairy tales exclusively as "children's literature," without interest for serious scholars.

Thus, analysis of Atwood's work is also a re-visioning of fairy tales, again to be appreciated without guilt as sources of inspiration and beauty. Hardly for children only, both oral and written tales dramatize basic human emotions and may be timeless works of art, among the greatest achievements of Western culture. Despite recent debunking of fairy tales' universal meanings (Zipes, *Fairy* 1–3; Bottigheimer, *Grimms' Bad* x, 15); despite oral, written, and cultural variations of folktales—often disproving assumptions of fairy-tale sexism—fairy tales continue to inspire us, either directly or as subtexts in films, television programs, musicals, operas, plays, and books. Recognition of fairy tales' connection to particular cultures need not necessitate disregard of their appeal or of correspondences to mythic, religious, and psychological texts (archetypes). Fairy-tale intertext in Atwood's work reverberates with mythic significance, giving us courage to face themes of sexual politics—in literature, society, and our lives.

Relating Atwood's use of fairy tales to her handling of mythic, biblical, and other popular or elite cultural stories, this book aims to offer a new reading of the Atwood canon and a fresh appreciation of fairy tales.

Chapter 1 introduces the folklore, feminist, and Canadian contexts necessary for understanding how Atwood deconstructs and revises fairy-tale intertexts by creating metafairy tales and other metanarratives. It also offers an overview of identifiable features and techniques in Atwood's intertexts. The first and second sections of this chapter explore how usual folklorist and feminist views of the Grimms' popularized *Märchen* or fairy tales differ from Atwood's and mentions the similarities between fairy tales and myths Atwood discusses in interviews and conversations. Referring to the feminist theories of Julia Kristeva and Hélène Cixous and to patriarchal amputations of the fairy tale and mythology, the second section focuses on the female artist as Medusa witch: Atwood uses metaphors of amputated and cannibalized female bodies to re-member not only her protagonists but also the fairy tales and myths embedded in her work. The third section briefly identifies my own standpoint and, for the benefit of other U.S. scholars, refers to broad differences in U.S. and Canadian literary history. The fourth section is an attempt to situate Atwood in reference to varieties of postmodernism, feminism, and postcolonialism and to illuminate her intertextual techniques, genres, and purposes.

Chapter 2 discusses Atwood's visual art in relationship to themes and images in her literary work, especially her poetry. This chapter explores the fairy-tale sexual politics of Atwood's watercolors, drawings, collages, book cover designs, and comic strips through her treatment of cannibalism, the Grimms' "Fitcher's Bird," and the mythic Triple Goddess.

Focusing on fairy-tale cannibalism and metamorphosis, Chapter 3 explores the Grimms' "The Robber Bridegroom" intertext in *The Edible Woman* (1969). In addition to her role as the Robber Bride,[6] literally consumed in marriage, Marian also plays Fitcher's bride, Sleeping Beauty, Rapunzel, Alice in Wonderland, Goldilocks, the Gingerbread Woman, and Little Red Cap.

Chapter 4, "Decapitation, Cannibalism, and Rebirth in *Surfacing*" (1972), discusses the narrator's psychic amputations in reference to the Grimms' "The Juniper Tree," the French-Canadian tales "The Golden Phoenix" and "The Fountain of Youth," and other embedded stories that emphasize shape changing, transformation, rebirth, new vision, and new power.

Exploring Hans Christian Andersen's "The Red Shoes," the film based on it, and Triple Goddess myth as intertexts, Chapter 5, "Dancing for Others in *Lady Oracle*" (1976), focuses on the double bind Joan Foster and all females face: they can "dance" *or* marry; they cannot do both.

Chapter 6, "Frozen Touch in *You Are Happy*" (1974), focuses on the Grimms' "The Girl Without Hands" and Canada's version of the "Rapunzel Syndrome," in which Rapunzel and the tower are synonymous. *You Are Happy*'s Circe and the volumes' other personae are symbolically handless, frozen in postures or stories, cut off from others, from parts of themselves, from their pasts. Like the girl without hands, however, Circe breaks through Homer's plot into her own story and begins to recover her ability to touch and feel.

Chapter 7, on *Life Before Man* (1979), again about the Grimms' "The Girl Without Hands," also discusses L. Frank Baum's literary fairy tale, *The Wizard of Oz* (1900), and the Victor Fleming film (1939) based on it. In addition, it refers to "The Juniper Tree," "Fitcher's Bird," "The Robber Bridegroom," "Little Red Cap," "Cinderella," "The Snow Queen," and numerous other intertexts from myth, Mother Goose, nursery rhymes, vampire and ghost legends, popular literature, films, music, art, comic books, and radio programs.

Chapter 8 discusses *Bodily Harm* (1981), originally entitled "The Robber Bridegroom" and using this intertext from the Grimms. Again, a character, Rennie, is not only married to death, but western culture and values are similarly consumed from within. To varying degrees this chapter also explores "Fitcher's Bird," "The Girl Without Hands," "Cinderella," *Oedipus Rex*, Pandora myth, fisher king legend, the biblical story of the fall, current critical theories, and spy stories.

Making reference to *Power Politics*, *True Stories*, and other Atwood texts, Chapter 9, "Bluebeard's Forbidden Room in *Interlunar* (1984) and "Bluebeard's Egg" (*BE*, 1983), focuses on the Grimm's "Fitcher's Bird," "The White Snake," "The Robber Bridegroom," and "The Girl Without Hands." In addition, goddess and snake myth, the Bible, visual art, and snake legends are intertexts in the poetry volume and short story. Here I explore the paradigmatic importance of "Fitcher's Bird" throughout Atwood's·work in reference to the female artist's marriage to death and Atwood's gendered landscape of violence, featuring Bluebeards and their victims and images of mutilation and dismemberment, including amputation of hearts and limbs as well as decapitation.

Chapter 10, "Off the Path to Grandma's House in *The Handmaid's Tale*," examines the Grimms' "Little Red Cap," Goddess, and biblical intertexts in the anti-apocalyptic world of *The Handmaid's Tale* (1985). Chapter 11, "*Cat's Eye* Vision," examines Atwood's "eyes and I's," in the novel (1988) and throughout Atwood's work, in reference to the Grimms' "Rapunzel" and Andersen's "The Snow Queen."

Since this study is the first to apply the folklore classification to the tales and motifs Atwood uses, the appendix lists numbers from these standard indexes: Aarne and Thompson's *The Types of the Folktale* and Thompson's *Motif-Index of Folk-Literature*.

I would like to acknowledge my appreciation to Margaret Atwood for her generous cooperation; to Dr. Norman London and the Canadian Embassy for the Canadian Studies Senior Fellowship, Faculty Research Program Grant, and Faculty Enrichment Grant that financed most of my archive research; and to the Association for Canadian Studies in the United States for the subvention to help publish the visual art. Kathryn Van Spanckeren and Judith McCombs read early versions of the manuscript, and I appreciate their comments and suggestions. Thanks to Katharine Martyn, Edna Hajnal, James Ingram, and other staff members of the University of Toronto Libraries, and to the University of Northern Colorado, its graduate school, and interlibrary loan. Special thanks to the members of my family for their patience as well as their support.

Margaret Atwood's Fairy-Tale Sexual Politics

Intertextual Contexts
and Purposes

Fairy Tales and the Medusa Artist

A chronicler of Toronto manners, mores, and marriages, with insights as perceptive as those of Margaret Drabble or Doris Lessing on English or Joan Didion on American culture, Atwood is much more than a comedy-of-manners writer. Rather than the realist she is sometimes called, Atwood is a fabulist. Particularly in the imagery of *Cat's Eye*, her work shares qualities of the magical realism associated with Gabriel Garcìa Marquéz, Salmon Rushdie, and Angela Carter: "Magic realist novels and stories have, typically, a strong narrative drive, in which the recognizably realistic mingles with the unexpected and the inexplicable, and in which elements of dream, fairy story, or mythology combine with the everyday, often in a mosaic or kaleidoscopic pattern of refraction and recurrence. English Magic Realism also has some affinity with the neo-Gothic" (Drabble 606–7). Like these writers as well as Charlotte Brontë, Anne Sexton, Toni Morrison, and the Quebecois writers Anne Hébert and Marie Claire Blais,[1] Margaret Atwood makes extensive references to fairy tales and blends fairy-tale elements into details of everyday events.

But echoes of fairy tales or literary folktales constitute more than simple influence or allusion. Throughout her career, Atwood has used numerous intertexts or texts within texts; frame narratives echo inner narratives' images, motifs, themes, characterization, structures, and even plots, self-consciously reflecting, and reflecting upon, intertexts. Scholars who know that Atwood is influenced by the Grimms' fairy tales (Castro 215, Sandler 14) partly realize the importance of Greek and Roman myth, especially the Demeter-Persephone theme and the quest pattern in Atwood's work (Pratt, "*Surfacing*" 139, Grace Stewart 94–95), and sometimes discuss her references to fairy tales, myth, the Bible, North American native folktales or legends, other literary works, films, television, comics, and even advertisements (Wilson, "Camera" 29), which may all incorporate folktale motifs. But they generally do not recognize that fairy tales are more important than simple allusions, influences, or indictments of gender conditioning (Rigney 9, J. Rosenberg 2); that, in fact, they function as intertexts from Atwood's apprentice poems of the early 1960s through *Good Bones* (1992) and *The Robber Bride* (1993) (Atwood Letter, July 6, 1993). Characteristically, Atwood's narratives interweave one or two fairy-tale intertexts most crucial to the frame texts' meanings with several other minor, usually parodic, ones also selected from popular culture. Sometimes, as in *Interlunar*, parallel fairy-tale, mythic, native, and biblical stories are interlaced.

Building upon Bakhtin's theories, the word *intertext* could refer to the dynamics of any text, an entire canon, or even a collection of essays, such as that by O'Donnell and Davis, about texts and intertextuality. According to O'Donnell and Davis, an intertext is "the continual play of referentiality between and within texts. This means that intertextuality, most directly informed by semiotics and derived from the work of structuralism, defines a text as always in process, continually changing its shape" (ix–x).[2] To some extent my book investigates the intertextuality of particular fairy tales ("Fitcher's Bird"), folklore motifs, and Atwood texts throughout Atwood's work. Rather than referring to any word or discourse, however, *intertext* in this study has the more restricted meaning of a "bounded" text—a published literary work, manuscripts of it, screened films, or recognized versions of the same fairy-tale type or motif—within a frame text. Using postmodern techniques discussed later in this chapter, Atwood often calls attention to or displays her intertexts, providing a self-reflexive context for the "double-voiced discourse" (Bakhtin 324) of what might be called intertextuality's dialogism. "Overtly parodic intertextuality" of fiction that is "at once metafictional *and* historical in its echoes of the texts and contexts of the past" characterizes postmodernism (Hutcheon, "Historiographic" 3).

This chapter discusses folklore, feminist, and Canadian contexts for understanding Atwood's intertexts. Investigating patriarchal amputations of fairy tales and myths and the related conception of the female artist as a Medusa witch, it relates Atwood's work to varieties of postmodernism, postcolonialism, and feminism. The chapter also offers an overview of Atwood's intertextual tactics and briefly suggests the purposes intertexts serve in her work.

The Jacob and Wilhelm Grimm fairy tales Atwood most frequently embeds in her texts include "Fitcher's Bird" (Perrault's "Bluebeard") (AT 311, 312),[3] "The Juniper Tree" (AT 720), "The Robber Bridegroom" (AT 955), "The White Snake" (or "The White Serpent," AT 673), "The Girl Without Hands" (or "Maiden Without Hands," AT 706) and "Little Red Cap" (or "Red Riding Hood," AT 333) (Atwood, Telephone Call 1985). Hans Christian Andersen's literary tales (especially "The Littlest Mermaid," "The Red Shoes," and "The Snow Queen"), French-Canadian tales, native North American legends, Greek myths, biblical stories, and other stories from popular culture (nursery rhymes, comic books, children's literature) also recur. As Atwood says in "The Curse of Eve—Or, What I Learned in School," it is difficult to create a fictional female character when our literary ancestresses include, among mythic, comic-book, nursery-rhyme, biblical, and mainstream literary stereotypes, mermaids with no tongues, Cinderellas with sackcloth and ashes, and Beauties with Beasts (*SW* 219–20). Atwood goes beyond stereotype, however, sometimes "reversing" and re-visioning fairy tales much as she has parodied and transformed myths in *Surfacing* and Gothic romance in *Lady Oracle*. A re-visioned fairy-tale sexual politics underlies Atwood's aesthetics and is evident from her earliest to her most recent work, including her fiction, poetry, essays, and visual art.

Since critics have sometimes missed or misread Atwood's numerous fairy-tale allusions, investigation of these intertexts is long overdue. Generally recognizing only explicit references to popular fairy tales, most Atwood critics assume that fairy tales function as straightforward, negative conditioning that destroys some of her characters (Jensen 29, 48; Rigney 66) and that "the only way to survive is to move beyond the kind of romantic, idealistic notions found in fairy tales" (Petersen, "Fairy Tale" 3). Others argue that Atwood's work refuses the affirmation of a particular tale (Grace, "Courting Bluebeard" 261), or that Atwood either imperialistically appropriates or privileges indigenous tales outside her own cultural group (Godard, "Tales" 57–58, 60; Goldie 102–3). Grace ("Courting Bluebeard" 245–62), Baer (27–32), and Petersen ("Bluebeard's" 131–38) each discuss Perrault's "La Barbe Bleue" or the Grimms' "Fitcher's Bird" in reference to one work, *Lady Oracle*, *Surfacing*, and *Bluebeard's Egg*, respectively; MacLulich discusses "The Gingerbread Boy" and *The Edible Woman* (111–29), Jensen briefly alludes to "The Little Mermaid" and "The Red Shoes" in *Lady Oracle* (30–32), Granofsky discusses fairy-tale morphology in *Surfacing* (51–65), and Rigney makes several provocative but brief general references to fairy tales, often without specifying individual tales (41, 42, 66–67). Barbara Godard, author of the most complete article, focuses primarily on indigenous tales but does not explore how particular tales function in different works ("Tales within Tales" 57–84). In general, Atwood scholars have not recognized that, like the Bible and myth, fairy tales are among Atwood's most significant intertexts.

In exploring Atwood's use of fairy tales, some discussion of folklore contexts is in order. I am following Tatar in referring to the Grimms' *Nursery and Household Tales* as fairy tales (*Märchen*), rather than folktales, literary tales, or fakelore (*Hard* 32–33). The extent to which the Grimms, especially Wilhelm, "doctored" the tales is well known: thus, *Nursery and Household Tales* (*Kinder-und Hausmärchen*, 1812–1857) live an uneasy double life as folklore and literature. The Grimms and Perrault are really popularized rather than traditional *Märchen* (Stone, Review 110), but they should not be considered literary folktales since they are a "far cry" from Andersen's literary ones. Fairy tales, associated with both literary and oral traditions, are "narratives set in a fictional world where preternatural events and supernatural intervention are taken wholly for granted. A fairy tale can thus belong to the category of folktales, but it stands in contrast to the folktale, which is sharply biased in favor of earthy realism" (Tatar, *Hard* 32–33). As the psychoanalytical folklorist, Alan Dundes, observes ("Interpreting 'Little Red'" 193–96 n. 228), the Grimms and Andersen, Atwood's primary sources, are also not "fakelore," "the cardinal sin in folklore" (Dorson, "Folklore and Fakelore" 335–43). Following Bottigheimer, I will usually refer to the Grimms in the plural. Despite the attention given to Wilhelm's "sins," the tales reflect the work of both brothers (*Grimms' Bad* xi).

As I will show, Margaret Atwood's plots, images, themes, motifs, and structures draw very heavily on fairy tales and their mythic and biblical associations. The appendix lists Aarne-Thompson tale types for fairy tales and Thompson classification numbers (*Motif Index*) for folklore motifs most significant to Atwood's work. I pay some attention to tale variants, and many of the motifs I discuss are recognizable in Thompson's index (e.g., Q451.1 hands cut off as punishment, B217.1.1 eating to understand the language of animals). But my focus here is primarily literary motifs (internally recurrent words, phrases, or narrative elements) and images, within Atwood texts and the Atwood canon and, secondarily, the folk motifs in the written versions of fairy tales that constitute Atwood's intertexts. Although Atwood sometimes calls attention to oral tradition and tale variants (*BE*) and appears to know nineteenth-century literary fairy tales, it is the Grimms' tales that usually form her intertexts and have primarily influenced her work.

Contrary to usual views of fairy tales, including those of the Grimms, the fairy tales Atwood interweaves into her own meta-fairy tales and other metanarratives are the "spinnings" of females that recall the Goddess's role as spinner of fate (Walker, *Woman's Encyclopedia* 957). Such tales thus prepare the way for Daly's Websters (Weavers of Words and Word-Webs) and Cixous' "female-sexed texts" ("*écriture féminine*," written by and through the body) (Cranny-Francis xiii, "Laugh" 482). German *Märchen* are "assumed to have originated in or to have passed through . . . the Spinnstube, for it was there that women gathered in the evening and told tales to keep themselves and their company awake as they spun. And it was from informants privy to this oral tradition that Wilhelm and Jacob Grimm gathered many of their folktales" (Bottigheimer, "Tale" 143). Contemporary folklorists complain about Wilhelm Grimm's moralistic alteration of oral versions, suppressing sexual reference and rendering women more powerless (e.g., Zipes, *The Trials* 17–18; Bottigheimer, *Grimms' Bad* xiii, 71); but Atwood prefers the Grimms to Perrault and is concerned with 1950s and 1960s sanitation of the Grimms (Atwood, Telephone Call 1987). Such sanitation, also evident in fairy-tale illustrations of this period, not only further restricts female action but highlights female passivity. As the narrator of *Surfacing* comments (61), because violence is considered "bad" for children and is often removed from children's storybooks or collections, the tales are compromised.[4]

However, Atwood's comments on fairy tales resemble Joseph Campbell's more than those of most contemporary folklorists, particularly folklorists who emphasize tales' historicity, regionalism, or expression of national cultural values more than tales' universality or psychic content. Acknowledging that her use of fairy tales and Gothic stories may seem patterned in a Jungian way, Atwood mentions fairy tales, the Bible, and myth together as influences on her work (Atwood Tape). Literary fairy tales have also been important.

> Myths mean stories, and traditional myths mean traditional stories that have been repeated frequently. The term doesn't pertain to Greek myths alone. *Grimm's Fairy Tales* are just as much myth or story as anything else. But some get repeated so often in the society that they become definitive, i.e. myths of that society. Certainly Biblical ones have been very important in our society (Hammond, Interview 114–15).

Atwood also uses fairy-tale, mythic, and biblical narrative patterns very similarly, sometimes simultaneously (*HT*), in her work. Myth and the Bible do, of course, use folklore motifs (see Aarne and Thompson), and some folklorists and scholars do consider myth to be folklore (Dundes, "Introduction" in Propp xiii) or the foundation of the folktale and other narrative forms (epic, drama, parable, romance, novel) (Liszka 1). Conversely, the folktale is considered the foundation of all literary narrative forms (Thompson, *Folktale* viii).

Northrop Frye, not only a profound influence on Atwood and many other writers and scholars but also Atwood's teacher at the University of Toronto, recognizes that the folktale concentrates mythical meaning; he uses references to fairy and folktales along with those to the Bible, literature, and popular culture to illustrate his theory of myths, including the quest-romance and its dragon-killing theme. For example, among sinister antagonists of the quest—the "victory of fertility over the waste land"—are fairy-tale witches and ogres of parental origin (*Anatomy* 188–203). Atwood, whose own work demonstrates this victory over a contemporary wasteland, read and appreciated the popular Pantheon edition of the Grimms' tales, including Campbell's "Folkloristic Commentary" on them (Atwood, Telephone Call 1987):

"The monstrous, irrational and unnatural" motifs of folk tale and myth are derived from the reservoirs of dream and vision. On the dream level such images represent the total state of the individual dreaming psyche. But clarified of personal distortions and pro-pounded by poets, prophets, and visionaries, they become symbolic of the spiritual norm for Man the Microcosm. They are thus phrases from an image-language, expressive of metaphysical, psychological, and sociological truth. (J. Campbell 861, rpt. in *Flight* 34)

Both Freud and Jung recognized that "fairy tale figures can be seen as representations of instinctual drives," and, if analyzed like a dream, "as the psychic potencies and personal tendencies of the dreamer him- or herself." Because "unconscious processes can be seen in their typical forms" in fairy tales (Jacoby 4, 13, 6), Jungian depth psychologists find them useful in therapy, noting that transference and countertransference "often occur in accor-dance with patterns that are vividly described in fairy tales": "The archetypal motifs of fairy tales abound in the dreams of people who are under the pressure of acute suffering and seek psychotherapeutic treatment. . . . and in the tale we [therapists] often find a surprising suggestion for the solution of the dream-er's problem" (Riedel x, viii).

Thus, although Atwood parodies sexist "truth" and drama-tizes the old, great stories in such "realistic" settings as urban Toronto or London or the insurrection-prone Caribbean, part of the unrecognized appeal of an Atwood text is that the images, characters, and structures are "magical": they have archetypal depth. A woman and mother seems to turn into a bird, an un-named woman makes love with a furred god and understands the language of animals after eating a magic mushroom (*Surf*), a woman wakes from a fairy-tale seven-year "sleep" to discover her "crushed eggshell" face in a mirror (*JSM*, "Looking in a Mirror" 24–25). A narrator lost in the mazes of Harlequin romance and her own psychological and narrative confusion watches her suc-cessive lovers metamorphose into skeletons (*LO*), and a fairy god-mother descends and ascends like Glinda in *The Wizard of Oz* film

(*CE*). Joan Foster (*LO*) and Offred (*HT*) live out the separations of Cinderella, Rapunzel, and Persephone from their mothers and Great Mother; and Offred experiences Red-Cap's timeless betrayal by the wolf. Like the others, Joan and Offred finally experience a fairy-tale transformation of sorts: they tell their own stories and, resembling *Surfacing*'s unnamed narrator, are able to begin again, unlimited in the space at the end of the novels.

On the other hand, however, Atwood's narrative closures reveal a use of fairy-tale intertexts that is paradoxical, deconstructive, or constructionist, rather than straightforward. Some of the psychic pain that Atwood characters, notably Marian MacAlpin (*EW*), Joan Foster (*LO*), Circe (*YAH*), and Offred (*HT*), experience seems to derive from their unquestioning ingestion of old stories or an already written plot line ("The Red Shoes," "The Robber Bridegroom," Homer's *Odyssey*, the biblical Bilhah story) that threatens to limit their life choices. In commenting on female literary myth, Atwood recognizes that myths of a particular society may be sexist:

> We all know what the Bible's attitude toward women is. However, I wasn't brought up a Christian, so I wasn't affected by those beliefs, except insofar as they were held by the general culture. . . . The subject of mythological religions interests me. . . . These forms appeal to me mythologically. . . . Women are interested in female religious figures now simply because we've starved for them, but that doesn't mean that we should desacralize men and that women should be made sacred. (Hammond, Interview 114–16)

Atwood has read more than the few well-known Grimms' tales, and she speaks much more favorably of them than do most contemporary folklorists and feminists:

> The unexpurgated *Grimm's Fairy Tales* contain a number of fairy tales in which women are not only the central characters but win by using their own intelligence. Some people feel fairy tales are bad for women. This is true if the only ones they're referring to are those tarted-up French versions of "Cinderella" and "Bluebeard," in which the

female protagonist gets rescued by her brothers. But in many of them, women rather than men have the magic powers. (Hammond, Interview 115; see also Oates 70–71)

Contrary to most people's views of fairy tales, Atwood says that "if anybody is passive, it's the prince." His mother may cast a spell on him, and the princess, who "has to go through all those interesting machinations to get him back," may even have to rescue him. "She's the one that has the magic powers" (Lyons 224–25).

The folklorist Stone implies that the heroines in popularized *Märchen*, including the tales of the Grimms and Perrault, are less satisfactory than those in "traditional *Märchen*." Still, considering the genre as a whole, she confirms that many *Märchen* heroines "are as resourceful and assertive as are their contemporary manifestations" (the characters in Zipes's "feminist fairy tales") (Review of *Don't* 110). Although the traditional tales are retold, edited, and somewhat censored, the recently published *Tatterhood* stories, including "Tatterhood" from Norway and "Kate Crackernuts" from the Orkney Islands, offer examples of "active and courageous girls and women in the leading roles" (Phelps xv, xvii). Of the forty heroines in the complete edition of the Grimms' tales, not all of them are passive and pretty; nor are the villains always women. Stone and Zipes both refer to the rediscovery of matriarchal and female-heroic features in folk and fairy tales, and Zipes sees these features even in the Grimms' "Cinderella" ("Things" 43, 45–46; *Don't* 6–7, 13; see also Graves, *Greek I* 94, and Walker, *Woman's Encyclopedia* 168). Folklorists point out, of course, that the Grimms' tales are hardly unexpurgated. They are often so busy detailing the Grimms' ideology and protecting against possible uncritical praise (Zipes, *Brothers* 110; *Don't* xi), however, that they underestimate not only the tales' profound meanings to writers and readers but also fairy tales' potential illuminations of postmodern, postcolonial, and feminist theories. All products of culture are, of course, ideological, including the commentary on the Grimms, Atwood's texts, and this study. Current scholarship on the Grimms suggests overkill, however.

Virtually all the recent folklore books about the Grimms detail their methodological and sexist crimes (Zipes, Bottigheimer, Tatar, and Ellis). Similarly, narrowly focused feminist studies on fairy-tale encoding of acculturation[5] continue to appear and are still quoted and reprinted (Zipes, *Don't* 4–11, 185–228, 258) twenty years after Lieberman's important 1972 article ("Some Day" 185–200). Andrea Dworkin's much-cited book, *Woman Hating*, is perhaps partly to blame for stereotypical oversimplifications of fairy tales. The mothers and stepmothers of "Snow White," "Cinderella," "Hansel and Gretel," and "Rapunzel"

> define for us the female character and delineate its existential possibilities. When she is good, she is soon dead. In fact, when she is good, she is so passive in life that death must be only more of the same. Here we discover the cardinal principle of sexist ontology— the only good woman is a dead woman. When she is bad she lives, or when she lives she is bad. She has one real function, motherhood. In that function, because it is active, she is characterized by overwhelming malice, devouring greed, uncontainable avarice. . . . she is the wicked witch. (41)

Without looking beyond the powerful godmothers of "Cinderella" and "Sleeping Beauty," or the third sister of "Fitcher's Bird" (all remnants of the Triple Goddess), we find exceptions, good women who are not passive. We may see the Grimms' Red-Cap as a passive "image of male desire," an object in the wolf's "gaze" and in "inscribed and prescribed male discourse." We may feel the tale is a male fantasy. As Zipes suggests, however, Red-Cap herself should not be blamed: "As long as we are encouraged to point our finger at Little Red Riding Hood as willing conspirator in her own downfall . . . , our minds and bodies will be prevented from grasping the fundamental issues of sexuality at stake in the story and in our lives" (*Don't*, 259).

Why is it still necessary to ram the stake through the heart of the Grimms' fairy tales? As Dundes begins to question in pleading for psychoanalytic approaches, now that the Grimm tales are classified and their sources and erroneous methods known (e.g., Ellis 77–79), why aren't folklorists more interested in interpreting fairy tales ("Psychoanalytic" 116–18, 120–21), such as comparing patriarchal and matriarchal tales[6] or, as Manley queries, examining the broader field of folklore's relationship to literature (unpublished article), its "rival sibling" (B. Rosenberg xi, 7, 24, 272)? Why do feminists, especially those outside the discipline of folklore, use the same examples (e.g., "Cinderella," "Snow White") again and again, sometimes with the implication that fairy tales should be forbidden reading,[7] at least for girls and women?

By and large, women's studies no longer stops with initial methods of examining male texts and gender roles in literature for sexism. With the help of Rhys's *Wide Sargasso Sea* and Gilbert and Gubar's *The Madwoman in the Attic*, we now listen for Bertha's story in the gaps of *Jane Eyre*. But we continue to read fairy tales through a phallocentric lens, blaming the apparently passive females for their passivity and seeing the wicked stepmothers or stepsisters as the incarnation of evil. What would happen if, instead of continuing to view fairy-tale females as objects, we restored their lost subjectivity and listened to the stepmother's version of "Snow White" or heard the voice of Sleeping Beauty's dreams? What does it feel like to be caught in a "fairy tale" where one's fate depends on a "prince" not only falling but staying in love with you? Fiction writers such as Charlotte Perkins Gilman ("The Yellow Wallpaper"), Doris Lessing ("To Room Nineteen"), and more directly Gail Godwin ("A Sorrowful Woman"), Angela Carter (*The Bloody Chamber*), and Margaret Atwood do examine these questions. But with few exceptions (Barzilai 260–72), feminist theorists and critics still fail to apply skills of reading muted subtexts or "absences" to fairy tales. As Barzilai implies (259), even Gilbert and Gubar's revisionist reading of "Snow White" (*The Madwoman in the Attic*

36–44) privileges the absent king's voice in examining female relationships. As the next section indicates, commentators also fail to examine classic fairy tales and fairy-tale subtexts for the displaced female power—Medusa power—that is restored in Atwood's and other re-visioned fairy tales. As subsequent chapters show, Atwood develops the theme of the sexual politics of art through re-visioned fairy-tale, mythic, and related intertexts about the female artist's marriage to death and her need to recover the "godmother" or goddess in herself.[8]

Like Charlotte Brontë, Virginia Woolf, Doris Lessing, Sylvia Plath, Remedios Varo, and Frida Kahlo, Atwood usurps patriarchal power by being a woman and an artist at the same time. Despite considerable acclaim and numerous awards including the prestigious Governor General and Trilium prizes, Atwood was recently labeled "Our Lady of Control and Bondage" (Symons 36, Conlogue C1). Often confused with her narrators, she has been accused of seeing people through microscopes and using her exotic "woman's temperament" to spy on the "real world" (Cameron 42–43, Columbo 38), presumably from the Rapunzel tower she describes in *Survival*. In the seventies Atwood addressed and categorized prejudices women writers encounter because they are women ("On Being a Woman Writer," *SW* 195–202). Recently, Atwood again admitted, "over the years I've been on the receiving end of every sexist bias in the book," including being called "Witch, man-hater, man-freezing Medusa, man-devouring monster. The Ice Goddess, the Snow Queen" ("If You Can't Say Something Nice" 20).

Atwood's characters and personae, who tend to be frustrated artists (see McCombs, "Fictive" 69–88 on fiction), are perceived similarly. Indeed, if Atwood, her characters, and some of her readers existed within a fairy tale, this kind of audience would illustrate a folk motif or fear of what it describes: D529.1, petrification when a woman's voice is heard. Because her characters' stories (e.g., *You Are Happy, Surfacing, Lady Oracle*), like other postmodern literature, are open and without closure, most scholars see the Atwood artist as a failure trapped by art (e.g., Grace, *Violent* 73, 77–78). From *Double Persephone*'s Gorgon in the garden (1961), *The Animals in That Country*'s Lady Frankenstein ("Speeches for Dr. Frankenstein" 1968), *You Are Happy*'s Circe (1974), and *Lady Oracle*'s Joan (1976), to *Interlunar*'s Eurydice and Robber Bride (1984) and *Cat's Eye*'s Snow Queen (1988), Atwood's artists embody the female artist's "double" or "triple bind" (Juhasz 1; Trinh 6; Atwood, "If You Can't Say Something Nice" 18).

Like Julia Kristeva and Monique Wittig's personae, Atwood's artists speak the forbidden unspeakable through amputated, crucified (Kristeva, "Stabat Mater" 197), "Dracularized" ("If You Can't Say Something Nice" 19), or cannibalized female bodies. By facing societal either-or's and refusing to "marry death"— being a wife rather than an artist, choosing art and dying like Plath and Sexton, or being the male poet's fickle muse (Graves's White Goddess) rather than an artist (Atwood, "If You Can't Say Something Nice" 17; Graves, *White* 9–10)—Atwood's female artist becomes a black Hecate speaking for all women. She is simultaneously the unnurturing witch, the devouring mother, and the female transformer Medusa, whose vision and touch turn flesh into stone or, in her guise as the Snow Queen, to ice. Fear of the female artist's necessarily Gorgon touch and vision (Davey, "Atwood's" 149) reveals more than sexist jealousy. As Chapter 2 demonstrates, not even Atwood's Persephone is, *in herself*, a Medusa monster (*DP*).

Marie-Louise Von Franz's insight into the origins of the witch image also clarifies why women artists are so frequently viewed —and view or create themselves (Grace Stewart 109, 178)—as monsters. Fear of the witch exists not just in fairy tales, "which, in the main, are under the influence of Christian civilization," but in our psyches, and, significantly, in history:

> In fairy tales . . . the archetype of the Great Mother, like all others, is split into two aspects. The Virgin Mary, for example, is cut off

from her shadow side and represents only the light side of the mother image; consequently, as Jung points out, the moment when the figure of the Virgin Mary became more important was also the time of the witch persecutions. Since the symbol of the Great Mother was too one-sided, the dark side got projected onto women, which gave rise to the persecution of witches; since the shadow of the Great Mother was not contained in any officially worshipped symbol of the Goddess, the figure of the mother became split into the positive mother and the destructive witch. In fairy tales innumerable witches and even the Great Mother appear. (*Shadow and Evil* 105)

As Atwood is aware, the Medusa, like Persephone once part of the Triple Goddess, is a monster only in patriarchal "amputations" of the myth, or when, like Hecate, she "is seen as the only alternative, as the whole range of possibilities for being female" (*Surv* 199). According to the Argives, Medusa was a beautiful Libyan queen later identified with the Libyan snake-goddess Lamia, a shape-shifting snake with a woman's head akin to the succubus and the vampire (supposed to devour her lover, Motif G262.0.1.1; similar to North American native devouring and toothed vagina legends, F547.1) (Leach and Fried 601, 1152). Medusa was beheaded after battle by the ancestral hero Perseus, who brought her head (possibly her ceremonial mask) back to Athens. In the patriarchal myth, Perseus is sent to cut off the head of the snake-haired Gorgon Medusa, who rivals the Goddess Athene and whose glance or ugly appearance turns men to stone. Perseus' success is guaranteed by several gifts: the three "Grey Ones" (Three Fates or Moirae) give him winged sandals, a magic wallet or bag, and a helmet of invisibility; Hermes gives him a moon-shaped sickle, and Athene a mirror. In Graves's iconographic interpretation, the Perseus story details the poet's relationship with the muse: Hermes attains poetic sight and the Palamedes invent the pre-Cadmean alphabet through the Triple Goddess's inspiration and protection. Paradoxically, this sexist story also describes the breaking of the Triple Goddess's power by the first wave of the Archaens, figured as Perseus, "the destroyer" (*White* 229–31; *Greek Myths I* 238–45).

As the serpent-goddess of the Libyan Amazons, Medusa is part of the Great Goddess, and she represents female wisdom and art. The female face surrounded by serpent hair symbolizes not only this wisdom, but the "wise blood" presumed to give women their divine powers. She is the past, present, and future; mother of all the gods; women's creative and destructive magic moon blood (menstrual blood); the Destroyer aspect of the Triple Goddess (Neith in Egypt, Athene in North Africa); and death. Medusa was veiled since the future is always "veiled": to see death's face was to die, to be turned to stone as a funerary statue; and the look of a menstruating woman was similarly taboo. The Perseus story was invented to account for Medusa's face on Athene's shield (Walker, *Woman's Encyclopedia* 629), thereby disguising the unity of Medusa, Athene, and Perseus' mother Danae in the Triple Goddess. The Perseus story thus literally appropriates womb power: it masks the secrets of menstruation, birth, and death; creates an adversarial relationship between female divinities; steals female wisdom; and fabricates male heroism out of female murder.

The Perseus legacy pervades Western culture. According to Annis Pratt, Medusa is threatening because she violates a worldview in which the triumph of male over female, civilization (culture) over nature, reason over emotions, and mind over body is assumed. In Jungian theory, the Terrible Mother is an obstacle "to be confronted, absorbed, and transcended in the process of 'individuation.'" In Northrop Frye's literary theory of the rebirth pattern, the hero begins in a "culturally determined 'green world,'" combats natural and often female monsters, and moves toward "a denouement in which society reaffirms its norms" (Pratt, "Medusa," 2, 4).[9] Once we see Medusa's real face, however, we again question these norms. By rupturing patriarchal structures, Medusa is anarchistic.

In phallocentric culture, all female artists, perhaps all females, *are* Medusas. When women laugh or refuse to reflect men at twice their size (Woolf, *Room* 60), women's art and vision freeze the colonizing other. Seeing and saying the forbidden, women artists and the body of the female text have been symbolically and sometimes literally castrated or decapitated to silence them (Cixous, "Castration" 486).

If the woman writer's position sometimes seems tragic in Atwood (Rigney 80–81) or other women's texts, part of the reason may be that we have all been conditioned to fear and suppress the Medusa self. Louise Bogan, Sylvia Plath, and May Sarton all write Medusa poems, but Bogan's Medusa traditionally freezes life, transforming it into "a dead scene forever" ("Medusa" 1611), and Plath's persona rejects her Medusa self as alien ("Medusa" 2210). Like Atwood, however, Sarton looks Medusa in the face. Sarton's "I" receives a healing gift: "I turn your face around! It is my face. / That frozen rage is what I must explore—/ Oh secret, self-enclosed, and ravaged place! / This is the gift I thank Medusa for" ("The Muse as Medusa" 1777). An Atwood artist-persona may create and deny a monster self-reflection ("Speeches for Dr. Frankenstein, *AC* 45). She may believe her role and life plot are dictated for her, already finished by the old stories (myth, fairy tales, the canon) or by male or societal storytellers ("Circe / Mud Poems"). But, like her Circe, most of Atwood's female characters do confront the albatross images hanging like withered hands around their necks ("Circe / Mud Poems").

Internal and external societal strictures against uncontrolled female creativity constitute gender thorns and walls confining the female artist to a fairy-tale tower. Women artists sometimes suffer from the internalized assumption that a woman cannot be both artist and woman (or artist, woman, and a particular nationality, ethnic group, race, or class). Similarly, they may have to overcome formalist expectations (predominant when Atwood began writing) that the artist must be a kind of Rapunzel: separate and distant from the work—necessarily a closed entity—from audience, and from life, society, history, and the world.[10] Rather than the female artist, it is formalism, "that great block of aesthetic ice" once preserved by English department "refrigeration apparatuses," that rigidly insists on "Literature beautifully preserved in a crystal cube, touching no one and nothing" (Katz-Stoker 315).

Current knowledge of feminist and deconstructionist revisionings of text, "story," and closure help us understand and appreciate Atwood and other female artists' achievements. Like Woolf, Rich, Brossard, Cixous, and Kristeva, Atwood reinvents form; her text is usually a metanarrative of the female artist's transformation from patriarchal Medusa monster in Rapunzel tower to woman artist courageous enough to draw on Medusa wisdom and her own artistic vision and "touch."

Like Anne Sexton in *Transformations*, Atwood explodes the phallocentrism of the popularized "Cinderella" story (AT 510A) in all her novels, enabling us to see its sinister mirroring in The Grimms' "The Girl Without Hands" (Chapter 6). Targeting especially Perrault and Disney versions[11] and Frye's "Cinderella archetype" (*Anatomy* 44), Atwood also deconstructs most current readings of the fairy tale. Contrary to what many feminists believe, folklore actually preserves information about the Great Goddess (Gimbutas, *Civilization* 226). "Cinderella" and many other fairy tales (e.g., "The Sleeping Beauty" or "Briar Rose") (Von Franz, *The Feminine* 20) are Goddess stories: the real mother of Ella (Hel or Helle) was the earth. The "fairy godmother" of later versions of "Cinderella" (Motif F311.1) represents "the dispossessed Great Goddess in retirement underground" and is still associated with the tree of life (Walker, *Woman's Encyclopedia* 168; Von Franz, *Interpretation* 9–10).[12] In Sexton's "Cinderella":

> Cinderella and the prince
> lived, they say, happily ever after,
> like two dolls in a museum case
> never bothered by diapers or dust,
> never arguing over the timing of an egg,
> never telling the same story twice,

never getting a middle-aged spread,
their darling smiles pasted on for eternity.
Regular Bobbsey Twins.
That story. (56–57)

Atwood, however, goes beyond Sexton's sarcastic pessimism to
re-member the fairy tale and the Triple Goddess myth behind it.
Atwood's characters, like many of the Grimms', will fail to live
"happily ever after." Like Doris Lessing and Marge Piercy's
works, Atwood's feminist, poststructuralist texts "break through"
phallocentric plots to "re-vision" the stasis of "happily ever after,"[13] a resolution not nearly as common in folklore as usually
believed. The Grimms' version of "Cinderella" (No. 21) actually
ends with the punishment of the "false brides," whose eyes are
pecked out at the wedding (Hunt and Stern 127; Zipes, trans.,
Complete 92). Even Perrault's better-known variant, with two
tacked-on morals mentioning Cinderella's graciousness but stress-
ing her indebtedness to a godmother, says nothing about everlasting happiness (Zipes, Beauties 29–30).

Recognizing how fairy tales, especially Perrault's and Andersen's overtly moral ones, reflect societal conditioning and historic patriarchal sexism, Atwood deconstructs phallocentric versions of fairy tales and similarly confining myths, in Lady Oracle
finally freeing even "The Red Shoes"' Karen and in You Are
Happy, Homer's Circe from written life scripts. Each of Atwood's
novels is a variety of the female Bildungsroman or Künstlerroman;
and the poems, prose pieces, and stories in other volumes are
arranged in a narrative progression. For example, we and the
personae of You Are Happy's other sections may learn from the
"Songs of the Transformed": the man who shut himself in
the "cask skin" of a bull, the corpse who advises us to "sing now/
while you have the choice" ("Bull Song" 31, "Corpse Song" 43).
In fairy tales, myth, and Atwood texts, transformation is not
always positive; generally at the end of an Atwood text, transformation has just begun.

Still, with few exceptions even in her poetry and short stories, Atwood's images of negative transformation are stages in a structural movement toward positive transformation. This positive transformation means that Atwood's women characters, frequently silenced artists like the unnamed narrator of *Surfacing*, face their monster selves and paradoxical societal strictures against female creativity, eventually seeing the hidden face of Medusa. Atwood's characters re-member the fairy-tale amputated bodies associated with the Grimms' "Fitcher's Bird," "The Robber Bridegroom," and "The Juniper Tree." They also regain amputated senses: speech (*BH*'s "The Robber Bridegroom"), touch (*LBM*'s "The Girl Without Hands"), vision (*HT*'s "Little Red Cap," *Surf*'s "The Golden Phoenix"), smell, taste ("Little Red Cap"), and hearing (*Surf* and *I*'s "The White Snake," "The Magic Snake"; "Little Red Cap"). Atwood's characters recover lost female power: not only their personal power—typically leaking away like electricity at the text's beginning (Elizabeth in *LBM*)—but power associated with the Great Goddess lingering in fairy-tale and Atwood godmothers ("Cinderella" and the tree-of-life goddess in "The Juniper Tree," as well as *LO*'s Aunt Lou).

I am not suggesting that comic characters like Marian, who worries about girdle advertisements near the beginning of *The Edible Woman*, suddenly turn into aspects of the Great Goddess and ritualistically sacrifice their male consorts at the novel's "end." Rather, Atwood's fairy-tale intertexts, like her mythic and biblical ones, often include either displaced or divided goddess figures (the third sister of "Fitcher's Bird"; Diana, Venus, and Hecate divisions of Little Red Cap, her mother, and grandmother). Thus, Atwood's metanarratives and metafairy tales resonate with goddess images (*Surf*'s mother, *CE*'s Mary), even when these images are parodied (*Lady Oracle*'s artist shadowed by secret fat lady and pulp writer identities). Of course, as Atwood says, "That doesn't mean that we should desacralize men and that women should be made sacred" (Hammond 114–16). What this resonation does suggest is that Atwood's texts mean more to us than we may be able to explain because they tell the untold and muted female subtexts of the old, great stories, now our stories. Atwood's texts also implicitly rejoin aspects of the Great Goddess and our split selves, helping us recover ourselves as Hecate Crone, artist, and Medusa.

As a U.S. scholar writing about a Canadian, I approach the subject of Canadian contexts with understandable hesitation. Any U.S. study of Canadian arts may be or seem imperialistic cultural appropriation. Obviously no U.S. reader can read as a Canadian, and no two Canadians read the same way. Still, U.S. scholars not only can but must read Canadian literature and conduct research in Canada. Thus, as an "other" who often finds the writing of Canadians, especially Canadian females, less "other" than that of many U.S. males, I have a few remarks.

Non-Canadian readers of Atwood need to address a number of aspects in which the cultural context of Canada differs from that of the United States. As recently as 1968 in the United States, the revised edition of the widely used *Norton Anthology of English Literature* represented nearly a hundred writers in 1,981 pages; although this second volume includes writers from the romantic period through the twentieth century, only six of them are women, and two of the writers, Ann Radcliffe and Elizabeth Jennings, are represented on less than a page. Volume 2 (*Since the Renaissance*, 1,859 pages) of the U.S.-published *World Masterpieces* (3d ed., 1973, ed. Mack, et al.), contains no women writers! In Canada, unlike the United States, women writers including Susanna Moodie, Anna Jameson, and Catharine Parr Traill have been considered part of literary history for much longer than Canadians have considered their own writing to be literature. Saying this, of course, does not deny that women writers in Canada as in the United States have been, and continue to be, viewed through a patriarchal lens.

Atwood is one of many feminist revisionaries who deconstruct patriarchal patterns and force readers to reread and reshape not only Canadian literature (*JSM*, *Surv*) but also history. Ironically, some distinct features of a rapidly changing Canadian literary scene not only affect Atwood readers and readers of Atwood in a Canadian context, but paradoxically suggest that Atwood is part of a variously described decadent establishment. For example, some Canadians, suffering from Canada's famous identity "amnesia" and reacting against U.S. cultural colonization (Atwood, "Canadian-American" 30, 24), resent the international attention Atwood attracts, especially in the United States, and even suggest that she, along with George Bowering and other Canadian writers known outside of Canada, has "sold out" her country (Mathews). In British Columbia, Atwood, like Northrop Frye, may be seen as "Ontario-centric." Even among feminists, Atwood is sometimes considered a major component of the white, anglophone establishment providing "both frame and ground against which women's writing in Canada is configured" (Neuman and Kamboureli ix–x). In Atwood's own parodic exaggeration, people who accuse her of "Thoughtcrime" (not toeing "some stylistic or ideological line or other") "probably think of [her] as the Goodyear Blimp, floating around up there in an overinflated and irrelevant way—just the Establishment, you know, like, who cares?" ("If You Can't Say Something Nice" 24).

However, culturally myopic U.S. readers with "Mr. Magoo eyes" (Atwood "Canadian-American" 26) are likely to overlook the fact that Canadian literature has its own frame and ground. Despite burgeoning Canadian studies programs (Metcalfe 203–4), many U.S. admirers of Atwood's novels, especially the best-selling *The Handmaid's Tale*, do not know that Atwood is Canadian or that she is also a poet and critic. Many U.S. readers would have difficulty naming even five other Canadian writers. Because Atwood often speaks about contrasts between Canada and the United States (*Surv*, "Canadian-American"), is active in both Amnesty and P.E.N. International, travels internationally, and is well versed in Canadian, U.S., and international literature, U.S. and Canadian readers who overlook her "difference" or *differance* are likely to misinterpret her work.

A U.S. audience may also find ignorance of Canadian literary theory problematic. Unlike some French and U.S. critics, who still center language and literature discussions in women's marginalization, the introduction to an excellent recent Canadian feminist anthology is concerned to address a many-voiced literature and extend consideration beyond Atwood and Margaret Laurence. Wishing to address prejudices against Quebecois, "native, colored, and immigrant writers" and against genres other than fiction and poetry, Neuman and Kamboureli do not even mention female marginalization in addressing Canadian literary history's "binary model of center and margin" (x). Other Canadian or Quebecois feminists, including Lorna Irvine, have primarily addressed this marginality; but while many of these critics are aware of well-known U.S. feminists and offer valuable insights,[14] few U.S. readers are aware of important Canadian criticism (See McCombs, *Critical* for reprints and her and Palmer's *Margaret Atwood* for annotated bibliography).

Through the efforts of the International Council for Canadian Studies, the Association for Canadian Studies in the U.S., the German Association of New Literatures in English, the Canadian Embassy Academic Affairs Office, and the Margaret Atwood and Margaret Laurence Societies, a growing number of U.S. and European scholars do research in Canada, including the University of Toronto Margaret Atwood Papers. Still, few English and women's studies teachers in the United States are aware of the Margaret Atwood who can be glimpsed only in the landscape of Canadian culture. Consequently, Atwood has often been taught in a cultural vacuum in the United States (See Wilson, Friedman, and Hengen).

In order to understand Atwood's use of fairy-tale intertext, brief examination of her texts' relationship to twentieth-century literary movements and other literature, the genres and tactics or techniques Atwood uses to embed intertexts, and the purposes intertextuality serves in her work is useful.

Like Salmon Rushdie and Gabriel García Marquez, Atwood, too long considered modernist, is now simultaneously claimed as postmodern and postcolonial (Griffiths 155). Other critics simply refer to Atwood's fiction as feminist (Greene, *Changing* 1; Cranny-Francis 141–42). The genres and techniques Atwood uses (metafiction, anti-fiction, self-conscious narration, intertextuality, magical realism, parody, irony, deconstruction of national and cultural myths) have more frequently been identified with the older and better known discourse of postmodernism (Wilson, "Deconstructing" 54–55; Hutcheon, *The Canadian* 1–25, 138–57, "Circling" 168–69). As Linda Hutcheon suggests, it can be argued that postmodernism is "politically ambivalent," meaning that "its critique coexists with an equally real and equally powerful complicity with the cultural dominants within which it inescapably exists." But even postcolonialism "continues to operate within the power field of [the] dominant culture, no matter how radical its revalorization of its indigenous culture" ("Circling" 168, 176, 170). As Bakhtin says, language is "ideologically saturated" (271).

Thus, given Canada's history of precolonial as well as neocolonial imperialism ("Circling" 167, 170, 176), the same questions can be raised about Atwood's works as about any of Canada's white, as distinct from Native, writers. Because of Atwood's valorization as an established international writer, newer, more marginalized, dissident, or insecure writers may unfairly choose to see her as neocolonial rather than postmodern or postcolonial. Postmodernism and postcolonialism overlap, experiencing what Hutcheon calls a "problematic site of interaction" in their concern with history and marginalization and their use of self-reflexivity, of allegory, and, especially, of irony as a "doubled or split discourse which has the potential to subvert from within" ("Circling" 168–70).

Similarly, feminism or feminisms overlap with both post-modernism and postcolonialism. Although useful for many writers, using Greene's definition of feminist fiction is also problematic, particularly in reference to the third world, if it appears to privilege feminism, pit it against other revolutionary movements, or reduce it to a literary technique: "whatever a writer's relationship to the women's movement, we may term a novel 'feminist' for its analysis of gender as socially constructed and its sense that what has been constructed may be reconstructed—for its understanding that change is possible and that narrative can play a part in it. Feminist fiction is the most revolutionary movement in contemporary fiction" (Greene, *Changing* 2). All varieties of feminism share with postcolonialism not only a dismantling of the dominant culture (in the case of the postcolonialist, from within this culture) but also "constructive political enterprise insofar as it implies a theory of agency and social change" (Hutcheon, "Circling" 169–72). Unfortunately, U.S. feminists are only beginning to investigate postcolonialism; not all feminists are postcolonialists, and not all postcolonialists are feminists. Since, in Hutcheon's definition, postmodern deconstruction lacks feminisms' constructive impulse ("Circling" 169–72, 183), feminisms do resist incorporation into postmodernism because of "their revolutionary force as political movements working for real social change" (*The Politics* 168). The term *postmodern* is generally associated with male writers; and feminists also find problematic assumptions intrinsic in some definitions of postmodernism, including the separation of reason and the body, supremacy of the West, and relativism (Greene, *Changing* 1; L. Nicholson 4–12).

Nevertheless, Atwood is a feminist writer who deconstructs phallocentric narratives, including modernist, colonialist, and other traditional patterns. Thus, although the debate over the meanings of the terms *modernist, postmodernist, postcolonialist,* and *feminist* and how they can be distinguished from one another is far from over, I am adopting the controversial positions here that, first, as the many, sometimes contradictory ways the term *post-*

modernist is used indicate, there is more than one postmodernist ideology and, by extension, more than one postcolonialism (including at least the sometimes "infected" postcolonial discourses of feminist, nonfeminist, third-world, ethnic, dominant, and mixed groups). Second, despite patterns rooted in the body (l'écriture féminine) and more common in the texts of a particular gender, neither phallocentric nor gynocentric criticism has convincingly demonstrated either gender's exclusive ownership of particular techniques and genres. Thus, consistent with unconscious intertextuality and marginal writers' adaptation or reconstruction of techniques and genres for their own purposes, I am assuming that technique and genre to some extent cross gender lines. Although feminists may create their own kind of postmodernism or Bildungsroman, inventing new terms obscures critique of "the canon."

Third, assuming that postcolonial discourse includes the techniques postmodernism illuminates, I see Atwood as what might be called a feminist postcolonialist (or a postcolonialist feminist). In other words, in incorporating fairy-tale and other intertexts into her metanarratives, Atwood synthesizes the often similar techniques identified with feminist, postmodernist *and* postcolonialist theory into a revisionist form. She prefers not to call this form an ideology, particularly to the extent that the term suggests an easily distinguishable "message" as opposed to a literary theme (e.g., *Margaret Atwood: Once in August,* "If You Can't Say Something Nice" 21).

Positing a feminist postcolonialism that incorporates and develops postmodern literary techniques is useful in discussing not only Atwood's texts but also those by Trinh Minha, Nadine Gordimer, Doris Lessing, Toni Morrison, and other contemporary writers. Although Rachel Blau DuPlessis, Anne Cranny-Francis, and Jack Zipes's recent discussions of feminist fiction do not directly relate Atwood's techniques to postmodern practice or discuss her intertextuality, their comments on feminist tactics and genres are illuminating.

According to DuPlessis, "Writing beyond the ending begins when authors, or their close surrogates, discover that they are in fact outside the terms of this novel's script, marginal to it" (6). Atwood and her personae do write "beyond the ending," as in *Bodily Harm*, beyond the ending the reader expects and the genre or canon would seem to dictate and beyond the ending of the intertexts they, and the book they are in, may parody. Even though DuPlessis's application of her theory to Atwood's *You Are Happy* differs from mine, her "Tactics of Revisionary Mythopoesis," partly based on Atwood's "Basic Victim Positions" in *Survival*, are useful in discussing the ways Atwood writes "beyond the ending."

Atwood uses the techniques of displacement, delegitimation, and decolonization in her feminist postcolonial narratives, including *You Are Happy*, other poetry, and fiction. According to DuPlessis, the technique of displacement is "a committed identification with Otherness" in order to give voice to the muted: the "noncanonical" or "other side" of the story.[15] "A change of point of view reveals the implicit politics of narrative: the choice of the teller or the perspective will alter its core assumptions and one's sense of the tale. By putting the female eye, ego, and voice at the center of the tale, displacement asks the kind of questions that certain feminist historians have" (108–9). DuPlessis defines *delegitimation* as "the critical creation of an unexpected story, in attempts to gain release from a colonial tale," roughly Atwood's "victim" position three: "To acknowledge the fact that you are a victim but to refuse to accept the assumption that the role is inevitable" (DuPlessis 110; *Surv* 37). Although DuPlessis doesn't refer to global postcolonialism in her definition, decolonization is the transition from "internalized colonial mentality to an anticolonial world view" that Atwood traces with her four positions (*Writing* 110).

Since Atwood says, "Insofar as you are connected with your society," position four, being an ex-victim, isn't possible until the society's position has changed (*Surv* 38), she paradoxically writes "post" colonially from position three in transition toward four. Even though her characters begin in positions one or two, they, too, generally "end" in transition from three. In Atwood's meta-narratives, her self-conscious narrators and personae also use displacement, delegitimation, and decolonization to tell the "other side" of fairy-tale, mythic, biblical, literary, other popular culture, historical, and life stories. Usually, they and most of us knew only one version anyway.

Jack Zipes and Anne Cranny-Francis suggest other tactical and genre considerations relevant to Atwood's fairy-tale intertextuality. Zipes considers Atwood's short fiction, "Bluebeard's Egg," like selected works of Anne Sexton, Angela Carter, Joanna Russ, Tanith Lee, Judith Viost, Jane Yolen, Merseyside Fairy Story Collective, and Olga Broumas, a feminist fairy tale. Authors of feminist fairy tales "challenge conventional views of gender, socialisation, and sex roles . . . [and] map out an alternative aesthetic terrain for the fairy tale as genre. . . . Created out of dissatisfaction with the dominant male discourse of traditional fairy tales and with those social values and institutions which have provided the framework for sexist prescriptions, the feminist fairy tale conceives a different view of the world and speaks in a voice that has been customarily silenced" (*Don't* xi). Placing the reworked fairy tale in the genre of feminist fantasy, however, Cranny-Francis lists Atwood's "Bluebeard's Egg" along with the selections in Zipes as metafictions. She refers to the "metanarrative function" of feminist intertextual revisions, sometimes involving [the narrator's] direct reader address and always revealing the ideologically determined discourses encoded in the traditional tales (85, 89, 94).[16]

Atwood's fiction and poetry texts are indeed feminist metanarratives, and, in reference to fairy tales, often feminist "metafairy tales," sometimes anti-fairy tales. Calling attention to themselves as art and commenting on, even parodying fiction, poetry, film, and other popular-art conventions, Atwood's texts resemble Virginia Woolf's *To the Lighthouse*, Joy Kogawa's *Obasan*, Amy Tan's

The Joy Luck Club, Louise Erdrich's *The Beet Queen*, and A. S. Byatt's *Possession: A Romance* in their self-consciousness about themselves and art. Thus, even Atwood's Bildungsromane (novels of education) are to some degree *Künstlerromane* (artist novels). When the text is, at least on one level, about fairy tales and uses straight or deconstructed fairy-tale form or style (including structure, language, characterization), it is, thus, a literary meta-fairy tale, including works as diverse as Rushdie's *Haroun and the Sea of Stories*, Barbara Comyns's *The Juniper Tree*, Byatt's *Possession*, and Toni Morrison's *Beloved*. If self-parody destroys the fiction or the poem's illusion of reality, as in *Surfacing*, the text becomes anti-literature (anti-romance, anti-novel,[17] anti-poem, anti-fairy tale), by definition a metatext or literary metafairy tale (Wilson, "Deconstructing" 60 n. 7; "Self-Conscious" 169–83).

In deconstructing her fairy-tale and mythic intertexts, allowing the muted or silenced subtext to speak, Atwood's metanarratives consist of more than two narrative strands interwoven in dialectic with one another: the frame narrative (always more than a revised version of the traditional fairy tale)[18] and the "embroidered" intertexts, usually heightened, exaggerated, or parodied. As is generally recognized, Atwood knows and skillfully deconstructs romance forms, including literary fairy tales, fantasy, the fantastic, Gothic and ghost fiction, detective fiction, the thriller, and the "true trash" or true romance of *Wilderness Tips*.[19] In keeping with these romance traditions, Atwood's intertextual narratives often resemble the interlace of medieval romance: resembling the decorated capital letters of illuminated manuscripts, medieval interlaced narratives "adhered to each other in an infinite sequence of echoes and anticipations" (Vinaver, *Form* 22; *Rise* plates 6, 7.[20]

In terms of image and scene, characterization, point of view, tropes and symbols, plot, structure, language and tone, genre, techniques, costumes and setting, ideology, and engagement of readers, Atwood's metanarratives typically display identifiable features and reveal similar techniques of intertextuality. Although this listing includes often interdependent techniques and is by no means exhaustive, it offers a beginning overview of Atwood's intertextual tactics. First, as when the mother feeds jays in *Surfacing*, Atwood often builds a scene on a powerful fairy-tale image. Second, she frequently reverses the gender of the hero, "heroine," or other characters, such as third sons in *Surfacing*'s "The Golden Phoenix" and "The Fountain of Youth," to shift females from object to subject. She sometimes doubles roles so that the same person may be both rescuer and rescued and, in terms of divided archetypes or foils, princess and step-mother or witch. Sometimes men comically play roles assigned to women in the intertexts. Third, displacing the "truth" of traditional texts and inherited patterns and giving voice to the silenced, Atwood shifts the point of view from the fairy tale's usual privileged, reliable, third-person narration[21] to unreliable third-person center of consciousness (reflector) or unreliable first-person narration (see definitions in Booth 153). Fourth, as with the fish bait and dead heron in *Surfacing*, Atwood uses tropes and symbols to enlarge the meaning of the ordinary, especially to make the literal symbolic: the dismemberment in all her novels' "Fitcher's Bird," the "treasure" the youth finds in *Surfacing*'s "The Three Languages," the prince's "rescue" and the princess' "awakening" in "Sleeping Beauty." Fifth, retaining the magical transformations of fairy-tale plots, Atwood displaces the original plot line so that the silent or marginalized subtext of female experience is central. For example, she makes the daughter and mother's feelings and motivations in "The Girl Without Hands" the focus of *Life Before Man*.

Sixth, keeping something of the fairy tale's binary opposition (Van Spanckeren, "Magic" 2) and its archetypal, structural movement from "negative" to "positive," Atwood changes the intertext's resolution so that marriage or heterosexual relationship does *not* complete the woman's story (*EW*); or, more commonly, she explodes and opens the resolution ("writes beyond the ending"). Seventh, Atwood transforms, bends, or blends either tones or genres. For example, she makes Fitcher and the Robber Bridegroom comic figures in *The Edible Woman* and simultaneously parodies and uncovers the tragic subtext in *Lady Oracle*'s flip costume Gothic. Eighth, Atwood uses irony as a subversive doubled or split discourse (Hutcheon, "Circling" 170). Ninth, although Atwood usually retains fairy-tale and mythic costumes (Offred's red clothing and basket in *HT*), settings (*LO*'s labyrinth, *CE*'s river of death / icy pool), and even props, just as she does events (the sibyl's trance in *LO*), plots, themes, and motifs (animal languages in *Surf*, dancing in *LO*)—thereby aiding readers' unconscious recognition of fairy-tale intertexts—she uses language to defamiliarize (Shklovsky 13–22, 48–49), transgress (York 6–19) and often parody these elements (e.g., the hierarchy of uniforms in *HT*). For example, pushing language into anti-language to resemble the anti-narratives of Beckett, Robbe-Grillet, and Sarraute, Atwood's "There Was Once" (*GB* 19–24) entirely deconstructs not only fairy-tale plots, readers, current critical approaches, and the genre but description, the sentence, and language itself. Tenth, using decolonization in a transition toward a postcolonial society, Atwood revises or "reverses" the norms or ideology of an intertext: for example, the danger of Red-Cap's going off the path becomes the danger of staying on it. Eleventh, and finally, by transgressing the conventions of language and culture (York 18) through puns, wordplay, figures of speech, and irony; using delegitimation (creating an unexpected story), and writing beyond the ending, Atwood engages readers in creation of the text and remythification of patriarchally amputated intertexts.

Atwood's fairy-tale intertexts thus foreground sexual politics and other political issues, including those of the postcolonial condition. As Zipes points out, fairy tales deal with issues of power. Atwood links sexual politics, already a subtext in such tales as "Fitcher's Bird" and "The Robber Bridegroom," to broader dominance and submission hierarchies, exposing issues of class; internal political fragmentation; and social, sexual, cultural, or religious orthodoxy. By doing so, she raises many of the same questions, and implies some of the same answers, as Riane Eisler and other feminists about the possibility of human survival and evolution. Contrary to most critical assessments, Atwood's often unrecognized fairy-tale intertexts usually offer hope.

Atwood's intertexts serve at least five connected purposes in her work: 1) to indicate the quality and nature of her characters' cultural contexts (Beran 4, 2); 2) to signify her characters'—and readers'—entrapment in pre-existing patterns; 3) to comment self-consciously on these patterns—including the embedded fairy tales, myths, and related popular traditional stories—often by deconstructing constricting literary, folkloric, and cultural plots with "transgressive" language (York 6–7, 17) and filling in the gaps of female narrative; 4) to comment self-consciously on the frame story and other intertexts; and 5) to structure the characters' imaginative or "magical" release from externally imposed patterns, offering the possibility of transformation for the novel's characters, for the country they partly represent, and for all human beings.

②

Sexual Politics in Atwood's Visual Art

"Fitcher's Bird" and the Triple Goddess

Few people are aware of Margaret Atwood's visual art. Until my recent publication of nine watercolors and one drawing (Wilson, "Sexual" 205–14; "A Note" 111–16), most of Atwood's art was hidden in private collections or in the University of Toronto Atwood Papers.[1] Some Canadians remember Atwood's *Survivalwoman* comic strip, drawn by "Bart Gerrard," or recognize that she designed the dazzling covers for *True Stories* (Oxford edition), *Murder in the Dark*, and *Interlunar*. Others comment on Atwood's clever cover design for *Good Bones* (1992) as if she had never done any previous visual art. None of these covers has appeared in a U.S. edition. Even *The Journals of Susanna Moodie* collages (1970), so integral to the volume's meaning but not published in either Canadian or U.S. editions of *Selected Poems*, have received surprisingly little comment (n. 13, 14). In general, Atwood is not considered a visual artist, and the striking parallels between her visual and literary imagery are largely ignored. Like many women artists working in media not traditionally displayed in museums, Atwood has had little encouragement to publish or exhibit her watercolors, drawings, collages, linocuts, and comic strips. Since the publication of *Cat's Eye* (1988, 1989), about a female visual artist, recognizing the diversity of Atwood's talents and exploring parallels between her visual and literary art have become imperative. Atwood's visual art not only presents memorable visual images; in many ways it epitomizes her fairy-tale sexual politics. The dynamics of this politics is examined here through works using the Grimms' "Fitcher's Bird," the Triple Goddess, and other intertexts.

Like her fiction, poetry, and essays, many of Atwood's visual works, sometimes untitled or undated, present Gothic images of female-male relationships in fairy tales, myth, legend, the Bible, literature, popular culture, and history. Female figures, sometimes evoking the Triple Goddess or her fairy-tale doubles, include a moon, an Eve-snake-tree, an underwater woman, an angel, a mother harpy with two chicks, a termite queen, a bride with a skull face, an urban woman "pasted" on an alien wilderness, an underground Persephone, an insulated woman, and the comic strip *Survivalwoman*. Males and females appear in watercolors depicting Mary Queen of Scots with her male executioners or oppressors and Frankenstein monsters with dead or passive female victims. Atwood's Robber Bridegroom holds the head of his female victim; and the medal-laden General of her parodic "hanged man," the basis for the *Power Politics* cover, holds a relaxed concubine. Where males appear separately from females, we find a submerged skeleton about to become a bird-god, a male harpy, and a comic dracula or "red-eyed person" (Atwood Tape).

As Atwood acknowledges, some of her references to fairy tales and Gothic stories "are close to patterning. Jungians would call them Jungian." Several watercolors were created while she was working on *Power Politics*. "The third section has lots of references to fairy tales and gothic stories." The Grimm brothers' tales, that she read when very young, have the "depth for [her] that certain Biblical stories and Greek stories also have." While she "doesn't think that doing visual art has particularly affected the literary art," she is more likely to paint when writing poetry than when working on a novel. As Atwood says, "Sometimes I paint things before I write about them; the thing appears as a visual image. On the other hand, sometimes I don't. Poets and artists . . . [shouldn't] think too much about processes—it interrupts work. The visual art and the rest of it are of course connected at some level. I don't really have any way of verbalizing it" (Tape).

This connection is most evident in cases where Atwood has designed, used, or adapted art for book covers discussed later in this chapter: *Double Persephone*, a linocut put into a flatbed printing press (1961, uncredited) (Tape, figs. 3, 4); *Journals of Susanna Moodie*, a photograph of a nineteenth-century plate (1970); *Power Politics*, a watercolor (1970, Plate 8) that is the basis for the William Kimber cover (1971); the Oxford edition of *Two-Headed Poems*, a Graeme Gibson photograph of Atwood Christmas tree ornaments (1978) (Plate 2); *Bodily Harm*, an undated watercolor (not used) (Tape, Plate 18); the Oxford edition of *True Stories*, a watercolor (1980, book 1981) (Plate 17); *Murder in the Dark*, a photograph of a collage (Coach House 1983) (Tape, Plate 16); and *Interlunar*, a watercolor of a landscape (Oxford 1984). For a writer who puts so much emphasis on hands and touch (Chapters 6–9), Atwood's "hands-on" involvement in book production is notable. Atwood often works on book covers just after writing the poems or fiction and, in some cases, she has designed the cover itself: *Double Persephone*; the Contact Press and first Anansi editions of *The Circle Game*, 1966; the projected cover for the Oxford edition of *Two-Headed Poems*, a magnified cell in process of division (not used) (Correspondence, 18 May 1978 letter to Bill, Atwood Papers); and *The Journals of Susanna Moodie*.

Many of these cover designs present motifs from folklore and myth discussed later (*DP*'s Eve-Persephone-snake, *PP*'s hanged man, *THP*'s two heads), and several are linked to literary images of sexual politics and the displaced goddess. For example, Atwood's cover for *The Circle Game*, made of sticker dots (Tape), is not a closed circle but a spiral frequently associated with the spiral labyrinth of the Mother Goddess (Walker, *Woman's Dictio-*

nary 14). For Atwood, it "suggests possibility of breakthrough."[2] Atwood's *True Stories* cover (Canadian edition, 1981) (Plate 17) and the commissioned *Bluebeard's Egg* cover (1983) both feature eggs in connection to fertility, sexual relationship, and power politics. This cover art, like that for *Two-Headed Poems* and John Alcorn's for *The Edible Woman* (first American edition, 1969),[3] is appropriate to the fabulous tone of both works.

Also, Atwood's use of her own photographs as a component in two book covers (*Murder in the Dark* and *Journals of Susanna Moodie*) is significant in interpreting her recurrent literary images of camera and photograph. Contrary to popular impression, Atwood is not only widely photographed: she is an occasional photographer who feels "some [of her photographs] are actually quite good." Atwood is interested in a photograph's ability to freeze time (Tape); it also seems to freeze characters in roles that are socially conditioned, desired, or feared. Thus, her literary works often feature couples turning reality or one another into photographs (Wilson, "Camera" 31). Interestingly, one of the few U.S. covers with any thematic connection to her works presents four small photographs of Atwood: three negative and one positive print (*True Stories* 1981).

When asked about any relationship between her recurrent and negative literary images of packaging and surfaces to either her experiences with commercial publishers or her decision to do cover art, Atwood says the negative images of packaging don't come from negative experiences with publishers, "although you might fit them in. I've been interested in packaging for a very, very long time." Like *Surfacing*'s narrator, when she was eight or nine years old she made a scrapbook that included numerous pictures cut from advertisements. Later, "when [Marshall] McLuhan brought out *Mechanical Bride*, I got it immediately and was very interested." But, she said laughing, "I don't consider my cover designs of my work to be packaging!" *Murder in the Dark*'s cover, which is not a parody, is "neither art [n]or merchandizing. It is a cover design appropriate to the book" (Tape).

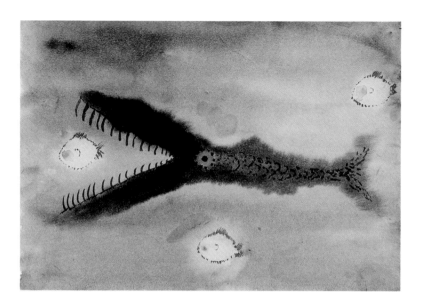

Atwood 1970

PLATE 3 *Fitcher's Bird.* Untitled Watercolor. Archive-labeled
"Death as a Bride." Signed, 1970. Atwood Papers; 15.2 X 21.8 cm.

atwood 1969

PLATE 4 *Mary Queen of Scots I.* Untitled Watercolor. Archive-labeled "Lady and Sinister Figure." Signed, 1969. Atwood Papers; 15.2 X 21.8 cm.

atwood 1969

PLATE 5 *Mary Queen of Scots II*. Untitled Watercolor. Archive-labeled "Lady and Executioner with Axe." Signed, 1969. Atwood Papers; 15.2 X 21.8 cm.

PLATE 6 *Frankenstein I.* Untitled Watercolor. Archive-labeled "Man Holding Woman's Body." Signed, 1970. Atwood Papers; 17.7 X 25 cm.

PLATE 7
Frankenstein II.
Archive-labeled
"Mourners at
Woman's Bier."
Signed, 1970.
Atwood Papers;
21.7 X 15.2 cm.

PLATE 8
Hanged Man.
Untitled
Watercolor. Cover
design for *Power
Politics* and basis for
William Kimber
cover. 1970.
Atwood Papers;
22.8 X 29.4 cm.

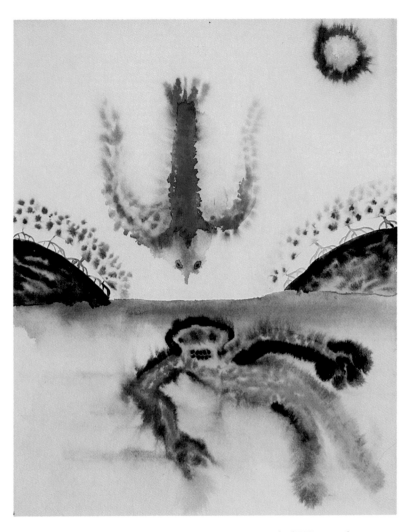

P L A T E 9 *Dream: Bluejay or Archeopteryx.* Untitled Watercolor.
Archive-labeled "A Bird Diving into a Submerged Figure." Signed,
1968. Atwood Papers; 29.8 X 22.9 cm.

M. atwood 1970

Plate 10 *Male Harpy.* Untitled Watercolor. Archive-labeled "Red Bird." Signed, 1970. Atwood Papers; 25.2 X 17.7 cm.

PLATE 11 *Portrait of Graeme Gibson.* Untitled Watercolor. Signed, 1974. Atwood Papers; 30 X 22.8 cm.

PLATE 12 *Termite Queen.* Untitled Watercolor. Archive-labeled "Insect in Red Gown with Bouquet." Undated. Atwood Papers; 22.8 X 29.7 cm.

PLATE 13
Mother Harpy and Chics.
Untitled Watercolor.
Archive-labeled
"Atwoods as Birds."
1974. Atwood Papers;
30.1 X 22.7 cm.

PLATE 14
Good Bones cover.
Collage. 1992. 20.3 X
14.2 cm.

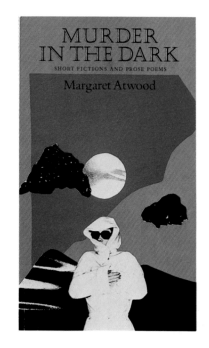

PLATE 15
Sphinx. Untitled
Watercolor. Signed,
1970. Atwood
Papers; 22.8 X 30.4
cm.

PLATE 16
Murder in the Dark
cover. Collage.
1983. 21.3 X 12.4
cm.

MARGARET ATWOOD
True Stories

PLATE 17
True Stories cover.
Watercolor. 1980,
published 1981. Atwood
Papers; 21.6 X 13.8 cm.

PLATE 18
Microscope Image. Untitled
Watercolor. Undated.
Atwood Papers; 15.3 X 22
cm.

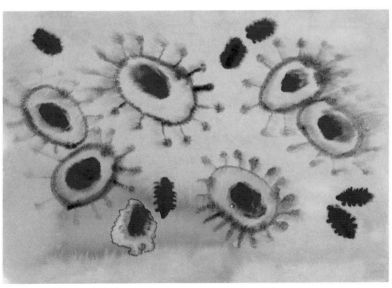

PLATE 19 *Angel.* Untitled Watercolor. Archive-labeled "Winged Creature." Undated. Atwood Papers; 30.4 X 22.8 cm.

PLATE 20 *Drowned Figure I.* Untitled Watercolor. Undated.
Atwood Papers; 19.2 X 15.3 cm.

PLATE 21 *Drowned Figure II*. Untitled Watercolor. Undated.
Atwood Papers; 19.2 X 15.3 cm.

Atwood has also commissioned (Canadian *Bluebeard's Egg*) or selected (the Canadian editions of *Bodily Harm* and *The Handmaid's Tale*) covers for her work (Tape). Although she did not see it until it was finished, she calls the American cover for *The Handmaid's Tale*, which draws attention not only to the wall (of execution, entrapment, control) but also to Offred as ironic "Little Red Cap," "a knock out! It's terrific!" (Tape). The farther away publishers are from her base of operations, of course, the less involved Atwood has been in cover designs. She usually sees American paperback editions of her work, but they almost never use her designs. She sees English ones if she happens to be in the country; but she has no say, if not lack of interest, in European ones. Some of Sweden's are "terrific" and Finland's "good" (Tape).

In other cases Atwood has created artwork not as illustration of literary texts but as a "parallel activity that had to do with the same body of material" (Tape): "Variations for the Termite Queen" (See Plate 12), *Dreams of the Animals* Broadside (197–), *Journals of Susanna Moodie* (Figs. 5–10), and particular poems in *Procedures for Underground*, *The Animals in That Country*, and *Power Politics*. Most of the archive watercolors are of this type. When she feels like it, she paints on a drafting table in the same office where she writes. Atwood has also done comic strips (Fig. 12) and illustrations for children's books.[4] Although in 1985 Atwood didn't plan any further artistic projects (Tape), her recent illustrations for *The CanLit Foodbook* (1987) and the collage for the cover of *Good Bones* (1992) (Fig. 1, Plate 14) suggest continuing interest.

Despite the extraordinary power of some of her visual art, however, Atwood resembles many other women artists (including her own narrator of *Surfacing*) in undercutting the value of her visual work: "I myself would not feel that too much should be made of these paintings . . . . (Atwood Letter, 29 September 1986). I paint images but am not a painter, if you understand the difference" (Tape). Often working in styles or media outside the mainstream, women artists may be denied formal recognition and thus lack confidence in their work. Finding it necessary to insist that some paintings are "done for fun" (Letter, 29 September 1986) and that some details in the archive watercolors are accidental, such as a red spot on her Sphinx (Plate 15) when someone dropped a cherry nearby (Tape), she maintains that others occur "just because I don't paint very well!" (Letter, 29 September 1986).

Thus, she doesn't take artistic influence too seriously but mentions Hieronymus Bosch and Pieter Bruegel (Tape). Both draw on folk tradition, even portraying the "big fish eat little fish" motif (Plate 1) to satirize humanity's self-destructive deception and greed, the oppression of the weak by the strong, and the anarchy of existence (Mieder 198–201). The atmosphere of Bosch's and Bruegel's work certainly resembles Atwood's literary as well as visual landscape, which might be variously considered Gothic, fabulist, super real, magical realistic, or surreal. Bosch and Atwood also share a central theme: metamorphosis.

In addition, Atwood and her friend, the visual artist Charles Pachter, have probably mutually influenced one another to some extent. Although aware that Charles Pachter's visual imagery is different from hers (see n. 2), Atwood owns art by Pachter and has respected Pachter's talent throughout her career. Well known in Canada for such paintings as *Ceremonial* (1973), *The Painted Flag* (1981), *Davenport and Bay* (1984), three *Mooseplunge* works (1976, 1984, 1986), and *The Supremes* (1985), Pachter deserves wider recognition. Both Atwood and Pachter interrogate popular culture, including myth (See Pachter's *Perseus Transfigured*, color lithograph and seriograph 1969), and are fond of word play (e.g., Pachter's *State of the Tarts*, acrylic 1984). Both share the gift of parodic and satiric wit and incisive cultural critique, and both have a talent for suggesting either depths or absences below surfaces. Compare and contrast, for example, Atwood's Susanna Moodie pushing up from underground (*JSM* Fig. 10) to Pachter's *Pioneer* (acrylic 1982), where the Moodie figure—like the English immigrants to Ontario she stands for—is missing legs and a ground to stand on (Welsh-Ovcharov 81). As he is aware, Pachter's *Two Plus One* (acrylic 1983, Welsh-Ovcharov 68), showing three bathers looking toward the ominous unbroken surface of impenetrably opaque water, recalls Atwood's poem, "This is a Photograph of Me" (*CG* 17, September 1992 Conversation). Pachter's insight into Atwood's work is evident in the way his art and even his print styles for his illustrated editions of her poetry foreground many of her central images, constituting a kind of visual commentary on her poetry (see these rare volumes, especially *The Journals of Susanna Moodie*). Atwood wrote a perceptive foreword to Welsh-Ovcharov's recent book, *Charles Pachter* (1992), which reproduces many of Pachter's visual works.

Like Atwood's poetry and fiction, her watercolors and drawings present recurrent, archetypal images of power politics, in which women and men may not only oppose but also represent aspects of one another, playing roles evoking Gothic stories, myths, biblical narratives, television, comic books, and nursery rhymes as well as fairy tales. Images of eating and food, prevalent in fairy tales and folklore, and even of edible and cooked or baked art also recur in both Atwood's literary and visual art, including some cover designs. In "Speeches for Dr. Frankenstein," *Power Politics*, *The Edible Woman*, *Lady Oracle*, *Bodily Harm*, an untitled undersea watercolor (Plate 1), illustrations for the *CanLit Foodbook* (Fig. 1), *Two-Headed Poems*' cover design (Plate 2), and the magic-marker drawing of a sliced, womb-shaped, amanita mushroom (*Amanita Caesarea, Egg, Cross-Section on Cloud* (Fig. 11), such images suggest power politics, the struggle for survival, and metamorphosis.

Thus, it is time to examine Atwood's visual and literary images together. My focus in this chapter is Atwood's visual portrayal of sexual politics through allusions to the Grimm brothers' "Fitcher's Bird" (Hunt and Stern 216–20) and to the mythic Great Goddess. *Fitcher's Bird* exemplifies Atwood's use of "The Robber Bridegroom," "Little Red Cap," "The Juniper Tree," and related images from fairy-tale, mythic, Gothic, biblical, and historical stories. This fairy tale is a paradigm of sexual politics underlying the menace of the room (or unopened door to the room) from *The Circle Game* to *The Handmaid's Tale* and *Good Bones*, revealing her recent fiction's unique continuation of fairy-tale themes, motifs, and images fundamental to her work. The Great Goddess, linked to numerous female heroes of fairy tales and myth, including the third sister of "Fitcher's Bird," is an emblem of Atwood's emphasis on cycle, metamorphosis, and rebirth.

In preparation for a specifically sexual politics, we will first examine Atwood's visual art depicting power politics and the struggle for survival through images of eating, cannibalism, and opposed doubles or foils.

The first illustration (Plate 1) is the untitled watercolor of an undersea setting, also common in Atwood's early literary works. It depicts a toothed dinosaurian creature about to swallow an oblivious small fish, which may in turn be swallowed by the large fish swimming intact inside the creature. It was influenced by National Geographic photographs of fish with phosphorescent markings (Tape) and may bring to mind the center panel of Bosch's *Garden of Earthly Delights*, portraying a whale swallowing a small fish. Both Atwood and Bosch's art works dramatize the ancient proverb about human nature, "big fish [creatures] eat little fish" (Motif J133.6), which not only depicts the food chain but implies that "the larger and stronger will devour (i.e. conquer) the smaller and weaker" (Mieder 178–79), a variation of Atwood's "power politics" theme.

Sometimes power and sexual politics involve symbolic but overt cannibalism (Motifs G10–49). Atwood illustrates her "Eating People Is Wrong: Cannibalism Canadian Style" chapter of *The CanLit Foodbook: From Pen to Palate* (which she compiled) with one of her visual jokes, a credited black and white drawing (Fig. 1) accompanying and inspired by Crad Kilodney's *The Last Secrets of Omega* (captioned "Chobey Eats a Salesman," 157, 163–64, excerpted from *Lightning Struck My Dick*). In this humorous

Eating People Is Wrong

9

CANNIBALISM
CANADIAN
STYLE

Tarte au Salesman Kilodney,
garnie de Hornrims

FIGURE 1. Tarte au Salesman Kilodney, Garnie de Hornrims; drawing for
CanLit Foodbook, 1987; 25.3 × 17.7 cm.

piece, the steaming tart appears to "eat" the salesman before Chobey does. Wearing horn-rimmed glasses and accompanied with briefcase and shoes, the anthropomorphic tart seems to invite us to participate in the feast. As Atwood says in her foreword, which she supports with selections from Leonard Cohen, Dennis Lee, Susan Ioannou, Libby Scheier, Bill Bissett, Jay MacPherson, Wayland Drew, Jeni Couzyn, George Bowering, Timothy Findley, Kilodney, and her own *The Edible Woman*, Canadian literature has "a surprising amount" of metamorphical and actual cannibalism (4).

In addition to introducing literary selections and recipes, including some from Atwood and her family, Atwood's other witty drawings also take an irreverent look at food and foodways: the *Canadian Tea Angel à la Johnson* (color) on the cover and in chapter 4, *Metaphorical Onion* (5), *Oeufs 'Kanadian' MacEwen* (19), *Poetic Apple à La P.K. Page* (33), *Poisson Rosenblatt* (77), *The Flying Supper* (95), *The Attack of the Giant Cinnamon Bun* (121), *Rat Jelly Ondaatje*, *Garni de Souris Mowat* (141), and *Wedding Cake Hodgins, with Spice* (173). Much as *The Edible Woman* subverts both the institution of marriage and one of the most common literary plots, *Wedding Cake Hodgins, with Spice* parodically reveals the "disaster" of social shindigs by stripping the groom of his pants, turning both bride-and-groom dolls upside down, and drowning them in the cake as preparation for consumption. Extending the joyous wedding brawl, including "the sound of a million teeth chewing" (179–80) in Jack Hodgins' *A Wedding Catastrophe* (*The Invention of the World*), Atwood implies that the wedding ritual, and by implication marriage, offers consummation in cannibalism. The fact that such art appears—and may for Atwood be—so effortless suggests intuitive genius more than calculated satire.

While the Christmas decorations (Plate 2) on *Two-Headed Poems'* cover (1978) only appear edible, they reveal Atwood's skill in culinary arts and, as Chapter 3 indicates, her interest in edible art. In addition to showing Atwood's sense of humor, this innovative engagement in folk art demonstrates her characteristic re-visioning of the traditional and her deceptive ability to reveal depths in familiar rituals. Ironizing her first idea of a dividing cell (Atwood Correspondence, 18 May 1978 letter to Bill), the two heads (Motifs F511.0.2.1 and T551.2) of *Two-Headed Poems'* cover, unable to "see" one another and each upside down from the other's point of view, image archetypal opposition in the title poem and throughout the volume. As masks for comedy and tragedy, they illustrate the tension between two modes of human and specifically Canadian response. Suggesting Atwood's other doubled images, characters, and plots, they may also refer to Julian Jaynes's double-head discussion (Bowering 49). In addition, they suggest Atwood's early poem, "The Siamese Twins" ("Fall and All" 60, Motif F523), about the anguish of male and female "opposite bodies" "Roped in one continual skin."[5]

In many ways the "Fitcher's Bird" watercolor (Plate 3) typifies the mood of the archive art. Based on the Grimms' fairy tale, "Fitcher's Bird" (Tape), it is one of many Bluebeard stories, including the recently translated "Bluebeard" and "The Castle of Murder" (Zipes 660–63, 670–71), the better-known Perrault "Bluebeard," and the anonymous English "Mr. Fox" (see Carter, *Old Wives'*; Yearsley 127–28). "Fitcher's Bird" is about a disguised wizard (sometimes death, the deadly sun, sin, a troll, or the devil) (Leach and Fried 150; Jobes, vol. 1 230) whose touch forces pretty girls to leap into his basket. When he takes them to his castle, he gives them an egg to be carried everywhere and keys to every room but one,[6] which he forbids them to enter (Motif C611). Most versions of the tale deal with three sisters: the first two are curious and open the door, discovering the chopped-up bodies of former brides; Fitcher/Bluebeard, seeing the egg's indelible blood stains, recognizes their disobedience (Motif D474.4). The third sister, who cleverly leaves the egg outside, passes the test and gains power over the wizard. Before escaping, disguised as a marvelous bird (Motif K521.1), she leaves a substitute (a decorated skull) to fool the groom and rejoins the severed pieces of her sisters (Motif E30), re-creating rather than destroying life. The groom, not the bride, dies in a communal execution that also destroys his friends and the skull-bride (Hunt and Stern 216–20).

The watercolor shows the ornamented skull that the groom and his friends mistake for his bride. But the female figure is also the death that the first and second sisters and earlier brides encounter in the room and, ironically, the death the man ultimately marries because of his expectations. The red flowers bleed down the front of the woman's gown, anticipating the bleeding flowers in *The Handmaid's Tale* (1985) and the consequences of "loving" "Bluebeards" in Atwood works embedding the "Fitcher's Bird" fairy tale, including "Hesitations Outside the Door" (*Power Politics*, 1971), "Three Jokes" (unpublished, Atwood Papers), *Bluebeard's Egg* (1983) (see Chapter 9), and *Good Bones* (1992). *Bodily Harm* (1982), whose original title was "The Robber Bridegroom" (Atwood Papers), *The Edible Woman* (1969), "The Robber Bridegroom" poem in *Interlunar* (1984), and *The Robber Bride* (1993) allude to the closely related Grimms' fairy tale, "The Robber Bridegroom," in which the groom actually eats prospective brides (Motif K1916; see Chapters 3 and 8). Atwood's watercolor, *The Robber Bridegroom*, pictures a man holding both an axe and a blond head. The head emits light (Atwood Telephone Call 1985). As in "Fitcher's Bird," the female protagonist in the Grimms' "The Robber Bridegroom" survives the sexual battle, in the first case by using her wits and in the second, by speaking. The third sister of "Fitcher's Bird," a figure who recalls Isis and other goddesses' ability to rejoin severed limbs, implies ritualistic metamorphosis and rebirth.

Atwood says the woman in Plate 4 is Mary, Queen of Scots, Anne Boleyn, or "someone like that" (Tape). In addition to "Fitcher's Bird," the figures suggest the dynamics of Mme. de Villeneuve's "Beauty and the Beast" or the Grimms' "Little Red Cap." Notice the visual contrast and tension between the apparent male, who seems primitive and menacing, and the somewhat prim female, whose dress is both formal and red,[7] the color of blood, death, birth, and passion and the color Marian in *The*

Edible Woman associates with being a target, a hunted rabbit. As the beheaded Anne Boleyn, one of Henry VIII's six wives who failed to produce a male heir, the figure is again one of the interchangeable wives of Bluebeard and a victim of patriarchal politics. As Mary Stuart (1542–1587), who was the daughter of Henry VIII's sister Margaret and thus not only Queen of Scotland but also a possible candidate for the English throne, the figure can suggest betrayed innocence, the absurd consequences of religious intolerance, or the no less deadly or abstract power politics between females (see Chapter 11). Much admired for her intelligence and poise in the moments before execution, Mary was beheaded, dressed in red, on orders from her cousin, Elizabeth I (Anne Boleyn and Henry VIII's daughter), who probably never met her.

Already missing the right hand that was, perhaps, too close to the bestial other, the lady resembles the narrator of *Bodily Harm* and numerous other Atwood personae recalling "The Girl Without Hands" (Hunt and Stern 160–65; see Chapters 6–9). Among other amputated pieces, their hands, their ability to touch and keep in touch, are missing (Motifs Q451.1, S161). Whether Anne or Mary, the figure of legend finally inhabits Bluebeard's castle and becomes a pawn in a series of relentlessly unfolding events. Her powerlessness is dramatized in being beheaded (Motif G335), a condition many Atwood personae fear and a fate female characters in male novels often suffer ("Women's Novels" in *MD*).

Atwood pairs the lady and sinister figure (Plate 4) with the watercolor of a woman and her executioner (Plate 5), again picturing Mary Stuart or Anne Boleyn (Tape). I am reminded of "Marrying the Hangman" (*Two-Headed Poems*, 1978), based on a true story of a couple who escaped death, in his case by becoming the executioner and, in hers, by marrying the executioner. In Atwood's poem, the woman must not only create the hangman but also convince him to exchange his face for the "impersonal mask of death, of official death that has eyes but no mouth." Atwood cautions that "there is more than one hang-man." As the female narrator asks, "Who else is there to marry?" (Touchstone *Two-Headed Poems* 49). Despite Atwood's preference for stories in which women are more than victims (Atwood Tele-phone Call, December 1985), the woman in the painting is victi-mized. Significantly, her head is already detached from her body, the axe is marked with red, and her dress, like both people's eyes, is the color of blood. Like many of the watercolor figures, the two appear to be mouthless (Motif F513.0.3), voiceless; his barlike eyes make him appear an automaton, like the Frankenstein below.

According to Atwood, the two 1970 untitled watercolors, archive-labeled "Man Holding Woman's Body" (Plate 6) and "Mourners at Woman's Bier" (Plate 7) deal with the Frankenstein story (Tape). Atwood earlier alludes to the folk motif of the golem (Motif D1635) in "Speeches for Dr. Frankenstein" (*AC*, 1968), originally published with Charles Pachter's woodcuts (1966). Again the figures make a striking contrast. He, like the "sinister figure" and executioner, is partly black and, in this case blocklike, powerful, robotic. Although he is "holding" the inert, pink, fluid body of the woman, he appears armless (Motif F516.1), incapable of touch as she is of action. Both are faceless, without features (Motif F511.1.0.1). Viewed through Shelley's *Frankenstein* and Atwood's "Speeches," the watercolor has a number of other dimensions. As Atwood says, *Frankenstein* is "a creation parable, where God forsakes Adam . . . because he can't face the grotesque creature that he's produced. But the monster's not *evil*. . . . He's totally innocent." In Atwood's poem, however, "The monster is the narrator's other self, and the process of writing that poem involved separating the two selves." In this case, "it's the monster who deserts his maker" (Sandler 15). Thus, while the watercolor may depict the monster holding the lifeless body of Elizabeth, Dr. Frankenstein's fian-cée, or more generally, the passive female victim in a battle of sexual politics, it may also show the monster holding his female creator. Stated another way, the female is being held by the monster she has created.

The subject of Plate 7 again is Frankenstein, and a number of questions arise. Is the dark figure framed in the doorway Dr. Frankenstein, who is viewing the results of his Faustian attempt to play God? If the dead woman is Shelley's Elizabeth, does the bouquet again serve a double purpose, so that marriage to an artist is simultaneously a funeral? Does the rootlike hair suggest a possibility of rebirth? Does the dead woman, like the monster, represent a part of Dr. Frankenstein, who appears to be either male or female creator, or, in this case, has the male creation murdered the female creator? Considering *Murder in the Dark*, does creation always involve "murder"? More generally, again a hidden part of the fiancé's personality victimizes a female. But what if she, like the persona in "Speeches for Dr. Franken-stein," is slicing loose a reflection that refuses to stay framed in the mirror?

Based on the hanging man card (XII) of the Tarot and also ironically suggesting the lovers card (VI), the signed watercolor (Plate 8), not credited in the book, is the original for the William Kimber cover of *Power Politics* (Anansi, 1971) (Tape) and a pattern for the theme of sexual politics underlying most of the archive watercolors. Intertextually and parodically, the cover suggests not only T. S. Eliot's use of the Hanged Man as the Hanged God of Frazer's *The Golden Bough* in "The Waste Land" (1922) ("Notes on 'The Waste Land'" 68) but also the Grail legend foreground-ing the characters' emptiness in *Surfacing*. The one able to read tarot cards or pages of the Egyptian book of mysteries, the *Book of Thoth*, traditionally knows and controls the secrets of the universe (Leach and Fried 1104). Thus, by putting her persona in this position, Atwood recalls not only the charlatan fortune tell-er, Madame Sosostris, of "The Waste Land" but also both Tiresias and the Eliot persona's genuine oracle role.

The right figure, the male, wears medals suggesting the wooden general with the statue concubine and this volume's other matched sets, with both projected and defensive false skins or disguises. As my students observe, if the work were turned upside down, it would be the man, not the woman, who would be powerless. Commenting on the actual cover that adds mummy wrapping to the woman and a suit of armor to the man, Judith McCombs asks, "Is he there at all? If so, is he a prisoner in his rigid iron role?" (Review of *Power Politics* 55, passim). Some question also exists about the complacent expression of the woman on the cover and the possibly voluntary arm and leg position, that seems to allow struggle. In any case, the woman's arms in the watercolor remind us of *Mary Queen of Scots I* ("Lady and Sinister Figure"), and the ritualistic position seems timeless. The man and woman are tied to or are extensions of one another, both victims/victors of prescribed or projected roles. Because of each figure's aura or halo, the roles seem to be either intrinsic or divine.

The bluejay watercolor (Plate 9), one of many Atwood works about bird-people (Motifs B50–59),[8] is a parallel activity for a poem from *Procedures for Underground*, "Dream: Bluejay or Archeopteryx" (Tape). The poem was first published in 1969 and suggests that the bluejay or its archeopteryx predecessor, a dinosaurian ancestor of birds, transforms into a bird-god, "his body sheathed / in feathers, his teeth / glinting like nails, fierce god / head crested with blue flame" (8–9). Like the crow in Atwood's *For the Birds* and the jays in both the unpublished story, "The Girl Who Flew" (Atwood Papers, Children's Literature), and in *Surfacing*, the bird in the poem suggests North American native legends of people who can "take on the shape of a bird at will" (Sandler 46). Like other birds the bluejay is also associated with mythic or fairy-tale metamorphosis and is probably linked to Canadian identity through the baseball team, the Toronto Blue Jays. In Plate 9, the Jungian dive adds another dimension to the persona's reflected shadow self.

According to Atwood, the watercolor of a red bird (Plate 10) is a parody of a harpy (Tape, Motif B52), the winged and clawed females the Argonauts pursued and the female death spirits and "rapacious wind goddesses" of Greek mythology (Graves, *Greek I* 128, *II* 230; Walker, *Woman's Encyclopedia* 374; Leach and Fried 482). The head is from an actual picture of Oscar Lewenstein, the London producer of *The Edible Woman*'s first projected screenplay, which Atwood wrote in 1970 (See Atwood Papers).[9] Suspended or frozen in space and time like some of Atwood's characters, this harpy also seems to be a takeoff on the U.S. bald eagle. As both the cover and content of *Good Bones* (1992) reveal, folkloric, mythological, and biblical birds, ranging from other harpies (Plate 13), the bird goddess (*Surf*), and the sphinx (Plate 15) to the destroying angel (Plate 19) and the little red hen (*GB* 1992, not the same story as the Grimms' "The Death of the Hen"), are significant throughout Atwood's work. *For the Birds* (1990) indicates Atwood's interest in real birds as well.

Atwood says the watercolor of her life companion (Plate 11) pictures Dracula (Motif E251) or a red-eyed person (Tape) and is a visual joke "done for fun" rather than an ominous figure (Atwood Letters to Sharon Wilson 1986, August 27, 1991). The devil, for instance, "as the slaughterer, the destroyer, the render in pieces, ... is called 'The Fiend, red of hair and eyes, who cometh forth by night, and doth fetter the fiend in his lair'" (Neumann 171, quoting from *Book of the Dead*). Atwood's devils and Draculas, like her goddesses, are usually parodic; and her recent work suggests a return to the parodic zest usually associated with her sixties and seventies work. In her "My Life as a Bat" (*GB*), for example, Dracula is invoked in a mock-heroic style befitting this watercolor: "O Dracula, unlikely hero! O flying leukemia, in your cloak like a living umbrella, a membrane of black leather which you unwind from within yourself and lift like a stripteaser's fan as you bend with emaciated lust over the neck, flawless and bland, of whatever woman is longing for obliteration, here and now in her best negligee" (101). This water-color also humorously illustrates and undercuts the kind of role projection that can contribute to games of "power politics."

Created throughout her career and ranging from the mythic, archetypal, tragic, and Gothic to the comic, parodic, and satiric, Atwood's visual female images evoke another figure evident in her literary texts: the Triple Goddess. Widely worshipped in Africa and all over Europe throughout the neolithic and Bronze Ages until around 2500 B.C., with a resurgence of interest today, the Mother Goddess was "suppressed and set aside in favor of those male-oriented, patriarchal mythologies of thunder-hurling warrior gods" (J. Campbell, *Masks* 626).

Robert Graves's *The White Goddess* (1948) is itself an important Atwood influence: "The White Goddess" is the title of the third chapter of her doctoral dissertation draft, "Nature and Power in the English Metaphysical Romance," and an early target of parody in her "The Triple Goddess: A Poem for Voices" (Atwood Papers; *Acta Victoriana* 8–13, cited in Godard, "Telling" 10, 29). As an aspiring writer, Atwood learned from Graves that women are to be "incarnations of the White Goddess [Muse] herself, alternately loving and destructive, . . . inspirations rather than creators" (Atwood, "Great Unexpectations" xv). A personification of "primitive woman—woman the creatress and destructress . . . [,as] Goddess of the Underworld [the Triple Goddess is] concerned with Birth, Procreation and Death. As Goddess of the Earth she [is] concerned with the three seasons of Spring, Summer, and Winter: she animate[s] trees and plants and rule[s] all living creatures. As Goddess of the Sky she [is] the Moon, in her three phases" of new moon, full moon, and waning moon (Graves, *The White Goddess* 386).

In extolling goddess worship, Graves ironically limits female possibilities. According to Atwood's *Survival* (1972), he "divides Woman into three mythological categories or identities. First comes the elusive Diana or Maiden figure, the young girl; next the Venus figure, goddess of love, sex, and fertility; then the Hecate figure, called by Graves the Crone, goddess of the underworld" (199). The Triple Goddess has been associated with Athena, Neith, Hera-Demeter-Kore, Eire-Fodhla-Banbha, Thetis-Amphitrite-Nereis, and Hecate-Artemis-Diana, all variants of the maiden, mother, and moon or maiden, nymph, and crone (Daly, *Gyn/Ecology* 75–78). The Crone, "not sinister when viewed as part of a process," is sinister when "seen as the only alternative, as the whole of the range of possibilities for being female" (*Survival* 199).

Atwood observes Canadian literature's tendency for Diana-Maidens to die young, Venuses to be absent, and Hecates to proliferate, often incorporating trapped Venuses and Dianas. "Ice women" by their own or other characters' definitions, they populate the fiction of Margaret Laurence, Anne Hébert, Alice Munro, Joyce Marshall, Sheila Watson, P. K. Page (*Surv* 199, 210, 205), and, as I will investigate, Margaret Atwood.[10] Viewing the history of fiction, in "The Curse of Eve" Atwood mourns the proliferation of "Evil Witches, White Witches, White Goddesses, Bitch Goddesses, Medusas" and other stereotypes of women (219). Despite Atwood's images of initially dismembered females, usually part of embedded fairy-tale or Gothic intertexts, her own work is more balanced. Deconstructing confining scripts for women, Atwood's literary and visual texts lay bare the muted and subversive subtexts of phallocentric mythology, restoring the displaced Hecate (often in her Medusa guise) to her context and allowing us to see her hidden face.

Like the Demeter and Persephone figures of myth, the godmother/witches of fairy tales, and the triple Marys of the Bible, all associated with the Triple Goddess, several of Atwood's characters are themselves double, triple, or multiple (*YAH*'s Circe, *Surf*'s narrator, *EW*'s Marian, *LO*'s Joan, *CE*'s Elaine). Some of her most recurrent literary and visual art images (birds, snakes, mushrooms, blood and the color red) are associated with the Great Goddess of Life, Death, and Regeneration or with the goddess's magical ability to create or bestow life with her hands, mouth, womb, and eggs (Gimbutas, *Goddesses* 163). Images in Atwood's literature include metaphoric, sometimes parodic, nymphs, venuses, and crones (*HT*); goddesses of earth (*LO*), sky (*Surf*), and underworld (*JSM*); and new, full, old, or dark moons (*Surf, I*).

Atwood's visual art also presents images linked to the goddess or her attributes: a female crescent moon, a black and white Eve/snake, an apparent angel, a mother harpy with two chicks, a mermaid and eggs, a sphinx, a termite queen, a drowned woman, a sliced-open mushroom/womb, invaded cells, a bleeding heart, and an almost totally covered or insulated woman. From *Double Persephone*'s snake in the garden to *Murder in the Dark*'s packaged woman, archetypal female images in Margaret Atwood's visual art, like many of her characters, are paradoxically debased, drowned, dismembered, and reborn. As in her fiction, poetry, and essays, Atwood's visual art confronts and transforms patriarchal amputations of the goddess, reawakening and humanizing, sometimes parodying, the "goddess" in everywoman.[11]

Atwood's book of poetry, *Interlunar* (1984), testifies to her interest in moon images; she did the moon drawing more than thirty years ago (Fig. 2). A moon also appears in the Termite Queen watercolor and either a full moon or the sun, usually with clouds about to cover it, occur in several other works of art, including *Murder in the Dark*. In the northern hemisphere, the crescent or new moon, the spring nymph or young girl incarnation of the sky goddess, cyclically follows the darkness of intermoon, the time when, according to "Interlunar," both earth and human beings return to themselves (102).

An image of eternal life (Sjoo and Mor 58), here the moon also symbolizes vision. Not just passively viewed but seeing, unlike most of Atwood's characters as we first encounter them, this Diana goddess is above the earth and its problems. Like many statues of the goddess, however, she is mouthless (Motif

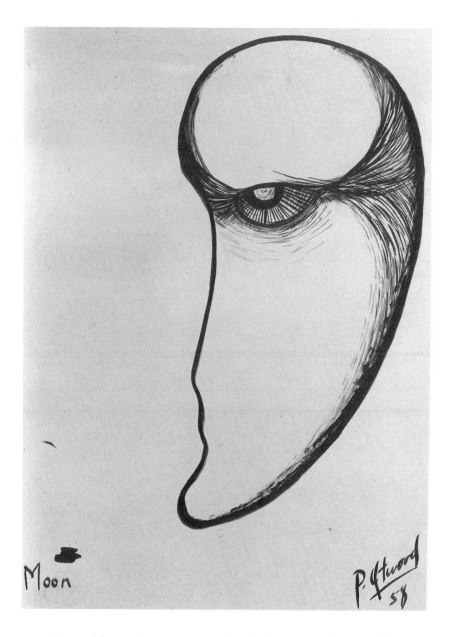

FIGURE 2. Moon; ink drawing; signed by P. Atwood, 1958; Atwood Papers;
23.7 × 31.7 cm.

F513.0.3) and thus voiceless, a quality Atwood associates with impotence. Like "New Poems"' moon (*SP II*), this skull moon is not, apparently, a goddess of mercy and could even be a target ("Not the Moon" and "Machine. Gun. Nest" 175–76, 165). Never caring or returning human regard, the moon in these poems, however, no longer sees. In "Galliano Coast: Four Entrances," the new moon, not anthropomorphized, "sheds grace without intention" on a paradise of loss (*SP II* 169). In "Not the Moon," fishing for the silver light or praying to the moon is futile: it is people, not nature or its mythic incarnations, who can answer questions, know names, and care about amputations and other horrors of war. The real "goddess," "not the moon, or anything we can see clearly," need not be any thing, but only "the light we see by," the inner vision (Motifs D1810.0.11, D1810.8.1) or third eye developed by the narrators of *Surfacing*, *Cat's Eye*, and *Murder in the Dark* (*SP II*, Oxford 176).

Atwood's treatment of the goddess in *Double Persephone* (1961) is again paradoxical.[12] This volume presents both white and black Eve/Snakes, simultaneously Demeter and Persephone, the serpents of wisdom and temptation, and the trees of life and knowledge/death in the double garden of creation and destruction (Figs. 3 and 4). Although this rare book of poems does not credit Atwood with designing and printing both covers, the linocut designs, finished in 1961 just after the poems (Atwood Tape), illuminate unrecognized dimensions of meaning: they suggest the Snake Goddess incarnation of the Great Mother, again depicted without a mouth. These covers suggest a well-known folklore motif of a snake body with a woman's head (B29.2.3), represented in Bosch's *The Hay-Wain* and *The Last Judgement* (see De Tolnay 118–19, 168–70). They also anticipate Atwood's later mythical, biblical, and fairy-tale snakes, including *Surfacing*'s association of snake and mushroom folklore, *You Are Happy*'s snake goddess, and *Interlunar*'s "Snake Poems" based on the Grimms' "The White Snake," North-American snake tales and legends, and snake goddess myth.

FIGURE 3. *Double Persephone*; front cover; linocut, 1961; Atwood Papers; 13 × 17 cm.

FIGURE 4. *Double Persephone*; back cover; linocut, 1961; Atwood Papers; 13 x 17 cm.

In the poems' text, the artist is apparently a Medusa-crone disguised as Atwood's first "dancing girl" ("Persephone Departing"), and her artificial, gorgon touch opposes the touch of life. Like the waters controlled by the snake goddess (Gimbutas, *Goddesses* 145), her garden paths become labyrinthine snake spirals. Here transformation, usually positive in Atwood's literary work, is viewed from its negative underside as flesh changes into statue, leaves into letters. Thus, if Atwood's female artist is a Medusa, turning life into stony art (McCombs on Davey's discussion, *Critical Essays* 11; Davey, "Atwood's" 135), Atwood reinforces Graves's injunction that the female be muse rather than artist. Or does she?

According to Graves, the first stage of European cultural development, the neolithic period favorable to poetry because of its dedication to the goddess-muse (*White Goddess* 9–11, 14), is epitomized in the Aegean icon depicting "a Moon-woman, a Star-son, and a wise spotted serpent under a fruit-tree." Although Graves briefly mentions a serpent goddess, his Serpent is the goddess's male lover, twin and foe of the Star-son lover with whom the poet (always male) identifies himself (*White Goddess* 387–89). Later Christianity associates Eve, the snake in the garden, and the tree of knowledge's fruit with the temptation and consequent fall of "man," a traditional misnomer for "men"; thus, serpents were associated with she-devils (Walker, *Woman's Dictionary* 262). Patriarchal heroes (St. George, St. Patrick, Perseus) traditionally slay the moon mother, associated not only with Eve but with the Catholic Church's Mary and Hinduism's Kali, in the shape of a great serpent, dragon, or sea monster (Sjoo and Mor 155).

In its ancient symbolism of female power, however, the snake stands for the power of life and enlightenment. "In Arabic, the words for 'snake,' 'life,' and 'teaching' are all related to the name of Eve—the Biblical version of the Goddess with her serpent form." Eve is associated with Lamia, the Serpent Goddess of Libya conventionally depicted with a woman's head and breasts, the Greek Medusa (Walker, *Woman's Dictionary* 388–89, 262), and

Hebrew legend's rebellious Lilith, part snake, subject of her own goddess cult (Sjoo and Mor 276–77), and emblem of the uppity woman. According to archaeologist Marija Gimbutas, in neolithic and chalcolithic eras, "The snake [is] the vehicle of immortality" and the snake's presence is "a guarantee that nature's enigmatic cycle [will] be maintained and its life-giving powers not diminish" (*Goddesses* 95). The snake goddess, like the closely associated bird goddess depicted in Atwood's watercolors of angels and harpies, represents "the feminine principle" (Gimbutas, *Goddesses* 145). Similarly, the Tree of Life that Christianity transposes into Tree of Knowledge and then Torture Cross symbolizes the cosmic energy of the Goddess (Daly, *Gyn/ecology* 79–81). On the cover of *Double Persephone*, Atwood breaks with traditional iconography by rejoining the goddess to both snake and tree. By doing so, she refeminizes the imagery and revisions patriarchal conceptions, such as Keats's icy femmes fatales in "Lamia" and "La Belle Dame Sans Merci" (both 1820), of women's roles in life and art.

Thus, not only is Atwood's first female artist, like the goddess and any woman, more complex than we have thought; so is Atwood's famous dualism (Grace, *Violent*). If, as "Her Song" suggests, "There are two kinds of death" and two immortalities, one natural and one artificial, *Double Persephone* presents them as phases of a cycle. Although the poems begin and end in a symbolic winter, "Pastoral" cycles through all four seasons and "Iconic Landscape" rocks day and night "round into one." Despite Demeter's periodic freezing touch and the poems' ominous conclusion with Persephone's impending departure to the underworld, Persephone is more than double. In terms of usual interpretations, however, we should not forget that she is at least double, in the world as well as the underworld, signifying spring as well as withered crone, nature as well as art, creator rather than muse.

Like many other Canadian works published before 1970, *Double Persephone*'s text may temporarily trap Venus and Diana inside a predominant Hecate; but, as Graves ironically reminds us, Hecate's Medusa mask warns the profane against trespassing on her mysteries (*Greek Myths* I 17). Persephone is more than a fickle femme fatale. From earliest times, the Goddess sacrifices herself to the earth. North American Natives' Corn Mother, whose limbs are severed, gives her blood to the earth so that her children, humanity, can cultivate corn. Similarly, Demeter-Ceres is "reaped as the grain with her own moon-shaped sickle" (Sjoo and Mor 165–66). Even in the best-known patriarchal versions of the myth, Persephone leaves the earth, not of her free will but because Hades abducts and rapes her, symbolizing male usurpation of the female mysteries (Graves, *Greek Myths* I 93). In *Double Persephone*'s last poem, Hades's black horses, finally overtaking Persephone's very breath, not only "Stamp impatient for her death" but threaten to trample both art and life.

If *Double Persephone*'s female artist, like that of the earlier "Speeches for Dr. Frankenstein," has a killing rather than magic touch, it is Graves's White Goddess, patriarchy's amputated substitute for the Great Goddess, that poisons, maims, and silences her. Viewed with its covers, *Double Persephone* presents both the societally debased goddess *and* her continually reborn antithesis: an image of female creativity and power. Although the poem series does not approach the power of *The Circle Game* (1966), rather than showing the female artist's inefficacy or impotence, *Double Persephone* confronts and works through the female artist's double or triple "bind" (Juhasz 1, Trinh 6).

Atwood's watercolors depicting a termite queen (Plate 12) and a mother harpy and chics (1974, Plate 13) and her collage of a harpy (cover of *GB*, Plate 14) are comic versions of the debased goddess. Her power truncated in sexist society, the Termite Queen Goddess becomes American television's "Queen for a Day," a prom queen, and a beauty pageant winner; the goddess's ancient image is parodically reduced to an insect's costume.

The satiric watercolor of the termite queen is an illustration for the "Variations for the Termite Queen" poem series (Atwood

Telephone Call, 29 September 1987) listed in early *You Are Happy* Tables of Content (*YAH* Manuscripts, Atwood Papers Box 13) and published in *Kayak* (1973, 3–6). This series, earlier called "The Life of the Termite Queen," has five parts: "The Termite Nest," "Her Arrival on These Shores," "Ancient Artifacts," "Cosmology," and "Her Destiny." The Termite Queen of these poems is an immortal and passive receptacle of "matter without form." In the nest, "Other termites cram food into her mouth and carry away / the eggs which emerge in due time regularly as sausages"; and blind soldiers, "all jaw," fight the war that surrounds her. Because statues of this goddess, like those of most fertility goddesses, have broken or gnawed-off arms and legs, she is a "sacred amputee," "the Holy Torso," and even her priests and priestesses have fingers amputated in her honor. Once evoked, her devotees must either abandon her or drag her with them. Yet, the Termite Queen's destiny is to lie undefeated but abandoned, "hoarding herself," while "the gaps where parts of her body / do not quite join fill with snow" (3–6).

Atwood's watercolor of the Termite Queen closely follows the second poem, depicting the goddess in gown and crown, wearing a World War One gas mask and carrying a bouquet of roses. Ironically pictured with Hecate's waning crescent moon but wearing the color of love, battle (Graves, *White Goddess* 70), and resurrection (Gimbutas, *Goddesses* 159) connected to the full-moon goddess, the pregnant Venus of the watercolor is a parodic violated Persephone, whose life, love, fertility, and fame are already shadowed by death (Cirlot 77–78, 207–08; Daly, *Gyn/ecology* 75–78; *Surv* 199). Targeted in the blood red that Atwood associates with victimization, the Termite Queen ironically anticipates the Handmaid breeders of *The Handmaid's Tale*. With a tiny head and huge, pregnant body reminiscent of Venus of Willendorf and other fertility figures originally serving matriarchal rather than patriarchal ends, this goddess is what Adrienne Rich calls "the eternal fucking machine" (*Of Woman Born* 285). Thus, she is one of the reflected or conditioned images

Marian, Joan, Rennie, Offred, and Elaine repudiate (*EW*, *LO*, *BH*, *HT*, *CE*).

Like her male harpy (1976) (Plate 10), Atwood's untitled watercolor (archive labeled "Atwoods as Birds," 1974 signed) presents an irreverent view of a bird deity and punctures pompous poses, including taking oneself too seriously (Plate 13). Also anticipating her pose as "Margarets Atwood" ("Review of Second Words" 251–53), Atwood undercuts critics' desires to see her as multiple. Identifying the figures as a mother harpy and chicks rather than one or several Atwoods, Atwood is interested in the idea of women (chicks) as birds (Tape), evident not only in contemporary slang but in the Grimms' "Fitcher's Bird." Harpies, mythological bird-people with the arms and breasts of women, appear in Greek mythology and folklore (Motif B52). Probably once the same as Valkyries, harpies were children of the ocean nymph Electra and came from a cave on Mounte Dicte, home of the Cretan Goddess. Their name meant "snatchers" or "pluckers," and they predate the Christian angel as a bearer of souls (Walker, *Woman's Encyclopedia* 374; Graves, *Greek I* 128, *II* 230). Later, however, they were considered hideous and feared, even confused with sirens and the furies (Leach and Fried 482). In addition to comically re-visioning the Goddess, Atwood parodies the societal inconsistency of viewing women as bitch-harpies as well as chic chicks.

Atwood's recent collage (credited) for the cover of *Good Bones* (Coach House, 1992)[13] is another humorous and satiric harpy (Plate 14; Motif B52). The figure, whose separate body parts are cut from magazine advertisements (Atwood, qtd. *Toronto Star*), has a beribboned hat, grape-cluster hair, sun-glass breasts, a tail of mascaraed human eyes, and a wing of lipsticked mouths. Although it will again be taken as a self-caricature in the style of Atwood's earlier *Survivalwoman* (Fig. 12), the harpy collage foregrounds the volume's bird motif and perfectly expresses its comically sarcastic tone. The figure especially suggests the protagonist of the volume's first story, "Bad News," featuring a Medusa harpy with a "literate" serpent hairdo and a siren howl (9–10). The disparity of using contemporary found materials to picture a classic figure focuses on the mass culture we all share and on its mythic and fairy-tale intertexts, too often distorted into stereotypes blocking our vision.

Like several untitled bird watercolors, such as *Angel* (Plate 19), the Sphinx watercolor suggests another goddess role, in this case the two-faced goddess of birth and death associated with the Sphinx (Walker, *Woman's Encyclopedia* 957). With the face of a woman, the body and tail of a lion, and the wings of a bird, the Sphinx is another well-known motif in myth and folklore (B51). As we have seen, it is one of several mythological or magical birds significant in Atwood's work. Unlike the best-known Sphinx of *Oedipus Rex*, whose riddle (Motifs H541.1.1, H761) is answered with "man," Atwood's female characters, often goddess parodies, have to find their own, gender-specific answers to the riddles of existence.

Among the important visual art that is not in the Atwood Papers are the cover (not pictured here) and collages published in *The Journals of Susanna Moodie* (1970), illustrating Canadian and gender survival. Because Charles Pachter's art for *The Journals of Susanna Moodie* (in the Art Gallery of Ontario and the National Library of Canada) was too expensive to reproduce, Atwood did the color painting of the Susanna Moodie family (Fig. 8, *JSM* Collage 4), privately owned but once reproduced by Gloria Onley, at the time she wrote the poetry. This was the original for the illustration of the family in the book. The untitled collages in *The Journals of Susanna Moodie* are "composed of a nineteenth-century drawing or painting with a twentieth-century watercolour bit superimposed on top of it." Atwood "did the watercolour bit and used the other stuff as collage material" (Tape).[14]

The photograph of the Canadian poet on the cover of *The Journals of Susanna Moodie*, placed at a ninety-degree angle to the wilderness horizon, introduces the volume's main themes. The cover and the six collages visually depict the poems' conflicts:

FIGURE 5. Moodie and the Wilderness, Journal I; untitled collage, *The Journals of Susanna Moodie* illustration, 1970; 22.4 × 12.6 cm.

FIGURE 6. The Wereman; untitled collage, *The Journals of Susanna Moodie* illustration, 1970; 22.4 × 12.6 cm.

FIGURE 7. Journal II; untitled collage, *The Journals of Susanna Moodie* illustration, 1970; 22.4 × 12.6 cm.

FIGURE 8. Susanna Moodie Family; untitled collage, *The Journals of Susanna Moodie* illustration, 1970; 22.4 × 12.6 cm.

FIGURE 9. Moodie, Journal III; untitled collage, *The Journals of Susanna Moodie*
illustration, 1970; 22.4 × 12.6 cm.

FIGURE 10. Moodie Underground; untitled collage, *The Journals of Susanna Moodie* illustration, 1970; 22.4 × 12.6 cm.

"the violent dualities" between the Moodie family and nature, between nature and civilization, between different facets of Susanna, and among Canadians. Both poems and collages dramatize metamorphosis and death-rebirth themes. When Susanna's husband "enters the forest/ and is blotted out" in both the "Wereman" collage and poem (Fig. 6), he begins the shape-changing process (*JSM* Collage 2; 18–19). Atwood's Susanna, and by implication Canada, progresses from being an urban woman "pasted" on the alien wilderness (Fig. 5) (*JSM* Collage 1)—the Persephone figure blind in her innocence—to the Venus bearing children and integrating with the landscape as she is "crept in / upon by green" (Figs. 7, 8) (*JSM* Collages 3, 4; 26). With her children dead and her face a pitted moon (Fig. 9) (*JSM* Collage 5), she is a Hecate aware of her "double voice" as she "revolve[s] among the vegetables" and orbits the apple trees (42, 48). The final collage (Fig. 10) (*JSM* Collage 6), an underground figure accompanying "Alternate Thoughts from Underground," is the Hecate who already pushes up for "Resurrection" and the beginning of a new cycle (56).

As we have seen, Atwood often relies on folklore, history, and myth to provide contextual resonance. Similarly, separate works together suggest motifs, also present in poetry and fiction, that illuminate them all. Thus, just as her poetry images amputated heads, hands, fingers, hearts, tongues, breasts, wombs, and penises, Atwood's visual art depicts sliced open, cut off, or separate body pieces as victims of power politics.

No wonder that the insulated woman of *Murder in the Dark*'s cover (Plate 16) (1983), shielding herself behind dark glasses and a hooded coat despite the dark masses beginning to cover the sun, is protectively layered! Elizabeth Campbell states that the cover belies and satirizes "the dying lady traditionally required for artistic creation" (10). This collage, composed from caviar, sun block, and wet-look bathing-suit advertisements in *Vogue* (Atwood Tape), also suggests *Bodily Harm*'s Rennie and all the other Atwood protagonists who use camera vision and fold or dangle their hands instead of reaching out. Life-tourists filtering their vision through the manufactured reality of mass culture (Wilson, "Camera" 51), their gaze is frequently colonizing. Atwood characters are often at least partly responsible for dismembering themselves (Motif F1035). Like the artist-personae of *You Are Happy* and *Interlunar*, the "I" of *Murder in the Dark* remembers, in this case through personal, mythic, and fairy-tale remembering (e.g., "Autobiography" 9, "Worship" 51, "She" 50), touching ("Hand" 59), and seeing ("Instructions for the Third Eye" 61–62). By creating and re-visioning images such as the bleeding bread of the Grimms' "God's Food" (Motif F991.3.1, No. 205)[15] for the eyes of our imaginations ("Bread" 41–42), the artist helps us open the eyes of our bodies so that we may "touch the light" and one another ("Hand," "Instructions for the Third Eye" 59, 61).

Dismemberment, a frequent feature in folklore and myth (e.g., Motif D1884), may be a means to re-memberment and rebirth for the goddess, the artist, and the reader. The broken heart of the Canadian *True Stories* cover (Plate 17) (Oxford 1981) may also be viewed in this context. Like the watercolors depicting Mary Queen of Scots or Anne Boleyn and their executioners (Plates 4, 5, both 1969) and Fitcher's bride (Plate 3, 1970), the cover of *True Stories* suggests the amputation and dismemberment of sexual politics as well as ritualistic metamorphosis and rebirth. As in the "Bluebeard's Egg" story (*BE*) and the Ogre's Heart in the Egg tale type (AT 302), *True Stories* associates hearts and eggs, linking the bleeding heart to real Bluebeards and the soul-killing games of sexual politics, causing "death" from love or a broken heart (e.g., Motifs T81, F1041.1.1).

This "broken heart," exposed like that of the split body in Frida Kahlo's "The Two Fridas" (Mexico City, Museo Frida Kahlo), has either burst or been clinically "opened," sliced, or ripped out. Unlike the Virgin Mary's exposed heart of compassion in *Cat's Eye* and the frilly Valentine-heart watercolors Atwood painted as possible covers (Atwood Papers), this heart suggests bodily harm and abortion: it is a running, fertilized egg, possible food for this and other volumes' Robber Bridegrooms. As in fairy tales, legends, myth, and popular culture, hearts in Atwood's works are usually hard (Motif W155), heavy, broken (Motif F1041.1.1), filled with arrows (See Kahlo's "The Little Deer" on the Canadian cover of *WT*), torn out (Motif S139.6), removed (Motif D2062.1), or eaten (Motifs Q478.1, G262.2), parodying her characters' failure to live "true romance." If the amputations in *True Stories* cannot heal like those of "Fitcher's Bird," the red egg still suggests possibility of new life (see Chapter 9). When "you" breaks the egg in the volume's final poem, "Last Day," "the sky / turns orange again and the sun rises / again and this is the last day again" (103). Mythic cycle again displaces despair.

Atwood designed the untitled watercolor of diatoms' *Microscope Image* (Plate 18) (Atwood letter 6 July 1993), as a possible cover for *Bodily Harm* (Atwood Tape). Earlier Atwood had suggested using a scientific slide of a cell or amoeba in the process of division for the cover of *Two-Headed Poems*, and she remarked on how much she would love this kind of "organic quality" (Atwood Correspondence, Atwood Papers). Literally, *diatom* means cut in two or to cut through. In the context of the book, Plate 18 suggests the food cycle, the fish eat fish motif, and by extension, cancer cells, Rennie's mastectomy, her lifestyle,and both psychological and colonial segmentation and invasion.[16] Rennie associates her cut-open breast with a wall painting in the Sunset Inn of a cut-open melon. She "fears that the scar on her breast will split open 'like a diseased fruit' and that a centipede, maggots, worms, or something. . . in the 'cellar' of her Griswold 'subground' will crawl out." In *Bodily Harm* the cell image symbolizes cancer of the female and world body and represents "all women, all victims and oppressors, all human beings, all" (Wilson, "Turning" 141, 138). Thus, the invaded cells of the body also suggest cancer of the earth. Because of the Goddess's stature as the mother of all, the womb of the earth, these diseased cells also suggest a colonized Mother Nature, prefiguring the demonic, fallen world of *The Handmaid's Tale* (Wilson, "A Note" 115; see Chapters 8 and 10).

Atwood says she drew *Amanita Caesarea, Egg, Cross-Section on Cloud* (Fig. 11) around 1980 with a magic marker and brushed it over with water (Tape). Literally, it features a cross-section of a poisonous amanita mushroom. Because its spores are called eggs, the clouds are black, and its laboratory cut is a Caesarean, it simultaneously suggests national (Roman, American, British) and gender imperialism or pollution[17] and a sexually and surgically opened womb, the kind of violation *Bodily Harm*, originally titled *The Robber Bridegroom*, symbolizes with Rennie's mastectomy. This drawing even seems to resemble the painting of a cut-open melon Rennie associates with her mastectomy. As in "The Robber Bridegroom" and "Fitcher's Bird" fairy tales, however, ritual rebirth follows dismemberment, in *Bodily Harm*, throughout Atwood's work, and, by implication, in "Amanita Caesarea."

The full moon is, as we have seen, associated with the goddess in her Venus aspect and, as in *Murder in the Dark*'s cover, dark clouds seem about to diminish her light. Certainly the spores or eggs, like the seeds of goddess iconography (Gimbutas, *Civilization* 223) symbolize the generation of life. The mushroom's heavenly position, on a cloud, suggests the magic mushrooms of myth, legend, folklore, and seventies' popularity and, since the cloud is black, possibly the poison of this mushroom. In *Surfacing*, eating mushrooms, associated with eating snake and the Grimms' "The White Snake," symbolically empowers the narrator to understand the languages of animals and the earth (see Chapter 4). According to Graves, the nectar and ambrosia of the gods and of the Eleusian Mysteries celebrating Demeter were really intoxicant mushrooms, including the *amanita muscaria* that induces hallucinations, prophetic sight, and erotic energy. "The Maenads' savage custom of tearing off their victims' heads" may even refer to tearing off the sacred mushroom's head (*Greek Myths*

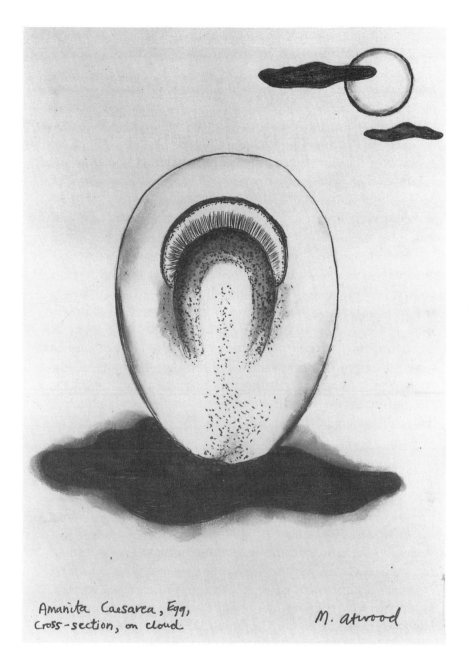

Amanita Caesarea, Egg,
Cross-section, on cloud

M. atwood

FIGURE 11. Amantia Caesarea, Egg, Cross-Section on Cloud; drawing, undated; Atwood Papers; 16.4 × 23.9 cm.; inside top horizontal and right
vertical pencil lines 16.0 × 23.5 cm.

I 9–10, 94). The ritual dismemberment and cannibalism of some of these rites, lingering symbolically in Christian communion (Walker, *Woman's Encyclopedia* 135–39) and relating to the magic cannibalism of "The Juniper Tree" (Motifs G61, E607.1), were probably originally attempts to partake of eternal rebirth in the Great Mother, whose womb wound healed itself (Sjoo and Mor 81–82). Thus, Atwood's imagery again transcends patriarchal and cultural violation by evoking the goddess's rebirth (see Wilson, "A Note" 115–16).

Angel (Plate 19) is one of several angel watercolors (Tape). Like *Double Persephone*'s Eve/tree/snake, Atwood's angels are at least double: "the others, and those who fell" ("An Angel" 43). Another sometimes parodic bird goddess or god, the angel in Atwood's work is often associated with disguise (Motif K1828). Many of Atwood's females run into trouble by trying to be the Angel in Coventry Patmore's popular nineteenth-century poem, "The Angel in the House," according to Woolf, the negative heritage and self-image the woman writer must kill ("Professions" 285). Sally, for example, parodically plays the angel in "The Girl Without Hands" ("Bluebeard's Egg"). See also the *Canadian Tea Angel à la Johnson* on *The CanLit Foodbook* cover. The angel-police of *The Handmaid's Tale* disguise themselves as the Bible's dark or destroying angels (Motif K1828.1), and the dark angel appears as a suicide voice to the narrators of *The Handmaid's Tale* and *Cat's Eye*. The destroying angel of Atwood's recent prose poem, "An Angel," is again suicide. "Heavy with anti-matter, a dark star," she is a "rebellious waitress" with the face of a grey egg (*SP II* 157–58; "Two Stories" 43–44; *GB* 109–11. Atwood recently abandoned a novel titled "Destroying Angels" that she was working on eight months before beginning *The Handmaid's Tale*.[18]

While Plates 20 and 21 are not as effective as many of the other artworks, these watercolors visually depict the drowned world so important in Atwood's early poetry, including "This is a Photograph of Me" (*CG*). The drowned or drowning woman, designed to accompany a poem in *Power Politics* (Tape), has a cut throat and is leaving her children behind as she sinks to the underworld. As the childless persona fills the blue cup in the poem, she remembers one of the old stories that, with this volume's tarot cards, seem to foretell her death by water: "it is the pond again / where the children, looking from / the side of the boat, see their mother / upside down, lifesize, hair streaming / over the slashed throat /and words fertilize each other / in the cold and with bulging eyes" (41).

The second untitled watercolor with a drowned figure (Plate 21) illustrates the ambiguous final poem in *Power Politics*, "He is Last Seen" (56) (Tape), a poem that has seemed to suggest not only the persona's powerlessness but the potential harmony between nature and humanity (J. Rosenberg 72). The androgynous figure[19] is journeying under water through clutching coral, holding what appears to be a wedding bouquet. On one level, since the poem persona imagines the "he" walking toward her "carrying a new death" and she may be already drowned, both male and female are spouses of death. The gift he carries in the poem, a glass paperweight of a scene depicting male and female hand in hand, under endlessly falling snow, is represented in the watercolor's wedding bouquet: the persona fears the *Citizen Kane* stasis of a glass-enclosed world and these socially prescribed roles. She sees him with a flat, scaled face and feels her actions cannot affect his. Thus, the safety of *Power Politics*'s final poem could be ironic; the volume would then end uncharacteristically for Atwood's poetry books, with the female narrator again projecting a "killer" role onto her "other."

On the other hand, perhaps what the two carry or expect is only death if it conforms to old patterns; perhaps the death prepares for rebirth. In any case, by the end of *Power Politics*, both the "I" and the "you" are peeling off the projected images of myth, literature, and fairy tales. Despite the tragic tone, both watercolors illustrate not only the kind of role portrayal or projection that characterizes narcissism (Motif N339.10) and games of "Power Politics" but also another archetypal means of symbolic death and rebirth. The last words of the volume are "firm ground and safety" (56).

Finally, conceptually if not chronologically, is the self- and Canada-parodying *Survivalwoman* (Fig. 12) of the seventies comic strip Atwood wrote for *This Magazine*'s "Kanadian Kultchur Komix" under the name, "Bart Gerrard." Atwood has done cartoons since she was five, and she and her brother used to create comic books for one another. Occasionally she still does them (Tape). The Atwood Papers also include the self-parodying "The Glamour and Fashion Page, or How to Achieve Effects You Would Not Have Thought Possible Even in Your Wildest Dreams!" In addition to giving the persona Atwood's curly hair, her early entry into high school, her sister-in-law Lenore, and even her Governor General's Award, this strip ridicules female fashions, conformity to changing definitions of glamour, and the role conditioning that makes female glamour seem more important than intelligence. Some of "Bart Gerrard's" "Kanadian Kultchur Komix" show Canadian Broadcasting Corporation executives meeting in a broom closet, the "Cultural Infiltration Agency" recruiting for an assignment in the Writer's "Onion" [Union] and the "Onion" thinking of changing its name to the "Writer's Lemon of Kanada" (Atwood Papers).

Pitted against fellow Canadians Boughtman, Rodentman, Labourlad, Gooseman, and the Ostrich People, and, especially, against the U.S. imperialist Sam the Ham, the *Survivalwoman* strip raises many of the still current issues Atwood discusses in *Survival* (1972): the invasion of U.S. culture, Canada's lack of identity, its failure to support its own culture, and national, cultural, and gender struggles to survive. Also known as "The Flying Kotex Limited," "the Fighting Failure," and—in a rejected stars-and-stripes version of her costume—"the Canadian dream," the maple-leaf-caped Survivalwoman wears an "S" on her chest mirroring Sam the Ham's. In Figure 12 Survivalwoman has a chance to rescue Pierre Truedough (Trudeau), almost confused with the popular author Pierre Burton. Like all of At-

FIGURE 12. Survivalwoman Comic by "Bart Gerrard" [Atwood]. "Kanadian Kultchur Komix," Comic Strip Series, *This Magazine*, 1979; Atwood Papers; 14.4 × 35.1 cm.

wood's personae, Survivalwoman strives for magic transformation and actually utters what she thinks is a magic word,
"Whammieq!" Resembling Atwood's literary works, the comic
humorously undercuts not only superpowers but "superpower"
and still foregrounds the real power of language. Because she is
tired of "just surviving" and attacks what she sees as her country's voluntary assumption of victim positions, Survivalwoman
points the way to the implied real survivors of Atwood's novels
and poems.

Using the Grimms' "Fitcher's Bird," the Triple Goddess, and
other intertexts to illuminate the struggle of ordinary females
and males to survive, Atwood's visual art foregrounds sexual
politics. Like such contemporary female artists as Mary Beth
Edelson, Judy Chicago, and Betye Saar, Atwood re-visions
Graves's White Goddess: "exorcising the patriarchal creation
myth through a repossession of the female visionary faculties,"
their visual art presents a new feminist myth (Orenstein 158). In
Atwood's case, however, her mythic art liberates through laughter as well as knowledge: its memorable images evoke, sometimes
parody, the eternally reborn goddess in order to celebrate humanity's ability to surmount victimization.

Tragic, comic, and inspiring, the images of sexual politics in
Atwood's visual art parallel those of her fiction, poetry, and criticism. Whether alluding to the literal consummation of "mates"
by the Robber Bridegroom or the wolf of *The Handmaid's Tale*; a
Bluebeard's deadly sexual test that culminates in his own death;
the female Frankenstein's creation of a monster who shadows
her; or the comic revelation of Bluebeard/the wolf as a pot-
bellied Scrabble-player, Atwood's images reflect, parody, and
transform the timeless roles to which we have been married. As
we shall continue to see, these images are far from hopeless.
According to *True Stories'* "Variations on the Word 'Love,'"

> This word is not enough but it will
> have to do. It's a single

vowel in this metallic
silence, a mouth that says
O again and again in wonder
and pain, a breath, a finger-
grip on a cliffside. You can
hold on or let go (Simon and Schuster 83).

③

Cannibalism and Metamorphosis in *The Edible Woman*

"The Robber Bridegroom"

In *The Edible Woman* (1969), Atwood's first published novel, the fairy-tale intertext focuses on food, recalling ancient images of witches, wizards, parents, and spouses, who, deliberately or not, eat the precious "food"—other human beings.[1]

The Edible Woman was written in 1965, the same year Atwood began doctoral study in Cambridge, Massachusetts,[2] a setting she uses for *The Handmaid's Tale* (1985, 1986). The two novels are more similar than they may at first seem: in addition to their implicit or explicit parody of graduate school (Atwood has joked that *The Handmaid's Tale* is an exposé of the Harvard English Department [1986 Conversation]), both novels are enriched with some of the same fairy tales involving dismemberment and cannibalism. Like "Hesitations Outside the Door," *Lady Oracle*, *Bluebeard's Egg*, and the "Fitcher's Bird" watercolor, both works draw on the Grimms' "Fitcher's Bird" (No. 46, AT 311), the tale about the groom who chops up brides who dare to open the forbidden door (Motif C913) and on the Grimms' "Little Red Cap" (No. 26, AT 333). Most important, as in *Bodily Harm* and "The Robber Bridegroom" poem and watercolor, *The Edible Woman* and

The Handmaid's Tale embed the Grimms' "The Robber Bride-groom" (No. 40, AT 955), a parallel tale in which a groom literally consumes fiancées. *The Edible Woman* also embeds or alludes to a number of other fairy, folk, and nursery tales involving cannibalism, metamorphosis through the act of eating, or a symbolic deadly consummation: "Hansel and Gretel," "The Gingerbread Boy," "Goldilocks and the Three Bears," *Alice in Wonderland*, "Peter Peter Pumpkin-Eater," "Cinderella," "Sleeping Beauty," and "Rapunzel."[3]

As Chapter 2 began to show, eating and food images are evident throughout Atwood's work. Of the tales that have most influenced Atwood, several ("The Robber Bridegroom," "The Juniper Tree," "The White Snake") (Atwood Telephone Call 1985) have predominant eating images. Atwood even discusses her fascination with cookbooks and eating habits (illustrating some of the foodways) in the "cookbook" she compiled as a P.E.N. International money raiser, *The CanLit Foodbook: From Pen to Palate—A Collection of Tasty Literary Fare* (1987). *Amanita Caesarea, Egg, Cross-Section on Cloud*, the photographed flour-and-salt Christmas decorations on the cover of *Two-Headed Poems*, the untitled watercolor of one creature eating another, and her illustrations in *The CanLit Foodbook* (Figs. 1, 11; Plates 1, 2) are visual expressions of this interest in food metaphors. According to Atwood, once a home-economics major who still is a good cake decorator, her interest in edible art was "part of the impetus for the cake in *The Edible Woman*, an anthropomorphic *objet* made of foodstuffs, such as candy brides and grooms and Donald Duck cakes in Woolworth's" (Atwood Tape). Resembling the *CanLit Foodbook's Wedding Cake Hodgins, with Spice*, picturing bride-and-groom dolls submerged head-first in the wedding cake (173, see Chapter 2), both cakes suggest that the "spice" is human flesh. Along with The Grimms' "The Juniper Tree," used in *Surfacing*, "The Robber Bridegroom" intertext is the basis for the cannibalism theme in *The Edible Woman* and throughout Atwood's work.

Even working in a company described as food (18), Marian in *The Edible Woman* consumer-product-tests a society in which everyone and everything, including nature, is product and consumer. Several critics have recognized that the central metaphor of this novel is food: "Living and eating are . . . metaphorically equivalent . . . eating is the means of individual identity. . . . To exist is an activity of daily transformation" (M. Nicholson 37). According to Page, "More than food gets eaten in life—our very souls and beliefs live by the conquering and consumption of other people's souls and beliefs" (9). No one has commented on Atwood's use of fairy-tale intertext, however, or on the significance of "The Robber Bridegroom" in *The Edible Woman*.[4]

In addition to satirizing contemporary societal cannibalism and revealing Marian's recognition of her complicity in it, the food metaphors in *The Edible Woman* resemble those of *Lady Oracle* (Wilson, "Fragmented" 52, 65–85): they can be linked to psychological and food disorders. Despite Atwood's indication of schizophrenia or other serious split-personality illness in an early draft of the novel,[5] the problems are anorexia nervosa (Cameron, "Famininity" 45–69) and, for Marian, its probable cause: the void of self associated with narcissism (see "Fragmented" 50–85 on *LO*) and conditioned female subservience. As will be evident, each of the protagonists in Atwood's novels is amputated, missing senses and even body parts. In *The Edible Woman*, Marian is symbolically mouthless. Resembling the expressionistic figure in Edvard Munch's *The Scream* (Boston Museum of Fine Arts) as well as the Bride in "The Robber Bridegroom," Marian closes her ears to her distress and is passive while we feel the effect of her mad world. We never hear her say "yes" to her engagement (84), and later her voice is feeble, "flannelly," when she is with Peter. Like *Bodily Harm*'s Rennie, Marian must find her voice and the identity it expresses.

Renouncing both eating (parody of Motif F1033) and voice, Marian ironically narrates the novel, with parts 1 and 3 in first person, 2 in a distant third person, suggesting alienation not only from society but from herself. Significantly, part 2 begins right after Marian mentions her two dolls and decides to throw them away as she cleans and gets organized (105–6; see n. 5). Employing techniques (such as reversal, inversion, exaggeration, circularity, terrible punning, rearrangement within a closed field, and incongruity) found in nonsense literature (see S. Stewart), Marian's surrealistic narration "gives an unfocussed, dreamlike effect to many of [the book's] hilarious but menacing events" (Stow 91). Paradoxically, Marian has mock-Gothic fears of eating, being eaten, suddenly changing into someone else, and being unable to transform at all.

From the first pages of the novel, the remarkable references to food, eating, and cooking are, like these characters' obsession with oral functions, more characteristic of fabulation than realism. As in *Lady Oracle* and several of her watercolors, Atwood develops a marvelous comic-Gothic. Marian is on her way to make breakfast as she encounters her roommate, Ainsley Tewce (originally Susan and then Angela Tusch) (*EW* manuscripts, Atwood Papers, Box 18). A professional tooth-brush tester who socializes with dental students, Ainsley is nursing a hangover from a party focused on "the insides of people's mouths." Feeling as if she is contained in a plastic bag as she rushes to her job with Seymour Surveys, Marian is immersed in the "soup" when she enters her hot-as-a-furnace office. Her company, "layered like an ice-cream sandwich," with her department being the "gooey middle layer" between men and machines, is under the watchful eye of Mrs. *Bogue*. Since Marian is neither man nor machine, Mrs. Bogue represents the only possibility of metamorphosis (*EW* 9, 12, 16, 18, 19, 22). Then the dietician, Mrs. *Withers*, asks her to pre-test canned rice pudding; and the accountant, Mrs. *Grot*, a woman "with hair the color of a metal refrigerator-tray," demands that Marian sign up for a pension plan in which people would "feed off [her] salary." Mrs. Bogue even recounts office folklore of interviewers breaking legs in meat-cleaver encounters and being smeared blood red in tomato-juice taste tests (19, 23,

16, 168). After handling a complaint about a fly in raisin cereal, Marian arranges respondents to a Moose Beer advertisement, which refers to "Manly flavour," "tang of the wilderness," and "hearty taste" associated with cannibal stories of the *Decameron*, Shakespeare, and the Grimms. Duncan, a subject who plays Baby Bear to Marian's Goldilocks, identifies "the pattern: . . . the husband kills the wife's lover, or vice versa, and cuts out the heart and makes it into a stew or pie and serves it up in a silver dish, and the other one eats it" (24–25, 53) (Motif Q478.1).

Preserved, baked in a witch's oven, and eventually served as food, Marian is, by turns, Gingerbread Woman, Cinderella, Sleeping Beauty, Rapunzel, Goldilocks, Alice in Wonderland,[6] Little Red Cap, the Pumpkin-eater's wife, Gretel, Fitcher's bride, and, especially, the Robber Bride.

The Grimms' "The Robber Bridegroom" ("Der Räuberbräutigam"), first published in 1812, is one of many Grimms' tales that use Marie Hassenpflug as a source (Zipes, *Complete* 717). "The Robber Bridegroom" is about a maiden who does not trust or love her prospective husband "the way a bride-to-be should" but feels "a secret horror" and "shudder[s] in her heart" when thinking about him. He insists she visit him and his guests Sunday in the dark forest, where he will scatter ashes so she can find the house. Feeling uneasy, she also marks her way with peas and lentils (Motif R145). When she reaches the dark and solitary house, it is "deadly silent" until a voice cries twice: "Turn back, turn back, young maiden dear, / 'Tis a murderer's house you enter here." The voice comes from a bird in a cage; otherwise, the house seems entirely empty as the maiden proceeds from room to room, coming at last to the cellar, where an extremely old woman, whose head bobs constantly, again tells her she is in a murderer's den: "You think you are a bride soon to be married, but you will keep your wedding with death." A kettle of water is on the fire; "When they have you in their power, they'll chop you to pieces without mercy. Then they'll cook you and eat you, because they're cannibals. If I don't take pity on you and save you, you'll be lost forever" (Hunt and Stern 200–201; Magoun and Krappe 151–52; Zipes *Complete* 153–55).

The maiden then hides behind a barrel, where she is told not to budge or move, just before the godless robbers return. They are dragging another maiden, whose heart bursts in two after she is forced to drink three glasses of wine: one white, one red, and one yellow (Motif F1041.1.1). The prospective bride realizes the fate planned for her as the victim is chopped into pieces and salted. The hiding maiden is almost discovered when the victim's chopped-off finger springs into the air, falling into her lap (in some versions, it lands in her bosom); but the old woman calls the robbers to dinner and drugs their wine. Both women escape, following the sprouted peas and lentils home, where the maiden tells everything to her father, the miller (Hunt and Stern 201–2; Magoun and Krappe 152–53; Zipes *Complete* 155–56).

On the day of the wedding celebration, the bridegroom appears with all the miller's friends, and each person is expected to tell a story. When the bride sits still and does not utter a word, the bridegroom says, "Come, my darling, do you know nothing?" She then relates a "dream," finally presenting the victim's chopped-off finger (H57.2.2.). Because the bride speaks, the Robber Bridegroom is executed: it is again the groom, not the bride, who marries death (Hunt and Stern 202–4; Magoun and Krappe 153–54; Zipes *Complete* 156–57). Tales closely related to "The Robber Bridegroom" have similar events. The ancient Greek version of "Fitcher's Bird" features a corpse-devouring death as the murderous husband (Leach and Fried 150); "The Castle of Murder" includes the old woman in the cellar, edible victims, and the tale-telling trap (Zipes *Complete* 670–71); and "Mr. Fox" features the warning, a woman's severed hand, the bloody chamber of "Fitcher's Bird," the bride's tale, and a cut-up groom (Carter, *Old Wives* 8–10; Grace, "Courting Bluebeard" n. 250).

"Robber Bridegroom" and related motifs figure prominently in *The Edible Woman*. In addition to explicit fear of marrying a cannibal (Motifs K1916, G81) and being chopped up and eaten, both the fairy tale and book feature distrust of the fiancé, path-marking on a forest journey (Motif R145), a visit to the bride-groom's home, unheeded warning, hiding, passivity, consumption of beverages, heartbreak, amputation, communal eating of precious food, assistance of an elderly "godmother," return to society, communal telling of the crime, presentation of an emblem representing the victim, and, finally, communal punishment/retribution. Dramatized through Marian's split, unreliable narration, most of these motifs occur comically in *The Edible Woman*. The novel also features or parodies motifs from "Fitcher's Bird," the Bluebeard tale about another dismembering groom and the curious "bird" who outwits him (see Chapters 2 and 9): disguise, enslaving touch, falling into an ogre's power (Motif G400), abduction by a monster (Motif R11.1), orders designed as tests, a forbidden chamber (Motif C611), amputated brides, stained honor, power reversal, a decorated substitute (Motifs K525, K521.1), the victims' re-membering and rebirth (Motif E30), revenge or punishment of the "murderer" (Motif Q211), and restoration of community.

Before Marian reaches the Robber/Fitcher's foreboding home, however, she has home, forest, or burrow encounters with a number of characters from popularized versions of other tales. Marian's roommate, Ainsley, plays the Prince to Len's Sleeping Beauty and Fish's Cinderella in the book's double parody of the "Cinderella"—"Sleeping Beauty" stories.[7] *The Edible Woman* is an anti-comedy in which the wrong person gets married (Atwood in Gibson 20–21); and the subplot mirrors the main plot, reversing the sexes of the Marian-Peter-Duncan triangle. Like Marian, Ainsley plays several simultaneous fairy-tale roles. She is a soulless, no longer little, mermaid (85) who, unable to please her first prince, catches another by becoming a fertility goddess. She is a "castrating," decapitating queen who manages to chop off her own as well as other heads in *Alice in Wonderland* (199). Preeminently, Ainsley is a Robber Bridegoom/Fitcher/wolf to double Marian's fiancé Peter, his pal Trigger, and witless "lady-killers" such as Len, who may be trapped and cooked in their own boiling cauldrons (variation of Motif K891.1).

Presiding over the excessively protected home from which our fairy-tale heroine travels (Heuscher 74) is the paradoxical "lady down below," whose modern realm has degenerated into the "lower regions" of a rooming house, in a district not as good as it used to be. Ironically, Marian fears the landlady's "heavenly thunder-bolts" and generally conforms to her "law of nuance," which forbids everything (274, 14). Like many of Atwood's witch or evil step-mother figures, including *Life Before Man*'s Auntie Muriel and *The Handmaid's Tale*'s Serena Joy, the woman down below wears symbolic gloves protecting her from touch. Obsessed with cleanliness and "the child's" innocence, she seems to burrow through the woodwork, ironically seeking evidence of what she considers evil. In contrast to the woman in Atwood's poem, "The Landlady," who is "a slab / of what is real, / solid as bacon" (*Animals in That Country* 14–15), the lady down below is the dark and Gothic side of the fairy-tale godmother. Like the other characters in this and any fabulation, she represents part of Marian. A "Rapunzel" enchantress who removes "the child" from others' hungers (Motif G204), she blocks Marian's escape from her "tower" (Motif R41.2), which is also Marian's conditioned self (see Atwood, *Surv* 209–10, and Chapters 6 and 11). Resembling the old fairy in Perrault's "Sleeping Beauty," the lady down below embodies a sleep-inducing curse (Motifs D1960.3, F316).

Unlike the warnings of the old woman in the cellar in "The Robber Bridegroom," those of the lady down below deny the existence of a cellar as well as the sustenance of life. Apparently covered with "an invisible plastic coating" impervious to dirt, she wears spotless gardening gloves, causing Marian to wonder "who she'd been burying in the garden" (93, 11). Although part of Marian is already swallowed and buried, she will emerge, like the Robber Bride, Little Red Cap, and Alice in Wonderland, from underground as well as background.

Avoiding Sleeping Beauty's spinning wheel (Motifs M341.2. 13, D1364.17), on which Len later becomes snarled (10, 220), Marian leaves "home" and journeys through the "forest" of Toronto, still a symbolic Sleeping Beauty (Motif D1960.3). Because a fairy-tale forest embodies isolation and noncommunity, it typically harbors witches ("Hansel and Gretel"), murderers and robbers ("The Robber Bridegroom" and "Fitcher's Bird"), dwarves ("Snow White"), and wolves ("Little Red Cap"). In the Grimms' tales, however, the forest is more dangerous for females than for males, suggesting a possible attempt to invert and eradicate the ancient belief in woman's control over nature (Bottigheimer, *Grimms' Bad* 102–5). In Marian's parodic forest, where she encounters a voice like cold oatmeal porridge and several parodic nursery-rhyme and fairy-tale figures, her passivity causes her to risk spiritual rather than actual death.

First, Marian enters the occupied house of the three bears (45, 50). The cadaverously thin baby-bear Duncan, fearing cannibalism but ironically ravenous for real and narcissistic food, also plays the mock turtle in *Alice in Wonderland*. The hairy papa Fish, in search of a Venus-womb, is eventually "caught" by a matrimonial angler; and the gourmet cook mama Trevor, a coconut-cookie king, also doubles as a contemporary "Prince Charming" (275). Marian next visits her friend Clara, whose doorway is marked with a nearly decapitated doll and a teddy bear leaking stuffing (29). In addition to playing the pig-holding duchess from *Alice in Wonderland* (212), Clara is a parodic mother-goddess / beauty queen. Resembling Atwood's watercolor of the pinheaded Termite Queen (Plate 12 and Wilson, "Sexual") when Marian presents roses to her, the eternally pregnant Clara is "being dragged slowly down into the gigantic pumpkin-like growth . . . enveloping her body." As Atwood says, "If you think you're a watermelon, you don't have to do anything, you can just sit around. . . . Life is very much simplified" (Gibson 26). Already consumed by her housewife role, Clara causes Marian unconscious worry that her own Peter is a "pumpkin-eater" (117).

Other important figures Marian meets on her archetypal fairy-tale journey include Joe, cannibalistic pumpkin-eater, who is also the worm-prince invading Clara's apple-core self (242); and the three office virgins, Cinderella's step-sisters, who unsuccessfully trail themselves "like many-plumed fish-lure[s]" for men "ravenous as pike" (114). In this fairy-tale Canada where pioneers journey through arborite-surfaced coffee shops, even the "wilderness" has been touched by "the knife and fork of man" (262).

The Robber Bridegroom's knife and fork are everywhere apparent in Toronto's urban "wilderness." To Marian, the pipes, boards, and blocks at Peter's uncompleted apartment building are part of the same system in which she and everyone around her participates: the "raw materials" disappear and are "transmuted by an invisible process of digestion and assimilation" into something else (231). As Marian enters this twentieth-century Bluebeard's castle, even the nearly empty building with its shining skin and orange-pink walls seems cannibalistic.

Marian first meets Peter, who resembles a cigarette ad and is rising "like a balloon" in his law firm, while eating ice cream in the shade. Since Peter is attracted to Marian's absence of "filling" (he sees her "as the kind of girl who wouldn't try to take over his life" [57, 62]), this appropriately chilled environment sets the tone for Marian's transformation into the puff pastry of the book's epigraph. Later, their dates continue to center on eating, a circumstance of some relevance to Marian's gradual renunciation of food. Consistent with *The Edible Woman*'s Gothic parody, Peter is a hunter who displays his collection of guns and camera-guns in his "murderer's den" (Motif K1916). He also flashes polished teeth while discussing fears of women predators (67). Peter begins to turn into a parodic and comic Robber Bridegroom, with touches of Fitcher, the wolf, and the pumpkin-eater, even before Marian meekly assents to marry him (Motif G81). Initially "disguised" as a bachelor-prince, Peter transforms first into a pro-vider of stability and later a home-movie man. As Robber Bride, Marian begins to distrust him but ironically fails to heed genuine inner warnings because she listens to the socialized voice of her lady below. Drinking gin and tonics rather than the Robber-victim's wine or Alice's size-altering beverage, Marian experiences heartbreak (Motif F1041.1.1), hides in passivity, and begins to turn into the victim who will be symbolically chopped apart and swallowed. Peter's authoritative touch, like Fitcher's, seems to enthrall her (Motif G400); and his matrimonial tests and secret or hidden identities seem to stain, "amputate," and consume similarly hidden facets of her personality.

Having dreamed that her feet are dissolving like jelly, Marian is surprised to find them moving after Peter brags about shooting a female rabbit through the heart and Ainsley unveils her pitcher-plant sex trap. Like Beatrix Potter and Lewis Carroll's rabbits, Marian runs away (Motif T311.1), while there is still time, away from the villain, the "killer" who stalks, traps, and touches her near the bed-"burrow" (Motif R211.3) where she becomes stuck (43, 72–73, 77, 79, 82–83). The morning after her engagement to this eight-eyed ogre (Motif F512.2.1.2), who has been "eating her" (Motif G81 and others, e.g., G312), her skull feels scooped out like a cantaloupe (79, 84). Previously, Peter had bitten her during bathtub sex and, after imagining a naked woman in a bathtub coffin, she had bitten back (61–63). Later, as Peter's steak disappears into his mouth (154–55), Marian, who has been feeling anemic for some time, identifies with a cook-book cow born with lines and labels for cutting. She symbolically serves him her heart (Motif Q478.1), a stale and belated token Valentine, as a cake (213–14). Continuing to find her delicious, he approves her decorated-cake hairstyle (214), says "yum yum" about her perfume (234), and, now that she's "been ringed," serves her to friends (180).

For one of these parties, a kind of prenuptial test, Marian endures a beautician's "operation" on her head in order to play the Russian Cinderella, Wassilissa, and her doll. Earlier, while looking at the doll whose fingers and toes she had once chewed off (105, 225), she gnawed on her own finger. As a child, Marian had not only operated on her sawdust-filled doll; like Wassilissa, whose doll protected her from being eaten by the Baba Yaga, she ritualistically served it food ("The Beautiful Wassilissa," rpt. Von Franz, *The Feminine* 143–47). Ironically, although the doll's teeth and tongue are still intact (*EW* 105), she, like the doll Marian becomes (Motifs D1620.0.1, D2006.1.6, D1268, T117.8), is unable to consume the food; in addition to her amputated extremities, the doll's face "is almost eroded" (see n. 5). After Marian is given another face for her Robber Bridegroom's party and imagines opening secret doors in his "castle," she discovers Peter the chef, holding a meat cleaver: she is no longer visible (228, 250). Although Marian is more than a victim of even a comic Robber Bridegroom, at this point she resembles the first and second sisters of "Fitcher's Bird," who will always bear the lines where they have been cut apart and reassembled (Atwood, *BE* 159; Motif E12.1): she is unable to become the conscious and clever bride or fiancée of either the Robber or Fitcher as long as she identifies with slaughtered rabbits, eaten cows, and amputated dolls.

In addition to Marian's consciousness of the forbidden chamber, her ambiguous relationship with Duncan "stains" her engagement to Peter (Motif D474.4) and follows many of the same "Robber Bridegroom" patterns. Duncan, too, is disguised: a wolf in baby bear's rather than sheep's clothing (AT 123B, Motif K828.1), he seems to project his emotional cannibalism (Woodcock, "Margaret Atwood" 315) onto Marian. A "changeling" from the underground who continuously changes "truths," Duncan's "identity" seems to spread out like an uncooked egg (*EW* 144, 101). Fearing that his mirror might one day reflect nothing, he smashes it, diagnosing his own narcissism. Even his "bear" protectors feel Marian will "gobble [him] up" (190), and she occasionally wonders if her Florence Nightingale role has that dimension (102). Nevertheless, feeding on endless preoccupation with self, a closed circle of meaningless words, and the nutriment of others, Duncan characteristically feeds Marian limitless supplies of nothing, licks his lips after she kisses him, and says, "I'm hungry" (263). Near the end of the novel, after gnawing his thumb and being alarmed by refrigerator sounds, Duncan jokes that Marian is "full of good things": perhaps he *has* tried to destroy her (286–87).

Like many of Atwood's other protagonists, however, Marian plays the Robber Bridegroom as well as the Bride: she participates in the mutual games of disguise and sexual politics that not only amputate parts of the other but also create the other as Bluebeard. Like the characters of *Power Politics* and *Bluebeard's Egg*, for most of the book Marian is unable to peel off both projected and defensive false skins, to stop playing or casting parts. Marian fears the void of self as much as Duncan, and possibly Peter, does. Wondering whether Ainsley, another gender-reversed Robber Bridegroom, is brewing aphrodisiacs and practicing voodoo, she jokes about chopping Peter into bits, camouflaging him as dirty laundry, and burying him in a ravine (94). Giving out bits of information about her engagement like candies, she looks down at the knives and forks on plates when asked how she caught Peter. Even Peter accuses her of "biting his head off" when he breaks a date (115–16). Although he doesn't make a believable Peter Rabbit and does try to assimilate his Cinderella when she's not in use as an ashtray stand (279, 213), Peter, too, is forced into shoes he cannot fill.

In *The Edible Woman* the fairy-tale intertext establishes a tone both comic and Gothic. Not only undercutting the reliability of Marian's vision and questioning the influence of popular culture, it parodies our expectations of "plot" in sexual relationship: the simultaneous anticipation of "Cinderella" "true romance" and fear of amputation by "Bluebeard." We are by no means assured that, for either male or female, it is possible to marry anyone but the Robber Bridegroom or death. Atwood sees *The Edible Woman*, unlike a traditional comedy, as a "circle." The social order in *The Edible Woman* is not reaffirmed, and it is more pessimistic than *Surfacing*. *Surfacing*, like *The Circle Game* (Tape), "is a spiral," because "the heroine of *Surfacing* does not end where she began" (Sandler 13–14). We have observed the "circle games" of sexual politics in *The Edible Woman*. As in "Hesitations Outside the Door," we are again left outside, in the room where Marian began, but it is with a possibility if not a resolution.

In fairy tales, being eaten is not usually the end of the story. True, the Gingerbread Boy does not return from the fox's stomach, but he, unlike Marian, is nothing but food (278). Like Gretel, Marian tricks the trickster and escapes the oven; like Fitcher's bride, she creates a substitute victim (Motif K525) that she pities (278), a cake-woman "creature" resembling a golem (Motif D1635, Van Spanckeren, "Magic" 4), a sugar puppet (Motif K525.1), and the straw doll decoy of the Grimms' "The Hare's Bride" (No. 66). As in true fairy tales, this kind of transformation and rebirth is still possible for the edible woman if not her partners. In the Grimms' "Little Red Cap" and "The Wolf and the Seven Little Kids," the wolf is cut open: like the goat kids, Red Cap springs intact from his belly, reborn and no longer either victim or food. Rather than the Robber Bridegroom's real destruction of Peter, Marian, or Duncan, the novel ends with a "comic parody of ritual cannibalism" (Onley 195–96): Marian's conscious swallowing of her cake woman.

Like Fitcher's bride, Marian tricks the prospective groom and his kind with a decorated substitute victim and leaves Bluebeard's castle. This time, however, the "bride" removes rather than donning the disguise as a marvelous "bird" (Motif K521.1). Marian and Duncan are swallowed in the snowy ravine, a "cavity in the city" associated with caves, the feminine earth-womb, and a door (Neumann 170). This is "as far down as you could go," and Marian thinks about "falling through." Before they go and Marian recognizes that she must act, however, Marian has "a vision of the red dress disintegrating in mid-air, falling in little scraps behind her in the snow, like *feathers*" (my italics 267–72). Again varying fairy-tale motifs (E30, D1884, F1035), Marian rejoins the severed pieces of her former victim self as she molds, joins, and later eats the "separate members" of her cake woman (276, 279). Marian even reverses the power dynamics of many fairy tales and has a revenge of sorts by confronting both Peter and Duncan with a marriage test. In this case, neither their ability to fight and play games nor her domestic skills and baking are at stake (e.g., Motifs H331.2.1, H331.4.1, H383, H383.1): she is not the prize. When faced with the smiling, "doll-like" pink sponge, the reality of the marriage to a doll (Motif T117.8) Peter seemed to desire, he leaves in alarm (277–79); and Duncan, himself a "universal substitute," absorbs the substitute woman without either expression or pleasure (149, 287).

Like the Robber Bride, Marian returns to society, presents an emblem of her victimized self, and tells her story, acting to re- claim swallowed pieces and to regain identity. Unlike Gold- ilocks, she doesn't even leave a mess. No longer trapped in a tower, burrow, or forbidden chamber but thinking of herself in the first-person singular again, Marian faces the "horrors" of both disordered life and apartment and penetrates through layers to discover another "floor" to reality (283–84). By baking, deco- rating, serving, and consuming the cake-woman image she has been conditioned to project, Marian announces, to herself and others, that she is not food.

Decapitation, Cannibalism, and Rebirth in *Surfacing*

"The Juniper Tree" and *French-Canadian Tales*

Surfacing (1972) again demonstrates fairy tales' continuing power to heal and transform, in this case personal, gender, and national fragmentation and alienation.[1] Filled with the "duplicity," doubleness, and irony of *The Edible Woman*'s comic, *Lady Oracle*'s Gothic, and *The Handmaid's Tale*'s apocalyptic romance, *Surfacing* opposes the fragmenting force of fake, censored, and socially "sanitized" fairy-tale images to the paradoxically real power of the main embedded tales: "The Golden Phoenix," "The Fountain of Youth," and "The Juniper Tree."

Atwood admits that she again draws on fairy tales in *Surfacing* (Atwood Tape and Telephone Call 1985). She names the Grimms' "Fitcher's Bird," "The Robber Bridegroom," "The Girl Without Hands," "The Juniper Tree," and "The White Snake" as particularly influential throughout her work (Telephone Call 1985); and all help frame the fairy-tale archetype in *Surfacing*. In this case, however, she uses French-Canadian as well as European tales. "The Girl Without Hands" (AT 706), like "Fitcher's Bird" and "The Robber Bridegroom," is again about amputation and rebirth of females betrayed by patriarchal father or husband (see Chapters 6 through 8). Atwood mentions "The

Juniper Tree" (AT 720) as a direct influence in the scene with the jays. "The White Snake" (AT 673), the Greek myth of Melampus, the Siegfried story (Motif B161.3), and several folklore motifs connect to one of the three French-Canadian tales that are self-consciously emphasized in *Surfacing*: "The Magic Snake."[2] The two other Quebecois literary tales, "The Golden Phoenix" (AT 550) and "The Fountain of Youth" (AT 551)—like the related Grimms' tales "The Golden Bird" and "The Water of Life," other French-Canadian stories, and native North American legends—also help structure the narrative.[3] At the same time, however, *Surfacing* sometimes transforms, subverts, or "reverses" constricting tales, much as Atwood has reversed comic, Gothic, apocalyptic, and mythic patterns in other novels.

Surfacing's themes, motifs, imagery, characterization, and structure are linked to the embedded fairy tales; and many of these tales share similar motifs. "The Juniper Tree" and "The Golden Phoenix," like the related Russian folktale and Stravinsky's ballet "The Firebird" (in Maxym 32–36), are about rebirth. Both present a singing phoenix, apples, decapitation, a magic tree, and improvement in fortune. "The Fountain of Youth," like "The Golden Phoenix," "The Juniper Tree," and *Surfacing*, features disguise, sleeping, successful and unsuccessful quests, magic renewal, vision, and rescue. "The Magic Snake," the tale similar to the Grimms' "The White Snake," dramatizes the power or wisdom to be attained—or lost—by special eating or drinking. "The White Snake" again features golden apples, the Tree of Life, disguise, tasks, and a successful quest. Like *Surfacing*, the Grimms' "The Water of Life," "The Juniper Tree," "The Robber Bridegroom," and "The Fountain of Youth" also present eating images. Since quests, ritual eating, and transformation figure significantly in all of these intertexts, it is no surprise that *Surfacing* also features these patterns. The French-Canadian tales help illuminate the fragmentation and reintegration of the narrator in *Surfacing*; "The Juniper Tree" portrays her struggle against symbolic decapitation and cannibalism.

Although *Surfacing* self-consciously comments on the embedded French-Canadian tales, "The Golden Phoenix" (AT 550), "The Magic Snake," and "The Fountain of Youth (AT 551), critics have not recognized these tales' significance. Instead, they have assumed that Atwood is either rejecting popular and mass culture (Goldie 104) or that she is "looking down on the oral traditions of those who are more marginal and peripheral than she is" at the same time as she appropriates these traditions (Godard, "Tales" 60).

Goldie argues, somewhat inconsistently, that popular and mass culture, including the French-Canadian tales and their original European folktales, are totally rejected in *Surfacing*, where "the source of truth" and "the true source of vision" are in Indian rock paintings (102–4). According to Atwood, however: "Nobody has really come up with the final answer for who made these paintings, what they meant, what they were of, why they were where they were. Indians still leave offerings at these sites. . . . But they've forgotten why they do it. There are various stories, which conflict" (Castro 14). Like *Surfacing*'s other religious or cultural rituals, including Catholic mass imaged as a festive birthday party, the significance of the elaborate rock paintings is lost. Apparently assuming that the unreliable narrator's initial view of her father's drawings is the final one, Goldie argues that "it is only with the native vision, the indigenous people, that an answer can be found" (102–3). He paradoxically concludes, however, that "In *Surfacing* the individual, without science, without elite culture, without popular culture, without mass culture, is left in insularity" (106).

While *Surfacing*, like Atwood's other work, provides few "answers," this metanarrative is far from nihilistic. Ironically, it is the very fairy tales of popular culture, seemingly so "dead" to the failed Cinderella narrator, that provide meaning. These stories within a larger story pattern the protagonist's movement—and similarly move us, consciously or unconsciously—away from despair to fairy-tale renewal. Atwood uses "The Golden Phoenix," "The Fountain of Youth," "The Magic Snake," and the closely related Grimm tales "The Golden Bird," "The Water of Life," and "The White Snake" similarly to her other intertexts. In addition to fairy tales, *Surfacing* recalls children's stories such as Dodgson's *Alice's Adventures in Wonderland*; Canadian bush stories; and Gothic, ghost, and science fiction. As in Atwood's other works, *Surfacing* draws on numerous other facets of popular culture, including Arthurian, shamanistic, wendigo, and loup garou or werewolf legends (Motif D113.1.1);[4] romance, animal fables, nursery rhymes; matriarchal, classical and biblical myth; songs, commercial art, magazines, comic strips, television, movies, products, literary tradition, even history and current events (see Wilson, "Camera Images" 36–37).

I also do not agree that, in Atwood's early work (*Surf*, "Canadian Monsters"), she appropriates but looks down on either Quebec or indigenous oral traditions or that she later (*BE*) "privileg[es] oral anecdotes of local experience over written narratives from other cultures" (Godard, "Tales" 57–58, 60, 82). Despite many fairy tales' patriarchal features, Atwood does not share some critics' scorn either for European *Märchen* or for translated French-Canadian tales (Telephone Call 1987). Although her handling of a motif varies over time, Atwood treats intertexts (regardless of source) as she pleases throughout her career, comically, seriously, tragicomically, or parodically. Her poetry and fiction, even her essays, embody a fairy-tale archetype in characterization, theme, structure, and imagery. Characters who "dance" for others—thereby becoming passively frozen, amputated, and cannibalized—evolve, change shape, or experience other ritual metamorphosis, often through magical eating, touching, or "drowning" in the natural world.

Often more humorous than their European counterparts, folktales of French Canada comprise animal tales, ordinary folktales, jokes and anecdotes, formula tales, and legends. Like the typical folktale, "The Golden Phoenix" features "repetition by three's, emphasis on trials and quests, the triumph of the youngest son, magic objects and supernatural helpers, marvelous transformations, and happy endings" (Fowke, *Folktales of French* 23). One of many Petit Jean (Ti-Jean) stories, "The Golden Phoenix" is about a third son's solution (Motifs H1242, L10) to the mystery of each day's stolen silver apple of wisdom (Motif F813.1.2). Unlike his supposedly smarter brothers, who cannot resist sleep-inducing wine and food, Petit Jean fasts; he then picks and hides the apple. When it is still stolen, he follows the thief's shining feathers (Motif B102.1, H1213) to the top of the Glass Mountain and then through a trap door, descending by basket into a well with sides as smooth as ice. Armed with a sword, he courageously faces three guardians of the cave—the unicorn, the lion, and the seven-headed serpent—decapitates both lion and serpent, who are able to re-attach their severed heads, and successfully passes into the great sultan's country. There he meets the sultan's beautiful daughter in a garden (Motif N711.3), where the golden phoenix sings its youth-bestowing song and the sultan announces the next day's triple game of hide and seek (the "catch me" motif, Granofsky 61). Although Petit Jean will marry the princess and choose a dowry if he finds what is lost and recognizes the disguised sultan, he must risk a real loss: the dearest thing he owns, his life.

The sultan is able to change his shape, first into a fish, then into a rose, and finally into a pear; but Petit Jean possesses a characteristic luck and is able to name what is hidden. He not only wins the princess but chooses the gold cage to which the phoenix must return each sunrise. Thus, "with the Golden Phoenix singing every night in the tree where the silver apple of wisdom" grows, "he and the Princess live "wisely and happily ever afterwards" ("The Golden Phoenix," Barbeau 7–25).

Like "The Golden Phoenix," *Surfacing* features a quest, trials, sleep, glass barriers, a cage, decapitation and re-attachment, disguise, parent images, descent, hide and seek, fasting and special eating, recovery of the lost, naming of the hidden, solution to mystery, a phoenix (Motif B102.1, B32), a magic garden (Motif

D961), songs, risk of the dearest thing, metamorphosis, and renewal. But Margaret Atwood re-visions the male-centered fairy
tale. At first resembling the elder brothers of "The Golden Phoenix," *Surfacing*'s narrator is a younger *daughter*. Closing her eyes,
sleeping through possibilities of wisdom and renewal and projecting her failures onto others, she must find the phoenix within
herself.

At the beginning of an early draft (winter 1964 or 1965) of
Surfacing called "The Transfigured Landscape" (later "Where is
Here"), the narrator sounds like the time-conscious rabbit in
Alice in Wonderland and is even named Maryann (later Myra), like
his servant (Mary Ann): "It was five twenty-seven exactly" as she
checked her watch (Atwood Papers, Box 21). Like Vonnegut's
Billy Pilgrim, however, the unnamed, fragmented narrator of
Surfacing has come "unstuck," not only in time but in place. Not
only a gendered person but a place—Canada—the narrator has
already lost her "dearest thing" in symbolic games of hide and
seek. Thus, she must dive into the void of who, when, and
where and into her past to name the unnamed—herself—and to
recover parents (heritage), previous selves (historical national
identity), and wholeness (unity). As in traditional French-
Canadian tales, patterns of three mark her journey, and "magic"
objects and "supernatural" helpers aid her on her quest, concluding in a fairy-tale ending: an ironically marvelous transformation.
Similar to Canadian animal fables, the French-Canadian tale
"Goldenhair," both French-Canadian and Villeneuve's "Beauty
and the Beast" (AT 425C), and the Grimms' "Snow-White and
Rose-Red" (AT 709), "Bearskin" (AT 361, Motif F821.1.3.1), and
"The Golden Goose" (AT 571), *Surfacing* parodically reveals
"prince" and "princess" when they remove "animal skins."

At the beginning of this anti-fiction (Wilson, "Deconstructing," 60–61) the narrator is, like the golden phoenix, symbolically caged, this time in the circle games of power politics. But
for most of the novel her voice, more like that of the littlest
mermaid than the golden phoenix, lacks regenerative power: she

is symbolically mute. Like Moira Shearer of "The Red Shoes" and all Atwood's footless "dancing girls," she has danced to the tunes and wills of others. Resembling her "friend" Anna and the princess of "The Fountain of Youth," she is a "captive princess in someone's head," in this case immersed in imitation of imitations, "the original nowhere" (194). Like *Life Before Man*'s Elizabeth, *Bodily Harm*'s Rennie, The Girl Without Hands, and Fitcher's first two brides, she has been symbolically amputated and chopped up; like Marian of *The Edible Woman*, Offred of *The Handmaid's Tale*, the bird boy of "The Juniper Tree," and the first Robber Brides, she, the land, and the country she represents have been symbolically dismembered and cannibalized, in this case by sexism, technology, imperialism, and cultural conditioning. Similarly, having lost the source of wisdom and power and carrying only an evil rather than holy "Grail" (Motif D1171.6) in the wasteland (168), she resembles kings in "The Golden Phoenix," "The Fountain of Youth," and "The White Snake": she is symbolically blind.

Ironically, however, the narrator-princess is also captive inside her own head, trapped in what she sees and says. Self-consciously constructing and deconstructing phony fairy-tale life-narrative, she offers both readers and herself unreliable narration, lying language, and word games (Wilson, "Deconstructing" 59–65). Thinking of her parents "as living in some other time, . . . closed safe behind a wall as translucent as Jell-O, mammoths frozen in a glacier" (*Surf* 11), the narrator's quest begins inside her own "glass mountain" (Motif F751), where she must face her internal beasts: self-deception, repression, and projection. "Initially feeling split-apart or double, she views everything through a wall of glass separating her head from the alien 'they' as well as from her body and feelings" (Wilson, "Camera" 37). The narrator is good at spotting "amputations," mutilations, or fakes: Madame's missing hand, the decapitated head on the U.S. penny, Joe's pots, and artificial faces, braids, and teeth (102, 66, 49–50, 144). Uncertain how she feels about an artificial womb, she rehearses emotions and even imitates herself (96, 132, 127). Layered for patriarchal consumption like a birthday cake in early photographs (129), creating watercolors and drawings of delicious bodiless princesses, and celebrating the "religion" of glamour, the narrator, like her country, ironically colludes in her own amputation and cannibalization.

The narrator finds it hard to believe that anyone in Quebec ever knew the volume of diluted Quebec folktales she is illustrating. Like her fabricated text of both self and life, the stories—translated tales of "the Other" (Godard 60)—and her drawings for them are missing something. As in Chrètien de Troyes's *Perceval* and the Fisher King legend, the sterility of her self is linked to the wasteland country and world she inhabits and symbolizes. There "the white birches are dying" and plastic-veined "Americans" spread like a virus, replacing human beings and senselessly crucifying birds (9, 61, 152). In "that country," Percival is a money-minded publisher. Mr. Percival apparently "amputates" any disturbing parts of the French-Canadian tales and completely omits any tales or tale types, such as loup garou stories, that might prove "too rough" (65) for his English, American, and Canadian audience. Framing the intertexts, Atwood's novel ironically opposes narrative about turning into a wolf (the narrator, her father, the narrator's drawing of the third princess) and taking off or putting on human skin (Joe,[5] the narrator) to this gap, or absence, in Percival's text. His edition of "The Golden Phoenix" substitutes lower cost yellow for red fire. In addition to association with the Triple Goddess (see Chapters 2 and 10), in alchemy the color red corresponds to the phoenix and, thus, signifies regeneration of universal life and completion of a process. In *Surfacing* it is also a sacred color to indigenous people and the predominant color of the rock paintings (*Surf* 122–23, Cirlot 241–42). Thus, Percival's commercial concessions diminish the tale's power, effectively "silencing" it as the narrator, her gender and country, the land, and the animals are silenced. The narrator is a commercial artist because her art teacher-lover says

no "real" women artists exist. Her phoenix, which should symbolize periodic destruction and re-creation, the triumph of eternal life over death (Cirlot 241–42), and self-renewal, resembles a
heraldic emblem or a fire-insurance trademark (*Surf* 61–62).

Similarly, the narrator's version of the giant guardian in "The
Fountain of Youth," sketched while Joe seems to trace her with
his eyes, is also debased: it looks like a football player (100).
Surfacing draws on several images or motifs from "The Fountain
of Youth": both highway and water journeys, an island, disguise,
sleeping, blindness, symbolic pillars of salt, ritual eating and
fasting, fish, and, most significantly, symbolic drowning and
renewal through magic water (Motifs D1500.1.18, D766.1). The
fountain image (Motif D1338.1.2), like the phoenix and both
gold and silver apples, is mythologically associated with the tree
of life (Motif E90) important in Christian, Judaic, Hindu, and
Islamic religions; thus, it can symbolize immortality, the center
or origin, the life force, and the inner life or soul (Cirlot 331,
107–8). According to Jung, who links the fountain with the
"land of infancy," an individual particularly needs this fount of
spiritual energy when life is inhibited or dried up (*Psychology and
Alchemy*, reported in Cirlot 108). When the fountain appears in a
garden's center, as in the paintings of Hieronymus Bosch, an
artist who influences Atwood's visual art (Chapter 2), it usually
represents the self or individuality (*Psychology and Alchemy*, reported in Cirlot 108; see Bosch's *Garden of Earthly Delights*).

In *Surfacing*, however, not only are the trees diseased; the narrator's literal and figurative gardens (Motif D961), like the bush
garden of Canada they represent, lack a fountain. The narrator
lives in the city, and she associates the only fountain in the
wasteland of narrator, gender, land, and country with her "evil
grail": her abortion disguised as a wedding. Possibly another
amputated imitation, like the narrator and her fake memory-
texts, this fountain is in the middle of the planned company town
and public flower beds of her youth. It features stone dolphins
and a cherub missing part of its face (14). Similarly, the oblong

family garden, created over years with a handbarrow "crucifix" and infested with witch weeds that must be burned to keep them from strangling vegetables, is artificial (94). Like the elder brothers of "The Fountain of Youth," for most of the book the narrator offers only fake renewal. While drawing the debased guardian of her fountain of youth, she recognizes that she has fed Joe [and herself] "unlimited supplies of nothing" rather than the water of life. "Like people isolated in a blank room who see patterns," he, too, "ha[s] to fill it up" and [becomes] "hooked on it" (101).

Again, *Surfacing*'s use of both fairy-tale and mythic intertext is not only ironic and parodic but symbolic: it is the nameless narrator's fairy-tale dreams and drawings and a censored contemporary edition of fairy-tales, not the "The Golden Phoenix," "The Fountain of Youth," or grail legend, that are dead. Just as Atwood's camera and photograph images not only dramatize fragmentation but also precipitate metamorphosis (Wilson, "Camera" 32), so a fairy-tale intertext—opposed to a void of values and magic—is a catalyst for the transformation of the narrator, and therefore her gender and country.

When the narrator sees the dead heron, senselessly hanging "like something in a butcher's window" but not even killed for food, she thinks about the king who learned to speak with animals in the third French-Canadian tale (see n. 2). Like other birds, including *Surfacing*'s jay and phoenix, the "helpful" heron (Motif B454) is associated with the goddess, the Tree of Life, and its restorative fruit. In addition, the heron suggests the sometimes caged soul, the generation of life, thought, imagination, supernatural aid (Cirlot 25–27, 141), and secrets. Reminiscent of both phoenix and fountain, *Surfacing*'s heron, like the fairy-tale, mythic, religious, historic, and nationalistic images it and other animals evoke, is "desecrated, unredeemed." The narrator wonders what people would hear if betrayed animals such as the beaver and heron, without spokesperson in a country and world devoid of magic, could speak: "accusation, lament, an outcry of rage"? Would "the Americans" of Canada and the world listen?

Unlike the dead tales and drawings or the narrator's faked album of memories ("a different version," with the "wrong parts" pasted over in the manner of her early narration), the heron's death is undiluted, "real" despite the anti-metanarrative's fiction (154–55, 169).

Ironically, the heron, like the fairy-tale animals it partly represents, does lead the narrator to a "treasure" of sorts (Motifs B109, B113.3, B160): the heron is the source of natural help that replaces folklore and myth's supernatural aid. Resembling the servant in the Grimms' "The White Snake," Siegfried of the *Nibelungenlied* (c. 1200) and of Wagner's *The Ring of the Nibelung* eats part of a serpent (Thompson, *Folktale* 260) (alternatively, bathes in or tastes its blood) (Leach and Fried 1010, 59) and attains the special wisdom associated with understanding animal language, in this case that of birds. Similarly, when the legendary Melampus learns the secrets of the earth, he grows "wise beyond measure" through understanding the languages of animals.[6] Seeing and "hearing" the heron, the narrator recognizes the difficulty of being human and feels "a sickening complicity" in all destruction, important steps to her and her country's metamorphosis. Re-membering the fairy tale, the narrator later engages in special eating so that she will hear other animal voices, including the voice of her own animal self.

Healing the amputations, not only of the narrator's phony fairy-tale illustrations but of her "censored" edition of fairy tales, *Surfacing*'s structure and plot echo fairy-tale patterns. Like typical Quebec tales, *Surfacing* features significant triple repetitions. The novel has three sections, three drawings of fairy-tale princesses, three "drownings" (one fake, one real, and one symbolic), and three main female characters (the narrator, her mother, and Anna); the narrator dives or immerses herself in water on three occasions, she initiates three other drownings (the bottled animals, bottled film images, and, symbolically, the "bottled" aborted fetus), and she is obsessed with three men (art teacher, father, and current lover).

Like some Francophone tales, *Surfacing* also has patterns of seven. Evans is supposed to take the group back on the seventh day, and the narrator, beginning to be her own prophet, tries to protect the others from the expected knowledge (100). Instead of having her "bushed" and guilty narrator either become or be disenchanted as a werewolf the seventh year, a common occurrence in loup garou stories (Fowke, *Folktales of French* 78–79) (Motif D791.1.1), Atwood parodies the pattern by structuring the narrator's meeting with her werewolf self, projected into a vision of her dead father, for the seventh day (218).[7] Since Bearskin (AT 361) spends seven years without washing or combing (Motif F821.1.3.1), the narrator's turning the mirror around on the seventh day, to see her matted hair and furless but dirty body, is similarly parodic.

Again like French-Canadian tales, *Surfacing* makes use of magic objects and supernatural helpers, some of which are ironic or parodic. The drawings and typescript of *Quebec Folk Tales*, the paint tubes and brushes, the photograph albums, the scrapbooks, her mother's leather jacket, her father's map, pictographs and books, the ring from her nonhusband art teacher, the Samsonite case—all her emotional luggage—are important in the narrator's quest. But in Atwood's reversed mythology all the false stories we tell ourselves, calling them truth, must be canceled. The jacket, associated with her mother's nature communication, and consequent assimilation, is slashed as an unnecessary husk (Motifs D720, D721.3), but, a reminder of transformation, it remains. As several critics note, the narrator, like the natives of this border area, engages in shamanistic ritual (Guèdon 105), leaving clothing offerings, eating special food, and evoking supernatural helpers—the spirits of mother, father, jay, and heron (e.g., Motifs B120–169). But these rituals simultaneously draw on fairy-tale and mythic intertext, and again, Atwood subverts the patterns (see n. 12). Ultimately, the narrators' parents dwindle (Motif F407), become what they were: human (221).

Atwood's and her narrator's use of translated and polished

French-Canadian tales is somewhat ironic. As an Anglo-Canadian in border-country Quebec, the narrator does not know the stories French-Canadians told around fires: they are not hers. But, in this sense, neither are those of native peoples, shamans, the ancient Greeks, the Christians, the Europeans, or some of her fellow Anglo-Canadians, whom she cannot distinguish from Americans, a word and concept long muddied by limitation of its reference to U.S. citizens rather than inhabitants of North and South American continents. Joe and David's "folklore" collection, "random samples," containing footage of a bottle house, a stuffed moose, a "captured" log, and a nude woman, comments on folklore snobbery and cultural and gender imperialism as well as fakelore, and a global twentieth-century wasteland as well as the Canadian and U.S. ones. Like all of us, Atwood's narrator is on "home ground, foreign territory" (14), inheritor of widely divergent traditions and "stories" only partly understood. Despite the ironic contribution of "anglophone" translations to French-Canadians' awareness of their own traditions and, therefore, ethnic identity (Godard, "Tales" 64), French-Canadian tales "belong to all European nations more or less" (Carpenter 222; Barbeau, "About the Stories" 140) and are meaningful to all of us. Like all folktales, the translated tales Atwood embeds reflect the cultures through which they have passed and, like all literary tales, are admittedly polished. While a few people may find Atwood's use of Quebec folklore inauthentic or imperialistic, the tales are not, therefore, discountable, particularly when they are, like the mirror in *Surfacing*'s cabin, "reversed." Unlike the narrator's dead drawings, published translations of the French-Canadian tales still emphasize shape-changing, transformation, rebirth, new vision, and new power.

Although *Surfacing* self-consciously comments on the embedded French-Canadian tales, its allusions to the Grimms' "The Juniper Tree" (No. 47, "Von dem Machandelboom," 1812, AT 720) are largely ignored. Baer recognizes Atwood's fondness for this tale, suggests some correspondences between "The Juniper Tree" and "Fitcher's Bird," and quotes from Atwood regarding Grimms' intelligent women, who often have magic powers (24, 27); but she does not discuss the larger importance of this tale, including its decapitation and cannibalism themes, in *Surfacing* and other Atwood texts.

As early as 1963, Atwood uses "The Juniper Tree," her favorite fairy tale (Oates 71), as an intertext in the poem, "The Little Sister." Unreliably narrated by the sister who thinks she is responsible for her brother's death, the poem anticipates *Surfacing*'s later images of decapitation, "stopped growth," "wordless voices," phoenix fire, and birds ("Five Poems" 29). According to Atwood, there is one scene in which *Surfacing* draws most closely on "The Juniper Tree." The narrator has a vision of her mother, who once broke both ankles attempting to fly, finally turning into a jay. In Atwood's "For the Birds," a girl must turn into a bird and understand bird language in order to understand birds' point of view (*FB* 9–10). Similarly, in Atwood's unpublished children's story, "The Girl Who Flew," although Kathleen's brother says she will never be able to fly, she changes place with a blue jay by walking through "The Mirror That Faces Both Ways."[8] In *Surfacing*, the unnamed narrator, who will also symbolically walk through the looking glass, sees her dead mother, hand outstretched, feeding jays. One perches on her mother's wrist, another on her shoulder. Then "The jays cry again, they fly from her, the shadows of their wings ripple over the ground and [her mother] is gone" (213). Throughout the book, the narrator links her Demeterlike mother to nature, transformation, magic, flying, and lifesaving or rebirth, themes and motifs from "The Juniper Tree" that are crucial to the narrator's own transformation. Like the narrator's and Atwood's own visual art, art from the fifth to the second-millennium B.C. "abounds in winged bird-woman images" of the Bird Goddess, who represents "the feminine principle" and other aspects of the Great Goddess (Gimbutas, *Goddesses* 138–47; see also Wall, "Goddess" 214–23 and *Callisto* 155–56 on Callisto myth).

The Grimms used Philipp Otto Runge as a source for "The Juniper Tree," and the tale shares some features with "The Golden Phoenix" and the better-known "Cinderella" (The Grimms' "Aschenputtel," No. 21, AT 510A) (Zipes, *Complete* 718). The mother and stepmother of "The Juniper Tree" both double and foil *Surfacing*'s narrator and her mother. As the story goes, long ago, a beautiful and pious woman cuts her finger while peeling an apple under a juniper tree. As the blood drops into the snow, she hopes for a child who, like Snow-White and Rose-Red, is "as red as blood and as white as snow." The snow melts, everything turns green, flowers sprout, trees grow, birds sing, blossoms fall, the juniper becomes fragrant, and the fruit grows. In the seventh month the mother picks and eats juniper berries, which make her sick. The eighth month, she asks to be buried under the juniper tree, and the ninth, she dies in happiness when she has the wished-for child and is buried beneath the juniper tree. Her husband's tears water the grave (Zipes, *Complete* 171–72).

After the husband remarries, the stepmother's heart is "cut to the quick" when she looks at the boy. Her daughter Marlene, who loves her brother, asks for an apple for him as well as for herself. Tempted by a devil, the stepmother slams the heavy chest lid so hard that the boy's head flies off and falls among the apples. Attempting to disguise her crime, the "bad mother" puts his head back on his neck, ties a neckerchief around it, and poses him in a chair with an apple in his hand. She tells Marlene that, if her brother doesn't speak, she should "give him a box on the ear." When the boy's head falls off, Marlene thinks she is the killer. Then the mother chops up, cooks, and serves her stepson for dinner to the boy's father, who eats with relish, refusing to share. Marlene weeps, as her father had for the boy's mother, and puts her brother's bones under the juniper tree (Zipes, *Complete* 172–74).

The juniper moves and mist, fire, and then a marvelous bird emerge. The phoenixlike bird repeats a song recounting the murder six times and receives a golden chain from a goldsmith, red shoes from a shoemaker, and a heavy millstone from apprentice millers. Returning home, the bird repeats the song for a seventh and then a final time, now issuing rewards and punishments. The golden chain falls around the father's neck and Marlene puts on the red shoes; but the stepmother's eyes burn and flash like lightening, she falls on the floor, and her hair stands up like flames of fire. The bird crushes her with the millstone; and out of the smoke, flames, and fire comes the little brother. Joining hands with his father and sister, he joyfully enters the house to eat (Zipes, *Complete* 174–79). The tale thus illustrates the cycle of nature, including fertility, death, metamorphosis, and resurrection. In addition, it features temptation, decapitation, and cannibalism, themes clearly evident in *Surfacing*.

Unlike "The Robber Bridegroom," demonstrating the exophagous type of cannibalistic story about an ogre, witch, or demon belonging to a race different from the victims', "The Juniper Tree" is one of numerous endophagous cannibalistic stories in the "perverted taste" cycle. Ironically for *Surfacing*, this tale (with Magyar, Scots,[9] English, Swedish, Breton, and Malagasy variants) is considered the best-known "unnatural mother" story, even though a stepmother replaces the mother. Probably connecting to human and animal sacrifice as well as to religious sacraments, cannibalistic stories may be linked to god-eating (theophagynous) ritual, transference of qualities, sin atonement, precivilization reversion, and even vampirism (Yearsley 38–41, 46–47, 49), all elements in *Surfacing* as well as other Atwood texts. Cannibalism in "The Juniper Tree" may suggest vampirism, human sacrifice, and religious sacrament. The innocent boy, "as white as snow and as red as blood," is both a scapegoat-victim and the resurrected son arising from the tree of life. Although *Surfacing*'s cannibalism theme is less explicit and sustained than that of *The Edible Woman*, *Surfacing* also depicts symbolic cannibalism: imperialistic and sexist power that wastes the wasteland of narrator, land, region, and country. In addition, the novel's ritualistic eating is linked to victimization and atonement, death and rebirth.

Cannibalism in *Surfacing* draws on "The Magic Snake," "The White Snake" (No. 17, AT 673) and "The Robber Bridegroom" (No. 40, AT 955) as well as "The Juniper Tree" and entails ordinary or religious eating that the narrator associates with cannibalism, "magic" foods or transformations linked to food, and shamanistic offerings or fasting. In the unreliable narrator's eyes, her acquaintances' and "Americans'" real or metaphoric meals, the food cycle, and by extension human relationships are cannibalistic. After Joe proposes to the narrator and she remembers the abortion she disguised as a wedding, the stains on Joe, David, Anna's, and her own mouth and plate seem "reddish-blue, vein-color." Earlier, remembering the childhood song about going to the garden to eat worms, she hooks a frog onto David's fish line and thinks: "It's a good thing our lives don't depend on catching a fish. Starvation, bite your arm and suck the blood, that's what they do on lifeboats; or the Indian way, if there's no bait try a chunk of your flesh" (107, 70–72). Like Atwood's untitled watercolor of a large fish eating smaller ones (Plate 1), *Surfacing*'s fishing expeditions depict smaller animals being swallowed by larger ones, who kill more for sport than for survival. "The Americans," deformed or "missing something" like all the main characters, chop up and kill animals to feed insatiable and unnatural "hungers." Unlike the father's hunger in "The Juniper Tree," however, such hungers spell death rather than rebirth.

Similarly, Catholic mass, which the narrator once imagined as "a sort of birthday party," becomes a more potent "cannibalism" after she encounters the "unsacred crucifix," the many commercial "X's" that replace the Tree of Life in her world and even mark the once sacred sites of rock paintings. In this antiapocalyptic world, where fishing is no longer linked to the redemption of either the Fisher King or Christ,[10] the animals, who are "substitute people," "die that we may live. . . . And we eat them, out of cans or otherwise; we are eaters of death, dead Christ-flesh resurrecting inside us, granting us life. Canned Spam, canned Jesus, even the plants must be Christ. But we refuse to worship; the body worships with blood and muscle but the thing in the knob head will not, wills not to, the head is greedy, it consumes but does not give thanks" (63, 164–65). The characters fish, hoping to eat peace, but there is no transferral of qualities, no resurrection for them or for the fish.

Later, the narrator burns the fairy-tale drawings, including her dead golden phoenix and edible princesses, and "X's" through artificial "husks," attempting to cancel her participation in cannibalism. Paradoxically seeking redemption through eating when she is both consumer and consumable, she tries shamanistic offerings (Motifs F406, F406.2) and holy food; "magic" red, yellow, blue, and green foods; mushrooms; and fasting in search of vision, hearing (the multilingual language of animals and the Goddess), and transformation. She even licks blood from her wounds and awaits a fur skin (Motif F521.1.1). Like the mother in "The Juniper Tree," who eats juniper berries and becomes the tree of life, *Surfacing*'s narrator must eat the right foods and become nature, "freedom feathering" her arms, like her own mother's, so that when she leans against a tree, she is a tree leaning (207, 212).

Eating in fairy tales frequently empowers, so the berries (raspberries rather than juniper berries), mushrooms, six-leaved plants, white roots, and "yellow fingers" the narrator eats (211–12) are significant if somewhat parodic. Leaves, such as four-leafed shamrocks, are associated with understanding animal languages; mushrooms, with hallucinogenic goddess rites.[11] The ritual dismemberment and cannibalism of some of these rites, lingering symbolically in Christian communion (Walker, *Woman's Encyclopedia* 135–39) and relating to the magic cannibalism of "The Juniper Tree" (Motifs G61, E607.1), were probably efforts to be eternally reborn in the Great Mother, whose womb wound healed itself (Sjoo and Mor 81–82). Like the snake, leaves, and plants in animal language tales such as the Grimms' "The White Snake" and the similar French-Canadian tale, the ritual foods in *Surfacing* continue the process the heron began, helping the narrator understand the language of the earth (see also Van Spanckeren, "Magic" 5 on the food's relationship to alchemy). As in "The Juniper Tree," one stage in the reincarnation of the "murdered child" (Motif E610.1.1, in this case the amputated parts of the narrator's psyche and of her repressed past as much as her aborted fetus), is special eating. After feeding the male "fur god with tail and horns" corresponding to her childhood drawing, she almost immediately has a vision of a female god feeding birds. She sees her mother, "The Juniper Tree"'s goddess of earth and rebirth, here associated with a bear as well as birds, turn into a jay and fly away (Motifs E323, D619). Identifying with the heron and the other silenced animals, the narrator symbolically wears an animal skin (Motif D100) (213–14).

Resembling a shaman, *Surfacing*'s narrator is also figuratively eaten, dismembered, drowned, and—like the stepmother/witch of "The Juniper Tree" and many other fairy tales—burned (Bottigheimer, *Grimms' Bad* 25, 27–28, 101–2). But she is not a shaman, and, contrary to what Godard suggests, shamanic or "native" tales are not preferred to "foreign ones" in *Surfacing* ("Tales" 57–58, 60, 82).[12] Rather than filling the void of who, when, and where, the "unsacred crucifix" and shamanic ritual help clear a space for "Juniper Tree" transformation. As in the fairy tale, cannibalism and ritualistic eating are part of a transformation cycle.

In addition to shaping theme, "The Juniper Tree" intertext is important to *Surfacing*'s setting, plot, motifs, and characterization. As mentioned earlier, the novel's forest scenes recall Gothic, ghost, science fiction, and Canadian bush stories as well as fairy tales in which a lost character flees or hides from a murderer, spirit, alien, witch, or the very condition of being "bushed" and attempts to mark or discover a path. Moreover, despite obvious differences, the sequence of "The Juniper Tree's" motifs both structure the novel's plot and parallel other fairy, folk, and popular culture references. The most important "Juniper Tree" motifs for *Surfacing* are sterility and fertility, parent images, the cross or tree of life, temptation, decapitation and dismemberment, disguise, eating, tears, magic, fire and mist, phoenixlike birds rising out of mist or flames (Motif B32), songs, sudden appearance and disappearance, metamorphosis, death and rebirth, and punishment and atonement.

In reference to characterization, at some point, the unnamed narrator resembles all of the archetypal characters of "The Golden Phoenix" and "The Fountain of Youth" as well as "The Juniper Tree." Her initial dismemberment, however, most resembles that of the boy in "The Juniper Tree," who is not only eaten but decapitated. *Surfacing*'s narrator loses her body rather than her head, however: "I realized I didn't feel much of anything . . . At some point my neck must have closed over, . . . shutting me into my head . . . it was like being in a vase . . . Bottles distort for the observer too: frogs in the jam jar stretched wide, to them watching I must have appeared grotesque" (126). Symbolically segmented but dressed up, like the boy, as "normal," the narrator has ironically managed to pass herself off as "divorced." Divorced from past and parents, separated from body and emotions, the narrator loses both personal and national identity by living in her head (reason). Her encounter with a "Robber Bridegroom" art teacher, who talks her into an abortion and convinces her that women cannot be great artists, is doubly amputating. She also lives in a society that reduces a woman to "a cunt on four legs" or "a pair of boobs" and Canada to a "split beaver." Bluebeards rationalize their amputation of women as fear of ball cutting, and "the power company" with which they are associated either amputates trees from the body of the earth or leaves them exposed like "splintered bones."

The narrator, like Madame and "the Americans," loses or is fitted with "fake" body parts, not because an evil stepmother chops her in two, but partly because "I'd allowed myself to be cut in two. . . . The other half, the one locked away, was the only one that could live; I was the wrong half, detached, terminal. I was nothing but a head, or, no, something minor like a severed thumb, numb" (129). As a child the narrator pretends her feet have been shot off and cuts out magazine illustrations of dresses without bodies. Later, as part of a career that feels like an artificial limb, she draws nearly bodiless princesses for *Quebec Fairy Tales*. Unconsciously, she casts not only her "friend" Anna but herself as a captive princess.

Like "The Juniper Tree's" stepmother, the narrator has been "tempted" by a "devil" (art teacher) and, at least in her eyes, becomes a "killer." Thus, resembling the elder brothers in "The Golden Phoenix," she closes her eyes, sleeping through possibilities of wisdom and renewal, and projects her failures onto others. Like the elder brothers of "The Fountain of Youth," initially she offers only fake renewal: her dead, compromised fairy-tale drawings.

Although the narrator, like her gender and country, has been chopped up and consumed by Bluebeards and Robber Bridegrooms and has slept the enchanted sleep of the princess awaiting rescue in "The Fountain of Youth" and so many other tales, she regenerates and rescues herself; and her metamorphosis is filled with fairy-tale and mythic allusions. She finally takes responsibility for the "paper house" in which she has lived: all the lies, compromises, and disguises in her "faked album, the memories fraudulent as passports" (169). Resembling the kings in "The Fountain of Youth," "The Golden Phoenix," and "The Magic Snake," the narrator's vision and wisdom clear; but unlike them she is her own restorative. Finding the dark grail, her own water of life, and special food, she becomes a "phoenix." Like Marlene and the father in "The Juniper Tree," the narrator symbolically "weeps"—she begins to recover feeling, including the pain in her relationships with the art teacher and Joe and her sorrow over the death of mother, father, and fetus. She "buries" the dead rather than self, memories, consciousness, what she is.

Like "The Juniper Tree's" initially sterile mother, who becomes the Tree of Life, the narrator achieves momentary unity with the land and living beings, becoming first part of the landscape, "a tree leaning," and then a place (212–13). Like "Juniper Tree"'s boy, who also changes shape, her segmented halves "clasp," her aborted potential self surfacing within her (Wilson, "Deconstructing" 63–64). Thus, she, like the youngest son in "The Fountain of Life," who is expected to drown, rises from water and anoints formerly blind eyes. Like her mother, the bird-boy in "The Juniper Tree," and the golden phoenix, she also rises from mist, smoke, and ashes after literally and symbolically burning her "evil grail" (168). Eating the food of wisdom, descending and being reborn as in "The Golden Phoenix," the narrator also resembles the king in "The Fountain of Youth": after anointment with regenerative water, she is fit for travel with new vision and power. Like the Robber Bride, she even finds her voice and the new language necessary to speak.

In contrast to "The Fountain of Youth," "The Golden Phoenix," and "The Magic Snake," however, *Surfacing* contains no actual giants, no magic water, no apple or leaf of wisdom, no phoenix. Since *Surfacing* is neither traditional fairy tale nor, as generally believed, archetypal romance (Pratt, "*Surfacing*" 139), the narrator's, and by extension her gender and country's, rebirth is not final. Atwood's wit being what it is, fairy-tale intertext sometimes sets up ironic or parodic correspondences. In keeping with the book's inversion of comic structure, rather than concluding, like "Cinderella," with the main character's marriage and reintegration into accepted social norms, *Surfacing* subverts reader expectations. "Hiding in the bushes at the end of the book, in slashed clothing rather than ballgown or Toronto chic and contemplating a man who is certainly no prince, she . . . is able to laugh" [Motif D1773], as more of us should (Wilson,

"Deconstructing" 64), not only at a "new kind of centerfold" but at re-visioned fairy-tale images and ending.

I am not suggesting that *Surfacing* is allegory or that all fairy-tale connections are necessarily intentional. Atwood's fairy-tale intertexts in *Surfacing* function similarly to those in her other works: they resonate in our memories and imaginations, heightening our perception of such fairy-tale themes as cannibalism, amputation, metamorphosis, and rebirth. In a world ultimately without magic or "happily ever after," where journeys cannot end, progress is spiral, and borders are neither visible nor capable of erasure (Wilson, "Deconstructing" 65), fairy tales underlie the novel's themes, motifs, imagery, and structure: they pattern the growth of the narrator, her country, all women, and all human beings.

Dancing for Others
in *Lady Oracle*

The Triple Goddess and "The Red Shoes"

The metamorphosis image, suggested in *Surfacing* by the phoenix, becomes dancing in Atwood's 1976 metafiction, *Lady Oracle*. Dancing is also an important motif in Atwood's poems, "Persephone Departing" (*DP* 1961), "The Circle Game" and "A Sibyl" (*CG* 1966), "Dancing Practice" (*PU* 1970), "There Is Only One of Everything" (*YAH* 1974), and "A Red Shirt" (*THP* 1978); short story collection, *Dancing Girls* (1977); and novel, *The Handmaid's Tale* (1985). For Atwood's initially footless (Motif F517.1.1) dancers, including her "dancing girls" (*DP*, *DG*), dancing paradoxically suggests captivity, freedom, and art. Nevertheless, dancing is a step forward for her artists. At the end of *Surfacing*, the narrator has transformed through immersion in water, growing and taking off animal skin, and laughing (Motifs D766.1, D1887, F521.1.1, D720, D1773), but her feet "do not move yet" (224). In *Lady Oracle*, the Proteuslike narrator has already undergone multiple metamorphoses and is engaged in becoming and creating: she retrospectively tells her own story, thereby inscribing her own dance over her socialized steps in the past.

The main intertext in *Lady Oracle* is "The Red Shoes" (Motif D2061.1.2) from Hans Christian Andersen's literary tale and Michael Powell and Emeric Pressburger's film of the same name.[1] In addition to making extensive references to other literary and popular culture, *Lady Oracle*, like *Dancing Girls*, "A Red Shirt," and *The Handmaid's Tale*, uses images from Hans Christian Andersen's "The Littlest Mermaid" and "The Ugly Duckling" (Motifs R138.1, L140ff), the Grimms' "Fitcher's Bird" (AT 311, No. 46), "The Robber Bridegroom" (AT 955, No. 40), "The Girl Without Hands" (AT 706, No. 31), and "The Shoes That Were Danced to Pieces" (AT 306, No. 133). *Lady Oracle* also evokes the three-headed Triple Goddess Trivia (Motif A123 .4.1.1, *LO* Manuscripts, Atwood Papers). Acting as a parodic metafairy tale by displacing and delegitimizing a sexist literary tale and analogous popular stories—telling "the other side" of the story (DuPlessis 108–10)—*Lady Oracle* also embeds folk motifs to suggest the character's genuine and continuous transformation.

Atwood's female characters in *Lady Oracle* and other works face the double and potentially triple bind of Moira Shearer's role in the film, *The Red Shoes*, loosely based on the Andersen fairy tale: they can "dance" (be artists, be "themselves," be "free") *or* marry (be conventional, be-for-others, conform to societal rules), but they cannot do both. As in "Fitcher's Bird" and "The Robber Bridegroom," a "Red Shoes" marriage is again a kind of death. Wishing to be a butterfly,[2] *Lady Oracle*'s Joan is forced to become an escape-artist. Like a slave pretending to dance so that she will be untied (Motif K571), Joan tries to be what her society wants her to be: a performer. She first dances as a brownie with red hair (Motifs F482.1.1, F482.5.1), a fat mothball, a circus fat lady, a voluptuous and parodic Triple Goddess, and a celestial nymph (Motif F642.5). Since dancing in folklore is often associated with enchantment, taboos, deception, captivity (K772, K826), and (especially for women) punishment, however, later she is the big/ Little Mermaid dancing on knives, Karen trapped in the dancing red shoes (Motif D2061.1.2), and a tired princess "danced" out (AT 306, Motif F1015.1.1) in costume-Gothic and life roles. After a fake suicide, a reunion with her lost real and Earth mother, and a dance with and for herself, however, Joan is no longer fixed in a role but symbolically reborn and in the process of becoming. Now resembling the Grimms' "The Girl Without Hands," she symbolically regrows her severed feet: like other Atwood personae, she opens the doors to split-off self, past, future, and relationship.

Contrary to most current critical estimations, *Lady Oracle* self-consciously comments on its many intertexts and still ends with a fairy-tale metamorphosis that is only partly ironic. While critiquing and parodying the either/or choices for women in "The Red Shoes" film, Atwood incorporates elements of Andersen's literary tale, "The Little Mermaid," in her comic but highly satirical metafiction. Hoping to please the prince, the mermaid (Motif B81) in Andersen's story sacrifices her tongue, beautiful voice, tail and, in my interpretation, any possibility of tale, in order to have human legs. Even though she symbolically "dances" on knives (Motif H1531.1) to win a husband, he marries someone else. Unlike the recent Disney version rewarding the "good" girl with marriage, the Andersen fairy tale offers only heavenly reward. However, the two Bluebeard tales, the Grimms' "Fitcher's Bird" and "The Robber Bridegroom," are about escaping marital dismemberment and, in the later case, cannibalistic consummation. They model re-membering: the possibility of women's becoming whole, being reborn, by re-membering (rediscovering), reading, speaking, and "dancing" their own texts as well as the old stories.

As in Atwood's other fairy-tale intertexts, the main image in both Andersen and Powell and Pressburger's *The Red Shoes* is female amputation. As we have begun to see, Atwood's women symbolically lose their eyes, tongues, heads or hearts, and bodies, breasts,[3] hands, or feet (Motifs Q451.0.1, S162) in phallocentric culture. Although three critics briefly explore the explicit fairy-tale allusions in the novel, they fail to recognize the complexity and irony of Atwood's vision. Like most feminist theorists (e.g., Daly 44, 90–91, 151–52, 266, 351–52), Jensen and

Rigney assume that fairy tales are necessarily role limiting for women. Thus, they also assume that fairy tales function as straightforward, negative messages in the novel and that Joan is destroyed by such conditioning (Jensen 29, 48; Rigney 66). Although Grace recognizes the affirmation of "Fitcher's Bird," she thinks *Lady Oracle* refuses it ("Courting" 261). Treating fairy tales much like other intertexts (including mythical, biblical, Gothic, historic, and popular stories),[4] Atwood subjects the Andersen tales to more satirical scrutiny than those of the Grimms. Nevertheless, embedded fairy tales and fairy-tale patterns in *Lady Oracle* suggest transformation for Joan Foster, other women, and society.

Most noticeably, Andersen's "The Red Shoes" is about worldly vanity and pride, its consequent punishment, and Christian redemption. It features three pairs of red shoes dramatizing female frivolity and overconcern with appearance. Because a poor little girl, Karen, goes barefoot in summer and wears ill-fitting wooden shoes in winter, a shoemaker's wife makes her a rough pair of red shoes, which Karen inappropriately wears for the first time in her mother's funeral procession. Convinced that the ugly shoes, soon burned, are responsible for an old woman's offering to take care of her, Karen also believes the mirror's pronouncement that she is not just pretty, but beautiful. Ironically imitating the queen's daughter, who "allow[s] herself to be stared at" wearing a second pair of red shoes, Karen deceives the kind old woman who cares for her and proudly wears the third pair of red shoes, again inappropriately, to confirmation. She thinks only of the red shoes. The third time she wears the forbidden red shoes she is on her way to communion. A red-bearded (Motif G303.4.1.3.1), crippled soldier, leaning on a crutch at the church door, is wiping shoes. When she puts her foot forward to be wiped, he comments on her pretty "dancing shoes." Slapping the soles, he tells the shoes, "Sit fast, when you dance" (*Complete Hans* 450–51).

Inside the church, all the people, even the monument figures, again look at Karen's shoes. Forgetting even to say the Lord's Prayer, Karen thinks only of the red shoes. As she starts to lift her foot to get into the carriage after the service, the old soldier says, "'Dear me, what pretty dancing shoes!' and Karen [can] not help it, she [is] obliged to dance a few steps." Once begun, her legs continue to dance, as if the shoes have "power over them." She cannot stop; her legs rest only when the shoes are removed and put into a cupboard. Still, Karen cannot stop looking at the shoes (*Complete Hans* 451–52).

When the old woman becomes ill, Karen neglects her duty by wearing the red shoes to a ball. Again she dances out of control, the shoes going as they will, out of the town, into a dark wood where the face of the old soldier replaces the moon. He repeats, "Dear me, what pretty dancing shoes!" Frightened, Karen wants to throw the shoes away, but they have grown to her feet and continue dancing. She has neither peace nor rest. When she dances by an angel holding a shining sword, he pronounces: "Dance ye shall . . . dance in your red shoes till you are pale and cold, till your skin shrivels up and you are a skeleton! Dance you shall, from door to door, and where proud and wicked children live you shall knock, so that they may hear you and fear you!" Although she cries, "Mercy!" she is unable to hear his answer and continues dancing. She knows she is forsaken and "damned by the angel of God" when she sees the old woman's coffin carried out. "Torn and bleeding" from being forced to dance over thorns and stumps, she finally comes to the house of the executioner, whose axe tingles to "strike off the heads of the wicked." Wanting to "repent of [her] sin," Karen asks the executioner to cut off her feet with the red shoes instead of her head. After she confesses, he complies and the shoes dance away with the feet into the forest (*Complete Hans* 452–53).

Using carved wooden feet and crutches, Karen twice tries to enter the church but turns back when she sees the dancing shoes. Repenting "heartily of her sin," she begs and is offered work at the parsonage. When biblical passages about "dress and grandeur and beauty" are read aloud, she shakes her head. Alone while others go to church, she calls for God's help and the angel appears, this time holding a green branch full of roses. As he touches the walls, they open, revealing the church and the pastor's household. The people tell Karen, "It was right of you to come." Karen says, "It was mercy." When her heart is so filled with peace and joy that it breaks, her soul flies to heaven, where no one asks about the red shoes (*Complete Hans* 452–53).

"The Red Shoes" has a straightforward moralistic story line. Because Karen sets "dress and grandeur and beauty" above religious and familial obligations, she is, for a time, condemned to do, unceasingly, that which she "wrongfully" chooses to do: dance. As in Andersen's "The Snow Queen" (written the same year) and the Grimms' "The Juniper Tree" and "Little Red Cap," the red shoes are linked to menarche and sexuality. Paradoxically, the red color also suggests not only Christian sin (Lederer 34), suffering, and martyrdom but the full moon or Venus phase of the Mother Goddess (see also Sciff-Zamaro 32, 35). According to Lederer, "Red is and always has been the color symbolic . . . of all that is forbidden at most times or to most people." The shoes won't come off because "Initially voluntary behavior becomes a part of our selves . . . . The slippers are 'the shoes we fill'—the role we play in life. They are 'the shoes we are to wear if they fit us,'" as in "Cinderella."[5] Thus, like the shoes Gerda wears in "The Snow Queen," Karen's red shoes suggest the "impure blood" of awakened sexuality and its consequences (Lederer 35–36).

But Lederer does not comment on the inconsistency of punishing only female sexuality. Feared and controlled in androcracy and androcentric religion (Eisler 92, 96–97), female sexuality is a subtext in most of Atwood's fairy-tale intertexts,[6] including "Fitcher's Bird" with its stained egg (see Chapter 9). Although dancing originally suggested the goddess's cosmic creation and was important in religious ritual for centuries, it later became associated with witches and devil worshippers (Motifs G247,

C51.1.5, G303.10.4.1, Q552.2.3.1), who often wore red. About the sixth or seventh century, Christian churches outlawed ecclesiastical dancing for being "too sensual and too much enjoyed by women" (Walker, *Woman's Dictionary* 89, 175–76). Thus, when Karen dances "out of control," it is no accident that the face of the old soldier (patriarchal authority) replaces the moon (matriarchy). Ironically from both early Christian and contemporary feminist standpoints, Karen wears the red shoes because she is female. Consequently, like some versions of oral fairy tales, "The Red Shoes" is gender biased. Underneath the moralistic text lies a subtext imaging and proscribing female world experience: girls or women who choose to dance or even express sexuality must willingly sacrifice their feet. In the words of Atwood's "A Red Shirt,"

> Children should not wear red,
> a man once told me.
> Young girls should not wear red.
> . . . . a Girl should be
> a veil, a white shadow, bloodless
> as a moon on water; not
> dangerous; she should
> keep silent and avoid
> red shoes, red stockings, dancing.
> Dancing in red shoes will kill you. (*THP* 1981, 101)

In perhaps her funniest novel, Atwood parodies the moralistic story of "The Red Shoes." Like Andersen's Karen, *Lady Oracle*'s Joan certainly "dances" out of control, in her addiction to escapism and repressive relationships as well as to eating. Consequently, Joan, too, has no peace or rest. She even experiences heartbreak. In *Lady Oracle*'s version of "The Red Shoes," however, Karen's over concern with beautiful appearance becomes the overweight Joan's reverse obsession: in battling her mother for her body, Joan asserts her presence and power and negates her mother's expectations by becoming ample, taking as much space as possible.[7] Whereas the monuments stare at Karen's red shoes, Joan's mother stares at her bulky daughter's defiant bathrobe and fuzzy pink slippers. Unlike Karen, isolated and offered no sustenance until her feet are chopped off, Joan stuffs cake into her mouth. Karen neglects her duties to the kind foster mother who dies disapproving of her behavior; refusing to be the product her "monster" mother desires, Joan neglects sometimes ludicrous duties to her husband, the "revolutionary" group, and her feminine role in order to write Gothic romances and play Lady Oracle. Because her mother also disapproves of her, Joan feels guilty for her death; but this mother's astral body returns for a reunion. Karen dances until her feet are "torn and bleeding" and submits to voluntary amputation; Joan cuts her feet dancing on her balcony and volunteers for symbolic amputation of will and talent. Karen is told she will dance until she becomes a skeleton; Joan penetrates the maze only to discover that Arthur and her other romantic dream images are really skulls. Finally, Karen, like the red-bearded soldier, is crippled and can move only on carved crutches; Joan, crippled by gender conditioning, carves her own "crutches" but is able to discard them without divine intervention.

As we have seen, the unforgettable image of the red shoes, grown to the feet and dancing of their own volition, transcends the moralistic story. It is this image, the artist context Michael Powell and Emeric Pressburger's 1948 film provides for it, and the fairy-tale subtext that structure *Lady Oracle*.

Such Andersen tales as "What One Can Invent" and "Aunty Toothache" sympathize with the difficult plight of the artist in the world. Although Andersen's "The Red Shoes" focuses on the image of dancing, significantly this fairy tale is not about art because Andersen's artists are implicitly male. Andersen's females can be muses, like "The New Century's Goddess" resembling Graves's White Goddess, or incarnations of stories, as in "The Will-o'-The-Wisp Is in the Town." Never treated as an artist, the female dancer or singer in Andersen's works (e.g.,

"The Red Shoes," "The Little Mermaid") is generally punished for vanity, often by male authority figures like "The Red Shoes"' soldier and Angel.

Michael Powell and Emeric Pressburger's *The Red Shoes*, a brilliant attempt to fuse music, ballet, painting, and film, makes the Karen figure an artist, but she is still punished for her aspirations. The film *The Red Shoes* frames its own fairy-tale intertext with a ballet and a larger romantic plot. Moira Shearer plays a ballerina who must, paradoxically, dance in order to live, but cannot live if she dances. As in the fairy tale, the shoes carry the dancer to death. This time, because she cannot choose between two masters and two professions, dancing *or* marriage, there is no redemption, even in death. According to *Lady Oracle*'s Joan, who weeps through four showings of the film: "The real red shoes [are] the feet punished for dancing. You could dance, or you could have the love of a good man. But you were afraid to dance, because you had this unnatural fear that if you danced they'd cut your feet off so you wouldn't be able to dance. Finally you overcame your fear and danced, and they cut your feet off. The good man went away too, because you wanted to dance" (368).

Victoria Paige, played by Moira Shearer in the film, is both wish-fulfillment dream and nightmare figure, emblem of both freedom and trap. Redheaded like her artist husband, Julian Craster (played by Marius Goring), and *Lady Oracle*'s Joan, Victoria is transformed in her tiara and tutu into a beautiful fairy-tale princess. She initially fulfills her dreams and seems to fly in her leaps. Dancing *The Red Shoes*, however, she imagines both Lermontov (the company head) and Craster as the evil shoemaker out to trap her. Pleasing Lermontov as Copelia doll but angering him as Juliet, Victoria dances parts that foreshadow her destiny. Forced to stop dancing for Lermontov in order to marry Craster, and then to leave Craster to continue dancing, Victoria is trapped in the red shoes. Symbolically pirouetting in ever narrowing circles, she gradually becomes a marionette controlled by a Stromboli master and finally by the shoes themselves, which literally dance her to death.

Wearing the red shoes thus takes on a number of gender-specific associations. Long an ideal image of female beauty and, therefore, the epitome of "the feminine," the ballerina is also an artist, married to her art instead of to a man and thus a "failure" as a conventional woman. More than writing poetry or painting, dancing as a ballerina exposes the contradictions inherent in female social conditioning and, especially, the female artist's "bind" (Juhasz 1; see Chapter 2). Dancing is a "fashionable" preparation for courtship (*LO* 44) and, thus, evidence of conformity to role conditioning. In order to dance with a dark, handsome stranger (who will presumably sweep the girl away to marriage), she must prepare for her role, enclosing her slim body in an appropriate costume and learning the "steps" of her part. Choosing to dance alone, however, without being part of a couple, is another matter entirely. Dancing as a ballerina is individualistic and self-expressive, therefore "selfish" and "unfeminine." Dancing thus takes on implications beyond compliance to role-conditioning. In *Lady Oracle*, dancing is initially an image of amputating feminine socialization. But it is also escape, self-expression, magical transformation, and, preeminently, art.

Like *The Handmaid's Tale*, whose Little Red Riding Hood is already eaten by the wolf when her tale begins (see Chapter 10), *Lady Oracle* begins near the end of the fairy-tale story, after Joan's mock suicide: despite her "death," her feet still adhere to the red shoes. But unlike the film character, Joan survives. Resembling *Bodily Harm*, the book is narrated retrospectively from a kind of "future present" after the events of the novel. In this case, however, we see not just the double vision of retrospective narration but the multiple vision of the artist-narrator and her ever-shifting personas, from the present of the novel's telling: the epic situation beyond the events of the book, the vision of multiple Joans in the novel's past, and even the character in the novel's present (Joan in Terremoto). As a conscious artist, Joan thus constructs both text and self by way of deconstruction (see Wilson, "Deconstructing" 65 on *Surf*): she deconstructs constricting fairy-tale, Gothic romance and life stories as she constructs the "science fiction" novel that revisions them and her earlier "alien" selves. Thus, we are able to observe both present and past Joans dancing *while* the artist Joan re-members and recounts her former life as dancer.

Three scenes, which Joan selects for the novel's beginning and end, illustrate the artist's analysis of her former Red Shoes dance. Paradoxically, the novel's first reference to dancing is an escape fantasy foretelling the fantasy's contradiction: the trap of the "real" red shoes, the punished feet. As we have begun to see, however, both Joan's lived and written texts demonstrate the duplicity and narcissistic mirroring characteristic of self-conscious fiction and postmodernism.[8] Disguised and using her "other" name, the character Joan remembers a previous Joan and that Joan's life with Arthur. Arthur "said he had never learned" to dance and disapproved of costumes. Behind this Joan is not only Atwood but Joan the artist. By ironically shaping the story of both past and "present" Joans for us and "the reporter" part of herself, this artist anticipates Rennie of *Bodily Harm* and the woman who names herself by using her voice in *The Handmaid's Tale*. Joan, too, becomes the "reporter" of "The Robber Bridegroom": "I would dab myself with perfume, take off my shoes, and dance in front of the mirror, twirling slowly around, waltzing with an invisible partner. A tall man in evening dress, with an opera cloak and smoldering eyes. As he swept me in circles (bumping occasionally into the dressing table or the end of the bed) he would whisper, 'Let me take you away. We will dance together, always'" (21). Knowing since childhood the consequences of dancing in the real red shoes,[9] an earlier Joan nevertheless surrendered her feet to punishment, even removing her other shoes to dance with the glamorous stranger whose image she created.

In the now of the epic situation, the artist Joan ironically combines Bella Lugosi's Dracula and Charlie Chaplin's Tramp with "Cinderella"'s Prince Charming. She undercuts the romantic with both the Gothic and comic, deconstructing the fantasy creation that ruled her life before "suicide." The ironic language of her self-conscious narrative ("As he swept me in circles . . . he would whisper, 'Let me take you away'") subtly reveals her recognition of this image's trap. Like the empty newspaperman with whom the film's Victoria dances a scene from *The Red Shoes* ballet, the image of the glamorous stranger once promised escape but kept Joan in socialized circles. Rather than participating in the energy and life force of a goddess spiral (Gimbutas, *Language* 279, 283; Walker, *Woman's Dictionary* 14), Joan's dance is static. Clearly neither the prince nor the stories about him provide Joan or the reader an exit from the patriarchally usurped maze once associated with the earth womb (Walker, *Woman's Dictionary* 14, 96).

Commenting that she will never be "very tidy," the frame-breaking narrator (Givner 139, 145) next remembers her mother signing her up for dancing school. Joan's mother hopes her daughter will become more socially acceptable, perhaps even lose weight so that her appearance more closely coincides with the feminine ideal (Orbach 74). Paradoxically, this supposedly sexual image also characterizes Greer's female eunuch, the castrated woman (*The Female Eunuch*) that Joan is in danger of becoming (Motifs Q451.10, Q451.10.1, S176). Lacking any identity except girlfriend, wife, and mother, even in frozen moments of the past (photographs), Joan's mother deflects her terrible anger about her own symbolic amputation by decapitating photographs of men. She finds her daughter's body, ample and impossible to overlook, an affront. Seeing Joan in her tutu—attempting not just to be pretty but to transcend the role and "fly" as a dancer—is too much: she arranges for Joan to be a dancing mothball instead of a butterfly. Mothballs kill growth, preventing a moth's development beyond the larval stage; as a mothball, Joan will supposedly "preserve," rather than question or transform, her caterpillar role and self. Ironically, however, dancing as a mothball—the parodic reverse of dancing as a ballerina—is similarly individualistic and self-expressive and, therefore, anarchistic of the fantasy product Joan's mother hopes to construct. Just as the artist-narrator deconstructs dancing as a fantasy escape, she makes sure that we recognize this second circular movement as "a dance of [repressed] rage and destruction" (51).

Finally, as artist-narrator Joan dramatizes a solitary dance on broken glass. This dance counters Joan's earlier fantasy dance with the mysterious stranger and breaks "the circle game" of the red shoes. Joan frees her mother as image of herself (and herself as failed image of her mother) by going through the glass barricade separating them from one another (*LO* 363), herself from her feelings, and female artists from their art (Grace Stewart 176–77). Joan also realizes the trap of her fantasies. After she kills that patriarchal construct, "the lady poet," in her fake suicide, Joan enters her internal maze to encounter the multiple identities of her Gothic characters, herself, and finally others (Wilson, "Fragmented" 79–80). Joan sees the entangled feet of her Gothic heroine, Charlotte, and decides to "dance for no one but myself. May I have this waltz? I whispered." True, she cuts her feet, "the real red shoes . . . punished for dancing," and compares her butterfly dance to a bear's "dance" on its hind legs "trying to avoid the arrows" (*LO* 367–68). Commenting on her unsuccessful role as an escape artist, however, even the character Joan recognizes that she wears the red shoes. She frees herself to be more than a "dancing girl" and to open more doors, to Arthur, the reporter, her Demeter self, and the future, thereby becoming the real artist who writes the book we read.

This incident illustrates that in addition to being a vehicle of socialization or escape, dancing in *Lady Oracle* and other Atwood works also draws on goddess myth, including the Demeter-Persephone story. As in "A Red Shirt," "red is our color by birth-/right." The red shirt the mother makes for her daughter "is stained / with our words, our stories":

This is the procession
of old leathery mothers,

the moon's last quarter
before the blank night,

mothers like worn gloves
wrinkled to the shapes of their lives,

passing the work from hand to hand,
mother to daughter,

a long thread of red blood, not yet broken.

Unaware of the fables and charms potent as "virginal angels dancing / on the heads of pins" and protected by the "private magic" of her mother's art, the daughter in "A Red Shirt" "hugs" the color red, runs in bare feet, and waves her red arms "in delight." As she dances, "the air / explodes with banners" (*THP* 102, 104–5).

Similarly, dancing in *Lady Oracle* becomes a means of self-expression, communion with other women, magic, transformation, and art. Scenes such as Joan's Brownie dancing (Motif F482.5.1), her tap dancing with the count, her choreographed affair with the Royal Porcupine, her fairy-tale godmother dance with the readers of her Gothic romances, her wedding scene ballet, the circus's harem dancing girls, and the fat lady's ballet steps on the high wire further show the varied functions of dancing in the metafiction.

Ironically, Joan's "release" from the red shoes comes not from "repenting" and agreeing to her amputation, as in the Andersen tale and as Joan tried earlier, but by becoming a different kind of dancer. As Grace Stewart indicates, the myths frequently used in literature to represent the artist—Daedalus, Icarus, Prometheus, Faust—assign women to mother, helpmate, beauty, muse, or troublemaker roles (107). If it is impossible to remove the red shoes that all women wear, Joan can still break through the constricting story lines of patriarchal fairy tales and myths.

Reliving in imagination a "costumed" life dance leading into Daedalus's maze,[10] Joan recognizes the shoes for what they are but chooses to dance nevertheless.

In Atwood's comic re-visioning, Joan ironically resembles James Joyce's Stephen Daedalus in being both a Daedalus and Icarus figure. Like Icarus, Joan flies too near the sun, falls into the sea, and "drowns." In recounting the story of her drowning, however, she encounters her amputated self-images as Karen, as her Gothic romance heroines, as Diana (the multibreasted fountain at Villa d'Estes), as Persephone separated from Demeter (Motif A310.1) and as Fitcher/Bluebeard's many Brides and wives (including their Venus and Hecate phases). She recovers her wholeness in the Great Mother (A3, A401), the three ways (Trivia) that are one (*LO* manuscripts, Atwood Papers). By embracing her multiplicity, the maze she is, she becomes "free," no longer trapped in prefabricated roles or lives that, like strands of her plot, are simultaneous but incongruous. Like Daedalus fashioning the once-denied wings of metamorphosis and rebirth (Motif 1021.1, see n. 2), Joan dances as an artist and structures her own story: "A Portrait of the Artist as a Dancing Fat Lady" (Wilson, "Fragmented" 53), the novel-maze we read. This comic *Künstlerroman* thus re-visions the traditional artist novel and re-members the matriarchal maze. Recasting the father-son quest story (Tindall 25–30) as a Demeter-Persephone tale, *Lady Oracle* passes on the "long thread of red blood" purged of phallocentric curses.

Although Joan deconstructs the gender-ensnaring plots and subtexts of embedded films, patriarchal myths, and fairy tales, she ironically experiences a genuine fairy-tale transformation. Expecting a Bluebeard killer rather than pretending invisibility, doing nothing, or disguising herself as someone else—ploys used before she realized she had options—Joan opens the door of her apartment to face the person behind it: a reporter she supposedly hits with a Cinzano bottle.

Whether or not the familiar-looking stranger behind the symbolic door (see *I* discussion) is "really" another person, "he" suggests an aspect of the multitudinous self Joan has always been afraid to see. In early drafts of this book Joan addresses a "you" resembling the androgynous "I"/"you" splits of Atwood's poetry and *Edible Woman* drafts (*LO* and *EW* manuscripts, Atwood Papers). A number of critics claim that when Joan visits the hospitalized reporter she is up to her old escape tricks again.[11] If the reporter is another person, however, the "something about a man in a bandage" is likely to be his vulnerability. His wound— corollary of her cut feet—again deconstructs the dangerous fantasy stranger and establishes a shared humanity. Earlier, Joan was disconcerted to discover that the man who untied her might have been the "daffodil man" who exposed himself, that her father—saver of lives—was also an executioner, and that all men might be both rescuers and destroyers. But in her "Red Shoes" / Gothic-romance life, she cast herself, and to some extent saw herself, as victim. This time it is she who hurts another and she who presents the yellow flowers. As the narrators of both *Surfacing* and *Bodily Harm* discover, "he" (or "they") is also "I." Planning to get Sam and Marlene out of jail and face Arthur, she now takes responsibility for her actions. No longer agreeing to amputation or, like Andersen's Karen, depending upon a male angel to open the maze enclosing and excluding her, Joan is a successful trickster who opens closed doors. Like Fitcher's third bride (the Grimms' "Fitcher's Bird"), she discovers that she is not a victim and that men, not necessarily Bluebeards, are also human and vulnerable.

Resembling the Grimms' Robber Bride ("The Robber Bride-groom"), Joan survives to tell her and her sisters' story. Thus, Atwood's fairy-tale intertext not only structures her metanarrative, including her character's positive transformation: it revisions the fairy tale and implies life beyond sexual politics. Again writing "science fiction" by shifting the point of view, in *You Are Happy* (Chapter 6) Atwood opens another already-finished story and gives voice to another alien, again a marginalized and silenced female artist.

Frozen Touch
in *You Are Happy*

*The Rapunzel Syndrome
and "The Girl Without Hands"*

In "Ice-Women vs. Earth Mothers," a chapter of her 1972 book, *Survival*, Atwood discusses Canadian literature's preponderance of sinister or life-denying women. Corresponding to only one aspect of the Triple Goddess, they demonstrate what Atwood calls the Rapunzel syndrome, a central dilemma in her poetry and fiction. In addition to the Grimms' "Rapunzel" (AT 310, see Chapter 11), "The Girl Without Hands" ("The Maiden Without Hands") ("Das Mädchen ohne Hände," 1812, 1857, No. 31, AT 706), one of the tales Atwood finds most influential (Atwood Telephone Call 1985), offers insight into how Atwood characters become separated from life. The folk motif of a maiden without hands occurs in Basile's "The Girl with Maimed Hands" (*The Pentamerone*) and is prevalent in medieval romance (Elizabeth Archibald cited in Tatar, *Off* n. 16). Grimms' "The Girl Without Hands" is also the basis for the title of Joyce Carol Oates's *Do With Me What You Will* (1973) (Stone, "Things" 43) and Sexton's poem, "The Maiden Without Hands," in *Transformations*. Atwood makes her interest in "The Girl Without Hands" overt in an unpublished poem of this title written for *Interlunar* (Atwood Papers, Box 13; see Chapter 9). However, Atwood uses the "Girl

Without Hands" intertext along with the Rapunzel Syndrome from her earliest to her most recent work. My discussion will focus on *You Are Happy* in this chapter and on *Life Before Man*, *Bodily Harm*, and *Interlunar* in subsequent chapters.

As McCombs indicates, Atwood's "apprentice years [preceding *CG*] are full of poems of frozen, freezing, caged, bottled, towered, lifeless women, poems that were published steadily in Canadian journals—which suggests that Canadian editors could recognize a character relevant to Canada" ("Politics, Structure" 144; Atwood Papers, Boxes 6, 7). For example, Atwood's Rapunzel in "Towered Woman" (1960) not only lacks a prince but even the ability to jump or sleep (60); and for "The Acid Sibyl" (1963), prophesying from a bottle, " . . . fresh air / Would be a form of suicide" ("Fall and All: a Sequence" 59). Canada's version of the ancient Triple Goddess, typified in E. J. Pratt's "Towards the Last Spike," Sheila Watson's *The Double Hook*, Margaret Laurence's *The Stone Angel*, Anne Hébert's "The House on the Esplanade," and Joyce Marshall's "The Old Woman," is generally a negative version of the Nature as woman (poetry) or woman as Nature (fiction) metaphor. "Not just an Ice-Virgin-Hecate figure, but a Hecate with Venus and Diana trapped inside" (*Surv* 199–200, 210), this Hecate is an extension of the Grimms' Rapunzel ("Rapunzel," No. 12, AT 310: The Maiden in the Tower).

According to Bottigheimer, "The single most pervasive image evoked in the popular mind by the term *fairy tale* is probably that of a maiden in distress leaning from a tower window and searching the horizon for a rescuer" (*Grimms'* 101). Thus, unlike the fairy tales with positive female images that Atwood prefers, "Rapunzel" may seem to embody the passive fairy-tale female that leads feminists to decry fairy tales' influence. Among the Grimms' "immured, incarcerated, or sequestered heroines" of this description are not only Rapunzel but Maid Maleen (No. 198), the king's wife in "The Pink" (No. 76), and Brier Rose (No. 50) (Bottigheimer, *Grimms'* 101–2). Predating the Grimms,

Danae was confined to a tower by Acrisius, who feared the prophecy that Danae's son would kill him. Generally known as a virgin impregnated with Perseus in a shower of gold (Walker, *Woman's Encyclopedia* 207; Kaster 47), Danae or Dana, like Eve, was "another name for the universal Triple Goddess." Thus, Danae's towered imprisonment, like the societal imprisonment of females so common in fairy tales such as "Rapunzel" and "Brier Rose," suggests fear of female power. Although "some critics see fairy tale enclosure or isolation as a remnant of archaic or exotic sequestrations experienced by pubescent girls and adolescent boys before marriage," Bottigheimer, like Atwood, sees the fairy-tale tower as "a socially created architectural structure," as opposed to a natural setting such as a forest. In the Grimms' tales females of all ages, but not males, are sequestered, just as gender rather than witchcraft determines whether they are burned at the stake.[1]

According to Atwood, the Rapunzel syndrome usually has four elements: Rapunzel, the wicked witch who imprisons her (Motifs $P_{272.1}$, G_{204}), the tower she is imprisoned in (Motifs T_{381}, $R_{41.2}$), and the rescuer. In Canada's version, Rapunzel is also silenced: she walks around with a mouth "like [a] clenched fist." She and her tower are synonymous: "These heroines have internalized the values of their culture to such an extent that they have become their own prisons." In most cases, "the Rescuer is not much help" (*Surv* 209–10). Such Rapunzels are found in every Atwood novel and in many Atwood poems and stories; in a sense, most of the fairy-tale intertexts incorporate the Rapunzel syndrome. As we have seen, Marian (*EW*), the narrator of *Surfacing*, and Joan (*LO*) all internalize negative cultural values and symbolically become what they wish to escape: a cannibal, a bodiless "American," and a narcissistic three-headed monster embodying its maze. Partly responsible for their separation from others and parts of themselves, they still transform and rescue themselves from their internalized isolation. The Grimms' Rapunzel learns that the power to change her situation resides in herself and can be expressed through her body (her hair and tears, Motifs F848.1, F952.1). Similarly, characters in *Two-Headed Poems*, *Interlunar*, *Bodily Harm*, *The Handmaid's Tale*, *Cat's Eye*, and especially *You are Happy* and *Life Before Man*, must choose to leave their imprisoning "towers" and "reinhabit" their bodies. Such Rapunzels recall other fairy-tale and mythic figures, such as Andersen's Snow Queen and Ice Maiden and the Grimms' Girl Without Hands ("The Snow Queen," "The Ice Maiden," "Girl Without Hands"), who are literally or figuratively "cut off." Exploring "Rapunzel" in greater detail, Chapter 11 discusses Elaine Risley, the main character of *Cat's Eye*, in reference to "Rapunzel" and "The Snow Queen." Although Atwood scholars have not discussed it at all, "The Girl Without Hands," like "Fitcher's Bird," "The Robber Bridegroom," "The Juniper Tree," "The White Snake," "The Red Shoes," and "Rapunzel," has archetypal significance in Atwood's work.

Atwood's watercolors demonstrate, among other amputations, the significance of the handless image throughout Atwood's work (see especially Plate 4, the first Mary Stuart or Anne Boleyn figure, and Atwood's mythological bird-people with claws rather than hands: Plates 10, 13, 14, 19. Even the monster's hands in the first Frankenstein watercolor (Plate 6) don't seem to belong to his apparently armless body, and many figures' hands are hidden or crossed rather than extended (Plates 3, 4, 5, 7, 8, 16). In the watercolors and *You Are Happy*, the victimization is of the *Power Politics* variety, so evident in the cover design of *Power Politics* (Plate 8): male and female games in an explicitly patriarchal setting. *Life Before Man* might initially seem different; as in *Bodily Harm* and *Interlunar*, however, the power politics in *Life Before Man* is still gendered, still conditioned by patriarchal institutions and values.[2] In *You Are Happy*, *Life Before Man*, *Bodily Harm*, and *Interlunar*, the imagery, theme, and narrative structure (from isolation, victimization and claws or handlessness to survival, regrown hands, and wholeness) are the most significant aspects of the fairy tale intertext.

The Grimms' sources for "The Girl Without Hands, a "mixed tale" resulting from a combination of at least two tales, were Marie von Hassenpflug, Dorothea Vichmann, and Johann H. B. Bauer (Zipes, *Complete* 717). The few general readers familiar with this tale, about a daughter whose father amputates her hands to save her from the devil, may be surprised to learn that, as in "Catskin" versions of "Cinderella" (AT 510B; see Tatar, *Off* 126–39), it is an incest story, with all signs of the incest suppressed. In unedited form, the major themes of the tales in the Grimms' collection are sex and violence, frequently incest and child abuse, but Wilhelm Grimm "systematically' purged . . . references to sexuality and masked depictions of incestuous desire" (Tatar, *Hard Facts* 10).

Although all seven editions of *Nursery and Household Tales* (*Kinder- und Hausmärchen*) use the same beginning, in the final edition of their notes the Grimms discuss two versions of the tale, "one of the two obviously having turned up *after* the 1812 *KHM* was published, and they say quite unreservedly that the second version . . . surpasses the other in inner completeness.'" Although they follow it in later editions, "they keep the *beginning* of the first manuscript. . . .[,] an admittedly inferior version of the tale[,]. . . . in their anxiety to soften depictions of serious intra-family violence" (Ellis 77–78; see Zipes, *Brothers* 127–30 for a translation of the 1812 version). Significantly, in the second tale, "the girl's father is the sole satanic figure" (Tatar, *Hard Facts* 10). As in some "Cinderella" variants, he demands his daughter's hand in marriage. In this case, before the lecherous father (Motif T411.1) drives his daughter out into the world when she refuses to marry him (Motif S322.1.2), he cuts off her hands (Motif Q451.1) *and her breasts* (Q451.9), sometimes her *tongue* (S163),[3] and makes her put on a white shirt. The Grimms filled the gap in motivation for the girl's leaving home with "a fairy-tale cliche—the devil," often used to incarnate forbidden desire (Ellis 78; Tatar, *Hard Facts* 10, *Off* 122). Regardless of obvious literary, psychoanalytic, and cultural interest in "The Girl Without

Hands," the Grimms' "unpardonable sin" of using a composite text, included in the term *fakelore* (Dundes, "Psychoanalytic" 118), has caused both "folk" (Degh 76) and folklorists[4] to disregard, berate, or reject rather than interpret the Grimms' version of this tale type. An archetype of patriarchal victimization of females, "The Girl Without Hands" should have a preeminent position in women's studies. As will be evident, many discussions of the Grimms' version, however, epitomize phallocentric collusion in disguising and displacing both crime and culprit. The central image of the tale symbolizes the handlessness afflicting most of Atwood's characters and a society ranking "grabbing"—including material acquisition—above a giving touch. More broadly, it epitomizes the cultural dismemberment—of both males and females—that interferes with the development of whole human beings and the egalitarian relationships they are capable of having.

The Grimms' "The Girl Without Hands" ("The Maiden Without Hands") has four main characters: the father, the devil, the king, and the girl. As published in the final edition (1857), the father, a miller, is gradually becoming poor, with nothing left but his mill and a large apple tree behind it. One day, as he is preparing to chop wood in the forest, he meets an old man who offers to make him rich if he promises, in writing, to give the stranger what is behind the mill. After the miller does so, he returns home and is met by his wife, amazed to discover the wealth in every chest and box of the house. It is she who recognizes that the stranger must be the devil and that the father has promised his daughter, who was behind the mill sweeping the yard (Zipes, *Complete* 118–19).

The beautiful and pious young girl lives the three years before the agreement is due "in fear of God and without sin." When the devil comes for her, he cannot take her because she has "washed herself clean" and drawn a chalk circle around herself. After the miller takes all water away from the girl, as the devil demands, the devil comes again and is frustrated because her tears have cleaned her hands. "Chop off her hands. Otherwise, I can't touch her," he says. When threatened that the devil will take him if he doesn't comply, the father asks her forgiveness (Zipes, *Complete* 119).

"'Dear Father,' she answered, 'do what you want with me. I'm your child.'" The father chops off her hands. But she weeps on the stumps, so that they are again clean, and the devil loses all claim to her. Admitting that he is wealthy because of her, the miller offers her a life of splendor; but she refuses: "No, I cannot stay here. I'm going away and shall depend on the kindness of people to provide me with whatever I need" (Zipes, *Complete* 119–20). After having her maimed hands bound to her back, she leaves and walks all day to a royal garden, with trees of fruit gleaming in the moonlight. She cannot enter because it is surrounded by water. Her prayers are answered by an angel, who closes one of the locks so she can walk through the moat and then enters the garden with her. When she eats one of the counted pears (apples in the 1812 edition) and hides, the gardener is silent (*Complete* 120).

The next morning the king asks the gardener why one pear is missing and is told about an armless "spirit" accompanied by an angel. The king, the gardener, and a priest keep watch in the magic garden under the pear tree until midnight and meet the girl (N711.3), not a spirit but "a poor creature forsaken by everyone except God." Saying that he shall not forsake her, the king takes her with him, has silver hands made for her, marries her, and puts her in the care of his mother when he leaves for war, asking specifically that she write if his wife has a child (*Complete* 120–21).

When the mother writes about the queen's baby boy, the devil exchanges the letter (Motif K2117) for one saying she has given birth to a changeling (or monster). Similarly, the devil exchanges the king's kind response for one demanding the death of both queen and son. When the king's mother again writes, the devil again substitutes different letters, the last one significantly ordering her to keep the queen's tongue and eyes as proof that she is dead. Unwilling to shed innocent blood, the old woman cuts out a doe's tongue and eyes, ties the child to the mother's back, and sends the queen and her son "out into the wide world" (Zipes, *Complete* 121).

When the queen comes to a wild forest and prays to God, an angel (sometimes the Holy Virgin—remnant of the Great Goddess) appears and leads her to a cottage (hut) with a sign reading, "Free Lodging for Everyone." Another angel dressed in snow white cares for them for seven years, when, "By the grace of God and through her own piety," the queen's natural hands grow back again (Motif E782.1) (Zipes, *Complete* 121–22).

When the king discovers the mistake, he vows to "go as far as the sky is blue, without eating or drinking" (Motif F1033) until he finds his wife and son. When he comes to the cottage, the angel leads him by the hand into the house, offers him food and drink he refuses, allows him to rest, and tells the queen her husband has come. "Sorrowful," the son who has thought his only father was "our Father that art in heaven," replaces the handkerchief over his father's face three times. Recognizing his wife after the angel fetches the silver hands (Motif H57.5), the king and the family are reunited (Motif S451). The couple eat a meal with the angel, remarry, and live happily ever after (Zipes, *Complete* 122–23).

Despite Wilhelm Grimm's changes between 1812 and 1857, making the maiden "more helpless, more stoic, and dependent" on an angel not present in the first editions (changes that may be psychoanalytically revealing about Wilhelm's life) (Zipes, *Brothers* 123–24), this tale's richness should not continue to be obscured by detailing its inauthenticity as folklore or its "negative" portrayal of females. Meanings of tales do change with time and with different audiences or readers: when we read the tale's "gaps," listening to the "voices" of the silenced females, we hear a story simultaneously old and new.

The most significant features of "The Girl Without Hands"

for Atwood's work are the fairy-tale sexual politics and the imagery of touch, hands, handlessness, and dismemberment. Like "Fitcher's Bird," "The Robber Bridegroom," and "Little Red Cap," the tale presents the violating, patriarchal touch of the "bad father," himself paradoxically "handless" in his incapacity for loving touch. Resembling the characters of other fantastic literature, those of "The Girl Without Hands" could represent archetypal aspects of a single personality; in patriarchy, however, they also dramatize "archetypal" gender relationships. Thus, father, devil, king, son, and father-god oppose mother, mother-in-law, daughter, and female angels and illustrate six kinds of touch: violating, pitying, absent, innocent, sustaining, and healing. "Male" touch splits into two opposing extremes mediated by a third possibility: 1) colonizing touch: the selfish father's betraying (Motif T411.1), punishing, and maiming touch (Q451.1, S161); the devil's intended and the king's actual owning touch; 2) the king's later pitying, absent, and sustaining touch; and 3) the son's healing touch and, by implication, a New Testament father-god's sustaining one. Similarly, despite patriarchal religions' assumption that the touch of a woman is the source of sin (Motif T336), female touch includes the daughter's "clean" hands and innocent touch, the mother's absent touch, and the mother-in-law and angels' sustaining touch. Thus, the father, devil, and king's hands both double and foil, as the daughter and mother-in-law's hands double the angels'. Mediating between are the hands of the mother, again doubled by those of the king. Finally, when the king's hands touch those of his son, Sorrowful, both persons' hands double those of the angel.

In terms of the tale's dismemberment imagery, incest has been described as a slicing apart, leading Dworkin to conclude that perhaps "incestuous rape is becoming a central paradigm for intercourse in our time." If "men, who are, after all, just family, are supposed to slice us up the middle, leaving us in parts on the bed" (*Intercourse* 194), it is hardly surprising that countless female characters of folklore, myth, the Bible, and literature, including Atwood's own, are symbolically amputated or split. "The Girl Without Hands" thus signifies the dismemberments of patriarchal cultures.

Even if one is unaware of the cycle's incest content— sometimes of a brother rather than a father[5] or of a mother and son[6]—the Grimms' miller is greedy and careless. Resembling the fathers of "Hansel and Gretel" and "Beauty and the Beast," he puts material wealth and his own welfare above his daughter's. Beginning to include the point of view of the violated female in the tale, Zipes suggests that the miller

> is a frustrated man, concerned about his inability to succeed— perhaps his virility—and he finds a way to vent his frustration by attacking his child and then rationalizing it. . . . His violating her is not treated as a crime but rather as an emergency; she is made to feel guilty if she does not relent. . . . the signs in this initial incident indicate that the narrator is expressing the difficulties a child feels in confronting an abusive father or mother. It is not a coincidence that the girl marries a man who also threatens to abuse her (with death or banishment). Aided by her mother-in-law (wish-fulfillment), she flees again. Only when the male (the father, the parent, the analyst) recognizes that *he* is the abuser and does penance for his misuse of power (seven years wandering), can there be a reconciliation. Only then will the maiden have her own hands, her own power, and be able to determine how she will live. (*Brothers* 125)

Although the king's kind "touch" culminates in a "natural" child rather than the "monstrous" product of incest, he, like the father-devil, is initially materialistic and aggressive. He counts each pear in his orchard personally. When the king takes the girl in, he supplies her with artificial silver hands, ornamental and expensive evidence of his wealth but useless to her.[7] When he leaves for war, he is primarily concerned about an heir, even though the king's absence threatens the queen, who is now dependent upon him in place of her father.

Anne Sexton's transformed "The Maiden Without Hands" helps us read Atwood's intertext by raising crucial questions about the king in the Grimms' "The Girl Without Hands":

Is it possible
he marries a cripple
out of admiration?
A desire to own the maiming
so that not one of us butchers
will come to him with crowbars
or slim precise tweezers?
Lady, bring me your wooden leg
so I may stand on my own
two pink pig feet.
If someone burns out your eye
I will take your socket
and use it for an ashtray.

Like the devil or wizard, the king in "The Girl Without Hands" initially seems to be a patriarchal exploiter, in Sexton's version attracted to the maiden's "stumps / as helpless as dog's paws" (81–83). His seven-year abstinence from food and drink before he may see her or his son is a time of growth paralleled by the seven-year period in which the woman's natural hands grow back. The son's touch recovers the human father, as opposed to the tale's devil and divine fathers.[8] Unlike the marriage to death in "Fitcher's Bird" and "The Robber Bridegroom," the "cleansed" marital touch of "The Girl Without Hands" can suggest today a heterosexual love that is sustaining but not violating, interdependent rather than dominating or colonizing.

Female roles in "The Girl Without Hands" are also more provocative than they may seem. Although the mother in the Grimms' version is not absent, cruel, or jealous (as in some variants) and does express dread at what her husband has done, she is powerless: the wealth belongs to the miller, and she is not consulted about the agreement, its penalty, or the daughter's continued presence in the home. Unlike Demeter's earth-freezing reaction, any response she might have to her daughter's violation and disappearance is unrecorded, another gap in patriarchal versions of female experience. The mother-in-law (sometimes cruel in variants) dares to substitute a (female) deer's tongue and eyes for her daughter-in-law's but cannot risk direct disobedience of her son.

When scholars interpret the maiden's role in the tale (rather than stopping with classification, comparison, or methodology), they do so in widely differing ways, ranging from her being the goddess of the coming year or a remnant of matrilineal descent (cited in Dundes, "Psychoanalytic" 135–36); having castration anxiety, masturbation guilt,[9] or an Electral complex (Dundes, "Psychoanalytic" 138–42), to fearing mental activity and participation in life (Von Franz, *The Feminine* 77, 83). Even today the girl is accused of projecting her incestuous thoughts onto her father: she is thus blamed for her own violation and bound arms (e.g., Dundes, "Psychoanalytic" 140–43). As Tatar points out with reference to Shakespeare's *Pericles*, "a daughter becomes tainted by her father's evil no matter what the circumstances" (*Off* 126). Unless scholars find the motivation of the Grimms' girl in actual or desired incest, she speaks in a way that puzzles them. On the one hand, she is a model of female compliance: "'Dear Father,' she answered, 'do what you want with me. I'm your child.'" After her hands are amputated, she has her maimed arms bound to her back (Zipes, *Complete* 120), further restricting her ability to interact with the world and implying internalized female conditioning. She also becomes more God-fearing in each edition (Tatar, *Hard Facts* 30). On the other hand, however, when offered material wealth and her father's "tender care" in exchange for betrayal and amputation, "inexplicably" she prefers the kindness of strangers and wandering alone rather than the "protection" of home! She also chooses to have evidence of her violation hidden from her and others' sight.

The Grimms' girl, like *The Handmaid's Tale*'s Offred (and millions of other women in phallocentric contexts), is "named" only in her relationship to men. In some versions of this tale type the handless maiden, like the Robber Bride, does tell her story, culminating in the punishment of the one responsible for her amputation (see n. 5). In the Grimms' version, however, the incest is concealed and the crime displaced: the father "protects" his daughter by cutting off her hands! Rather than being empowered through speech, the Grimms' maiden is left waiting, cloistered in the generic cottage in the woods (Bottigheimer, *Grimms' Bad* 102). The untold "story" of what she feels and how her hands grow back, like those of Fitcher's chopped up victims (Chapter 9), is the material of Atwood's, and our own, fairy-tale re-visionings. Once we "listen" to the point of view of the silenced female, we begin to hear and create new stories.

As a creative artist, Atwood is undoubtedly drawn to powerful images of amputation and handlessness in "The Girl Without Hands." In supplying contemporary contexts for images and stories from the Grimms and Andersen, *The Wizard of Oz*, myth, and history in her own tales and poems, Atwood's artistry resembles that of her friend, Jay Macpherson, who uses Noah and ark intertext in *The Boatman* (1968).[10] In her unpublished manuscript poem, "Girl Without Hands," "Only a girl like this / can know what has happened to you" and other contemporary Rapunzels. On her way to work, the poem's persona becomes aware of her symbolic handlessness as she walks through "ruins" "quickened" in sunlight: "and you can't hold it, / you can't hold any of it. Distance surrounds you, / marked out by the ends of your arms / when they are stretched to their fullest." Re-visioning and empowering the Girl Without Hands, in this poem Atwood paradoxically gives her the healing "touch" (Motif D2161.4.16) her alienated persona needs and anticipates the healing hands the narrator of *Cat's Eye* holds out to her internalized Cordelia: "If she were here she would / reach out her arms towards / you now and touch you / with her absent hands / and you would feel nothing, but you would be / touched all the same" (Atwood Papers, *I* Manuscripts).

In *You Are Happy* Atwood fills in the gaps in two classic stories "written" by phallocentric society and attributed to men: the Grimms' "The Girl Without Hands" and Homer's episode of Circe and Odysseus in *The Odyssey*. Much venerated and imitated, *The Odyssey* has since antiquity constituted a central part of cultural education and functioned as an intertext in countless works, including those of such Atwood influences as Tennyson (e.g., "The Lotus Eaters," "Ulysses"). By re-visioning both texts, Atwood remythifies both fairy tale and myth.

As several critics have noted, hands occupy a central position in Atwood's work, and, as images or motifs helping to structure Atwood texts, they are usually related to voice and vision. Atwood admits: "Hands are quite important to me. The hand to me is an extension of the brain. And if you read theory on the development of the human species, everybody says that the ability to use the two is central; they are part of one another. I don't think of the brain as something that is just in your head. The brain is also in your body. . . . And the brain is certainly in the hands" (Lyons 229). As *Life Before Man*'s Elizabeth and *Bodily Harm*'s Rennie demonstrate, Atwood's main characters and personae usually progress from symbolic handlessness or inability to touch, to "regrown" hands and renewed touch, including compassion and love for others. In the eyes of Atwood's narrators, the hands of sinister Atwood characters—"lady killers" such as the commander (*HT*) and, comically, the gun-carrying Peter (*EW*), or gloved "witches" such as "the lady below" (*EW*), Auntie Muriel (*LBM*), or Serena Joy (*HT*)—literally or symbolically murder or freeze life. The importance of hands in *You Are Happy* (1974), however, has largely been overlooked or misinterpreted. According to Frank Davey, Atwood's female artists, including *You Are Happy*'s Circe, possess the "gorgon touch."

> From the Medusa of *Double Persephone* who yearns for a man who will resist her transforming gaze to the woman of the final poem of *You Are Happy* who sees her lover awaken from a sculptural pose, Atwood

concerns herself with the tyranny of atemporal modes—mythology, stylization, ritual, cultural stereotype, commercial image, social manners—and with the contrasting richness of kinetic reality. Yet for Atwood art itself seems inevitably to possess the 'gorgon touch' and to work to transform life into death, flesh into stone. Almost all of her major personae are the artist-as-transformer: Medusa the statue-maker, the Power Politician who transforms her lover into a comic-book hero, Susanna Moodie who can remake her husband into her 'idea of him' (*JSM*, 19), Circe who can make men into animals or 'create, manufacture' hierarchic lovers (*YAH*, 47). . . . Atwood's poems circle back on themselves, recreating one central drama of artist-woman engaged in an unsuccessful struggle to escape art for mortality. ("Atwood's" 149, 51–52)

Davey seems to expect that women, at least, must paradoxically resolve what he sees as an unending struggle between temporal and atemporal, that, in other words, they must choose between being women and being artists. In a later study, Davey admits that Circe and Odysseus of *You Are Happy* presumably proceed into a deconstructed story that is "not frozen yet"; although he is more tentative about whether Circe still uses language and art on her envisioned "second" island, he feels she abandons her "magic" (*Margaret* 46–48).

Critics have not only underestimated creative touch in *You Are Happy* but also have failed to question whether the Atwood artist necessarily has—or has ever had—Medusa touch. George Bowering speaks of Atwood's early poetry persona as a "runic stranger" and "spectator," unable to touch until *Two-Headed Poems*, written four years after *You Are Happy* and supposedly presenting Atwood's "new voice" and new persona: the persona of *Two-Headed Poems* "has put out her hands, often into the dark, and they touch" (46, 48). Although Jean Mallinson notes "a difference" in *You Are Happy*, a tendency to speak from "the midst of things" rather than from their edges, she, too, speaks of the earlier "gorgon touch" and reads the "catastrophe" of its risked creation in "Speeches for Dr. Frankenstein" in terms of Atwood's own anxieties about creation. Preferring not to read *You Are Happy*'s poems as a progression, Mallinson stresses the artist's feeling of loss in her addiction to creation (38, 23, 35, 31; also see Grace, *Violent* 67, 72–73, 77–78). In the two stages of Atwood's poetic and fictional development that Judith McCombs describes, *You Are Happy* is chronologically Stage I Gothic realism (initially 1964–77, then 1966–77): "the Closed, Divided, Mirroring World" of female Gothic elements, with *Two-Headed Poems* marking the beginning of Stage II: the realistic "Open World." McCombs recognizes that the act of writing, "which Atwood argues is by definition creative and free," could characterize Atwood's Victim Position Four, that of the creative nonvictim (*Surv* 38). Still, she states that in Atwood's fiction, at least, her "portraits of the artist have thus far been either of the maimed, the soldout, and the parodied; or else of the mythically distanced, curiously faceless opening through which art speaks" ("Fictive" 69, 71, 86; "Politics, Structure" 142–43, 151; "Literary Introduction," *Margaret* xii).

But the touch of Atwood's artists is not necessarily deadly or maimed, distanced or distancing; and, at least in Canadian poetry, Medusa, stone, and rock images are often positive (Pratt, "Medusa in Canada" 16, 18, 29). Like the vision that often accompanies it, freezing and frozen (severed, severing) touch neither prevails before *Two-Headed Poems* nor ends with *You Are Happy*; nor is it confined to Medusas, females, artists, Atwood's fiction, or Atwood's poetry.[11] In fact, when, Circe, the "Medusa figure" of *You Are Happy*, finally gets to tell her side of the sexual-political story, we discover that her transforming touch can create another island and a story full of possibilities taken up in the volume's final section, "There is Only One of Everything." "His" [Ulysses'] empty hands (greedy, killing) are no more innocent than those of the handless maiden's father, Peter and Duncan (*EW*), the wooden General (*PP*), "the Americans" (*Surfacing*), Cordelia (*CE*), or any of Atwood's narrators before their epiphanies. Throughout Atwood's work, both male and female touch can bind and paralyze. In speaking of the female artist's Gorgon touch, Davey apparently confuses Atwood's tourists with the genuine artists they gradually become. Life tourists such as *Surfacing*'s narrator, cut off from their bodies and other people, are characteristically amputated and sometimes amputating: they are either symbolically "missing" a hand, foot, heart, breast, eye, ear, voice, and even mouth, or they are disabled, with stunted senses and maimed genitals or extremities. Atwood opposes such characters' initial "tourist vision" (see Wilson, "Turning" 29–57) to the "third-eye" or eye-witness vision they develop as artists, when they symbolically regain lost senses and body parts, including open, outstretched hands (*SW* 348; "Hand," "Instructions for the Third Eye" *MD* 59, 61–62).

Circe's section in *You Are Happy* ends very much as *The Animals in That Country, You Are Happy*, and most of Atwood's poetry volumes do, with the persona's loving touch, wholeness rather than fragmenting disguise, and a tone of peace rather than irony: "open yourself like this and become whole" (95–96). According to Constance Rooke, "hands *are* the language through which Atwood attempts to rival and replace the language of men. . . . They speak *instead* of words, in 'the other language' which the narrator of *Surfacing* acquires in her descent" (163). As we have started to see, the world in which Red-Cap supposedly dallies (Chapter 10) must be included in an Atwood persona's life journey. In addition to speech and touch, all the senses—including taste, hearing, smell, and especially vision—are essential to the character's metamorphosis. But without empathetic touch (see also Rubenstein on *BH*, "Pandora's" 273), taste may be symbolically cannibalistic, hearing distorted, vision freezing, and language lying. Since Atwood's Rapunzel is afraid of being cannibalized, her hearing, vision, and voice initially fail to project beyond her narcissistic walls.

Paradoxically, people symbolically without hands often play more than one part in Atwood's fairy-tale sexual politics: they are both victimizer (the witch, the snow queen, the patriarch) with "untouching" or destructive touch, and victim (Rapunzel, "The Snow Queen"'s Kay, the girl without hands) with severed touch. But just as there are more than two victim positions in *Survival*, with Position Four transcending game (39), naked hands in Atwood's works (as opposed to gloved or maimed ones, claws, and talons) can belong to survivors, gardeners, workers, prophets, lovers, the audience, and, yes, creators, who can tell unfinished stories and envision worlds beyond the closed tower or ice palace of narcissism.

As we have begun to see, the artist's necessarily "Medusa touch" is not only a stereotype of Atwood criticism (see also Grace, *Violent* 77–78; J. Rosenberg 82) but of the female artist. Louise Bogan's 1923 poem "Medusa" illustrates the tradition by self-consciously paralleling her poem with Medusa's "dead scene" (Gilbert and Gubar, *Norton* 1611). Like May Sarton and Hélène Cixous, however, Atwood revisions Medusa touch ("The Muse as Medusa," *Norton* 1777; "The Laugh of the Medusa" 488, 494). Once part of the Triple Goddess, the Medusa is a monster only in patriarchal "amputations" of the myth (Chapter 2), or when, like Hecate, she "is seen as the only alternative, as the whole range of possibilities for being female" (Atwood, *Surv* 199). If the body of the female text has been castrated or decapitated to silence it (Cixous, "Castration" 486), if all female artists are Medusas who freeze the colonizing other by seeing and saying the forbidden, Atwood's Circe, like her Persephone (*DP*), is another laughing Medusa finally unveiled. Evidence in the evolving manuscripts as well as in the finished volume supports that *You Are Happy* is another narrative of the freed Rapunzel artist and her regrown artistic "touch." Thus, like the creator-narrators of *The Circle Game, The Animals in That Country, Surfacing, Lady Oracle, Murder in the Dark, The Handmaid's Tale,* and *Cat's Eye,* Circe "ends" with a new beginning resembling that of *Two-Headed Poems,* grounded not in stony touch but in touch as secure and lasting as stone: "your hand is a warm stone / I hold between two words. . . . / It begins, it has an end, / this is what you will / come back to, this is your hand" ("You Begin," *THP* 110).

Although Atwood made significant changes in the arrangement and composition of *You Are Happy* as she worked on the volume, it has a four-part structure.[12] Part 1 presents public and private power politics; Part 2, ironic warnings; Part 3, "the mythical substructure underlying our political and personal behavior," leading to choices; and Part 4, the process for rejecting confining mythology and gaining wholeness (adapted from Grace, *Violent* 64 and J. Rosenberg 73). But because Circe and the final speaker break with conventional structures of poetry, closure, and consciousness, most critics see them as failures trapped by art and find Part 4 unconvincing (Grace, *Violent* 73, 77–78). Like the stories of *Surfacing*'s and *Lady Oracle*'s narrators and those of other postmodern artists, *You Are Happy*'s personae write "beyond the ending."

You Are Happy uses techniques of displacement ("a committed identification with Otherness" in order to give voice to the muted), delegitimation ("the critical creation of an unexpected story, in attempts to gain release from a colonial tale"), and, although DuPlessis does not agree, decolonization (x, 108, 110). In reference to "The Girl Without Hands" and *The Odyssey*, *You Are Happy* displaces the tale's Christian focus on the rewards of silent and passive female suffering and the epic's patriarchal focus on an adulterous warrior hero. Unraveling both phallocentric plots to demythologize devils, angels, gods, goddesses, and archetypal heroes and to give voice to the muted and marginalized, *You Are Happy* uses delegitimation by putting human touch at the center of the poetry narrative.[13] The volume also decolonializes, striving toward postcolonialism, not only by putting the colonized character at the center of the story but also by undercutting the whole conception of imperialism: "Don't you get tired of killing. . . . Don't you get tired of saying Onward?" (51). In addition, *You Are Happy* suggests a better way of being.

The characters of the first and third sections remind us of

those in *Power Politics* (1971). Wearing and projecting Bluebeard/
victim false skins, including the cover design's mummy wrapping and armor, *Power Politics'* characters both desire and fear
"love without mirrors" and its adjacent horrors, amputation or
nothingness: "If we make stories for each other / about what is
in the room / we will never have to go in" ("Hesitations Outside
the Door" 50; see Chapter 9). As in *The Circle Game* and *Power
Politics*, *You Are Happy's* characters have already faced, and face
again, "the menace of the room": not only the assumption or
projection of monster/ victim roles but also the literal and figurative dismemberment of killing touch. *Power Politics* begins with
the persona's hooked eye and a "you" whose hands (initially
pocketed) project her into a bad movie (1–3). *You Are Happy*
begins with a female persona whose skin remembers the imprint
of "you"'s now "burnt-out" and "useless" touch ("Useless,"
"Memory"). Facing you's "green and lethal" eye gun and images
of both murdered and suicidal wrists, she identifies with the
badly filmed man in "Newsreel" when his blindfold slips, allowing him to see his own execution (8–14). The "I," slipping like
the narrators of *The Edible Woman, Surfacing*, and *Life Before Man*
into the distancing third person, tries to write a Gothic story to
account for the loss, just as "you" invents the image of a dead
sheep ("Gothic Letter on a Hot Night," "November"). She also
"repents," uses her hands to dig into "the archeology of manure"
beside "the temple to the goddess / of open mouths," faces objects of their shared past ("these things I will never be able / to
touch, that will never touch me"), and decides to burn the dead
"weeds" of the relationship so that, phoenixlike, she can "begin
over" (18–23).

Nevertheless, the first section ends with the touch of the Snow
Queen and images of death and negative narcissism (Motif
N339.10): mirrors, crystals, and ice. The persona has not yet left
her Rapunzel tower or regrown her cut-off hands. The mirror's
icy touch, "firm and glassy," gives "you yourself," "beautiful and
frozen." From a distance, she and "you" in "Newsreel" might

have appeared happy, the walls just part of the scenery; now she knows that she is trapped behind the wall, which is not really a mirror. A passive fairy-tale princess, this voice, blending with those of other sections, awaits "the releasing word" that can open a door in the wall ("Tricks with Mirrors"), much as the more conscious persona of *Power Politics*, possibly still frozen in place, awaits her curved glass death ("He is Last Seen" 56).

The final poem of Part 1 backs up to the ironic long shot of its beginning, making this section self-reflexive and circular. The couple in "You Are Happy," so cold they can think of nothing but cold, "walk separately" along a hill that might have been part of the scenery in "Newsreel." Although the poem has been read literally, as an attainment of happiness, at this stage the persona is as self-deceptive as those of *The Edible Woman* or *The Circle Game*. Drafts of "You Are Happy" help demonstrate the poem's irony. As Atwood worked on the poem, she made the description bleaker, partly by adding ironic adjectives to undercut the literal meaning of "you are happy," reinforcing the tone and cohesiveness of this section. The stone becomes "raw," the sea "brown," the deer "headless," and the "shoving" wind hostile. "Unused" picnic tables (picking up the initial tone of "Useless"), erosion, "gravel / rasping on gravel," and a "glaring" road are added (see Atwood Papers, Box 13, *YAH* handwritten drafts). The "headless" deer recalls the "shattered faces" of "Newsreel" and the headless baby of "Chaos Poem" while predicting the next sections' mutilated or chopped up body parts (Part 2's, "Bull Song," "Owl Song," "Song of the Hen's Head"; Part 3's forest of spines and antlers, the mud woman, and chopped off hands).

The awaited "releasing word" can, however, signal ironically negative transformation and further entrapment rather than a simple freedom. Although the personae of "Songs of the Transformed" in Part 2 are ostensibly a pig, bull, rat, crow, owl, siren, fox, hen, corpse, and several worms, they still suffer and symbolize human follies as they encounter or use gouging, mutilating, crushing, and gloved touch. The transformations are both other and self-induced, both part of a natural process and mythical. They range from the incarnation of greed and parasitic taking ("the skin you stuff so you may feed / in your turn," "Pig Song" 30; "Rat Song" 32) to the abandonment of humanity for disguise (a bull's "cask skin" impervious to all but a disguised killing touch, an orator's crow "uniform," and a femme fatale's irresistibility) ("Bull Song" 31, "Crow Song" 33, "Siren Song" 38–39), to the planned revolt of the underground worms ("Song of the Worms" 35). Because the songs tell of "the crimes done by hands" ("Owl Song" 36) and voices, they are warnings and protests. Murderous claws threaten to grow through hands (Owl Song" 36–37). We learn that if the touch of the "Word" can be a decapitating "siren song" of power, ironically it can also make the powerless articulate ("Song of the Hen's Head" 41–42). Rather than becoming skinless and mute, "swollen with words you never said / swollen with hoarded love," we are told to "sing now" ("Corpse Song" 43–44).

In Part 3, "Circe / Mud Poems," Circe, once a character in Homer's story of Odysseus and Ovid's story of Aeneus (*Metamorphoses*, XIV cAD 8; see Woodcock, "Metamorphosis" 267), now sings her own song. Like the final section's persona, she becomes an artist, moving from deformed or sterile art of the past to the creation of new, open worlds in our "now." Initially, however, Circe is an alienated Rapunzel with severed and severing touch:[14] this Circe's emblem is actually the "clenched fist" with which Atwood associates Rapunzel's mouth (*Surv* 209–10). In this case the fist is withered and chained around Circe's neck. Thus, Circe is the desert island she inhabits. Although Ulysses' boat "glides as if there is water," Circe's landscape is a forest "burned and sparse," and the shore on which he lands is dry. Unlike some Atwood Rapunzels, however, Circe still has words, even if they have "wrecked" and left skeletons rather than flowers. Her "front porch is waist deep in hands" from "clamouring suppliants," whose limbs ironically seem to fall off because they assault the words they beg from her. A collector and dispenser of amputated and "muted syllables" rather than Homer's or Part 2's siren or *Power Politics*'s lying story teller, Circe is a poet and a snake Goddess.[15] The "touch" of her words can transform flesh into "wrecked words" for which she, like the suppliants, initially takes no responsibility.

> it was not my fault, the snouts
> and hooves, the tongues
> thickening and rough, the mouths grown over
> with teeth and fur . . .
> I did not say anything, I sat
> and watched, they happened
> because I did not say anything.
>
> It was not my fault, these animals
> who could no longer touch me
> through the rinds of their hardening skins (48).

Atwood's revisions of poem drafts (e.g., from "do" to "say" above) generally emphasize Circe's creative abilities, her power with language. Atwood experimented with a Circe more like Homer's witch, whose destructive magic touch turns men into swine, and in the previously published "Fall and All" (1963) had combined a conventional Medusa and Circe with the witch from "Hansel and Gretel" (AT 327A, "Fall and All: a Sequence" 58). She also considered several parodies of goddesses for *You Are Happy*, but she didn't use these poems (Atwood Papers, Box 13: "[Variations for the] Termite Queen," Oracle poems). Atwood's Circe of the published *You Are Happy*, a "seer" who is inconsistent about the extent of her power, "displaces" not only Homer's characters (Lauter 15) but also phallocentric text by providing alternative models of myth, the goddess, the quest, sexual relationships, and art. Circe has no wand, and her moods fluctuate from bragging, bitter, regretful, angry, and revengeful to passionate, thoughtful, and loving. She fears "that other" part of herself, the queen of the two dimensions Lauter associates with Hecate (70), the one who wears a teeth necklace and can make herself "deaf as an eye" (*YAH* 63). Circe believes that her amulet of dead fingers, "not something that can be renounced" (58), wants to keep her in its grip. Also in the grip of Odysseus' story and male-female power politics, she is initially in the same position as Part 1's woman ("Tricks with Mirrors"), passively waiting and even narcissistically mirroring the other (56).

While Circe, Odysseus, and Penelope all tell stories, in Atwood's text Circe is the only one who breaks out of the prescribed plot[16] (of Homer, the male lover, society, "martial mythology" [Lilienfeld 125], and even matriarchal myth), deconstructively envisioning a new Circe and Odysseus. Like her foil Circe, Penelope is associated with the waxing and waning of the moon, and she, too, has "her version" of the story. In Circe's mind, however, Penelope is conventional, ladylike, without Circe's passionate appetites, anger, assertiveness, or honesty.[17] Penelope's dialogue for suitors, "in perfect taste," "will include tea and sex / dispensed graciously both at once." Circe's word "weavings" demythologize traditional heroes and heroic narratives (see Lauter 66, 68) and remythologize Great Goddess "spinners,"[18] but Penelope's (re)woven history is the only version of the Penelope-Odysseus-Circe story that Odysseus will believe or hear (65).

As long as she is in her prescribed role as moon goddess, Circe is a chained fist automatically rubbing ancient rituals. Without abandoning her "magic," Circe develops it into art: she chooses the unknown, unwritten world of human touch. She is no longer interested in pig men, Daedaluses, or "men with the heads of eagles" (Motifs D152.2, D352.2) and searches instead for "the others," "the ones who have escaped from these / mythologies with barely their lives; / they have real faces and hands" (47). As the Circe of Atwood's drafts states more directly, however, genuine human beings are as hard to find in this story as in *Surfacing*, *Life Before Man*, or "reality" as Atwood helps us see it: "The only thing I can tell you is that you will become what you are. In all these years, no man has remained human" (Atwood Papers, *YAH* manuscripts).

Odysseus wears armored skin over his disjointed body, and his vacant hands, not innocent, "know how to take." Resembling the hands of Jake, Josef, and the handless maiden's father (*BH, CE,* "The Girl Without Hands"), they are "killer's hands," holding Circe's arms and head down as his boots submerge the boat's wooden body; Odysseus' extorting fingers grope into her flesh and force her body to confess with "tongueless and broken" words (*YAH* 50–51, 54–55). Even his hope hardens and "gleams / in [his] hands like axes" (53) as his teeth "remain fixed, / zippered to a silver curve." Although Circe is afraid of human touch (her withered fist amulet "wishes to hold on" to her and mutters "worn moon rituals"), the dead fingers finally stutter and give up when their command for Odysseus' transformation fails.[19] As in *Surfacing,* human passions and will finally supplant divine power. When Circe begins to trust Odysseus, she opens like a severed hand and clutches at a deceptive freedom (57–58). Unfortunately, Odysseus, one of Atwood's life tourists, thinks he is writing a travel book and, unaware of his own sexual repression and cannibalism, helplessly disappears into his "white plot" (64). He is no artist, however: as the traveler shaping mud rather than clay, he creates pornography rather than sculpture.

It is the pseudo-artist, not the artist, whose touch dehumanizes. Because of Odysseus' violating touch, Circe is tempted to become one of only two roles offered her in patriarchal discourse, either the accepting mud woman incapable of touch, a decapitated and amputated Venus earth goddess "beg[inning] at the neck and end[ing] at the knees and elbows,"[20] or her opposite, a Medusa snow queen (Hecate), offering only ice, a crystal wall, and a puzzle (61, 67). Having begun "handless," however, she is not interested in being shaped by any kind of external touch, matriarchal or patriarchal, including being "that other," Homer's witch (63), who synthesizes both possibilities by using her hands to dehumanize but being mastered nevertheless. Homer's story "is ruthless" for Circe not only because it is finished, resolved, even reversible (68–69), but also because, as a classic, it is a cultural icon that privileges phallocentrism and dictates female otherness.[21] Thus, Circe, her role as a woman, and women's roles in general have already been "read," marginalized, and frozen within the canon. Like the Grimms' handless maiden, Homer's Circe is silenced.

Atwood's Odysseus is more than a hero shouting "Onward," however, and both more and less than a killer representing a "dominator society" (Eisler xvii, xix, 166–68). Like Circe he is flawed, with skin under his disguises, and he, too, is scarred, even moon marked with the sickle sign (60) of the harvest, which can suggest his growing similarity to her in a relationship that could become supple, even androgynous (Lilienfeld 126, 128). Because of what they both signify, however, the "Circe / Mud Poems," like *You Are Happy* as a whole, promise hope for a society beyond "circle game" amputations and beyond domination and submission paradigms.

Atwood's Circe is a poet who can create new visions. There are at least two islands (an early draft even says two "possibilities"). Circe begins another, fluid story, on a second island where neither she nor Odysseus is frozen in roles: "The second I know nothing about / because it has never happened; / this land is not finished, / this body is not reversible." Unlike Homer's jerky repeating script, in which "the events run themselves through / almost without us," or the final poem of Part 1, with ice crystals, a headless deer, and brown water, her unfinished land is, in November, lush with astonishing orange apples, an unfrozen stream, melting snow, and the track of a deer (69–70). This is a world of Art rather than Nature, a magical reality outside of relentless time, but it is neither closed nor antithetical to becoming. Circe speaks to her readers' freedom to create their own possibilities. Neither Circe, the persona of the final section, nor Atwood's other female artists can be dismissed as sirens or Gorgons (Grace, *Violent* 78).

Atwood's Circe, like her author, has much in common with other contemporary artists, both visual and literary. "Hang Up"

(1966), by Eva Hesse, a rectangular frame with a thin, flexible rod looping out and back from it, is process art that refuses "to declare its meaning or to locate an inner 'truth;' the frame presents a self-contained object, but the line which registers the mark of the artist is drawn in space, not captured permanently on a surface." Alexis Hunter's "Considering Theory" (1982) is one of a series of feminist deconstructionist paintings that use visual parody, in this case a woman biting the Christian snake, "to expose the oppressive patriarchal nature of Greek and Christian myth" (Chadwick 314, 350, figs. 193, 233). Similarly, literary artists such as Alain Robbe-Grillet and Nathalie Sarraute aspire to throw off the mummy wrappings of constricting plots, characterization, and traditions, including the notions of formalist unity and static permanence, and appeal to the reader or viewer for creative assistance in inventing the work, the world, and one's own life (Robbe-Grillet 27, 31, 156).

Helping us understand this kind of experimentation, Julia Kristeva, one of many poststructuralists to call into question any boundary between fiction and criticism, "redefines the text as a dynamic 'working' of language through the desires of the speaking subject as he or she responds to the concrete socio-economic forces of history. . . . the writer confronts the ideological givens of his or her culture's discourse and displaces or decenters them by deploying the linguistic signifier in forbidden or unanticipated ways" (Davis and Schleifer 185). Through Circe's and the other personae's forbidden speech (sometimes in genre-bending prose poems), Atwood's text fills in the gaps of the Grimms' "The Girl Without Hands" and Homer's *Odyssey*. It extends into a future space similar to that of *Bodily Harm*, deconstructing and decentering patriarchal myth and oppressive literary traditions and remythifying the female artist.

Part 4 of *You Are Happy* takes up not only Circe's journey into a different dimension but also the deconstructionist technique and positive tone of her final poem. It begins with the self-conscious narrator's parodic "lord's prayer" to her abandoned body for its forgiveness and her and "our" healing and resurrection. In this "First Prayer," implying that possibly the whole section consists of prayers,[22] she asks for her body's descent (rather than ascension) from *the wall* where she has nailed it and speaks for a community of numbed and disabled owners who have gloved, displayed, and warped their loyal bodies, preferring the Snow Queen's word games and puzzles to touching and loving (72–73). "Is/Not," now addressed to the persona's "fellow-traveller" on a journey, explicitly connects to Circe's journey and continues the speaking of the forbidden, her anger "which does not need to be understood / or washed or cauterized, / which needs instead / to be said and said." Calling attention to her "saying" as to her praying ("Permit me the present tense"), she is aware of herself as an artist, "not a saint or a cripple," speaking "against the grain" as she and her antagonist fight their way "not out but through": "This is a journey, not a war, / there is no outcome, / I renounce predictions / and aspirins, I resign the future / as I would resign an expired passport" (74–76). "There is too much" to be said, however, and in "Four Evasions" "the old words reappear / in the shut throat" (78). The persona feels cold and crippled by the evasions of her senses and envies you's imagined inner sun and phoenixlike rebirth ("Eating Fire"). Still, the "four auguries" counter the four evasions: a binoculared man feeds birds in icy rain, the pockets release their hands to allow blind decoding by touch, they feel "greed for the real" and gather specifics, and an owl blesses them ("Four Auguries" 84–85).

In "Head Against White" the persona is inspired by the other's hands, "open and held / out, not empty, giving," and her touch returns. To move beyond "the mirror's edge," return from her "hermitage / of ice to the land of sharp / colours" and "rise up living" is difficult (77–83, 89, 91). Again, Atwood supplies no closure except for the statement in "There is Only One of Everything" that can be made "only once and it won't / last": "I want this. I want / this". As in "Hesitations" of *Power Politics*[23] and Section 3 of *You Are Happy* (70), the final poems of *You Are Happy* "end" lacking even the easy punctuation of a period, which instead may occupy an unorthodox position in the middle of the line (86, 91, 93, 96). Rejecting history and mythology—the Greek gods and minotaurs, "Book of Ancestors"' Mexican copper hawkmen (Motifs D152.1, D352.1), the endless snow and eternally running figures of *Power Politics*'s glass paperweight—the persona does not need to be a daughter of the sun god, Helios (as Circe is), or a phoenix to realize the potential of this volume's predominant sun image, shining on the cover, on the section title pages, and now in every poem of this section. She appreciates the uniqueness of what she touches with her fingers in this moment and inhabits "the season of peaches/ with their lush lobed bulbs/ that glow in the dusk" ("Late August" 93). The walls of their "death patterns" crumble. Ironically, no longer expecting miracles, she reenacts the gesture of Atwood's re-visioned Girl Without Hands (Atwood Papers, *I* manuscripts): she touches another with mortal hands and a miracle occurs "without blood, the killed / heart" of ritual sacrifice: undefended, "you open / yourself to me gently. . . . to take / that risk, to offer life and remain / alive, open yourself like this and become whole" ("Book of Ancestors" 96).

The voice of Part 4 blurs with those of Circe and *You Are Happy*'s other personae, and its final word is "whole." Like the Grimms' Girl Without Hands, *Life Before Man*'s Elizabeth, and *Bodily Harm*'s Rennie, *You Are Happy*'s characters begin the process of recovering human hands (Motif E782.1) and human touch.

$\boxed{7}$

Regrowing Touch
in *Life Before Man*

"The Girl Without Hands"
and The Wizard of Oz

Investigating fairy-tale intertexts in *Life Before Man* may surprise some readers. As Margaret Atwood jokes, the characters of this novel are confined to a square mile in which nothing enters and only a dead body leaves (*Margaret Atwood's Once in August*). Despite agreement that she usually draws on romance traditions, few readers (e.g., Carrington, "Demons" 68) have questioned Atwood's assertion that *Life Before Man* is a realistic novel (*Margaret Atwood: Once in August*). Atwood wanted details of dialogue, characterization, and setting, even the location of a telephone on the corner of Dupont and Spadina in 1976 and the 1977 salary for a job like Lesje's, to be exact. Thus, she constructed "realistic" backgrounds even for minor characters; consulted with people working in paleontology, taxidermy, and media relations at the Royal Ontario Museum; and hired Donya Peroff and Peter Boehm as research assistants. Her "Questions for Peter Boehm" include asking him to check the wording on the Queen's Park War Memorial that Nate sees when he is running, asking him to describe the Timothy Eaton Memorial Church and the St. George and Bloor Medical Arts Building where Muriel and Elizabeth respectively go, and verifying the form of the United

Church of Canada funeral service that is held for Muriel. Atwood asked Donya Peroff to record colors and atmosphere in the Ministry of the Environment where William works, interview people like Lesje with Lithuanian Jewish grandmothers, and even sketch real 1970s Toronto neighborhoods (Atwood Papers, Box 32, *LBM* Research Materials).

The novel makes frequent reference to real restaurants (the Colonnade, Varsity, Fran's, Murray's, the former Courtyard Cafe), bars (the Pilot Tavern), subway stations (Ossington, Woodbine), stores (Eaton's, Nick Knack's), and hotels (the Selby, the Park Plaza); and, in addition to its global, gender, and national themes, it does have important local and regional implications. *Life Before Man* simultaneously satirizes Toronto's museum specimens in their fossilized social strata and their contemporary "Toronto chic" facade further developed in *Bodily Harm*, *Bluebeard's Egg* (Davey, "Life" 29–30; Smith 258), and *Cat's Eye*: the pink-cheeked, urban sophisticates who must beg "scraps" of passion from the ethnic hybrids to whom they condescend.

More symbolically and universally, the novel, first titled *Notes on the Mesozoic* and *Notes from the Lost World* (see Atwood Papers, First and Second Typed Drafts), seems to present life *before* genuine human beings appear on earth. Like the characters of other Atwood novels, these life forms appear to be inhabited by ghosts, trapped in old stories, and symbolically "missing something." If Atwood characters of other fiction initially lack eyes (particularly *BH*'s Rennie, *HT*'s Offred, *BE*'s Sally), ears and nose (Offred), mouth (Offred, *EW*'s Marian), body (*Surf*'s narrator), and feet (*LO*'s Joan), the segmented characters of *Life Before Man* especially lack "hands" (Motifs F515.0.1, Q451.1): the ability to touch others and a world authentically "there," in the present.

Rather than being the dreary, pessimistic novel that most critics and sometimes even Atwood (*Once in August*) perceive it,[1] however, *Life Before Man* again uses unrecognized fairy-tale intertexts that offer hope. As in *You Are Happy*, Atwood uses the

Grimms' "The Girl Without Hands" ("Das Madchen ohne Hande" (1812) (No. 31, AT 706) and "Rapunzel" (1812) (No. 12, AT 310; see Chapters 6 and 11 for synopsis) in *Life Before Man*. L. Frank Baum's literary children's fairy tale, *The Wizard of Oz* (1900), and Victor Fleming's film of the same title (1939) are also major intertexts. This novel's most important related intertexts, interwoven with "The Girl Without Hands" and "Rapunzel" and, in most cases, also important to other Atwood texts, are the Grimms' "The Juniper Tree" (No.47, AT 720), "Fitcher's Bird" (No. 46, AT 311), "The Robber Bridegroom" (No. 40, AT 955), "Little Red Cap" (No. 26, AT 333), and "Cinderella" (No. 21 "Aschenputtel," AT 510A); and Andersen's "The Snow Queen" (1846).

Here, the intertexts serve at least four interrelated purposes, the same ones usually evident in Atwood's intertextuality: 1) to indicate the quality and nature of her characters' cultural contexts (Beran 200), 2) to signify her characters' entrapment in preexisting patterns, 3) to comment self-consciously on these patterns, the frame story, and the embedded intertexts, often by deconstructing constricting plots and filling in the gaps of female narrative, and 4) to structure the characters' imaginative or "magical" release from the externally imposed patterns, offering the possibility of transformation not only for the novel's characters, but also for the country they partly represent and for all human beings.

Numerous secondary intertexts deserve more extended commentary than is possible here. They include Russian and possibly Ukrainian-Canadian fairy tales,[2] Mother Goose's "Little Nancy Etticoat," "Little Miss Muffet," and "Ladybird"; the nursery rhymes "Lady-bug"[3] and "Hourglass"; the folktale "The Spider and the Fly;"[4] Washington Irving's "The Legend of Sleepy Hollow" (1820);[5] Lewis Carroll's (Charles Dodgson's) *Alice's Adventures in Wonderland* (1865) and *Through the Looking-Glass and What Alice Found There* (1871); Arthur Conan Doyle's *The Lost World* (1912); Coleridge's "Kubla Khan"; Ovid's *Meta-*

morphoses; *Virgil's Aenead*; and Dante's *Inferno*. Triple Goddess myth, including both matriarchal and patriarchal versions of the Demeter/Persephone and Medusa myths and the Isis-Osiris and Orpheus-Eurydice myths (AT 400); vampire and ghost legend; and Halloween folk tradition all also constitute secondary intertexts. Other texts that influence *Life Before Man* include those cited or planned for the epigraphs (Björn Kürten's *The Age of Dinosaurs*, Abram Tertz [Andrei Sinyavsky's] *The Icicle*), Naum Grzywacz's notes from the Warsaw ghetto) (Atwood Papers, *LBM* manuscripts), Julian Jaynes's *The Origin of Consciousness in the Breakdown of the Bicameral Mind* (Carrington, "Demons" 68), and the Bible—especially parodic or ironic allusions to Revelations, the parable of the Prodigal Son, and the story of Salome and John the Baptist.

Life Before Man's literary allusions include *The Arabian Nights*, Wordsworth's "Intimations of Immortality," Poe's "The Raven,"[6] Shakespeare's Romeo and Juliet, Flaubert's Madame Bovary, Kafka's "An Imperial Message," Vonnegut's *Breakfast of Champions*,[7] J. M. Barrie's *Peter Pan*, Sara Josepha Hale's "Mary Had a Little Lamb" (*Annotated Mother Goose* 127),[8] Joyce Kilmer's "Trees," John McCrae's "In Flanders Fields," and Rider Haggard's *She*, and the first film and book of Bram Stoker's *Dracula* (1897, film 1931), H. G. Welles's *Invisible Man* (1897), and Gaston Leroux's *The Phantom of the Opera* (1911). Allusions to art and music include Marcel Duchamp's painting, *Nude Descending Staircase*; Tchaikovsky's *The Nutcracker Suite*; the Christian hymns, "Away in a Manger" and "Jesus Christ is Risen Today"; Harry Belafonte's music; the children's song, "The Farmer in the Dell"; and the English national anthem, "God Save the Queen" (Beran 201, 212). Popular films, *King Kong* (directed by Ernest B. Schoedsack, Merian C. Cooper, 1933), *Jaws* (directed by Steven Spielberg, 1975), and *Fiddler on the Roof*; 1950s radio programs, "Our Miss Brooks" and "The Green Hornet" (Beran 212); and comic books, "Superman" and "Spiderman," are also important to *Life*

Before Man's imagery, characterization, themes, structure, or genre.

As in *Power Politics, You Are Happy*, and the earlier novels, sexual politics is again an important theme, but this novel, like "The Girl Without Hands," investigates it within disrupted middle-class family life. Supposedly, in *Life Before Man* the main "power" figures are Auntie Muriel and Elizabeth, and the main combatants (Muriel and Elizabeth, Elizabeth and Lesje) are female; certainly the consequences are no less devastating than those in heterosexual dispute. Still, the "object" of Elizabeth and Lesje's dispute is a man, Elizabeth uses Chris in a self-confessed "male" manner, and even Nate imagines Chris carrying off the female prize or murdering Elizabeth if he fails as traditional male protector (235–36). The disputed territory in both triangles is status within or outside of the patriarchal institutions of marriage and family.

Life Before Man uses a "Cinderella" ("Ashenputtle") intertext (Grimm No. 21, AT 510A) that can only be outlined here. The "Cinderella" cycle, with at least five hundred different versions in Europe alone, is about "an abused daughter" who marries a prince (Thompson, *Folktale* 127). Atwood subverts and parodies this basic marriage plot, essential to the comedy genre, in all of her novels and many of her poetry volumes (see Gibson interview on *EW*, 20–21). Often, as in *The Edible Woman* and *You Are Happy*, she reveals its dark underside. In different ways resembling the Girl Without Hands, both Lesje and Muriel feel like abused daughters; and Elizabeth, abandoned by both parents (Motifs S321, S301) and unsuitably touched by Uncle Teddy (136), is one. But Lesje's "prince" is already married when she meets him, Elizabeth's kills himself, and both Lesje and Nate must get out of relationships with those failing to qualify as "true" bride or husband. Instead of hoping to fit into a feather, gold, or glass slipper (Motif H36.1), Elizabeth marries Nate like trying on a shoe. Martha, the rejected princess whose gold shoe falls off on the way to having her stomach pumped, flourishes after the rejection, even making the prince feel "diminished" by her plans to attend law school (275). It is dinosaurs that do the dancing (LBM 23, 310) and "ghosts," including Elizabeth's dead mother and Nate's dead father, who provide what is hardly supernatural aid. Instead of a wicked stepmother (Motif S31), Lesje has rival warring grandmothers and her older opponent Elizabeth; Elizabeth has her Auntie Muriel. Instead of wicked stepsisters (Motif K2212.1), Lesje has evil and comic doubles, Elizabeth and Martha; Muriel has her favored "irresponsible" sister; and Elizabeth has the catatonic "twin" shadow partly responsible for her initial role rigidity and inability to have a successful marriage.

Like Dorothy of *The Wizard of Oz* film, the Girl Without Hands, and to some extent Alice and Ichabod, *Life Before Man*'s characters live in a black and white wasteland. This black and white world not only stifles the technicolor sensual world of imagination, either "lost," "over the rainbow," down the rabbit hole, or "through the looking-glass," but fails to provide a sustaining family, meaningful values, or environment for growth. Like Ladybird, Nate and Elizabeth fear that their house is on fire and their children gone (*LBM* 252; *The Real* 87): on one level, *Life Before Man* portrays a symbolic burning house similar to the literal ones, such as in Anne Hébert's poem, "Manor Life," that Atwood finds characteristic of Quebec literature (*Surv* 228). In this case, despite the characters' background or ethnic makeup, they all at some point live outside the structure of the nuclear family. Thus, rather than having to burn down the ancestral house in order to escape it, as Marie-Claire Blais's characters do in *Mad Shadows*, *Life Before Man*'s characters worry about it burning down or falling apart around them. Comparing and contrasting to "The Girl Without Hands," *Life Before Man* reveals largely absent parents, especially fathers. Nate's father dies, Elizabeth's abandons the family, and although Lesje's father still lives with her travel-agent mother, their influence in this Romeo and Juliet

feuding family is minimal. Even Nate leaves the marriage if not
the children. With the important exceptions of Nate's sustaining
mother and Elizabeth, who becomes so, mothers are also scarce.
Elizabeth's mother, dead, was an alcoholic who left Elizabeth
and Caroline with her unloved, unloving sister Muriel, one of
Atwood's best examples of a witch mother. Chris's parents beat
him. Rather than the idealized Norman Rockwell family life of
the 1950s, these characters have fragmented families.

This fragmentation not only signifies the disappearance of the
traditional nuclear family, however, but the creation of alternative strategies. The characters' familial amputations are, like
those of the Girl Without Hands, not necessarily permanent: if
they don't have access to angels in huts "free to everyone" and
lose faith in airy "pleasure domes," they still manage to create "a
dwelling over the abyss" (302). Their "cut-off hands" and other
body parts begin to grow back by the end of the novel.

All of the intertexts, allusions, and influences are worthy of
discussion, but I will focus on three classes of imagery that
convey themes of sexual politics and the fragmented family in
Life Before Man and the central intertexts. Showing the movement
from handlessness to hands or touching throughout Atwood's
work, these images are isolation or alienation; mutilation, amputation, or fragmentation; and magical transformation. As in *You
Are Happy*, the characters of *Life Before Man* are frozen in Rapunzel's tower (Motif R41.2), dismembered or missing parts of their
bodies, and living the amputated roles of characters in "The Girl
Without Hands," "The Snow Queen," *The Wizard of Oz*, and
"The Legend of Sleepy Hollow."[9] For most of the book they are
unable not only to draw on the power of their bodies by growing
new hands, feet, heads, hearts, mouths, or eyes, but either to
confront their problems or to touch anyone else without making
that person freeze in place.

As we have begun to see, the bleakness so many readers observe in *Life Before Man* can be explained in part by the isolation
all of the major characters experience. Social isolation is a well-

recognized stylistic principle of fairy tales, including the Grimms' (Lüthi, *European* 38), and it is also apparent in re-visioned or deconstructed fairy tales. Underneath *Life Before Man*'s surface realism, Elizabeth, Nate, Chris, Lesje, and Muriel individually experience both the exile and amputation of the Girl Without Hands in the forest, before she finds her sustaining angel and hut. Atwood's use of time-dated, multiple, unreliable, third-person centers of consciousness, with occasional sections of fragmented first-person narration, brilliantly separates the characters from one another, themselves, their position in time, and us, challenging us to notice the discrepancies and make the connections. Because the book uses interior monologue and time shift, including two chapters out of order in the otherwise relentless march of time, readers are also able to contrast the way we see the characters with the way other characters view them. Until the last few pages, these characters symbolically occupy separate, hermetically sealed, museum display cases. Although they see shadows and outlines of other specimens through their glass enclosures, they are unable to communicate or to touch.

Indeed, Chris (dead before the novel begins), Elizabeth (inhab-ited by Chris's "ghost"), Lesje (preferring dinosaur daydreams of prehistory and invisibility to anything her present life offers), and Nate (waiting for a "female healer" [Motif A454.1] to rescue him from outside the window of life) do not even exist in the same dimension. Lesje Green, really Etlin—Ukrainian and Jew-ish Lithuanian without knowing the customs or language of ei-ther group—and Chris Beecham—lower class and one-fourth French instead of the Métis he pretends—feel "foreign" to the Williams and Muriels who supposedly form Toronto's "core": "where the heart should be" (121). Even Nate Schoenhof, from a lapsed Mennonite family and "about as German as a newt" in early drafts of the novel, has a well-known, anglicized German name that Atwood changed from *Schoendorff* to *Schoenhoff* to *Schoenhof* (Atwood Papers, Box 30). His name signifies not only his inability to achieve middle-class success but his ironic absence of both home (*hof*, a pastoral home, farm, court, or yard) and community (*schön dorf*, a beautiful village), including the "green" vision so necessary to early poetry personae and *Surfacing*'s narrator. Lesje and Chris are also ethnic hybrids, and even Elizabeth speaks two languages, "genteel chic" and "street": her upper-class "haute wasp" manner (put on with Nate's name) is facade (148, 96). Ironically, every alienated character thinks others belong, but alternative points of view, actions (William's attempted rape, Martha's "suicide attempt"), and even bits of conversation (e.g., at Muriel's deathbed) suggest that no "core" exists: alienation is universal. Chris is unable to survive in this kind of world. Lesje's self-vision as Alice in Wonderland, *Lost World* explorer, implies the impossibility of having a home or coexisting with someone else in the present. As both Elizabeth and the Girl Without Hands might, she hungers for "a mother's blessing." Like Dorothy, Little Nancy Etticoat, Little Miss Muffet, and Ichabod Crane, Elizabeth and Nate battle their dark self-visions, for Nate, especially the "headless horseman." Elizabeth battles the Wicked Witch of the West, the melting candle ("The longer she stands, / The shorter she grows") (*Best Loved* 81), and the black spider.

Like other Atwood characters who function as both camera and photograph, *Life Before Man*'s characters also "'snapshot' the present and even the future, converting it into a past . . . or a 'safe' souvenir. . . . [V]iewing existence as a filmstrip, one frozen moment at a time," they impose "frames" on existence. These frames not only distance them from others and life, however, but also threaten them and, by implication, Canada with extinction. Ironically caught like the Royal Porcupine's frozen animals in the stopped action of their separate pasts (Wilson, "Camera" 32, 41–42), they are just as imprisoned in Canadian-made Rapunzel towers and Snow Queen palaces as the personae of *You Are Happy* and *Cat's Eye*. Alienation—from oneself, others, a dividing country, and a wasteland society or world—is image and theme in most of *Life Before Man*'s fantastic intertexts.

This degree of alienation seems to be intrinsically amputating or fragmenting, and the intertexts and allusions highlight internal and external fragmentation or mutilation. Lesje and Chris are, as mentioned, split ethnically. All the characters have, or are perceived to have, some degree of internal division. On a comic Gothic level, the characters paradoxically alternate roles as the Robber Bridegroom, Dracula (159), Fitcher, werewolf (133), or cannibal-witch *and* their victims, symbolically cannibalizing, sucking dry, or murdering others because they feel so empty.[10]

As in "The Girl Without Hands," in varying ways sexual politics splits and amputates each of the four main characters. In addition to their roles as handless persons, Chris (Davidson and Davidson, "Prospects" 211), Elizabeth, and Nate are even married to death ("Fitcher's Bird") or the devil ("The Girl Without Hands"). Elizabeth, ill and thirty-nine, is Venus verging on Hecate, still containing the maiden, in this case a maiden whose innocence has been violated. She is orphan, daughter, niece, sister, mother, wife, lover, "whore," and snob. Ironically and parodically, she is the Girl Without Hands, Rapunzel/Witch, Dorothy/Witch, Florence Nightingale savior, the Queen of Wonderland, Robber or Fitcher's victim, and not only Cinderella and the prince but the stepmother and stepsisters. She is Madonna and Medusa, Salome, Kilmer's sucked mother earth, Duchamp's fragmented nude, Persephone as Snow Queen under the ground, Isis sleeping with Osiris after his death and dismemberment (259), a reversed Eurydice hearing Orpheus sing in an ether rather than nether world, Marlinchen ("The Juniper Tree"), Snow White's stepmother, both spider and fly, a dragon lady, a female vampire,[11] a professional exhibiter (Museum Special Projects), and a survivor. Similarly, Nate is "segmented man": fatherless son, husband, father, lover, absurd hero (Camus 49, 89), toy maker, and toy. He is ironic and parodic Girl Without Hands and King / Sorrowful, Rapunzel and Prince, Scarecrow and Tin Woodsman / hired hand, Sultan (*The Arabian Nights*), Gift of God, Fitcher / Robber Bridegroom and victim, Romeo, and

"Cinderella" Prince. Another segmented man who literally divides his body from his head, Chris is preeminently demon lover as well as parodic false wizard, the "headless horseman," the decapitated boy ("The Juniper Tree"), the decapitated John the Baptist, one of the queen's chopped off heads and the Cheshire cat (*Alice in Wonderland*), Fitcher / Robber Bridegroom and "brides," Dracula and victim, Cinderella and prince, Orpheus, Osiris, and Hades.

Lesje and Muriel are similarly divided. Lesje is maiden verging on Madonna, daughter and granddaughter, "brain," lover, muse, and toy as well as Girl Without Hands, Rapunzel in treetop (Motif N711, see Bottigheimer, *Grimms'* 101–4), parodic Cowardly Lion, Robber and Fitcher bride, Alice in Wonderland, the spider's fly, the wolf's lamb, Scheherazade (Motif J1185.1), Cinderella, the Invisible (Wo)man, and Juliet. Muriel's deathbed conversation and incongruous funeral service suggest her different facets, including Girl Without Hands and Father, Rapunzel, and Witch. Even Elizabeth, Nate, and Lesje's mothers and fathers, Martha, William (not only William Canadian but Jaws and Dracula), Lesje's grandmothers, Caroline, and Uncle Teddy seem split. Since the action of the book includes events leading to Quebec's 1980 referendum vote on separation from Canada, even the characters' country seems on the verge of a split, at least temporarily averted at the same time Nate, Lesje, and Elizabeth heal their internal divisions.

Like *Life Before Man*'s other intertexts, *The Wizard of Oz* suggests characters' movement from isolation and mutilation or fragmentation to the beginnings of transformation. Baum's *The Wizard of Oz*, parodically referred to as the "Wizard of Ooze" in one of Atwood's Kanadian Kultchur Komix (Atwood Papers, Artwork),[12] is mentioned several times in *Life Before Man*. *Wizard* "aspires to being a modernized fairy tale, in which the wonderment and joy are retained and the heart-aches and nightmares are left out." Baum states that "the old-time fairy tale [Grimms and

Andersen], having served for generations, may now be classed as 'historical' in the children's library." He sets out to provide a series of newer "wonder tales" that eliminate "the stereotyped genie, dwarf and fairy" and "all the horrible and blood-curdling incidents devised by their authors to point a fearsome moral to each tale. Modern education includes morality: therefore the modern child seeks only entertainment in its wonder tales and gladly dispenses with all disagreeable incidents" (1900 "Introduction"). Much more than simple entertainment, *The Wizard of Oz* inspired thirteen sequels by Baum and additional ones, including several film versions, by other authors after his death. Victor Fleming's first, most popular film, MGM 1939, stars Judy Garland (Dorothy), Frank Morgan (Professor Marvel), Ray Bolger (Hunk/Scarecrow), Bert Lahr (Zeke/Lion), Jack Haley (Hickory/Tin Man), and Billie Burke (Glinda).

An African-American film (*The Wiz* with Michael Jackson and Richard Pryor), a sequel, *Return to Oz* (directed by Walter Murch), and many animated versions (including one with Lorne Greene's voice, 1982, and a sequel, *Journey Back to Oz*, 1971, with the voices of Liza Minnelli and Mickey Rooney) demonstrate the story's universality. *Life Before Man* significantly parallels both the book and Fleming's major film version (1939) of *The Wizard of Oz* in characterization, structure, setting, and imagery.

Both book and film versions of *The Wizard of Oz* begin in a gray, dismal wasteland that is not "home" and that threatens to turn Dorothy as gray as her surroundings (Baum 3). Dorothy has a truncated family (a dog, gray aunt, and uncle rather than parents) that does little laughing: the book's Aunt Em is upset by laughter (2), and the film version of the character not only stops Dorothy from playing but also tells her to stop imagining things. In the film, Dorothy wants to go to a place where there isn't any trouble, so she runs away from home and meets Professor Marvel (not in the book), Oz's traveling magician double who sends her home. In both film and book, Dorothy and Toto, alone inside the house, whirl into the air when they are caught in the still middle of a cyclone. Nearly deafened, Dorothy worries that she will be "dashed to pieces." When the house falls, however, Dorothy opens the door to a different reality, a lush green world of sunshine, flowers, and brooks (5, 7–8). But Dorothy realizes that she wants to go home and journeys down a yellow brick road leading to the Emerald City of Oz, where the Wizard is expected to fulfill her desire. Dorothy's first two companions on her quest are initially rigid, without purpose, in passive roles imposed upon them. The Scarecrow, stuffed with straw and existing only to scare away crows, can't escape the position in which he is tied until Dorothy uses her hands to help him. The Tin Woodman, rusted in place and unable to speak clearly, can't reach the oil he needs without the hands of others. Although he groaned for over a year and might have lost voice as well as mobility, no one had come to help (38–39). Even the Cowardly Lion, who roars loudly and attacks smaller creatures, is afraid to venture outside the forest until he meets Dorothy. Again, Dorothy supplies a hand, in this case of friendship.

Like *Life Before Man*'s characters, Dorothy and her three companions are missing something: the Scarecrow a brain, the Tin Woodman a heart (Motif D2062.1), and the Lion courage; and as they tell their stories, they develop a common purpose. Because he has become an object of ridicule to the crows, the Scarecrow believes that brains "are the only things worth having in this world" (33). A patchwork rather than a whole being, the Tin Woodman first chopped off his legs, then his arms, head, and body with his enchanted axe; but although all have been replaced with tin, he thinks he has lost his desire to marry because he lacks a heart. The Lion cannot live up to his world's expectation that he be the king of the beasts. Because he has roared every time he is frightened, he believes he is a coward.

Striving to reach the Emerald City to satisfy their greatest desires, all become objects in the Wicked Witch of the West's one-eyed telescopic gaze (Motif F512.1). Her sister, the Wicked Witch of the East, disappeared, beginning with her feet, when

Dorothy's House fell on her (13). Similarly, in the film the name of the Wicked Witch of the West's alter ego, Miss Elvira Gulch, implies dryness. The Wicked Witch of the West melts away when confronted with the possibilities of new life inherent in Dorothy and symbolized by the water she splashes. Oz's "bad" witches, like Atwood's Auntie Muriel and Mrs. Smeath, are insensitive to life and free choice; they epitomize sterility and enslavement.

After many adventures in which members of the group help one another, including awakening from a deadly sleep in a poppy field, they reach the Emerald City and attain new vision with green spectacles. The Great and Terrible Oz, using special effects to appear as a gigantic disembodied head and other marvels, proves to be only a magician (a good man but a bad wizard). Before taking the Scarecrow's head off to substitute bran, pins, and needles for most of the straw, Oz gives the Scarecrow his real gift: the messages that "Experience is the only thing that brings knowledge" and that the Scarecrow will have to find out for himself how to use his brains. Similarly, the Tin Woodman decides that he is willing to disregard his patches and bear unhappiness, and the Lion learns that his confidence is inside him: "True courage is facing danger when you are afraid" (153–54, 59–61). Encompassing all these ideas, Dorothy's discovery is that she needs no balloon to carry her over the "desert" to "home": *she* has the power to go any where she chooses (205–6). The only magic the characters need is belief in themselves.

Life Before Man deconstructs and collages intertexts to present the same theme. Chris, Elizabeth, Nate, and Lesje, closer to Kansas than to Munchkinland, most assuredly do not fly "over the rainbow." If their Toronto has a yellow brick road, it initially seems almost circular, like Queen's Park Road, and leads back to a museum of the past. Or, like Bloor Street, it runs from ethnicity to the center of commerce. Even if their Toronto is viewed as a world-class city or "the Paris of the Northeast" rather than

Hogtown (Atwood, "Canadian-American," 381), it still isn't the Emerald City. While *Life Before Man*'s Toronto may abound with humbugs who exaggerate their and other characters' qualities, its inhabitants are neither good nor wicked witches. *Life Before Man*'s characters are lonely inhabitants of a closed, gray urban world, where they typically wear boots to protect them from the symbolic as well as literal snow of Canadian myth and literature (*Surv* 65–67). Nevertheless, *Life Before Man* is about alienated characters who resist the inertia and safety of habit rather than slavery to the Wicked Witch of the West and learn the "magic" of self-confidence. They finally extend hands to others and move feet toward "home." As we have begun to see, resembling homeless Dorothy and *Wizard*'s other characters, *Life Before Man*'s characters have truncated families, live in a world where Hecate swallows Venus, and are encouraged to "silence" or amputate part of themselves. All are finally dissatisfied with playacting meaningless roles and quest for the "missing parts" of themselves they potentially have.

Of all *Life Before Man*'s characters, Elizabeth is most like Dorothy. The cyclone that pulls Dorothy up at the beginning of her story is the whirlwind void that sucks up Elizabeth (and to some extent other *LBM* characters), and characters of both books fall back down to earth near the end. Inside her house, Dorothy lands on the Wicked Witch of the East in lush Munchkinland and receives powerful silver, in the film ruby, slippers (Motif D1532.3). Elizabeth, leaking power, is drawn into a nightmare despite her structured life. As the novel opens, Elizabeth's carefully lined up shoes, neither ruby nor silver, are locked in place rather than taking creative steps, either to adventure or to a real home. Despite the absence of mother or father models in her own life, Elizabeth manages a "mummy" role that both encases and supports her. She worries that her daughter Nancy, like "Little Nancy Etticoat," is already melting into the nothingness Elizabeth feels (252). After Chris's death, Elizabeth imagines telling a psychiatrist that she's "already been down that particular yellow brick road" of her past and has found out that "there's no Wizard of Oz" (99).

Ironically, however, Elizabeth has always expected sex to be magic and Chris, especially, to be a kind of Wizard. Faced with the tragic consequences of her and others' actions, for much of the book she does not really believe that she has choices (99). Having lived life torn between Glinda the Good—her romanticized version of her alcoholic mother—and the Wicked Witch of the West—a similarly exaggerated version of the "Auntie" Muriel who raised her (139)—Elizabeth has unsuccessfully tried to escape her past, including identification with her catatonic sister. In addition, she has tried to build a new identity (Queen Elizabeth, haute wasp) and keep her "Kansas" house intact by holding onto the companion of her life's journey.

Like *Wizard*'s Dorothy and the other surviving characters of "life before man," however, Elizabeth literally falls out of her dream world. In Elizabeth's case, it is a negative, Gothic one. Elizabeth falls first in her kitchen when *The Wizard of Oz* seems to run backward: before she recognizes that she wants to be saved from marriage to death (Fitcher, Dracula) (205), "dry ice" associated with the dead Chris begins to "eat" color. She falls again at Aunt Muriel's funeral, where, in a folkloric scene bringing to mind the end of the world for the witch in "The Juniper Tree" (see Chapter 4), her witch self dies. Although she cannot disregard Hecate's "waning moon," she no longer needs to inhabit either *Wizard*'s wasteland or Emerald City. Nor will she continue to wait for a demon lover in Xanadu with its walled greenery, "sunless sea," Rapunzel towers, and "caves of ice" (Coleridge 683–84). As we shall see, Elizabeth learns that after going back she can go forward: despite the parable of the foolish person who builds on sand rather than rock (Matt. 7.24–27), *she* is able to create her own "home" or greenness in a wasteland or over the abyss (300–302). Not really a mummy, she rises from her own ashes.

Unable to live up to Elizabeth's expectations of a lover and unable to face continued isolation, Chris is an ironic Wizard of Oz. Not only a fake magician but also a person who has faked at least some of his identity and family background, Chris is also a tin man, a patchwork of cut-off pieces. Paradoxically both the weightiest character in the book (Elizabeth describes him as a weight leaning on her and resents the power he has over her) (23) and as invisible even in life as Lesje sometimes wishes to be, Chris wants to be felt but not seen (89). Although he sticks a plastic eye with a red iris in the center of his forehead (Motif F512.1.1), his theatrics cannot produce mystical third-eye vision (Motif D1810.8.1) or the magical power he and others seek (171). Initially as mysterious as the wizard or a demon lover to Elizabeth, Chris colludes with her to concoct theatrical costumes, sets, and roles almost as elaborate as the Wizard's. A professional "taxidermist" and "glorified custodian of dead owls" (172), Chris still ironically resembles his stuffed owl, dead despite the feathers and eyeless (Motif F512.5) rather than wise.

Reversing the Wizard's appearance as an enormous head on a throne, "without a body to support it or any arms or legs whatever" (Baum 97), Chris becomes a body without a head (Motif F511.0.1), a literalization of Atwood's many images of decapitation. Literally in pieces after he blows off his head, Chris is associated with several myths, fairy tales, and legends about decapitation and segmentation, especially the Grimms' "The Juniper Tree," the Osiris and Orpheus myths, and "The Legend of Sleepy Hollow." A playactor used to disguise, he even dons suit and tie and shines his shoes before he blows off his head (17). Indicative of the fantasies that constitute their relationship, their affair begins when Elizabeth seeks leftover scraps of fur for doll clothes. Predictably, she eats up his hints of being a son of a romantically poor trapper in "the north," part French and Métis, "that mythical hybrid; archaic, indigenous, authentic as she was not." From English River, a town named after the "enemy" English Elizabeth thinks she personifies to him, Chris supposedly exacts "payment" of her white flesh and presumably white blood.

Although we cannot know their accuracy, Elizabeth's perceptions, somewhat supported by Nate's and Chris's reported dialogue and actions, are revealing. Ironically, Chris may have cast Elizabeth as his magician. "She had what he wanted, power over a certain part of the world; she knew how to behave, what fork to use, what went with what. . . . She had that power and she'd let him see it and touch it," promising "transformation, a touch on the shoulder, knighthood." But Elizabeth, who has her own mythological scenarios, including Chris as a feathered or furred God, Dracula,[13] demon lover, Fitcher, and ghost, loses interest in his humanity and steps back to reveal his nakedness, "showing him that he was after all only a vacation, a beautiful picture on a brochure, a man in a loincloth whacking the head off some nondescript coconut" (160–61). After he has shattered his head, Elizabeth fears that "Part of him has been left behind" (159). She has trouble remembering him whole and, as Isis does for Osiris, Elizabeth decides to collect his pieces—the fur scraps that seem to constitute him—and scatter them, in this case over a snow-filled ravine, so that his soul can rest (151, 158). Significantly, Chris exists in the novel exclusively through other characters' fragmentary, unreliable memories. Since Elizabeth, Nate, and Lesje each contemplate suicide, and Martha enacts a fake suicide, Chris symbolizes the grayness or amputating alienation threatening to overtake the characters as well as Canada, the gray-skyed, "morbid nation" that identifies itself with the dead (57–58).

From Elizabeth's point of view, if her husband Nate is no wizard, he at least brings her cups of tea and takes out the trash. Nate is a combination of the stuffed Scarecrow and the patched Tin Woodsman, who has apparently chopped off both head and heart. Like the Scarecrow, the slim Nate is a failure in his job, from one point of view a ridiculous figure even he seems to scorn. Nate is so ineffective in the traditional role of "guarding" his home and marriage that his wife's lover, Chris, even seeks his help in attempting to spirit Elizabeth away. Like the Scarecrow, the Tin Woodsman, and Elizabeth, Nate seems unable to "move" on his own (change his life) and unwilling to use either his brain or his heart. Like the Tin Woodsman and *Life Before Man*'s other characters, he has progressively "chopped away" his identity, family background, and supports, diluting his relationships with others. Not wishing to be his mother's son any more than Elizabeth wants to be the child of her parents and Auntie Muriel, or Lesje of copulating grandmothers, Nate is Nathaniel, gift of God. He thinks he lacks the courage to be the son of his dead "hero" father. Like Ichabod Crane, Nate is afraid to face the "headless horseman," Chris, and with him, awareness of his own insignificance and eventual death. But unlike Crane, Nate eventually paces his detached Peter-Pan shadow, carrying it with him rather than running from it. Seeking the Tin Man's heart, the Scarecrow's reason, and the Cowardly Lion's courage, Nate learns that he, too, must be his own "Wizard."

Lesje, Cowardly Lion with Oz daydreams, is also cut off from home and identity. Like the Tin Man and other *Life Before Man* characters, she is "patchwork." Although Lesje seems to believe that her brains are more important than anything else, she resembles *Wizard*'s Scarecrow by not using them in her personal life. Like Elizabeth, Nate, and *Wizard*'s Dorothy, Lesje misses "magic" in her black and white life: this "Alice"'s search for a "Wonderland" in prehistory symbolizes the characters', and our own, failure to live in the present. Rather than roaring like the Lion to disguise her fear, Lesje characteristically covers her mouth with her hand as she speaks. She is also an Oz ventriloquist: comparable to *The Edible Woman*'s Marian and *Lady Oracle*'s Joan, she does not take responsibility for her own voice or hands (actions) until late in the book. Much of the time, she seems to pretend that she is voiceless (Motifs S161, S163, Q451.3). Split between grandmothers, ethnic backgrounds, mind and body, and men, Lesje is accustomed to watching mutely and appeasing (144–45): she is more comfortable cataloging specimens or being a distant observer in prehistory than living in the present. Even when William attempts to rape her, Lesje wonders whether his "turning into someone else" is her fault (186). She avoids direct confrontation with William by locking herself in the bathroom, reading a book on Ichthyosaurs until he goes to bed, and silently moving out when he is gone. Even buying a stove and refrigerator for the house she and Nate rent is "a serious commitment" (192–94).

Lesje finally asserts her right to a relationship and her rights within a relationship by "roaring" at Nate, refusing to keep her voice "down" any longer: "*The children.* He thought all he had to do was to say *the children* and she would shut up, like magic" (292). Rather than swallowing the Lion's "magic" substance to gain courage, Lesje chooses a future by flushing her birth control pills down the toilet, allowing her body its intrinsic magical power to transform and reproduce.

By the end of *Life Before Man*, Elizabeth, Nate, and Lesje—all artificers like Marvell/Oz and Dorothy—also open a door to a green world within themselves; and they attain their "green vision" without donning the Wizard of Oz's green spectacles. Although, as Atwood says, "They all make concessions to reality" (Atwood Papers, Box 32, "Nan's Major Points"), they do so imaginatively, in an atmosphere of change. Elizabeth, whose "falling house" has survived Nate's departure, plans a picnic on her crumbling but still standing porch. Nate, no longer in a "rigid" Scarecrow or Tin Man posture, plans a similar life-celebrating picnic with Lesje in the country. Lesje gains courage and finds her voice. Resembling *Surfacing*'s narrator, she grows a symbolically new self that could lead to the more highly evolved human being promised by the novel's title. Neither Elizabeth nor Nate will abandon their children, and Nate and Lesje will build another family together. "The Girl Without Hands" intertext makes this transformation more apparent.

Unlike *Lady Oracle* and *The Handmaid's Tale*, *Life Before Man* does not directly allude to its major fairy-tale intertexts, "The Girl Without Hands" and "Rapunzel" (see Chapters 6 and 11 for summary). Still, these tales provide the frame for the other intertexts, modeling the transformational structure and supplying images, motifs, and even occasional details of plot. To some extent, all of Atwood's protagonists initially have the problem Atwood describes as characteristic of Southern Ontario: they don't touch (*Margaret Atwood: Once in August*). Like the Girl Without Hands, they all carry burdens despite their "bound" arms. In a larger sense also dramatized through Dr. Minnow's ironic comments on the "sweet Canadians" (*BH*) and Atwood's own discussion of Canadians' "Porky Pig" noses, clinched-fist mouths, and victim positions ("Through" 332; *Surv* 36–39), "The Girl Without Hands" intertext could suggest Canada's famous colonial mentality, a related "neutral," even isolationist, foreign policy, or an understandable fear of imperialistic "others." As portrayed in the novel's characters, settings, and symbols, the Canada of *Life Before Man* is an encircled museum, filled with fossilizing dinosaurs such as the gliding Pteranodon, possibly "unable to touch down anywhere." Twelve years before Canadian studies scholars discuss the "immense and cataclysmic change" approaching a Canada "mired" in "issues of native rights, all types of international trade realignments, ethnic discrimination, the marooning of arts and culture, and . . . mounting difficulties of crime, environmental degradation and health deterioration" (Konrad 1), Nate passively watches his country fall apart. The only one of *Life Before Man*'s major characters interested in politics, Nate characteristically watches from a distance, on television. Despite Aunt Muriel's concern with "a decent home," *Life Before Man*'s Toronto is even comically "incestuous" (216). In keeping with the novel's other amputations, Toronto is also "heartless." Without being limited to Canadian levels of meaning, however, the novel also portrays colonizing touch, including that of the Gorgosaurus: "It's a stomach on legs, it would swallow the world if it could," and the Deinonychus: it balanced on one foot while using its special claw for disemboweling (238, 30, 121 141).

Symbolizing the effects of living in such a fragmented, fragmenting world, Chris is not only unable to establish a place for himself—including relationship, home, and a sense of balance—he is unable to survive. In order to get out of their "Ice Age" and have any connection with the world, their country, or other people, Elizabeth, Nate, Lesje, and Muriel must all to some extent regrow mutilated or amputated hands along with other body parts.

As the *You Are Happy* discussion indicates, hands and touch are essentially positive, negative, or somewhere in between. In Atwood's work hands can carry burdens, communicate and express the self, establish relationship, and touch the earth; they can act, love, pity, sustain, heal, applaud, and create. "Gloved" or as symbolic or literal claws, they can also lie, betray, threaten, paralyze, violate, maim, disembowel, cannibalize, or kill. Between these clearly positive and negative poles, hands express their owners' doubts and fears. Thus, hands can resist commitment, establish distance, or attempt to conceal. Just as Atwood's characters frequently use and suffer from their and others' blind or distancing gaze, they must come to terms with the debilitated, and debilitating, touch that parallels characters or personae's missing tongues, voices, ears, heads, feet, hearts, and genitals.

More evidently than most of *Life Before Man*'s characters, Chris does have hands. Although his "huge, thick knuckled" hands are powerful (173), they either dangle helplessly or become violent fists. Like the others, he needs "a hand," preferably magical, but this ironic Rapunzel looks to the wrong person for rescue and marries death (Davidson and Davidson, "Prospects" 211) instead. Elizabeth remembers him "Gripping her hand across the table as though, if he let go, she w[ould] slide down past the edge of the table, the edge of some cliff or quicksand, and be lost forever. Or he w[ould]." Chris is never able to escape from the tower (Motif R41.2) to which the characters not only are confined but confine themselves: "There was your room and there was everything else outside, and that barrier between the two." Elizabeth imagines Chris carrying his rented room on Parliament Street "around with you like a smell, it was a smell like formaldehyde and the insides of old cupboards, mousy, secretive, like musk, dusky and rich. Whenever I was with you I was in that room, even when we were outside, even when we were here. I'm in it now, only now you've locked the door" (24–25). In an unsafe neighborhood and barely furnished, the room seems disordered, with nothing in the right place, just as, to Nate and Elizabeth, Chris's speech, clothing, and manners always seem deficient. Chris makes a point of parking illegally and aggressively revving the engine of his mufflerless car (174), and he seems to relish scenes. We can't know all the factors that contribute to Chris's suicide, but, as the Davidsons suggest, "Chris's death might be his judgment on himself for trying to solve a crisis by thinking it through"—the 'rational' basis for his suicide—as opposed to living it through" (211).

Like *Bodily Harm*'s Rennie, Elizabeth is a Girl Without Hands (Motifs F515.0.1, Q451.1). At the beginning of the book, she is so alienated from herself, others, her past, her world, and the present that she lacks any kind of meaningful control over her life: her hands have become useless "rubber gloves." Like the Girl Without Hands and many of Atwood's personae, Elizabeth also has other symbolic amputations. She feels invisible, she hears voices from above (Motif F966), she is growing "deaf," and "her voice has been stolen. . . . She has nothing to write with . . . . [and] The only power she has left is negative" (251–52). Like other Canadian Rapunzels, her body is her internalized "tower," but its external shape is her room, "barricaded" with an "invisible thread" stretched across the threshold to keep others out. Feeling out of body, she rigidly lies on her back in a characteristic position approximating the dead Caroline's ("arms at her sides, feet together, eyes open"). From a bed that no longer seems hers, she watches the cracks in her life and the ceiling:

"She can't move her fingers. She thinks about her hands, lying at her sides, rubber gloves: she thinks about forcing the bones and flesh down into those shapes of hands, one finger at a time, like dough" (12–13).

Elizabeth may not literally be a victim of incest despite her father and Uncle Teddy's overtures, her mother's relationship with the son of her father's lawyer, and her own sharing of two men with a coworker, who even has sex in Elizabeth's bed. Still, in many ways she is an abused child. Like the Girl Without Hands, she lacks sustaining parents and is exposed to possible harm (e.g., sitting in her night gown on the laps of her father's drunk friends) (149). When her "rounder" father walks out and her mother's passive arms and legs prove as useless as her doll-like "porcelain face" (149), Elizabeth literally and symbolically feeds the family. Like the Girl Without Hands, Elizabeth also feels she has been sold, chooses to leave the place that is not home, does her best to hide her amputations, and even trusts to the "kindness" of strangers. As a teenager Elizabeth enjoys going to "the edge" with leather-armed men and pushing back in time (178). After her mother's funeral, she uses anonymous sex like a car crash in order to let go of her mother's dead hand (177–79), only to be crippled and imprisoned first by Aunt Muriel's and then Chris's "touch" (123).

For much of her life, sex is Elizabeth's one means of touching and being touched; before she meets Chris, she doesn't realize the extent to which this touch has been counterfeit. Later, without even the "arm" of Nate's companionship (99), Elizabeth "wants anyone, just some arms that aren't hollow and knitted" and feels she must either warm her own cold hands (205–6) or have degrading sex with strangers, such as the spider-handed salesman (229). Looking into a mirror on her thirty-ninth birthday and tracing "the shadow of her face as it will be in twenty years" (247), Elizabeth is Snow White's stepmother. Having substituted male regard for missed parental "mirroring" (see n. 2 and Wilson, "Fragmented" 50–85), Elizabeth is now supplanted by a younger woman. "[L]ocked in this house" with crying children, leaking roof, and crumbling foundation, she is locked out of Nate and Lesje's life together (251). Elizabeth's crossed wrists recall Caroline's in her coffin.

Hands can be powerful, however, and once Elizabeth linked her arms with those of other girls in a chain to show that she wouldn't stop for anybody (180–81). Elizabeth frequently wears leather "hands" or gloves, including when she uses her voice like a rock on Chris (99, 236) and when she attends Muriel's funeral. Despite her preference for sitting or lying with hands folded or crossed after Chris's death, she "holds things together," develops projects, makes columns of bills and income, and makes a point of hugging Janet (23, 139, 250). But although Elizabeth hands Nate money, thinks she can control Nate's relationship with Lesje "with one hand tied behind her back," and even makes Lesje shriek when she puts one hand on her shoulder (150), Elizabeth is "leaking" power. Feeling out of body like Caroline, for much of the book she sits passively in her Rapunzel room with empty hands.

Elizabeth and her situation slowly begin to change on April 13, 1977. Trying her symbolically silenced voice (Motifs S161, S163, Q451.3) and amputated (Q451.1.1) or numb hands and feet, she is finally able to confront Muriel and her own anger directly and honestly. Remembering that she was, like the Girl Without Hands, "sold" (Motifs H914, S211), she "feels the ground sliding from beneath her feet." As she stands without costume, telling Muriel to get out of "her house," she uses her hands decisively: Elizabeth cracks her Rapunzel shell at the same time as she shatters one of her cherished bowls filled with nothing, complete in itself as she had tried to be. Even moving formerly rigid feet to dance in celebration (216–19), Elizabeth begins to establish that she is making a sheltered living space—a something from nothing—for herself and her children. Although she temporarily resumes a static Caroline position, by September 3, 1977, Elizabeth recognizes that her legless pose as a stone Buddha is "cutting off the circulation in her legs": being a statue may mean immobility rather than serenity. She begins to regain her lost ears (Motifs D2161.3.5, F511.2.4) as she hears Auntie Muriel's voice in what she thought was her own (260–62).

But it is not until the hospital scene (Friday, April 14, 1978) that Elizabeth, who has "practiced not caring," recognizes her own culpability. Cradling vengefulness and looking at Muriel's stubby hands, Elizabeth remembers running and pulling Caroline away from her one-gloved mother's touch. She is able to hear Muriel, ironically saying "You never listen to me," at the moment she recognizes "her own treachery" (279–80). The scene ends with Elizabeth extending to another what she denied her real mother: she takes the dying Muriel's hands. Although Muriel's "elastic-sheathed barricades" make the idea of her giving birth unimaginable (*LBM* 278), in a surprising early version of the scene, Elizabeth even calls Muriel "mother": "Sadness grips her. Nevertheless, nevertheless, she whispers: It's all right, mother. Mother, it's all right" (Atwood Papers, Box 30, *LBM* handwritten drafts). Consistent with Atwood's usual practice of burying overt or simplistic motives as she revises, the published version of the novel more subtly establishes Elizabeth's association of Muriel with her real mother. As in similar scenes of reaching out near the end of *Bodily Harm* and *Cat's Eye*, Atwood suggests a healing of the past.

After taking the dying Muriel's hand in her own, Elizabeth begins to have the strength of her playground hand "chain" without its destructiveness. At Muriel's bizarre funeral, "The children are attached to [Elizabeth's] hands." Snorting with stifled laughter into cupped hands, Elizabeth notices that many people are actually crying and recognizes that Muriel, like herself, "might be other than what she seemed." In a passage parodying the narrator of Vonnegut's *Breakfast of Champions* (234), she realizes that, in a sense, she can make other people appear and disappear (see n. 7), even make a transparent world solid. She is the creator of her own reality: her life is in her hands (298–302).

Atwood's written comments from Edinburgh to her editor, Nan Talese, about *Life Before Man*'s galleys are illuminating: "No, Elizabeth doesn't have a breakdown. . . . No, she isn't going to retreat from the world. . . . The last scene, in the Museum looking at the Chinese art show, indicates that she is able to formulate a vision beyond the personal (which has obsessed her until now) . . . the fact that she is able to think of this at all indicates a possible direction for her . . . outwards, if not upwards" (Atwood Papers, Box 32, "Nan's Major Points," *LBM* Correspondence Re. Revisions, Publication, etc.). When the Oz and Rapunzel Witch image of Auntie Muriel is buried along with Elizabeth's sterile self-projection, Elizabeth is able to leave her symbolic desert, reinhabit her body, and regrow hands (Motif E782.1) that extend to others.

Auntie Muriel is handless Girl, trapped Rapunzel, cruel aunt, and amputating or imprisoning witch (Motifs S72, G205) or devil. In response to inquiries from her editor before the book was published, Atwood said, "I see A. M. [Auntie Muriel] as a *given*, that thing that cannot be overcome or changed within itself" (Atwood Papers, Box 32, "Nan's Major Points," Life Before Man Correspondence Re. Revisions, Publication, etc.). Although Muriel, like Elizabeth, usually wears Virgin-Mary blue dresses, coats, and robe in *Life Before Man*, she is the archetype of *Survival*'s Canadian Hecate. Unlike the touch of Nate's mother, who worries about atrocities all over the world and nurses armless and legless men at the veteran's hospital, Muriel's touch seems crippling, incinerating (132, 123, 296), or freezing, as if she is "a mammoth or mastodon . . . recently dug out of an iceberg" (120). Elizabeth's exaggerated view constitutes most of what we know about Muriel. As we have seen, however, we gradually discover that Elizabeth, who literally cannot "stomach" a day with Muriel, projects her own sense of "treachery" and "worthlessness" onto her aunt. Muriel did at least offer her destitute sister financial support (281). Still, Muriel's actions and conversation also reveal a lonely, unloved, and unloving person.

In Elizabeth's Auntie Muriel stories, Muriel is the epitome of "old" Toronto's "blue-law ways": in the hierarchy of Muriel's Great Chain of Being, partly "graded according to skin color and religion," sexual organs are at the bottom. Muriel was brought up by "a domineering father who stunted her" in a patriarchal society punishing her for strong personality and good mind rather than beauty. Her narrow-mindedness, vindictiveness, and lack of charity are symbolized in her "stumpy fingers," often white-gloved and once forced to embroider (119–23). Like Margaret Laurence's more human Haggar Shipley, identified with a blind marble angel in the Manawaka cemetery (*The Stone Angel* 1), however, even Muriel proves to be "a bleeding statue, a miracle": her "witch" self "melts" as Elizabeth takes her "blinded hands" (280–82).

Nate, too, has built isolating walls around himself without feeling at home; occupying "the spare room" and frequently sitting alone in a bar, he retreats to the basement to work with his symbolically withered hands. His expectation of marriage as protection may be partly responsible for his parodic role as Rapunzel princess and abused orphan Girl. According to Elizabeth, Nate has "wanted a woman to be a door he could go through and shut behind him. Everything was fine as long as she was willing to pretend she was a cage" (162). Unlike the other characters, Nate knows the importance of touch, but his is often impotent. He has revealing fantasies about smashing his hand through the kitchen window, strangling Elizabeth, accidentally "breaking" Lesje, hitting or killing Chris, reaching through the bathroom door to Lesje, and leaping through a lighted window to a female healer (Motif A454.1) and life (17, 258, 174, 163, 133–34). As his similarities to the Scarecrow, Tin Woodsman, and the other characters suggest, however, Nate is initially locked in place: he is another of Atwood's static "wooden" Pinocchios awaiting the spark of life.

Nate is not really powerless: he just thinks he is (Atwood Papers, Box 32, *LBM* Correspondence Re. Revisions, Publication, etc.). Like the personae of *The Circle Game* and other volumes, he can't always touch what he needs or do what he thinks about: he is outside the window watching "Victorian Christmas-card" images of happiness ("The Circle Game" 52). He quits his job as attorney because he wants to return to "the wisdom and simplicity of the craftsman." In creating an unusual gouge tool, however, he actually carves a new hand for himself, wooden rather than the silver hands of the Girl Without Hands. Like the people who make "dead" totems again warm with "hands holding warm / hands holding / the half-formed air" ("Some Objects of Wood and Stone" 75), every time Nate picks up his gouge, "there [is] another hand close within his own"; he feels "secure, rooted, as if by carving them himself he's made them already old." He has the pleasure all Atwood characters seek or miss, of "Holding, holding on" (201), but this hand is not yet alive.

Still, Nate's "withered" hands are wiser than he: it is his hands that grope through the dark "by a touch that is also a smell" for metamorphosis, relationship, and "the ethical life" (197, 83). Preparing for further metamorphosis, his hands shave (43), touch Lesje, stop making toys, substitute for his mother's as they hand out leaflets about Mountie wrongdoing, and even anticipate being grasped as "a kindred spirit." Like Elizabeth and readers of *The Journals of Susanna Moodie* ("Alternate Thoughts from Underground" 56), he has trouble believing in a solid earth (303–4; see Fig. 10). He also believes that the petition he is collecting signatures for is futile.

Although he would like to "feel at home" among "the apathetic, the fatalistic, the uncommitted, the cynical," as he earlier sought the protection of maternal female healers, he finally realizes that he is responsible for his life. Knowing that "The world exists apart from him" and that no "Imperial Message" (*LBM* 276, Kafka 13–15) or absolute truth exists, "he refuses to be defined" (Sartre's being-in-itself).[14] By the end of the book, Nate gives up trying to overtake his headless shadow and knows that he will eventually die. But Nate is also reborn. Unlike *The Circle*

Game's lovers whose bones grow "flesh" again, Nate is a "settler" who survives ("The Settlers" 95). Despite being "an evolutionary mistake" (having a right leg shorter than a left), Nate begins running toward a future, a transition that is signaled by the shift in his narration from present to future tense: he, like the grass beneath him, "strains upwards" and outward. Instead of waiting to be rescued or assuming the traditional male role of rescuer, Nate plans "uncharted" expeditions in the country to "fields" he could never enter with Elizabeth (313–14), a green world lying beyond games and resembling *The Circle Game*'s final "fields of our open hands" ("The Settlers" 95). "Possible day[s] shimmer ahead of him." Although he cannot predict what will happen, he knows that he and Lesje will go *home* together (*LBM* 313–14). By rejecting a prescribed role and acting—establishing a relationship with Lesje without abandoning his children and committing himself to causes even if they may be futile—he does achieve new hands (276, 306).

Lesje, too, is handless maiden and Rapunzel, distant from life even in daydreams about the past. The tree from which she watches dinosaurs in prehistory is linked to several Grimms' fairy tales about females isolated and silenced for years.[15] Even though she plays "invisible woman" and "life tourist," Lesje initially is "encased" like her mother, who has "drawn herself together into a sphere . . . [and] become impenetrable, compact, plump" to survive "Montague" and "Capulet" feuds. When Lesje's parents had desired "transformation and change," they "began the trek north but got stuck halfway up, on a nondescript street south of St. Clair" (113). Although Lesje also lives in Toronto's "heart," it seems frozen, the "fossilized burrow" of the book's epigraph rather than home. The brilliant colors of Lesje's fantasies, including "a sun more orange than her own has ever been," suggest suppressed emotions, desires, and ethnic identity; but Lesje spends her time cataloging fossils, hiding not only her teeth but her appetites and needs, and wearing "protectively colored" clothing (18, 26, 93).

Alone and a "tourist" in her own "country," "Lesjeland," Lesje is "farsighted" even when she's not behind binoculars: her dinosaur daydreams are "clear-edged," "but her own hand," and everything else in her personal life, is "a blur" (92, 157). She not only shrinks from the "kiss" of the Ukrainian summer camp song but from the "touch" of any real relationship (18–19, 93). Lesje settles for the appearance of being happy with a person, William, who is supposed to remain all surface (195–96). Lesje once moved between dueling grandmothers in a "waystation" neighborhood to facilitate her mother's work at a travel agency. Next, she is "a cliff hanger" with William. Then, without a sense of anything having ended or begun, she camps out with Nate as he moves back and forth between Elizabeth's house and theirs (268, 20, 192).

Like those of other Atwood characters, Lesje's problems manifest themselves in symbolic sensory deprivations (of touch, sight, hearing, speech, and even taste) and bodily amputations (of arms, hands, fingers, eyes, ears, mouth, voice, head, heart, genitals, legs, feet). Although this Rapunzel does have hands, which she imagines being clasped by two raging grandmothers refusing to meet one another, Lesje has been pulled in two mutually exclusive directions and continues to feel paralyzed. Thus, although Lesje considers William a "doll," it is her hands that characteristically "dangle" from her wrists, much as Chris's do in his relationship with Elizabeth (295, 129, 234). Lesje's one commitment is to her career. Professor Summerlee of *The Lost World* fantasy, so instrumental in her decision to become an archeologist, holds her hand as William never will (45). Outside of cataloging museum specimens, if Lesje does use her hands, she usually uses them passively as a chin rest (169) or negatively, to cover her mouth or to close and lock doors.

Lesje is also unable to express anger except through her internalized grandmothers who yell obscenities (Atwood Papers, Box 32, "Nan's Major Points," in *LBM* Correspondence Re. Revisions, Publication, etc.). Feeling that she is the child of two grandmothers speaking different languages, Lesje closes her ears—she doesn't really listen to the stories that might give her a personal history (269)—and does not develop a voice of her own. Lesje also seems to be without feet (167) for dancing or changing her life (Motifs F517.1.1, Q451.0.1, S162). In her choice of William, less capable than flesh-eating dinosaurs of inspiring her fantasies, she is even without genitals.[16] Instead of "dancing," as Joan Foster does by the end of *Lady Oracle*, or creating "balance" in her own life by expressing her feelings, Lesje comically imagines Deinonychus "coping" with its environment by balancing on one foot and disemboweling with the other. Lesje suitably watches this "dance" "from the immunity of her treetop" (141).

Like Elizabeth, Lesje is not a literal victim of incest, but she, too, has been "cut up" and "orphaned" in family disputes, ironically because of too many, conflicting, parental figures. Like both the Girl Without Hands and Elizabeth, Lesje hides the evidence of her amputations. She goes into the world without "a mother's blessing" (269), paradoxically appearing as a ministering angel in Nate's fantasies (Motif D2161.5.5). Lacking the voice to protest her victimization and to become a nonvictim, Lesje pretends compliancy with her parents, associates, and lovers. In her relationship with Nate, she is in danger of becoming Hay's "seduced and abandoned" Rapunzel, who twists her "heartstrings to a rope" for the faithless prince to climb ("Rapunzel" 121). Ironically, Lesje's "incestuous" relationship with Nate, the husband of a coworker who also sleeps with Lesje's companion, precipitates William's attempt to reclaim the disputed "territory" of Lesje's body. More significantly, the relationship helps Lesje reclaim her own body and move into new territory.

Despite Lesje's personal "fog" (157), by the end of Part 2 she is not only able to reach out to Nate but to offer him healing touch (Motif D1503.9): "He's letting her in, letting her listen in. She isn't sure she wants this. Nevertheless, her hand moves up, drawn to his mysterious wound, touches his forehead. . . . He's making a gift of himself, handing himself over to her, mutely. . . . She opens her arms. One of his arms goes around her." She expects to hear glass breaking, and they each have many problems to work through. Still, the relationship, like the bottle of wine Lesje drops, remains "intact" (116). Until Lesje discovers that she and Nate have made love in Elizabeth's bed, Lesje "does not see this happiness as having any necessary result." When she discovers this "incest," Lesje feels unclean: "this is a violation, . . . she has trespassed." Saying only, "This is Elizabeth's room" (169), Lesje recognizes Elizabeth's own enclosed space and Elizabeth's "territory." Previously, symbolically watching life from a tree, she had seen herself as a herbivore safely outside of life's "carnage." In Elizabeth's game of Lifeboat, Lesje escaped when she was unable to think of a reason that she should live except to identify the bones. Now, however, she is involved: she faces the competition and plans her "move." Lesje almost expects even the dinosaurs to "reach down their fingers in friendly greeting" (310). Although she later clutches a knife and again considers escape, she adopts one of the Lifeboat game's survival solutions. Rather than being eaten, cannibalizing others, or passively waiting for the bones of civilization to appear, Lesje, like the other characters, takes her life into her own hands (155–57, 293).

Life Before Man's fairy-tale intertexts again model the "magical" transformation needed in its gray country and world. Used both seriously and parodically, *Life Before Man*'s "Rapunzel," "The Girl Without Hands," and *The Wizard of Oz* intertexts offer hope by implying characters' imaginative release from externally imposed patterns.

⑧

The Artist's Marriage
to Death in *Bodily Harm*

*"The Robber Bridegroom" and "The Girl
Without Hands"*

Written within a few years of *Bodily Harm* (1981), Margaret Atwood's *Murder in the Dark, Bluebeard's Egg,* and *Interlunar* (including the previously published *Snake Poems,* 1983) share intertexts,
motifs, themes, and techniques similar to those in *Bodily Harm.*
In varying degrees these works use fairy-tale intertexts alongside
mythic, biblical, native, and/or literary ones (Dante, T. S. Eliot)
to portray "hollow" wasteland artists who are figuratively, sometimes literally, married to death. Like the narrator-illustrator in
Surfacing, these *"solde"* females and males, sometimes contrasted
to heroic artists, are divided from others and from parts of themselves but are seeking transformation. Connected themes include
sacrilege or debasement of art and of the sacred, natural, and
human; humanity's simultaneous attraction to destruction (poison, murder) as well as to creation; and the artist's heroic/ironic/
parodic journey out of the underworld (wasteland/prison/hell).
Other themes these works share are sexual/textual/cultural politics; the colonization of the alien "other"; and transformation
toward individual and global wholeness, healing, and wisdom
(sometimes through special eating). Among shared motifs in
these texts are magic, dismemberment, vision, cannibalism and

ritual eating, silence versus speech or singing (poetry), hands, and the folk motif, also used in *Double Persephone* and *Procedures for Underground*, of descent to the underworld of the dead (F81).

In *Bodily Harm*, the Grimms' "The Robber Bridegroom" (No. 40, AT 955), "Fitcher's Bird" (No. 46, AT 311), "The Girl Without Hands" (No. 31, AT 706) (Wilson, "Sexual" 209), and a deconstructed combination of the Grimms', Perrault's (AT 510A), and Disney's "Cinderella" are major intertexts. In addition, *Oedipus Rex* and Oedipus folklore (AT 931), goddess (especially Demeter, Pandora, Hecate) myth and related fisher king legend, the biblical story of humankind's fall (A1331.1), current critical theories, popular detective stories and games, spy stories (Vitale), and other popular culture texts (see Wilson, "Turning" 136–45) playfully reflect and refract one another in *Bodily Harm*. Canadian riddles of the Robber Bridegroom type (AT 955C),[1] Sir Walter Scott's *Ivanhoe* (Patton, "Tourists" 153), and John Berger's *Ways of Seeing* are also important (see Carrington, "Another" 50; Irvine, *Subversion* 39). Fairy-tale and other intertexts in *Interlunar*, *Bluebeard's Egg*, and *Murder in the Dark* are discussed in Chapter 9.[2]

To varying degrees, most of Atwood's work is, on some level, about the artist's marriage to death. Atwood's comic and serious artists include the poetry personae, Marian, *Surfacing*'s narrator, Joan, Nate, Offred, Elaine, and such short fiction protagonists as Julia ("Lives of the Poets"), Joel ("Ugly Puss"), Loulou and the poets ("Loulou; or, The Domestic Life of the Language"), and Joanne ("True Trash"). In *Lady Oracle* (1976), dancing in the red shoes all women wear means at least amputation of talent, goals, or desires: a psychic death. In *Bodily Harm* and *True Stories*, the marriage to death can be literal; and even in *Interlunar*, *Murder in the Dark*, and *Bluebeard's Egg*, the political and cultural implications of this theme have moved from subground to foreground. Because potential artists in these works are married to death, the "robber" is not simply a male or even patriarchy *per se* but the kind of dead or death-worshipping culture Riane Eisler associates with "the Blade" rather than "the Chalice" (xvii–xx), societies in which art and the artist serve commercial, military, and colonial ends. By being part of this increasingly global culture, Atwood's artists thus become not just victims but "robbers" of life colluding in their own and their world's "cannibalism" and "dismemberment." Ironically already in the kind of personal, urban, or societal hell Lessing portrays in *Briefing for a Descent into Hell* (1971), in *Bodily Harm*, *Murder in the Dark*, and *Interlunar* Atwood's artists descend into an inner and sometimes external healing or purifying landscape. Their initial self-deception sometimes makes them more parodic than heroic; and when they return to "ordinary life," they may again face speechlessness. Although such protagonists' life quests follow a deconstructive pattern, they still resemble those of medieval romance, where journeys (and thus texts) never end.

Originally entitled "The Robber Bridegroom" (Atwood Papers, Typescripts, Box 33), *Bodily Harm* resembles *The Edible Woman* and the short fiction, "A Travel Piece" (*DG*), in again using the Grimms' "The Robber Bridegroom" intertext (Wilson, "Sexual" 209; "A Note" 115). This fairy tale about a suitor who chops up and eats prospective brides and the woman who witnesses and tells about his crime dramatizes personal, interpersonal, aesthetic, national, political, and "earth" survival problems in a cannibalistic world.

Much more than source material for understanding Atwood's intentions or the changed vision many critics see (Patton, "Tourists" 165, 151), "The Robber Bridegroom" intertext is, with "The Juniper Tree," the basis for the cannibalism motif throughout Atwood's work and for distinctive features Irvine and others find in *Bodily Harm* (*Subversion* 40). Along with "The Girl Without Hands" and the "Fitcher's Bird" fairy tales with which Atwood associates it, "The Robber Bridegroom" intertext illuminates the book's splitting of subject and object; disembodied, italicized language fragments; apparent narrative dismemberment; multileveled themes of cannibalism and dismemberment; surrealistic tone; patterned doubling; unreliable narration; and metafictional frame. Significantly, it structures the breastless and symbolically handless Rennie's transformation toward wholeness.[3]

An "artist" married to death, as are protagonists in virtually all of Atwood's work, Rennata Wilford is the bride of the Robber Bridegroom, Fitcher and the father/devil ("The Girl Without Hands") in the novel's deadly sexual and global politics. Like all of us—male and female—however, she is married to the human condition, including her own relentlessly approaching death. As she discovers, because there is no longer an inside and outside, a here and there, there is no separation between the robber and his band or culture, the robber and his land, the robber and the bride, or the bride and other women. Thus, little separation exists between the man who breaks into Rennie's Toronto apartment (the man with the rope) and other men, the man with the rope and Rennie, Rennie and other women, Rennie and world imperialism, or Rennie and an invaded mother nature. Although she is a "sweet Canadian," Rennie is no more exempt than *Surfacing*'s narrator: she resembles "The Americans" who keep dictators in power either through foreign aid or CIA manipulations. A food specialist (*BH* 170) like *The Edible Woman*'s Marian, Rennie is literally and metaphorically eating and being eaten: Rennie's eyes "twin and reflect" those of the Robber and the closely related Fitcher and Devil father ("The Girl Without Hands"). Thus, Atwood's postcolonial themes and postmodern techniques are perhaps more evident in *Bodily Harm* than in any of her other work.

Not only is another evolving female "artist," Rennata Wilford, married to death, but Western and third-world culture and values are similarly consumed, internally and externally. As Patton suggests, the Caribbean country Rennie visits is also a "girl" in danger of being consumed by "robber bridegrooms"' cannibalistic imperialism ("Tourists" 165–66). Massively involved," not only by literal and metaphoric cancers but also by consciousness, Rennie becomes a cell in the global body: she must "turn inside out" to connect the personal and political in order to create and to speak rather than to colonize (see Brydon 181–83) and consume.

As in *Surfacing*, where disease is symbolically spreading up from the south (9), the main narrator of *Bodily Harm* exists in a diseased landscape that is her body, her "art," her nation and world, and the earth, all characterized with the "out of control" motif. Not only her own cancerous cells but also her relationship with Jake; her trendy articles; pornography; crime; Ste. Agathe and St. Antoine's government, revolution, and prison; Toronto's urban sprawl; Western imperialism; and, by extension, the narrative itself seem out of control.

Rennie is a parodic fisher king whose knights are more interested in killing dragons than in rescuing her or attaining the holy grail, a female symbol of regeneration (228; Walker, *Woman's Dictionary* 90). She lives in a world, not just one country, where "Ellis [not Christ] is King." The "Prince of Peace" and the fish symbol are reduced to campaign poster decoration, and Christ (parodically Prince and Minnow), no longer a savior, is either ineffectual or dead.[4] In Atwood's feminized "Wasteland,"[5] neither Rennata Wilford, the island probably named after a saint (Agatha) whose breasts were cut off (Goodwin 114), nor Rennie's world can be healed by patriarchy's "bionic cock" (109). In *Bodily Harm* we can no longer fail to see that the cancer is already within the narrator (see n. 6) and that she is the wasteland she seeks to escape, first by living on its surface and then by taking a more literal "vacation." As the narrator's aborted fetus and sliced-apart body in *Surfacing* symbolize personal, national, and societal dismemberment, Rennie's cancer and mastectomy, evidence of a "break in" on multiple levels, suggest similar, more explicitly global themes: the cell image symbolizes cancer of the female and world body and represents "all women, all victims and oppressors, all human beings, all." Thus, the invaded cells of the body also suggest cancer of the earth. Because of the goddess's stature as the mother of all, the womb of the earth, these diseased cells also suggest a colonized Mother Nature, pre-figuring the demonic, fallen world of *The Handmaid's Tale* (Wilson, "Turning" 141, 138; "A Note" 115).

Again Atwood simultaneously develops these artist, sexual-political,[6] and global themes through re-visioned fairy-tale, mythic, and related intertexts about marriage to death and the need for the female artist to recover the godmother or goddess in herself. In this case Rennie is a simultaneous parody of Fitcher, the Robber, and the devil-father of "The Girl Without Hands" and their victims, Cinderella, and both patriarchal and matri-archal versions of Pandora, Mother Earth, and Eve in the Garden of Eden. Rennie is Barthes's "zero" or absent author, Rennie's and Atwood's readers, a parodic fisher king, and Berger's seen and acted upon woman (*BH* epigraph from *Ways of Seeing*). She is also Oedipus, the smart/dumb detective who discovers that he is the murderer in his life text; and Tiresias, the blind oracle. Si-multaneously, she is also some of these texts' re-visioned hero.

Initially, Rennie is both cannibal (imperialist) artist and read-er/consumer at the same time as she is the consumed "bride" in *Bodily Harm*'s at least six interlaced levels of "Robber Bride-groom" story (Motif K1916): the personal body (disease, mortal-ity), personal relationships (sexual politics, competition, friend-ship), the world of literature and culture, the national/political/global arena, the human condition, and the earth body. In the Grimms' "The Robber Bridegroom," disruptive female speech depends upon paternal and patriarchal absence or permission (see Chapter 3 for summary). Symbolically, like the caged bird, the old woman in the cellar becomes the voice of the girl's sub-conscious: the old woman is able to offer warnings and help only insofar as the robbers do not know about them. After the Robber Bride and the old woman escape from the Robber's den, the Bride tells her father about the Robber's crimes; the marriage feast goes on as scheduled. After each of the wedding guests and presumably the Robber has told a story, the Robber Bride-groom's condescension ironically releases silenced—internally and externally repressed—female rage: "'Come, my darling, do you know nothing? Relate something to us like the rest.' She replied: 'Then I will relate a dream'" (alternatively, "'Well, my dear, can't you think of anything? Tell us a good story.' 'All right,' she said. 'I'll tell you a dream'")" ("Rope Quartet" epigraph same as Hunt 204; also see Zipes, *Complete* 156). "This is how I got here, says Rennie,"[7] as she begins the story that the Robber Bridegroom requests and we read; some drafts of the novel even use an epigraph from the fairy tale (*BH* 17; Box 33 *BH* drafts, Atwood Papers).

Both the fairy tale and *Bodily Harm* present dreamlike stories that challenge readers' realities. In "The Robber Bridegroom," recounting the Robber's murder and cannibalism of another prospective bride, the Robber Bride undercuts her narrative with the increasingly sarcastic statement, "My dear, it was only a dream" (Zipes, *Complete* 156). *Bodily Harm*'s recurring question, "What do you dream about?" (see Irvine, *Sub/version* 47), is now Rennie's "last wish, it's all she really wants to know" (*BH* 220). Asked by a Rennie seeing literal or symbolic death not only in her dreams but everywhere she goes, in everything she eats, and in everyone or everything she touches, the question is, like its "Robber Bridegroom" corollary, still directly or indirectly answered with death (Paul's dreams of a hole in the ground, Minnow's actual death). Even Lora's answer, that she dreams of bearing "a son for Prince" (149), fosters the destructive system underlying the book's action. Like the Robber, however, we are surprised at the form, content, and real effect of the "dream."

As in the Grimms' "The Robber Bridegroom" and Atwood's *Surfacing* (Wilson, "Deconstructing" 53–69) and *True Stories*, *Bodily Harm* breaks the fictional frame supposedly separating dream or fiction and reality, suggesting the "truth" of fiction and the fiction or multiple stories of "truth." In the case of the fairy tale, when the Bride produces the severed finger of a formerly dismembered and cannibalized bride at the end of her "dream" tale, the Robber and his band are "actually" tried and executed

(Zipes, *Complete* 155–57). One of the voices in "True Romances" warns us that one day we will discover such a severed finger in the bottom of our own breakfast coffee or tea cup. *Bodily Harm* again subverts our desire to know the "true story," lying among all the other stories, "multiple and untrue / after all" and yet all the more believable for the disclaimers (44, "True Stories" 11, Simon and Schuster *TS*). As Paul says and Rubenstein discusses, there are at least three versions of everything in this novel (135, "Pandora's Box" 260). Resembling some of Angela Carter's fiction, Rennie's dreams blend into her and our realities.

Also reminding us of Iris Murdoch's texts, Rennie's self-conscious narrative, including Lora's parallel self-conscious narration "snaking" through hers (see also Kolodny 98), punctures the story illusion. The comments parodying popular genres and the book we are reading make *Bodily Harm* not only metafiction (metaromance) but anti-romance. Discussing publication of the story Minnow wants her to write, Rennie tells him, "I can't think of anyone who would touch it. It isn't even a story yet, nothing's happened. It's hardly of general interest" (122). Later, when her Sunset Inn room is broken into, "This, thinks Rennie, is an exceptionally tacky movie. . . . It's not even a good lunchtime story" (142). She recognizes that her relationship with Paul "is the biggest cliché in the book, a no-hooks, no-strings vacation romance with a mysterious stranger" (198). As Atwood points out, by using the point of view of one of the females outside the central action of a conventional spy story (Vitale n.p.) and never totally uncovering the mysteries it poses, the book undercuts even its thriller story. Parodying the narrative form of "The Robber Bridegroom," Atwood first breaks the "frame" separating the Robber's known but unauthored text (his unacknowledged cannibalism) from the Bride's narrative, and then, more radically, the frame between the Bride and Rennie's narratives.

A parodic fusion—of metaphysical detective story, spy thriller, the ghost story, the Gothic romance, and the doctor/vacation romance—that Atwood calls an anti-thriller (Draine 379), *Bodily*

Harm is, on one level, also an anti-comedy like *The Edible Woman*. Rather than resolving the action through marriage of the wrong people (Gibson 20–21), however, *Bodily Harm* begins with marriage, in this case a profoundly ironic marriage to death. Despite its deconstructed romance form, *Bodily Harm* is sometimes mistaken for novelistic realism (Kolodny 97, 100). Like *The Handmaid's Tale*, it is paradoxically grounded in "demonstrable realities" and recounts actual events: in this case pornography depicted in the Canadian Film Board documentary *This Is Not a Love Story* and a failed revolution on a Caribbean island Atwood visited but prefers not to identify (Kolodny 96–97, Castro 222). After reading *Bodily Harm*, readers may be afraid to face what is in their own cellars, closets, and bedrooms.

Prior to her Caribbean experience, Rennie is a camp, post-structuralist author: if not yet appropriately "dead," she is the impersonal blank, "replaceable by something else" (Clayton and Rothstein discussing Barthes and Foucault 4), that contemporary critical theory seems to approve.[8] Atwood admits Rennie could be the writer of the novel, *Bodily Harm* (1983 National Women's Studies Association Workshop, cited in McCombs, "Fictive" 88). If, as Kristeva suggests, "the creator" "is not an individual . . . , not an identity," but "the one who produces a text by placing himself or herself at the intersection of this plurality of texts" on their semantic, syntactic, or phonic levels, creative subjectivity is a "kaleidoscope." "On the basis of this anonymity, this zero where the author is situated, the *he/she* of the character is born" (Waller interview 281, *Desire* 75).

If we apply Kristeva's theory more literally than she might to Rennie's narrative, we could call Rennie's uncommitted life-style journalism the art of the faceless stranger. For Rennie's similarly escapist readers, such "faceless" writing falls into an existential void not only of Platonic substance but also of authorial and reader presence. The Toronto art world of *Bodily Harm*, also represented by *nouveau wavé* Jocasta, is as comic as Atwood's other parodies of current "trends" both in the arts (the Royal

Porcupine's "con-create" freezer art) and in criticism of them (Charna's catalogue comments in *CE*).[9] With the possible exception of *The Handmaid's Tale*, however, *Bodily Harm*'s authorial, reader/critic, and literary parody has a darker side than in any other novel. Rennie's colonialist discussion of what she eats in the Sunset Inn and what people wear on St. Antoine's streets could, for hundreds or thousands of people, constitute "the Caribbean." Similarly, writing flip articles on such topics as boredom for the ironically named *Visor, Crusoe,* and *Pandora* magazines, Rennie assumes the passive females and active males of Berger's warning *Bodily Harm* epigraph and thereby perpetuates rather than challenges a view supported in some versions of fairy tales and myths: "A man's presence suggests what he is capable of doing to you or for you. By contrast, a woman's presence . . . defines what can and cannot be done to her" (*Ways of Seeing*). *Bodily Harm* self-consciously foregrounds the irresponsibility of Rennie's authorship and innocuous "pieces" in its own internal parodies: "What To Do If the Thief Visits You" and Madame Marvelous's "Problem Corner" in *The Queenstown Times* (23–24, 126).

In *Bodily Harm*'s satiric pluralism of texts and intertexts, pictures of a calendar sunset, a rat in a vagina, a judge in *Pandora*'s "Woman of Achievement Series," the gallows of the prison (ironically named Fort Industry) where Rennie and Lora are incarcerated,[10] a winking sun in *Leisure* magazine, an "exposed" brown-skinned woman on a Heather Cooper poster, and a tourist brochure's woman in a modesty-paneled bathing suit (65) exist side by side with "Rex Morgan" comic strips, Dell mysteries, the game of Clue, and Rennie's "mental films" or superficial "camera vision" (see Wilson, "Turning" 136–45). Refracted by the Grimms' fairy tales and, as we shall see, by myth and *Oedipus Rex*, these interacting postmodern texts structure the larger postcolonial text that Rennie writes and we read.

Of course, we, like the novel's characters, are "under no obligation to see" (166) or to reflect on a pluralistic void. Despite a common "marriage to death," "few can read" what matters on

St. Antoine or anywhere else in Atwood's world: until the Robber Bride speaks, few can read the Robber Bridegroom's hidden
text. Prior to the "massive involvement" that eventually turns
Rennie into the subversive writer of the book we read, Rennie's
life, her unvalidating notebook, and the eyes of the sun-glassed
men (Paul, Marsden, Ellis's minister of justice and his body
guards) responsible for deaths in Ste. Agathe's short-lived revolution resemble the *nouveau wavé* book, *Death by Washing Machine*,
after page 63. Despite subground conditioning and motives reek-
ing of "authorial" intention, they all look "blank" (232, 117, 239).
Like the never seen but omnipresent dictator Ellis and the absent
Paul, who simply disappears from the book after performing as
"the connection," Rennie thinks of herself as invisible (Motifs
J2337, D1980).

Although Daniel suggests after Rennie's mastectomy that she
should think of her life as a clean page and write whatever she
likes, Rennie and her life are, of course, already partly inscribed,
despite her admission of emptiness ("empty" is not the same as
"clean" 79–80), her frequent wearing of Diana white, and her
repudiation of her small town Ontario background. She even
complains to Jake about his doodling inscription of her (96; see
Irvine's somewhat different discussion of male inscription,
Sub/version 50–53). Despite the narcissistic absence of self (Wilson, "Fragmented" 50–85) implied in Rennie's looking at herself
from the outside—through the male gaze—at her body under
glass during the mastectomy, and at others through reflecting
sunglasses, *she* is reflected in what she sees or reads, including
others' efforts at nonimpingement: their reflecting sunglasses. In
addition to mocking the absent author of both formalism and
poststructuralism, Robbe-Grillet's zero narrator, and the "faceless stranger" of the news and of Rennie's, Atwood's, Berger's,
and our own fictions, *Bodily Harm* deconstructs the absent reader: "he" and "they" are also "I." As in the art gallery cheese and
grapes of *Cat's Eye*, the taste of death—a major "Robber Bride-

groom" motif—is omnipresent. *Bodily Harm* may thus (unintentionally?) deconstruct borders between author, narrator, reader, text, and intertext.

Atwood ridicules the concept of the dead or missing author: "I think I am a writer, not a sort of *tabula rasa* for the Zeitgeist or a non-existent generator of 'texts'" ("If You Can't Say Something Nice" 22–23). Nevertheless, she is uncomfortable with simplistic autobiographical readings of her works and prefers to "cover" both author and authorial "intent" (signified with a paper bag in Michael Rubbo's autobiographical film, *Margaret Atwood: Once in August*). While she stops short of Beckett's "Crritic!" as the final insult (*Waiting for Godot* 48), she jokes about kicking deconstructionists and seems to repudiate poststructural readings of literary criticism as texts among other texts, that is, as a variety of, or of the same status of, literature (Conversation 1991). Ironically, it is her own literary criticism that not only establishes a Canadian literary tradition (*Surv*) but also speaks movingly about the writer's moral responsibility and the opportunity books give us "to review, to re-view what's being presented": "I've implied that the writer functions in his or her society as a kind of soothsayer, a truth teller; that writing is not mere self-expression but a view of society and the world at large, and that the novel is a moral instrument. *Moral* implies political. . . . By "political" I mean having to do with power: who's got it, who wants it, how it operates" (*SW* 357, 353).

We may be more aware of Atwood's soothsaying voice (Motif D1712) in her recent work, such as *The Handmaid's Tale* (1985) and "Three Chronicles" (1990). Although a number of critics have stated that 1981, the year both *Bodily Harm* and *True Stories* were published, marks a turning point (see Rigney 103; Patton, "Tourists" 151), however, Atwood's moral commitment does not begin with *Bodily Harm*. Like *You Are Happy*'s Circe and many of Atwood's other poetry or fiction artists, Rennie does not remain faceless.[11] By "spying" as the Robber Bride does and telling her multileveled story (the one Minnow, the Deaf and Dumb Man, and Lora want her to tell and the one we read), Rennie, too, becomes a soothsayer speaking for the voiceless.

However, Rennie also resembles the Grimms' Robber Bride, first in disregarding her instincts against following "the path"[12] and later, after seeing and hearing the Robber Bridegroom's text, in initially "remain[ing] still and . . . not utter[ing] a word" (Zipes, *Complete* 156). For much of the book Rennie is the kind of escapist reader targeted in *Lady Oracle*, this time of several subspecies of the romance genre including "the ultimate male writing": the voyeuristically dismembering and devouring genre of detective fiction (Patton, "Tourists" 169) parodied in *Bodily Harm*'s deliberately complicated and unsolved or unresolved mysteries.[13] Ironically, as Patton suggests, if Rennie had not been "bookless" on the plane (she finishes the thriller purchased in the Toronto airport before she reaches her "destination") and so undefended against conversation with Dr. Minnow, she might never have become involved in Caribbean politics and might have avoided jail ("Tourists" 162). Rennie reads murder mysteries on the night of Ste. Agathe's first election since the end of British colonial rule. Even in prison she wishes for a book and tries to shield herself from reality, paradoxically in this case the *story* of Lora's rape, by recasting it as media entertainment (Wilson, "Turning" 142–43). As a voracious reader of stories littered with female bodies, Rennie is again both Robber and Robber Bride.

In order to subvert both the thriller and travel romance form as well as Rennie's method of reading (predicting the murdered victim, guessing the killer, and skipping to the end to discover "the truth"), Atwood obfuscates narration, genre, settings, characterization (Irvine, *Sub/version* 40), structure, and plot. She denies possible expected endings or even a resolved ending (Rennie's rape, murder, or marriage) while offering two alternate future-tense conclusions (see Atwood's comparison to nineteenth-century double endings in Castro's interview 320–21). Engaging the reader in a narrative game of Clue while Rennie reads clues to her own involvement as murderer, victim, and detective, Rennie's retrospective, unreliable narration has caused more than one reader to misread details of plot or structure as Rennie initially misreads her life.[14]

The name of Rennie's friend Jocasta helps us recognize the comic *Oedipus Rex* intertext that not only carries tragic "Robber Bridegroom" themes but also foregrounds Rennie's insufficient "reading" ability. In addition to providing the basis of Freud's Oedipus complex, *Oedipus Rex* is based on myth explaining the Triple Goddess's suppression (Graves, *Greek II* 13). In the play, Jocasta is symbolically married to death from the moment she gives birth to the son she will marry. In *Bodily Harm* Jocasta is an incestuous mother only of lame *nouveau wave'* trends. Like Lora always on the move, she embraces trends when, in changed form, they return to her. Thus, as "oracle" of the future and Rennie's braver alter ego, she is also a likeable Tiresias, the physically blind prophet of Sophocles' play. She even recommends the gender-shifting experience Tiresias embodies (140–41; Motif D513.1): based on the seven years Tiresias is supposed to have spent as a harlot, he judged that women experience more sexual pleasure than men (Graves, *The Greek Myths: II* 11).

Rennie plays Oedipus, Creon, and Tiresias roles. As a blind detective, naively obtuse but convinced of her own cleverness in solving riddles, Rennie is a parodic Oedipus in danger of being devoured, and not by the Sphinx (Motifs H541.1.1, H761, B51; Plate 15). She is even an "oracle" in her job. Although editors think she sees into the future, she tells them, "I see into the present, that's all. Surfaces" (29). In order to become a genuine Tiresias figure, the soothsayer who speaks against "bodily harm" rather than either the raped and murdered victim or the evil murderer her reading seems to predict, Rennie reads clues and tries to detect the "author" of the crime: her cancer, the book's many robberies, the rape and selling of females and the third world, Minnow's death, Lora and the Deaf and Dumb Man's beatings, world imperialism and corruption, and all the book's other "bodily harm" and betrayals. Before the "break in," the break into her consciousness, Rennie, like Oedipus, symbolically blinds herself so that she will not see what she begins to know about herself and her "Toronto-chic" life (Motif J2412.2; Davey, "Life" 29; Smith 258).

Also like Oedipus, Rennie was symbolically maimed in child-hood. Her grandmother, who eventually "loses" her own hands, never lost her temper but locked Rennie in the cellar with un-clean, crawling things. Accustomed to being silenced and con-trolled, Rennie, too, hides her misgivings (shuts them in the "cellar")—in her case about such matters as Jake's sexual bond-age games, the pornography exhibit, her frivolity compared to the happy, successful judge she interviews, the possibility of being responsible for her own cancer—behind a precarious pride so that she will be able to continue her life. Rejected as well as abandoned by her father (Motifs S321, S301) and remembering her grandfather mostly for cutting holes in women's stomachs and amputating men's legs (53–56), Rennie even becomes, in a sense, "incestuous," particularly with Daniel and the older Paul. She wants a strong male to "father" or passively protect and take care of her.

Like Creon, Rennie even "banishes" the person her Griswold subground identifies as the culprit: herself, first from Griswold and then from the scene of the first break-in. If the exact loca-tion, weapon, victim, and crime seem unclear because of the book's surrealistic spaces and times and doubled imagery, events, and characters (Irvine, *Sub/version* 44–45, Rubenstein "Pandora's Box" 263–64), the novel's clues still lead to everyone's complicity in a continuing crime. Paradoxically, Rennie's Griswold training has its uses. She knows how to read events in terms of the narrow Griswold version of the biblical fall: one gets what he or she deserves. Everyone is, therefore, guilty (a murderer) and is pun-ished (murdered). Unlike the English woman at the Sunset Inn, however, both Rennie and the reader are denied the Griswold gossip detective's malicious joy of discovering and reporting.

The biblical story of the fall is, like the fisher king and *Oedipus Rex* interstories, intertwined with several levels of "The Robber Bridegroom," "The Girl Without Hands," and Pandora intertexts. Reversing the pattern of fisher king legend and fairy tales, Adam and Eve "fall" from innocence in paradise to knowledge and death. Although with the completion of the pattern they may return to paradise in the form of heaven, their transformation—from immortal to mortal beings in a similarly transformed setting—is, at least at this point, negative. As in so many fairy tales ("The White Snake"), myths (Demeter/Persephone), and children's books (*Alice in Wonderland*), the transformation is linked to eating, in this case the forbidden apple (Motif C621.1). In *Bodily Harm* a nameless, hidden or "underground" evil invades Rennie, the cells of her body (93), her consciousness, and her relationships—including those with Minnow, Jocasta, and Lora. In addition, evil invades other female and male bodies, Ste. Agathe's political coalition, and the novel's real and remembered settings: Rennie's apartment, the Toronto art world, Paul's garden, an abandoned coconut plantation, Lora's childhood (cellar) apartment, the twin Caribbean islands of Ste. Agathe and St. Antoine, Ste. Agathe's dock where Rennie and Lora hide, the prison where they are jailed, Rennie's room at the Sunset Inn, the cellar of her grandmother's Griswold house.

This cancer or cannibalism is symbolically suggested by rats (in vaginas, in Lora's apartment, in the prison), maggots, fleas and other insects, crabs and snails, and by the motifs of nibbled flesh (Lora's fingers, Rennie's mastectomy), massive involvement, and something or someone "out of control" (cell division, the revolution, the government, the prison) (see, for example, 78, 160, 80, 225, 151). Since Atwood's motifs characteristically begin to reverse as her narrators regain amputated senses, in *Bodily Harm* self-birth, growth, and flying overtake disease, death, and the fall as, at least mentally, Rennie moves "out of control" to report what is under the surface.

In terms of the biblical intertext, *Bodily Harm* tantalizes readers with thriller forewarnings and premonitions of evil and death in "paradise," giving ordinary details of setting a partly parodic charge. Images of hell, the underworld, mortality, death, and the Garden of Eden's snake (Motifs A63.6, G303.3.3.6.1) quickly replace stereotypical images of humdrum Toronto and the Caribbean as paradise. Descending and crossing over, as her name suggests (Carrington, "Another" 61–62), Rennata (Rennie) enters an underworld where dead people elect the government, the head of the government is invisible, and the Minister of Justice dresses like an undertaker (199, 203). In *Snake Poems*, snake imagery connotes goddess power and shamanistic vision rather than biblical sin or evil, and Oedipus myth links Tiresias' oracular powers to snakes (Graves, *Greek Myths: II* 10–11). The snake in *Bodily Harm* (Rubenstein, "Pandora's Box" 261), however, is a phallic coiled-snake rope. The first clue the police, Rennie, and reader-detectives discover, the rope on Rennie's bed warns of bondage, invasion, possible dismemberment and cannibalism, and, ironically, of the massive involvement that readers as well as Rennie encounter in tying seemingly separate events and narrative strands together.

"Rope Quartet" was an early title for the book that became *Bodily Harm* (Atwood Papers, Boxes 33–35). Although Atwood cut at least one passage dealing with rope, there are still fifteen or so references to ropes and people, objects, or activities associated with rope, including the man with the rope and his doubles, the rope, the coil, tying, binding, strangling, and hanging.[15]

Playing against the biblical fall and the disease and mortality it brings, "ropes" in *Bodily Harm* usually suggest the evil of "bodily harm." After Rennie's plane "falls" and lands, "the heat slips over her face like thick brown velvet." Although she thinks she is escaping not only the man who left a coiled rope on the bed of her Toronto apartment but also the breast cancer that ties her to a dying body, her Sunset Inn room contains another coiled signifier. Close to a picture of a cut-open melon and a lamp featuring a mermaid with exposed breasts (see Wilson, "Turning" 141) and next to the Bible by her bed, Rennie finds a mosquito "coil" from the Blood Protection Company (37, 47). Since she ironically overcompensates for learned Griswold prudery by metaphorically sleeping with the Robber or death throughout the book—sometimes confusing symbolic rape with love—her descriptions of the coiled rope, coil, and other ropes are ominous and surrealistic.

If the island country of St. Antoine and Ste. Agathe is a parodic Eden, "bush garden," and Gethsemane, then Rennie is its parodic Eve / Pandora and Robber Bride / Girl Without Hands. Jake, Daniel, and Paul share roles as ironic Adam, Robber, and Devil-father, and Paul and Marsden, especially, as coiled snake and Judas (222). Right before Marsden stops Rennie and Lora from leaving Ste. Agathe, Paul (possibly covering his own tracks before heading south) accuses Marsden of being the new CIA agent. Lora even approximates a "hiss" (227). Although we never know for sure who the agent is and who kills Minnow, evil and betrayal permeate all the book's settings, including hypocritical Griswold with its punishing cellars.

Usually Rennie associates both rope and coil, like the mosquito netting that guards against being bitten in bed on the islands, with the bed and sex. After seeing Keith's bound women pieces and film clips of strangled and abused women in the police pornography collection, Rennie has trouble with Jake's holding her so she can't move during sex (185–88). Several times after the Toronto "break-in," including once in Paul's bed (Lora, too, finds this experience "like being with someone who wasn't there," 191), Rennie dreams that the man with the rope is in bed with her. After the Sunset Inn break-in she wants "A warm body, she doesn't much care whose" (42, 193–94, 143). Ironically, Rennie parodies the policeman's presentation of pornography, including the kind of strangled women Rennie reads about on Paul's bed, as entertainment for "normal" (heterosexual) people.[16] She does so by indirectly contrasting the book we read with her earlier stories. Once, Rennie would have served the man with the rope as an entertaining lunch story: "She would have told it at lunch, with the strawberry flan. . . . [but] the story had no end, it was open-ended. . . . And when you pulled on the rope, which after all reached down into darkness, what could come up? What was the end, *the end?* A hand, then an arm, a shoulder, and finally a face. At the end of the rope there was someone. Everyone had a face, there was no such thing as a faceless stranger" (41–42). The rope reaches down into darkness, suggesting the folk motif of the rope to the lower world (F96).

At the end of this rope, however, is a hand. In addition to suggesting the presence of evil, ropes in *Bodily Harm*, like the character Paul, symbolize connection and signification. Although for most of the book this connection is "someone's twisted idea of love" (42) rather than genuine love, touch, and communication, the motif suggests how all of Rennie's experiences, all of the settings and the separate pieces of narrative, eventually braid into the "rope" of narrative Rennie throws to us. Since ropes in *Bodily Harm* are not intrinsically evil, hands used either like binding or saving rope focus the book's opposition between Robbers and Lovers. If any one strand is followed to its terminus, we find hands, either of the Robber/Devil-father—the many-faced person with the rope who does evil (imperialistically controls, beats, rapes, tortures, amputates, or "eats") because it is possible—or the lover: the one who gives, who pulls the other to safety, through instead of down. Ironically characteristic of Atwood's postcolonialist vision, the lover can be a wiser ex-Robber.

In keeping with *Bodily Harm*'s "Robber Bridegroom," "Fitcher's Bird," and "The Girl Without Hands" intertexts is another implicit "murder" of the Grimms', Perrault's, and especially Walt Disney's "Cinderella" story. As we have begun to see, on the sexual-political level of the six-dimensional Robber Bridegroom narrative, most of the men Rennie and her alter egos Lora and Jocasta encounter are in some sense robbers or betraying devil-fathers rather than princes. To *Bodily Harm*'s unreliable but developing narrator—a Rennie who has just become aware of her mortality—the male strangers in her life, with and without known faces, are comically and parodically if not seriously the ultimate Robber Bridegroom with whom she has a brief affair: Death, or in other guise, time, who will eventually "get" her (79). Understandably, after the first "bite" is taken out of her, she is frequently nauseous and uncomfortable when she recognizes that others have been "nibbled" (129, 80). In *Bodily Harm*'s nonchronological narration, Rennie's first bedroom encounter is not with a lover but with the rope the Ovaltine-drinking intruder leaves on her bed. In the "romantic" Caribbean, the fast-growing love vine strangles everything in the garden (180–81), and the island country considers chopping up women (an activity Rennie associates with cookbooks) less offensive than stealing (201). Despite Lora's story of love at first sight, Prince, of course, is neither the Prince of Peace nor a fairy-tale prince. Certainly not (except comically and parodically) the Prince of Darkness Rigney suggests (110), Prince fails to be either Lora, Rennie, or his country's rescuer in this book's enactment of the Rapunzel syndrome (see Chapter 11). Like Minnow—a potential rescuer whose icons (minnow, whale) suggest Atwood's food chain watercolor (Plate 1)—Prince is eaten by the "sharks."

In addition to the men Rennie has sex with and the actual robber or man with the rope who breaks into the false security of her existence, robbers include many doubles: the older policeman who investigates, the robber in a bathing suit, Marsden, Ellis, Prince, Lora's stepfather Bob, Lora's rapist, the prison guard Morton, and even Dr. Minnow. Although it is Rennie who is "hungry enough to eat an arm" when Minnow, "his bottom teeth clasped over the top ones like folded hands," takes her to lunch (120), his tour of St. Antoine and its prison parodically foreshadows and even helps determine her entrapment in the Robber's "cellar."

Again parodically, however, instead of the Robber and Fitcher's successive chopped-up and eaten brides, Rennie has successive "grooms" whose amputating abilities, like her own, threaten their societies. Each of the men Rennie has sexual relationships with and several other characters (male and female) still use touch (hands) to control, like a rope that ties one in place. Sometimes comically, each also "amputates" or "eats" her. But Atwood repudiates the male bashing both fans and foes gratuitously assume in her work: *Bodily Harm*'s Robber Bridegroom intertext is not a simplistic equation of men with the bodily harm of the novel's title. Still, if no one, female or male, is exempt from the cancer with which humanity is invaded, it is already apparent that one level of symbolism deals with the evils of what "he" and the patriarchy or androcracy do with what Eisler calls "the blade": rape, war, guns. Although not linked either to "The Robber Bridegroom" or "The Girl Without Hands" intertext, other discussions of *Bodily Harm*'s sexual politics and hand imagery (see especially Irvine, *Sub/version* 39–53; Rubenstein, "Pandora's Box" 259–75) also make brief treatment of the Robber/father's amputating hands possible here.

If there is a parodic Prince Charming in *Bodily Harm*, he is obviously Jake, all surface and style without any depth. Few readers would argue his already apparent Robber/"Devil" qualities. Resembling *Interlunar*'s artful Robber, Jake has long canine teeth (21) and is expert at designing attractive packages and "layouts" for consuming Rennie. From his point of view, women exist as objects, such as warm wet washcloths, to be arranged for his convenience and pleasure; if Rennie's body is not available, he is entitled to a substitute (180). In Rennie's mind, Jake's "lovemaking" blurs with scenes and implements of paradigmatic female bondage: footage of bound or strangled women in the pornography collection, whips, Keith's sculpture of chained women, Lora's story about a man who wants to tie her to a bedpost, and pornographic "snuff films."

Since Jake uses his hands as a binding rope, symbolically removing Rennie's hands, his actions, along with the poster he picks for Rennie's Toronto apartment, epitomize the sexual-political crimes of the Grimms' "The Girl Without Hands": "Jake liked to pin her hands down . . . to hold her so that she couldn't move" (185–86). In Rennie's bedroom Jake hung "a Heather Cooper poster, a brown-skinned woman wound up in a piece of material that held her arms to her sides but left her breasts and thighs and buttocks exposed. She had no expression on her face." Like the Girl Without Hands, the bound woman is upright, physically able to move but in her case unaware that she might walk away from her conditioned bondage.

The poster's ironic title, "Enigma" (97), even reminds us of the "enigma" some critics find in the Grimms' "The Girl Without Hands" (Chapter 6). Like Rennie, *Lady Oracle*'s Joan, and the woman on *Power Politics*' cover, this "triply" bound woman (Trinh 6) still wears the "red shoes." Even before Rennie is able to make connections, she recognizes one facet: "Being in love was like running barefoot along a street covered with broken bottles" (94). Rennie associates this poster with Keith's pornographic tables and chairs featuring bound women locked into degrading positions: "The women were dressed in half cup bras and G-string panties, set on their hands and knees for the tables, locked into a sitting position for the chairs. One of the chairs was a woman on her knees, her back arched, her wrists tied to her thighs. The ropes and arms were the arms of the chair, her bum was the seat" (185).

In "The Girl Without Hands," after the incestuous father sells his daughter to the devil, he cuts off her hands and sometimes her breasts. Far from being simply an altruistic healer or a source of compassion in the book (Carrington, "Another" 61), Daniel resembles Jake in amputating and using Rennie. As Rennie's surgeon, Daniel is, in a sense, an abusive "father": he consciously abuses the trust of a privileged relationship in which Rennie feels like a "child" hoping to earn "a gold star." Even though he knows patients in Rennie's circumstances are prone to low self-esteem, he violates his oath by having sex with her (211). Although Daniel uses his "healing hands" (Motif D1503.9) to save Rennie's life and to comfort her after her partial mastectomy, the same hands literally amputate part of her breast and the person under it, just as Prince's grandmother Elva uses her "magic hands" (Motif D996) to carry the box with the machine gun. Parodically, Daniel is even a cannibalizing Robber who frequently takes her to lunch, but he doesn't want "to be stuck with the whole package. She might be the icing on his cake but she sure as hell [isn't] the cake." Rennie imagines a "lineup," "a harem" of Daniel's patients, "each with a bite taken out of them, one breast or the other" (139, 129). However, Daniel is not really a "devil." Like *Lady Oracle*'s Joan Foster, Rennie learns that people don't fit neatly into the Gothic romance categories she and Jocasta enjoy nailing them into; she resents Paul's playing a similar game with her, pronouncing her "nice" after he realizes her genuine need for companionship.

Paul supposedly "deals" with the devil (191). If he is not "a buffet casserole or a spare room" Lora has the right to give away (162), he is, like Lora and ironically Rennie, still "for sale," apparently providing guns, including the gun that kills Minnow, to anyone who asks. However, unlike amputating Jake, whom Rennie thinks is afraid of her because she has "the kiss of death on her, you c[an] see the marks," Paul ironically helps Rennie recover touch. He does not look away from her mastectomy, "the missing piece, the place where death kissed her lightly, a preliminary kiss." Although death seems to be as real to Paul as life and he cannot stay in the present, paradoxically, momentarily, he still achieves, and gives, the gift of loving rather than robbing touch. Like the protagonists of all the novels, Rennie realizes that "This much will have to do, this much is enough . . . . she's solid after all, she's still here on the earth, she's grateful, he's touching her, she can still be touched" (179, 181–82).

In terms of *Bodily Harm*'s sexual politics, Rennie is "afraid of men and it's simple, it's rational, she's afraid of men because men are frightening" (256). Significantly, however, she says this when she sees a man victimized and recognizes her own culpability for the system. Not just females are victimized by men, and the patriarchy is partly supported by women. "There's no longer a *here* and a *there*" (256): as *The Handmaid's Tale* literalizes in the "particicution," she, too, holds the rope.

The evil of the coiled rope and Robber or devil-father's amputating or colonizing hand is not confined to sexual politics. Without noting "The Girl Without Hands" intertext, a number of critics have commented on Rennie's "symbolic handlessness" and "the emblematic episode of the severing of hand contact": her grandmother's "prying [her] hands away finger by finger" (Lucking 81–82). Having learned silence and the ability to look without touching, Rennie resembles *Life Before Man*'s Elizabeth in going through life with folded hands, culminating in Rennie's initial inability to find her hands with Lora (*BH* 210, 253). Some scenes in *Bodily Harm* remind us of the Amnesty International reports so familiar to Atwood. Black and brown people, men as well as women, political suspects and prisoners are all tied with ropes. In one instance, while pairs of women suspects have their hands tied behind their backs, men are tied together in bundles of three or four and stacked like cargo in the hold of a ship (237).

The backgrounds of Atwood's scenes can be overlooked only at the reader's peril (Wilson, "Turning" 138–41). Referring also to a man's "ropy arm" helping Rennie into the boat and a boat with "looped ropes thick as a wrist," Lucking notes another historical use of ropes: the gallows (85, 89) Rennie looks at but does not see, first as a tourist and then outside her and Lora's cell window. Readers, too, sometimes overlook the ironic language of this scene: "Rennie opens her eyes. She fails to see the point, but it's something to do. . . . 'There's nothing to see,' she says when she's back down" (241). Later, after dreaming that the man with the rope's eyes "twin and reflect her own," she sees the victimizer's face in her own. Rennie breaks through into a different dimension of consciousness as, from the same window, she sees the archetypal face of the victim. She witnesses apparently breastless figures endure a hair-cutting "ceremony" more physically brutal than the traditional one for Jewish brides: the deaf and dumb man, tied to other prisoners with rope, is sliced with a bayonet, kicked, and tortured with a cattle prod. "The deaf and dumb man, who has a voice but no words . . . wants her to do something, pleading, *Oh please*" (254–56).

Like the coiled rope and other means of death, bondage, and torture, the gallows and marriage to death are at the other end of the motif *Oh please* and in the background of everything Rennie reports throughout the book. Rennie recognizes that she, like most of the book's other characters, is not only Robber Bride but also Robber. Even if she doesn't directly kill, she, too, has exploited others' rights to their own lives, values, or taste; silence about "raw material" supports colonization.

In the much-discussed prison scene after Lora has been beaten, Rennie regains her hands (Motif E782.1). Like Fitcher's third bride who puts the dismembered pieces of her sisters back together and magically revivifies them, Rennie pulls Lora, and her own reborn self, "through" with a saving "rope." Despite her and all human beings' marriage to death, she symbolically gives birth: "she's gritting her teeth with the effort, she can hear herself, a moaning, it must be her own voice, this is a gift, this is the hardest thing she's ever done. She holds the hand, perfectly still, with all her strength. Surely, if she can only try hard enough, something will move and live again, something will get born" (263–64). Rennie passes on the gift of loving or healing touch to Lora, and "magically," by extension, to the "handless" grandmother she could never before touch. By acting to help another, as her mother and Elva had, she also symbolically "clasps hands" with the duty-bound, red-knuckled mother she, like her father, once escaped. In addition, she links hands with the breastless women in Daniel's "lineup" and with all women, with the deaf and dumb man who once blessed her with his touch, and with all "lovers" and saviors rather than Robbers or killers. As Atwood's "Five Poems for Grandmothers" and both title and content of Irvine's *Two-Headed Poems* discussion indicate,[17] "one woman leads to another" and, I might add, to the other.

By extending her own "good-fairy" hand (95–96, see also Rubenstein, "Pandora's Box" 265), Rennie symbolically collapses time to transform her grandmother from the once-menacing and then impotent witch in her mind into the no longer frightening godmother or goddess of her earlier dream. Sequentially following Lora's "Hansel and Gretel" newspaper story and parallel childhood memories, Rennie's dream "told" her that her mastectomy was not her only amputation. "Bound" in the bedsheet when she partly awoke, wearing a white gown tied in the back, Rennie searched for her hands in bureau drawers. As the narrators of *Surfacing, Lady Oracle, Life Before Man,* and *Cat's Eye* must do with their "framed" images of gods or monsters, she lets the past go so that she will not be "stranded" without hands either there or in "the future." Both past and future are now present: in a scene recalling the narrator's vision of her mother in *Surfacing,* "[Rennie's] grandmother smiles at her, the hummingbirds are around her head, lighting on her hands. Life everlasting, she says" (263–64, 106).

Finally, in addition to being Robber Bride, Robber, and Girl Without Hands, Rennie is also both patriarchal and original matriarchal versions of Pandora. Sometimes usefully discussed (Rubenstein, "Pandora's Box" 266, 274; Irvine, *Sub/version* 43), the Pandora myth has unrecognized significance as an intertext in *Bodily Harm,* particularly when Pandora's "first woman" connection to Eve and other goddess figures is explored. Like Eve, Pandora is sometimes seen as a temptress (Motif F34) and has been traditionally blamed for all human ills, including disease (Motif A1337.0.1.1) (Leach and Fried 1152, 843). In best-known patriarchal versions of the story, Pandora was given a box or jar containing all the evils that can trouble humanity. Although she was told not to open it, she was curious and did so and the evils spread over the earth. The box contained one good, however: hope (Kaster 128). The box Rennie carries, stored under her bed and later in Paul's bedroom closet, is paradoxically not only a metaphor for the vagina and womb and all the book's literally and symbolically invaded inner spaces but also the kind of phallic rather than matriarchal "snake" closely linked to the man with a rope and his break-ins. Rennie is afraid to touch the box and worries that it might hatch (155). In a sense, it does, breaking the thin shell separating "life-tourist" Rennie from real experience so that she can be "reborn" (Wilson, "Turning" 144–45; see also Page's poem, "The Permanent Tourists" 186–87).

If we supply motives in the nightmare, the literal and symbolic box is the reason the robber breaks into Rennie's bedroom, both in Toronto and at the Sunset Inn, and a major reason that she is arrested on the fairy-tale seventh day of her stay. By extension, Atwood implies, all women, innately possessors of "the box," ironically resemble Kafka's Joseph K. in being under "suspicion," "on trial" in their and others' eyes—in Rennie's case, the dissecting gaze of Marsden and other men—and therefore guilty without knowing why (*The Trial*). Traditional interpretation of archetypal feminine symbolism, including the mouth, the breasts, and the womb, suggests why, revealing an unconscious basis in male sexual frustrations, fear, and envy: "as container, [the Feminine] also holds fast and takes back" (Neumann 45). As Dworkin suggests, "that slit which means entry into her— intercourse—[and/or human beings' associations with it] appears to be the key to women's lower human status. . . .She is defined by how she is made" (*Intercourse* 123).

Literally, Pandora is the all endowed, with one quality from each of the gods, or all-giver, like the earth-goddess Rhea, made out of the earth in the underworld. Like Persephone, in matriarchal myth Pandora is an underworld goddess associated with Hecate and Ge, the earth mother, sometimes called Pandora (Walker, *The Woman's Encyclopedia* 767–68). Pandora's box was originally a honey vase or jar symbolizing the womb and used as a vessel of death and rebirth. Thus, contrary to what many believe, the womb-box traditionally contains the blessings and benefits of humankind. A number of folk motifs associate a box with the moon, magic, underground kingdoms, love, and even money (*The Woman's Encyclopedia* 767; Thompson, *Motif* v 6, 91).

In Hesiod's misogynistic version of the story, however, Pandora, in herself part of the gift from the gods, has become "a deathly vessel of the Feminine" designed to enact revenge upon "mankind" (Leach and Fried 843; Walker, *The Woman's Encyclopedia* 767–68; Neumann 172). Thus, from this point of view, Pandora's box suggests another myth and folktale motif apparently rooted in male fear or envy: the castrating toothed vagina (vagina dentata, F547.1) found in North American native, Chaco, and Guiana tales, in male dreams, and in Jung's archetype of the Great Mother. "The hero is the man who overcomes the Terrible Mother, breaks the teeth out of her vagina, and so makes her into a woman" (Leach and Fried 1152, Neumann 168–69).

Ironically, although vagina dentata tales may suggest a reversed-gendered "Robber Bridegroom," still with cannibalism and sexual-political themes but with female victimizer and male victim, they also remind us of the rat no woman would put into her own vagina[18] and of the tendency to view goddess iconography "through the lens of 20th century bias" ignorant of its religious and social context (Gimbutas, *Civilization* 223).

As in patriarchal versions of the Pandora myth, the womb in *Bodily Harm* anticipates the womb in *The Handmaid's Tale*: it is "packaged." Pandora's box no longer belongs to Pandora: it is the property of a faceless stranger who, in this case, uses more than one woman to deliver it. Ironically, the box returns to "poison" both owner and carriers. Thus, as in Hesiod's "anti-feminist" version, it contains a curse (Walker, *The Woman's Encyclopedia* 767). Again ironically, in *Bodily Harm* even the healing hands of the grandmothers (the matriarchy) now carry the means of destruction and betrayal (the machine gun). Guns supplied by the American "connection," Paul, presumably for a coup d'état, not only keep the current dictator in power: they kill his opposition (Minnow, Prince). Dr. Minnow jokes that one can't eat culture; but disguised as food, the box facilitates Robber-Baron cannibalism of the island (118). In terms of the Pandora version most people know, Rennie brings on her own and others' undoing not only by touching but by looking into the forbidden box (Motifs C533, C321), apparently especially damaging actions when a woman performs them (Motif H1557.4).

Again, however, Atwood remythifies and heals amputations, not only those of Rennie and the book's other characters but also those of the novel's male and female readers, of myth, of fairy tales, and of all women. Ironically, Rennie's error really is in not opening the box and her eyes sooner, in remaining passive under a colonizing gaze and touch and depending upon "the phallic opening power of the male" (Neumann 170) to disclose even her own inner spaces, her own "forbidden room." For example, she is fascinated with Daniel's secret knowledge of what is under her surface, but even she is annoyed with her "fluffiness" and irritated to be "seen through" as she quietly listens to Paul tell her who she is (74, 76, 135–36). As other motifs are reversed, however, Rennie shifts from being "opened" to actively opening. Like Fitcher's brides and Pandora, who do the forbidden, Rennie does open the box and finally does open the forbidden door: into Paul's extra bedroom, where the box is hidden (196), and into her own "underworld," "earth-womb" or "goddess" power associated with both door and regeneration (see Neumann 170, Walker, *Woman's Encyclopedia* 156). In discovering the Robber's identity and choosing to be a lover rather than a robber, Rennie is reborn, not as a goddess but as a human being. As in some versions of the myth, hope, the possibility for her world's rebirth, remains.

Throughout the book Rennie literally is missing part of a breast: not only her ability to "feed" (sustain, nourish, comfort) another but also the regenerative power once associated with the sometimes multibreasted source of nourishment—milk/rain—or Giver of Life in general (Gimbutas, *Language* 31–33, *Civilization* 222), and, in human rather than superhuman terms, necessary for Rennie and other characters' psychic health. Like other goddess attributes, including the womb, breast symbolism is too frequently subjected to the same kind of disparagement as are women and parts of their bodies: as objects of both external and internalized gaze,[19] breasts are, thereby, stripped of natural, historical, religious, and personal meanings. Viewed as a burden or trap, part of a heavy "feminine" package one might need to lose in order to be taken seriously or, paradoxically, to be a full human being (a man), such externally defined breasts are part of the antiquated dualism entrapping not only Atwood's characters but all human beings. Structuralists caught by our inability to see and account for our own standpoints, most of us (including feminist theorists) can talk about patriarchal conditioning without recognizing how much what we see is still distorted by it. Not just worn like clothing to be displayed or, as Jake advises, flaunted, breasts are part of the body Atwood's artists sometimes have difficulty accepting. Much as Atwood's *Cave Series* deals with both physical and mythological womb (31; other poems in *Interlunar* drafts, Atwood Papers), to the extent that Rennie's body *is* metonymically *Bodily Harm*'s landscape, the twin islands she initially visits as a tourist may even be seen as her breasts, and those of a personified, no longer sacred Mother Earth.

Symbolically, Rennie also lacks other body parts closely related to senses (touch, vision, speech, hearing, even smell and taste) amputated or cannibalized by "the system": family, gender, national, patriarchal, and Western colonialist conditioning. If she can't literally become whole, like St. Agatha (Goodwin 114), Rennie can symbolically regain her breast and *Bodily Harm*'s four other most important parts of the body: her mouth, hands, heart, and womb. She can learn to love and respect first herself and then the other, communicating this through touch and speech. Since Rennie's invaded cells, organs, and senses also represent cancer of the earth and a colonized Mother Nature (Wilson, "A Note" 115), her healing prefigures the possibility of the earth's healing.

Some readers deny Rennie's transformation, insisting she is still in jail telling the story we read to Lora and that she only dreams her release (Carrington, "Another" 52). As I have already suggested here and elsewhere ("Turning" 143–45), Atwood deliberately denies closure, especially the cliché endings of "happily ever after" and marriage as solution, in *Bodily Harm* as in other novels and many stories and poems. As in *Dancing Girls*' "Lives of the Poets," she often does so by shifting to the future tense (208–9). The manuscript drafts of *Bodily Harm* are particularly revealing, demonstrating that, in addition to the two alternate future-tense conclusions Atwood compares to nineteenth-century double endings (Castro 320–21) in the published version, Atwood actually experimented with and rejected two more resolved endings. One conclusion is similar to the published version with two very significant differences: Rennie does not connect Lora's hand to her grandmother's, so that when she is on the plane and feels a shape of a hand, she has "forgotten whose hand it is" (Atwood Papers, Early Typescript *BH*, Box 35). However, the other variant reads: "You can fly, she says . . . she's back, flat-land criss-crossed by roads, buildings foreshortened by the height, there's snow on the ground already, her shadow's on it, blue-grey, beneath her feet the scarred earth rises up to meet her" (Atwood Papers, "Rope Quartet" typed draft, Box 34).

Rather than landing or almost landing the plane, in the book Atwood uses the flying image that is associated with art, imagination, and the transcendence of growth and that will also "close" *Cat's Eye*.[20] Like *Bodily Harm*, Rennie "ends" in "the air," flying in a plane with faith in its and her ability to fly. The magical scene of holding Lora's hand and the lyrical tone of Rennie's resolve to be a subversive writer leave little doubt about her transformation or about the "magic" that can empower human beings: "She will never be rescued. She has already been rescued. She is not exempt. Instead she is lucky, suddenly, finally, she's overflowing with luck, it's this luck holding her up" (166). In order to read ourselves as well as Atwood, we must like Rennie read the subtexts—including intertexts of sometimes amputated myths and fairy tales—and make connections.

⑨

Bluebeard's Forbidden Room
in *Interlunar* and "Bluebeard's Egg"

"Fitcher's Bird," "The White Snake," and Other Tales

Like *Procedures for Underground, You Are Happy,* and *Bodily Harm,*
Interlunar (1984) is about the female artist's marriage to death,
her gradual empowerment, and by extension, the empowerment
of all artists and human beings. Major intertexts include the
Grimm's "The Robber Bridegroom," "Fitcher's Bird," "The Girl
Without Hands," and "The White Snake"; goddess and snake
myth; the Bible; and visual art. The title story of *Bluebeard's Egg,*
examined in the second part of this chapter, also embeds the
Grimms' "Fitcher's Bird" in exploring an individual's—and a
culture's—marriage to death.

Unfortunately, although Atwood was first known as a poet,
most of her poetry volumes are either out of print or were never
published in the United States, and even in Canada her recent
fiction attracts more critical attention than her recent poetry.
Since Atwood "is one of the best poets of her time" and since her
recent poetry reflects the dominant themes of all her writing,
including her literary criticism and history (Woodcock, "Metamorphosis" 266), serious readers of Atwood's work need to address her poetry. The *Selected Poems* volumes are a good place to
start, but Atwood's poetry volumes fit together into a whole that
can be altered with the omission of even a single poem. Atwood's

original book covers, generally used only in Canadian editions, also become part of the text's themes and imagery.

Irvine has commented on what she sees as *Interlunar*'s shift in tone to "the role of poetry (and the poet) in a world hovering on the brink of catastrophe" and to "poems on the edge" (Review 3). As Van Spanckeren notes, however, "Journeys or quests involving sinking into an unconscious realm run throughout Atwood's poetry, from her earliest books to her most recent, as does death as a wellspring of creativity" ("Shamanism" 189). Atwood's sensuous cover design, prepared specifically for this volume—as was Gibson's back cover photograph reflecting the salt marsh by his and Atwood's Norfolk house[1]—points the way for her characters' transformation. Reproducing the seascape watercolor Atwood is working on in the *Once in August* film, it reflects land and a red sun rather than suggesting the darkness of interlunar—the period between old and new moons. At odds with the potential or actual violence of some of the poems, the cover realizes the promise of the title poem.

As in many of Atwood's literary works, including some of *Interlunar*'s poems, the *Interlunar* cover depicts two worlds, "Reflection and Reality" (the title of Mendez-Egle's collection on Atwood): the watery underworld of the mystic or artist's unconscious and the supposed "real" world of ordinary experience. Although reflections in Atwood's work can suggest the artificial, "the doors through which death comes and goes" (Cocteau's *Orphée*), "separation of the unconscious and conscious mind, narcissistic obsession, a schizoid split, tension between subject and object, duplication or projection of the self, or other fragmentation," they can also suggest the way Atwood's texts deceptively mirror her intertexts and, as in *Lady Oracle*, even themselves. Like camera images, reflections can also be a vehicle for transformation (Wilson, "Camera" n. 51, 32), the same kind of "way out and through" as *The Circle Game*'s cover and *Interlunar*'s final poem, the latter conveying the characteristic tone of peace and trust that usually "ends" Atwood's volumes. According to Lorna

Irvine, "[*Interlunar's*] doublings, at first confusing, then paralyz-
ing, gradually become maps, reflections for the reader to follow.
Having decided for life, and the poem, the poet generously holds
out her hand to her readers, showing us the darkness we fear but
giving us the poem's instruction and delight" (Review 6).

Interlunar is divided into two sections, "Snake Poems," origi-
nally separately published in a limited edition (Salamander
Press, 1983), and "Interlunar," further divided into three parts.
Both sections use similar intertexts to present similar themes,
variously described as gender, language, and power (Irvine,
Review 2) or tenacious survival and constant metamorphosis
(Woodcock, "Metamorphosis" 266). The Grimms' "The Robber
Bridegroom" (No. 40, AT 955) and "The Girl Without Hands"
(No. 31, AT 706) and related fairy tales—"Fitcher's Bird" (No.
46, AT 311); AT 400, the search for the wife; and folk motifs
from goddess and classical myths (Orpheus-Eurydice, Persephone) and Native North American tales (Takánakaps ã luk,
Orpheo) about being married to death—form important intertexts in the second, "Interlunar" section of the combined volume. "Interlunar" again depicts cannibalized or dismembered
artist-personae (the characters and alter egos of the "I" in each
story): No Name, Orpheus, Eurydice, Persephone, the Robber
Bride (ironically), the Robber Bridegroom (in a draft of the volume), the Girl Without Hands, the nameless woman singing to
Genghis Khan, and the witch in "Harvest." The female poet-
quester and many of her characters must, like *Bodily Harm's*
Rennie and *Life Before Man's* Elizabeth, reach out to others and
nature in order to close their gaps.

Although *Snake Poems* has no explicit reference to either "The
Robber Bridegroom" or "The Girl Without Hands," it uses goddess and snake myth, the Grimms' "The White Snake" ("Die
weisse Schlange" 1812, AT 673, No. 17) and variant or similar
European folktales,[2] the Genesis story of humanity's fall, and
visual art intertext to suggest the symbolically dismembered persona's "marriage" to a kind of living death. In the "Snake Poems"

section, the empty, sick female artist, divided between an "I," a "you," and an alien-other "it," attempts to gain wholeness, wisdom, and power through dreaming, ritual eating (including taking god into her mouth) and re-membering her snake identity with native American snake gods and the Great Goddess (especially Eve/Lilith, Eurydice, Medusa or Lamia—the shape-changing Libyan snake goddess).

For *Snake Poems*' female artist, masked like some versions of Medusa, snake symbolism is as paradoxical as her and other women writers' double or triple bind as goddess/muse and "woman/native/other," a bind Atwood discusses in both essays and lectures (see Chapters 1 and 2, Juhasz 1, Trinh 6, "If You Can't Say Anything Nice" 18). In the Salamander edition the letters of *Snake Poems*' title form a snake pattern, and both the volume's structure and the narrator's attitudes toward snakes follow a serpentine motion once associated with the Great Goddess and with North American native songs invoking the snake. The snake once symbolized not only immortality and the power of life and enlightenment but specifically female power: female genitalia, "the feminine principle" (Walker, *Woman's Dictionary* 387–89; Gimbutas, *Goddesses* 145), fertility,[3] magical shape-shifting (Leach and Fried 601), and the oracular. Virtually every culture had some form of serpent mythology. This female power is illustrated in Delphyne (Gaea or Hera, the Womb of Creation), who was worshipped with her serpent-son and consort Python at Delphi's shrine of Mother Earth. Since "snake women" were literally killed by Northern Hellenes allied with Thraco-Libyans who captured the goddess's shrines,[4] the persona reads her own—by extension, all females'—speechlessness in the snake's mute and then "husk" voice.[5] In the first poem, "Snake Woman," *Snake Poems*' female poet announces her loss with the flippance signifying her and her culture's diminished sense of magic and value. She confesses that, like the Eve/Lilith/snake of *Double Persephone*'s cover, *You Are Happy*'s Circe, the snake goddesses of

Crete and Libya, Medusa, and Eurydice, she was once "a snake woman." Archetypally and parodically, she recalls not only snakes' touch and odor but also the matriarchal goddess power—and men's fear and desire to kill it—she tapped when she touched or carried snakes, sharing their identity (8). But as the volume proceeds, we discover that the killers or robbers of life, reminiscent of *Surfacing*'s "Americans" and *You Are Happy*'s Odysseus, are not all or only men.

In "Lesson on Snakes" the "I" adopts a sometimes sarcastic role as the teacher of "you" and begins the self and cultural lessons she must re-member as she proceeds on what we finally discover is a journey. Presenting "exhibits" in the detached tone that begins "A Women's Issue" (Oxford *TS* 54–55), here the persona deconstructs one of the main "lies" responsible for her and her society's marriage to death: the Judeo-Christian story about the devil in the form of a snake (Motif G303.3.3.6.1). "In Arabic, the words for 'snake,' 'life,' and 'teaching' are all related to the name of Eve—the Biblical version of the Goddess with her serpent form" (Walker, *Woman's Dictionary* 389). Thus, the "I" seems to represent the Eve/snake voice the persona has lost in patriarchy, the goddess "voice" silenced when her symbols were appropriated and converted—making the snake an icon of the (female) demonic. Thus this voice also represents dedication to life and creation. "The snake is a mute / except for the sound like steam / escaping from a radiator" and, though cause exists, cannot scream. "It's hardly / the devil in your [ordinary or Edenic] garden." Striped like a moose maple, the snake might even represent a graceful Canadian "antidote" to "mice." Even so, "you," obsessed with "what you think is your way," would stop its dance. Not only the "male" robber and readers of both genders, "you," like the snake, is part of the speaker's self.[6]

In "Lies About Snakes" the "I" insists that legends about snakes' metamorphoses into women, and vice versa, are "lies" (9–10); but like most of Atwood's personae and her alter ego snake with "a throat / like the view down a pink lily," she has "a double tongue" ("Lesson on Snakes" 9) and a double-voiced discourse. As in *True Stories* and *Murder in the Dark*, if an artist/persona reveals societal "lies," the "true" story still "lies / among the other stories" (*TS* Oxford 11): "by the rules of the game, I must always lie" (*MD* 30). Still, the glass snake is neither breakable nor transparent, and its sensuous "observed-female" movement ("hips in a tight skirt") to no music differs from the dance of many women and artists. Not conditioned by the kind of external gaze we initially associate with "you," "snakes are alone / . . . The time they keep is their own" (10).

In "Bad Mouth," however, the snake's carnivorous "endless gullet" is parodically the "evil glove" of the Beatles' *Yellow Submarine*: the artist-persona makes it symbolize "sheer greed." Now the "I" in search of her own "natural" voice again sees snakes as death, not creators or singers but killers who become first "you" and then "us" and "them." Seeming to project her own desire and frustration, she finds "no fellow feeling" between her and snakes: they cannot scream but can reductively silence: the "Constrictor constrictor" "squeeze[s] the voice from anything edible." Ironically, the alienated persona again sees snakes as alien: "The reason for them is the same / as the reason for stars, and not human" (11–12). Like "all peoples . . . driven / to the point of eating their gods" (Motifs V30.1, A192.1.2), in "Eating Snake" the persona admits eating snake in a parodic communion. Skinned, derattled, decapitated, and mounted, denied its ouroboros association with eternity, the snake is reduced to "mere lunch / metaphysics with onions" (13).

Nevertheless, in the next poem, "Metempsychosis" (Motif E614.1), the persona again identifies "you" with the snake: "Who were you when you were a snake?" The snake now has a voice (her lost voice) (Motif B211.6.1) she listens to as it "proclaims resurrection." Even more telling, the snake becomes "Your lost child whispering *Mother*, / the one more child you never had, / your child who wants back in" (14). As in Atwood's earlier poems

("Tricks with Mirrors"), the "I" and "you" ambiguously blend—much as "I" and "she" do in fiction (*EW*). In this case, "you" gradually supplants "I." "Snake Poems"' artist persona begins to heal the kind of internal split or amputation we see throughout Atwood's work, a healing marked, as in *Surfacing* (Chapter 4), by the recovery of lost aspects of the self—the child. Illustrating this and other works' Demeter-Persephone theme, as the snake goddess (Mother Goddess) was her (oracular) mother or muse, the narrator is now the reborn snake's—and her own—mother.[7] The narrator also echoes T. S. Eliot's "The Hollow Men" and "The Waste Land" in seeking "that voice of husk rasping in the wind": her own voice.

As in *Surfacing*, Atwood uses the Grimms' "The White Snake" (No. 17, AT 673) in her "The White Snake" poem to portray the persona's artistic quest for voice, identity, and connection, not only to other (audience, lover, anti-self) but to body and nature. Similar to the Norse myth about Siegfried and the Greek one about Melampus, this tale, like its Estonian and Finnish analogues, goes back to medieval literary sources. Along with other tales about animal languages (AT 670, 671, 517), it generally depicts good fortune for the one who learns the languages (Thompson, *The Folktale* 83–84). Although another well-known story pattern suggests that Adam learned the language of animals from Eve (Motif B217.8), the persona in "Snake Poems" must not only relearn what she has lost but remember its possible cost. In "The White Snake" she recalls the man who ate a white snake, hoping to understand the languages of animals (Motif B217.1.1). Like most fairy tales, the Grimms' version of "The White Snake" is about the transformative power of eating (Motif D551), in this instance the unfolding of forces (represented by animals) within the individual, and about humanity's relationship with animals and nature (Lüthi, *Once* 70). Hearing animal voices of three realms (earth, water, and air) helps a young man accomplish seemingly unsolvable tasks in the unknown, including fetching an apple from the tree of life and marrying a proud princess whose heart changes when she eats from the apple (Motif D1905.2) (Zipes, *Complete* 67–70).

In Atwood's reconstructions here and in *Surfacing*, however, "The White Snake" tale becomes tragic and cautionary to the female artist interpreting it. Although the fairy tale's "isolating technique" allows the sacrifice of a horse because it is not the focus of interest and the white snake because it "is only a means" in the Grimms' tale (Lüthi *Once* 70), Atwood characteristically adjusts the focus. According to legend found "at the dark of the moon [interlunar] / by the forks of roads, under three-leaved trees, / at the bottoms of unsounded lakes," the white snake is secret, "covered" food appropriate for the artist's archetypal transformation. Significantly described by the visionless persona as lacking eyes and resembling "water freezing" (15), the white snake also suggests the freezing isolation of the Rapunzel artist.

By framing her and her artist-persona's re-visioned tale with words to remind readers that the white snake belongs to story rather than nature, Atwood creates the double vision more overt in the second section of "Interlunar." She also ironically suggests resolution to her artists' splits. In order to understand nature and thereby attain wisdom, both the artist-persona and her alter ego "character," the snake-eating man, paradoxically "eat" "unnatural" food, in the man's case, the unmediated sacred food, god (Motif V30.1); in the persona's case, the mediated "food" of story *rather than* of nature or divine inspiration. Serving as a warning about either/ors not only to the persona but also to critics who see female artists as Medusas (see Chapter 1 and Davey, "Atwood's" 149), Atwood's re-visioned man ends up "paralyzed" and mute, hearing words but unable to create art or communicate in any way.

Anne Sexton's images in her earlier poem, "The White Snake" (*Transformations* 1971), may have influenced the shift in tone and resolution Atwood makes in her "The White Snake." In Sexton's parodic poem, the burden of wisdom is a "no exit," and the fairy-tale marriage between strangers is a coffin. When animals speak to "Dame Sexton," the artist-persona thinks "that the voice / of the spirits had been let in—/ as intense as an epileptic aura—/ and that no longer would I sing / alone." But after the animals help the snake-eating man, in Sexton's as in the Grimms' tale, we never hear of them again. Sexton's snake eater, like "Dame Sexton," experiences "the aura" and is the artists' alter ego. This "traveling man" is so good at satisfying his and the princess's hunger, however, that he ends up as food. In a box with his tongue lying in the princess's mouth "as delicately as the white snake," Sexton's artist resembles the Robber Bridegroom's victim: he marries death (*Transformations* 11–15).

Similarly, throughout most of Atwood's *Interlunar*, becoming and being an oracle in either Yeats's or Sinclair Ross's tower (see Atwood, *Surv* 185–86, 209–10) can be painful and lonely. In Atwood's "The White Snake," the ironic transformation of "the sacred body of living snow into raw meat" also has its price:

> The sound poured over him
> like a wall breaking, like a disaster:
> He went blind in an instant.
> Light rose in him filling his mouth like blood,
> like earth in the mouth of a man buried.
> Human speech left him.
> For the rest of his life, emptied and mute
> he could do nothing but listen
> to the words, words around him everywhere like rain falling.

In this version of the story, the wisdom gained through animal speech is overwhelming: gaining hearing and enlightenment, the seeker loses sight and speech. Having sold his soul (Motif M211), the Faustian artist wedded to words loses the ability to shape them. Choosing ignorance might be preferable.

Thus, although the snake's voice begins to speak in the dry landscape of the persona's interior wasteland, even appearing in her dreams, it does so through paintings of the Quattrocento (literally "four hundred," short for mille quattrocento: fifteenth century or the Italian Renaissance) ("Psalm to Snake," "Quattrocento" 17–18). The gender-reversed quester of "The White Snake" is afraid of what she must learn. Since the Madonna and child rather than the fall of humankind seem to predominate in the Italian Quattrocento, Atwood's poem brings to mind fifteenth-century Dutch paintings in which the snake represents a marriage to death. The reference to what resembles the exile from paradise of Bosch's *Garden of Earthly Delights* crossed with *The Hay Wain* and *The Last Judgment* seems to promise no happiness or love. The Lamia snake, "vertical and with a head / that's face-coloured and haired like a woman's" (Motif B29.2.3)—as in Bosch's *The Hay Wain* and *The Last Judgment*—and the Aztec apple, "no apple but a heart / torn out of someone" (Motif S139.6), remind us of Atwood's own covers for *Double Persephone* and *True Stories* (Figures 3, 4; Plate 17): "This is the possibility of death / the snake is offering: / death upon death squeezed together, / a blood snowball." Also suggestive of *Life Before Man*'s Elizabeth and *You Are Happy*'s Mud Woman and "First Prayer" personae, this artist recognizes that devouring the apple means that "you slide down into your body as into hot mud." Like Rennie in *Bodily Harm* and Elaine in *Cat's Eye*: "You feel the membranes of disease / close over your head, and history / occurs to you and space enfolds / you in its armies, in its nights, and you / must learn to see in darkness" ("Quattrocento" 19).

Seeing in darkness is indeed what this volume's personae— and we—must learn. Having eaten and thus cannibalistically and parodically brought the kingdom of god "within you," the persona sees the world shine "as it never did before," learns prayer, and hears the snake speak: "Love is choosing, the snake said" ("Quattrocento" 19). One part of the persona sings a "Psalm to Snake" as she inscribes the trail it makes in the "blank sand" with the voice she has lost: the snake is "an argument / for poetry," "a voice from the dead," a "long word." Using Cixous's "feminine economy" ("Castration" 488), in "Psalm to Snake" and

"After Heraclitus" the snake can talk with its body, "letter / after letter formed on the grass, / looping its earthy hieroglyphs" (17, 20). The questing persona knows the snake symbolizes resurrection and might provide her a name, the answers to her sickness, and power. Instead of holding its "darkness" in her hands or praying to it, however, she/"you" kills the snake with a shovel, "old blood on its blade" (20–21), again recalling the actions of the insensitive "Americans" in *Surfacing* and of all the human beings who have resisted the wisdom and power they seek.

In the final poem, "Blue Snake," however, the snake is a spirit (Motif F401.3.8) resurrected in this section's female artist. It "winds through" the landscape of her/your head into the deserted "temple" of a head no longer split off from the body of Mother Earth and swims over the "toppled stones." The persona again hears the snake speak/sing (Motif B214.1.10) in its/her ancient flute voice, paradoxically "the voice of things beginning and ceasing." Although the "you" cannot answer its question (why she is here), what it says is what she already knows but must retell herself. She knows "This has gone far enough." As it glows transparently and then dissolves into rock behind her, she turns away from the snake because, no longer "alien," it is again part of her: she knows that she must follow the snake-winding river "home" (22–23). Especially in the context of the *Interlunar* volume, rather than ending the journey, "Blue Snake" prepares for a new beginning: the second section, "Interlunar"'s "descent" in "Doorway."

Published after Salamander Press's *Snake Poems*, the title section of *Interlunar* is more closely related to the "Snake Poems" section than might be readily apparent. In "Interlunar," the shape-changing artist persona creates other questers drawn from old stories: goddess and classical myth, European and native American fairy tales, individual and collective history, and the arts. As in *Murder in the Dark*, these characters are alter egos for the female poet behind them. Their quests into the underworld are part of hers and (simultaneously poetic and human) are as much for hands (touch) and vision (especially the third eye) as for a mouth or tongue. Although snake imagery is not explicit, the biblical story of the fall lingers behind the images of hell, monsters, fearful metamorphosis, burning, torture, massacres, and other killing; and earlier associations of snakes with the goddess continue in the Eurydice poems. These personae, divided between creators and destroyers, are again initially married to death. Often literally or symbolically dismembered, they are even "eaten" or consumed by death, symbolic disease, the colonizing other, or what "Singing to Genghis Khan" sarcastically presents as a male existential dilemma.

Behind all the voices that double and foil her own is again the female poet quester on her journey for—and with—words. She moves away from herself in part 2 and back to self and us in part 3. "Interlunar" motifs include death, disease, dirtiness, eating, journey, power, hands, healing, dark versus light, reflection and "reality," and blindness and vision. Themes of destruction, condemnation, the holy, sexual politics, love, creation, germination or fertility, and metamorphosis link the characteristic three parts. Beginning in fading November sunlight, the "Interlunar" section moves from part 1's alienated "I"—passively waiting and powerless to touch and speak ("the hand unspoken" 29) ("Doorway")— to part 2's fairy-tale, mythic, and other "fictional" characters, part 3's naming of the poet's journey, and finally to the title poem's paired "I" and you"—hand in hand at the edge of a doubling lake (103).[8] As in the "Snake Poems" section, "Bluebeard's Egg," *The Handmaid's Tale*, and most of Atwood's work, *Interlunar*'s "end" is a new beginning: the couple is poised to enter the darkness of intermoon on yet a new journey from dark to now promised light.

The marriage-to-death theme, announced in the first poem, "Doorway," and explicit in "The Healer," "Nomads," "Valediction, Intergalactic," "Letter from Persephone," the three Orpheus and Eurydice poems, and many others, reaches a climax in the second part's "The Robber Bridegroom." "Interlunar"'s first part is filled with images of powerlessness, inertia or waiting, indifference, dying, and barbarism, culminating in the urban hell of "A Sunday Drive." Unlike "Snake Poems," where the goddess is associated with creative or artistic magic, the matriarchal power in this section initially seems to be Canada's black Hecate (with Venus and Diana trapped inside) as a variety of paralyzed Rapunzel artist (Atwood, *Surv* 209–10, 177). The doorway associated with the archetypal quest, based on both goddess and priestess caves (wombs) of inspiration, is prototypically, physically, and spiritually within the female persona (see n. 16; Neumann 170; Walker, *Woman's Encyclopedia* 154–56). Nevertheless, feeling "without power," like *Life Before Man*'s Elizabeth, she is "Waiting to be told what to say." Although she has potential power, it is linked to a murdered girl and inert: "Power of a door unopened" ("Doorway" 29). A black stone "in the dirt at the back of the garden" is "the same thing" as God, and the sun is "only one version" (Before" 31). Despite recurrent death images and suggestions of archetypal descent, "Nobody here / needs anyone raised from the dead, it's too / confusing" ("The Healer" 38).

Even the healer and the saints don't seem to know what to do with their artistry: "What am I to do with my hands in this tidy place / filled with those who do not want / to be truly healed?" asks the healer, who sometimes thinks her "life is over and there will be / repetition but no more story" ("The Healer" 38). Like the girl in "The Girl Without Hands"—a poem in *Interlunar*'s manuscripts that makes explicit the volume's concern with touch (Atwood Papers, Box 71)—symbolically, the saints are handless, in addition to being mouthless, dismembered, bodiless, and nearly eyeless: "What they touched emptie[s] of colour." They eat air, their bodies are like "drained pillows," and pieces of them, including hands, "litter history" ("The Saints" 40–41). Although they see things most people cannot and are, thus, doubles for the artist, they epitomize the paradoxical negative or black-hole power pervading this part and paralleling the second part's "energy / of an open socket, a dark / vortex in the wall" ("Three Denizen Songs" 65): "They drift through the atmosphere, / their blue eyes sucked dry / by the ordeal of seeing, / exuding gaps in the landscape as water / exudes mist. They blink / and reality shivers" ("The Saints" 40–41).

"Nomads" anticipates the self-deceiving female persona and the murderous sexual politics of "The Robber Bridegroom" published and draft poems. The voice of "Nomads," craving for arms to embrace her and even the trees to love her, already knows "the hole *No* makes / in the center of her forehead / where the eye was once that could / see it coming." Like the couples of *Power Politics* and the narrator of *Cat's Eye*, she disguises and projects love onto the landscape and her own death onto the man "devoid of features" (42). "A peach in boiling water," the "I" of "Valediction, Intergalactic" suspects that she prefers "the airless blaze of outer / space to men" (43). "Precognition"'s "you" supposedly considers the poem's Saint Dimorphia or Cassandra[9] figure a landscape "rich in curios" such as "a clay goddess you picked up at a stall" (44).

In the next poems love becomes "the dormant phase / of a disease," and you's skin "tastes faintly / of the acid that is eating through you" ("Hidden" 46, "Keep" 47), even as, Proteuslike, you's body, "liquid" in the persona's keeping hands, ironically doubles her own shape-changing and anticipates the luminous "quickening" of the third section's "The Skeleton, Not as Image of Death" ("Keep" 47, 90). The first part of the "Interlunar" section ends with "Anchorage"'s paradoxical "killer" and "swarming" water, "Georgia Beach"'s emptiness, and "A Sunday Drive"'s sibilant stagnant sea, "bombed out and burning" city (Bombay), and "maze of condemned flesh." This part thus reaches the peace of "burial by fire" in the ironic urging to give up "the last illusion," the desire to be loved (48–52). Called "Mother" by beggar children colonized in her gaze, pointing toward the second part's "flesh stutters" of the "left-handed mothers" ("Letter from Persephone" 63),[10] the persona is now linked with a Hecate/Kali whose reign extends beyond Canada: "I have never felt less motherly. / The moon is responsible for all this, / goddess of increase / and death, which here are the same. / Why try to redeem / anything? . . ." (51–52). Despite the persona's sense of futility, the images of decay, death, and burial resemble those in Eliot's "The Waste Land": part of the goddess's moon cycle, death makes possible the persona's descent and ultimate rebirth.

The fairy-tale intertextuality of "Interlunar" is most evident, and important, in part 2. This part not only continues the tone of "A Sunday Drive" (reconciliation to the impossibility of love) but also makes the evocation of hell explicit. The first poem, "One Species of Love," describes, without further comment, a Hieronymous Bosch painting depicting a seated man by a "blunted" lion, a hill "shaped like a mound burial / or a pudding," a creature "part bird, part teapot, / part lizard and part hat" emerging from an eggshell, and a "half-sized," winged woman suspended above his head.[11] Marking death, metamorphosis, and a new beginning in a manner parodying Yeats's "Second Coming," the poem's monster image reminds us that metamorphosis is not necessarily either positive or tragic. Like the painting, however, the poem is ironically removed from time. Further, the love seems to come more from the blue woman, holding one hand "in a gesture of benediction" and pointing with the other toward the ground, than from the new species. Rather than an angel of God, she is a half-sized woman the color of the background, the "serene eye-colour" of the sky as likely here to denote "lack of a body" as holiness or distance. Thus, in Atwood's re-visioned and parodic iconography, the woman seems to represent the questing poet (Irvine, Review 4), sometime "monster," present throughout this and other volumes. In addition, the woman represents the paradox of her and her viewer or "reader's" vision or enlightenment as well as the need, of both poet and world, for vision and love ("One Species of Love, After a Painting by Hieronymous Bosch" 55–56).

Subsequent poems in this part's stony and lunar underworld continue to dramatize paradox: the silent, timeless world of art and mass art (political thrillers, drama, film, opera, songs, ballet, painting, poetry, myth, biblical stories, published fairy tales, witchlore, commercial art, and even history) that again moves and speaks (e.g., "Giselle in Daytime"). Part 2's poems present narcissism's hollow "echo" and cannibalistic hunger versus the "seed" of love and the sustenance of art (both "Orpheus" poems, "Eurydice," "Singing to Genghis Khan"). Some of the poems are about Demeter's lost, dismembered and dismembering sons rather than daughters ("Robber Bridegroom," "Letter from Persephone"). Many are about the female and female poet as Venus, Hecate, Martian, witch, and captive sex partner, or about the poet as political prisoner ("Eurydice," "Three Denizen Songs," "Harvest," "Letter from the House of Questions"). Finally, this part's poems are about the need to awaken from Sleeping Beauty's dream (Motif D1960.3), to regain ears, eyes, mouth, fingers, hands, heart, and head, and to be a poet oracle and seer ("Eurydice," "Orpheus [2]," "Reading a Political Thriller Beside a Remote Lake in the Canadian Shield," and two manuscript poems cut from the published volume: "The Girl Without Hands" and "The Robber Bridegroom II").

"Giselle in Daytime" refers to Adolphe Adam's romantic ballet, first produced in 1841 in Paris and based on the tragic Theophile Gautier story and legend recorded by Heinrich Heine. It presents a postmodern "blank page" (Isak Dinesen story), a familiar landscape holding young girls in dresses made of "paper / not written on." The river is "unmoving," the tree "is dead, like everything / here. Nevertheless," as a girl holds a stone in her hands, the tree shakes out green flowers, "which has never happened before, / which happens every day, / which she does not notice" (57). Orpheus moves from a similarly frozen story in past tense ("Orpheus [1]") to present and finally future tense ("Orpheus [2]") (which resembles *Bodily Harm* and much recent Atwood work). Eurydice, "so chilled and minimal: moving and still / both," gradually understands (through the questing poet) how Orpheus uses her. Thus, we know by the end of this part that "this paper / world . . . is the real world / also" and that the fictional plot about power, about "men who pretend / to kill because they must," is as real as the dead lake beside the (writing, and now reading) persona ("Reading" 79).

Orpheus, the Robber Bridegroom, Genghis Khan, the amputator of the Girl Without Hands in this volume's draft poem, and those who hunt witches, torture prisoners, and begin massacres are all to some degree Atwood anti-artist killers, with the "materialistic and instrumental values" (Davey, *Margaret* 34–35) responsible for the dismemberment or cannibalism of others and sometimes of themselves. By making Eurydice, the Robber Bride, the old woman seer (the unpublished "The Robber Bridegroom II"), Persephone, the nameless singing woman ("Singing to Genghis Khan"), the witch, and other females either narrator or subject of most part two poems, Atwood again revisions the mythic, fairy-tale, and historical intertexts in which women are silenced.

Atwood's three Orpheus-Eurydice poems seem to draw on Jean Cocteau's play *Orphée* (1926) and its two film versions (1950, 1959) that anticipate some of Atwood's own irreverence and illusion breaking. The Brazilian film *Black Orpheus*, Bela Bartók's opera *Duke Bluebeard's Castle*, classical and goddess myth, the medieval English romance *Sir Orfeo*, Christoph Gluck's opera *Orfeo ed Euridice*, and indigenous Takánakapsãluk and Orpheo folklore are also probable intertexts. All of these works advance imagery, motifs, themes, and structures parallel to Atwood's in *Interlunar* and other volumes. Classically, Orpheus (possibly identical with Dionysus) was a Thracian musician who charmed the stones and trees to dance or gather around him. Orpheus was a muse's son, and his myth, also a North American indigenous tale, embodies "a story theme found all over the world, the folk-tale type of the descent to the underworld in search of a lost wife" (AT 400, F81.1). Linking the Osiris cult of ancient Egypt to the religious revival of the first century B.C. that became Christianity, the Orphic mysteries symbolize death and resurrection. Orpheus, dismembered and decapitated for failing in his mission to Hades, revealing divine secrets (Leach and Fried 834), denouncing the Maenads' sexual orgies, or advocating either male homosexual love or patriarchal-ascetic ideas (Walker, *The Woman's Encyclopedia* 746–47), is more than the "torn God" whose flesh was eaten in Orphic mysteries (Leach and Fried 833–34). He is a poet who "looks back" and a god of oracles, a "speaking head" (Motifs D1610.5, D1311.8.2, D1615.7) continuing to sing and teach about the afterlife after being laid in a sacred cave. The cave, earlier associated with Rhea and other mother goddesses, was an entrance to the underworld, a site for religious ceremonies, and a means of regeneration (Walker, *The Woman's Encyclopedia* 747, 154–56). Like Eurydice/Persephone, Orpheus embodies the Atwood character's symbolic decapitation, dismemberment, cannibalized body, duality, and death-rebirth. Orpheus is also a prototype for the oracular speaking heads most obvious in *Two-Headed Poems* but evident throughout Atwood's work.

Paradoxically, since Orpheus' descent into hell is traditionally considered to double that of Persephone, Aeneas, St. Paul, and the poet Dante (Leach and Fried 834), and since goddess myth reveals Eurydice as another creator/destroyer associated with the cave, Eurydice becomes both double and foil of Orpheus in the same way that Atwood's Robber Bride and Robber Bridegroom double. As "Black Mother Night," Hecate with her serpents, and "'Universal Dike,' or Tyche, Goddess of Fate" (originally a matriarchal fury), Eurydice was equated with Persephone and other aspects of the goddess. Only later did she become Orpheus's wife and ironically die from a snake bite (Walker, *The Woman's Encyclopedia* 745–48, 287). Diminished in the same way as Atwood's Circe (*YAH*), the great goddess of the wheel is invoked in Atwood's "Eurydice": "O handful of gauze, little / bandage, handful of cold / air" (61).

Tied together with a rope resembling that between Lucky and Pozzo in *Waiting for Godot*, Atwood's Orpheus and Eurydice typify the complex androgynous pairing of Atwood's males and females, found among characters as diverse as *Lady Oracle*'s mother and her boyfriends and *Bodily Harm*'s Rennie and the man with the rope. Both a killer *and* a creator, first a "you" and a "he" other and then a "he" subject, Orpheus like Eurydice and Persephone descends to the land of the dead.[12] In his case bearing "the image" of what he wants to create, the Orpheus of "Orpheus (1)" hopes to sing Eurydice into existence. According to Eurydice, however, Orpheus is another of Atwood's Narcissus lover/artists who confuse reality with an image and the other with him/herself or an object: "You could not believe I was more than your echo." In Eurydice's account she holds love in her hand "even in this land of no memory, / even in this domain of hunger." Orpheus "cannot believe without seeing" and seems to need her for selfish reasons: "This love of his is not something / he can do if you aren't here" (58–61).

True, where Eurydice is she is "used to silence" and "numb, like an arm/ gone to sleep." But when a creator/destroyer is reduced either to a muse or to an artistic image cut off from both artist and audience, Eurydice (and behind her the questing poet) feels like "a white curtain blowing / in the draft from a half-opened window / beside a chair on which nobody sits" (58–61). Paradoxically, however, even though Eurydice has left her body "cooling and whitening on the lawn," the quester characterizes her—and the Girl Without Hands of this volume's manuscript poem (Atwood papers, *I* drafts, Box 71)—with a nurturing touch the "killers" lack. Despite the Medusa prohibition against looking at her, Eurydice retains arms and hands and is a "handful." Through the poet persona who gives her voice, she / the poet also reaches an important realization: "it is not through him / you will get your freedom" (61).

Initially no more able than most of Atwood's personae here or elsewhere to view the other as subject, Orpheus changes by "Orpheus (2)," presumably as the direct result of his time in the underworld while we read about the Robber Bridegroom, Persephone, and other underworld characters in the second part's other poems. As the quester explains: "he was not wandering among meadows / all this time. He was down there / among the mouthless ones, among / those with no fingers, those / whose names are forbidden" (78). His journey thus doubles those of the female poet, Eurydice, the Girl Without Hands, and as we shall see, the Robber Bride. It also brings to the surface "Interlunar"'s implied political commentary.[13] Ironically, this singer, whose irresistible music compares to the Pied Piper's (D1427.1), faces a more than hostile audience. In some ways he resembles the woman singing to Genghis Khan for the same reason Scheherazade tells stories, so that she will not be murdered or become a Robber Bridegroom's food.[14] Khan "will not be consoled / by her or pleasure or any / thing, for being / alive on this earth / . . . . For the verb *to die*" ("Singing to Genghis Khan" 68–69). Similarly, the Orpheus of "Orpheus (2)," on one level about the Chilean folk musician Victor Jara, sings for those without mouths, fingers, eyes, and names, those who have been amputated and "eaten into" by the refusers of life. Like Khan, Orpheus knows "the horror of this world."

Contrary to Atwood's frequent demythification, "Orpheus (2)" mythifies Victor Jara's historical resistance. When a military Junta led by Augusto Pinochet overthrew (with CIA support) President Salvador Allende's government in 1973, Jara was confined in the detention center at the Santiago sports stadium, the stadium of Atwood's poem and the stadium where Jara's friend Pablo Neruda (winner of the Nobel Prize and Allende's Ambassador to France) had read poems a year earlier (Chavkin 213, Garza 101). Jara's resistance song, "Chile Stadium," was composed there. Mentioning horror and rooted in the horror of political torture and assassination, the song precipitated Jara's own

death. Internationally famous for songs about political and eco-
nomic injustice, Jara continued singing resistance songs when
soldiers splintered his guitar. Then they broke his hands with
rifle butts. "When he still continued to sing they beat him to
death" (Chavkin 231, Garza 101). Becoming "A literal man without hands,"[15] Jara had been noted for sensitive, expressive, and
caressing hands and, like Atwood, had devoted several poems to
the subject of hands (Joan Jara quoted in Chavkin 213–14).

The persistence of Atwood's Orpheus resembles that of the
previous poem's female forming words in the dust with broken
fingers ("Letter from the House of Questions," 76–77). They are
both poetic heroes, Camus's absurd artist-rebels. As for "Interlunar"'s central female persona behind them, "Creating is living
doubly." Like Camus, the French Resistance fighter who invites
us "to live and create, in the very midst of the desert" (*The Myth
of Sisyphus* 69–70, v), the quester's Orpheus becomes a model for
her, both model and foil for her other characters, and a model of
all the artists who continue to speak despite political or societal
efforts to amputate and silence them. Orpheus knows the tan-
gibility of his failure but still chooses to sing to "the already
dead":

> They have cut off both his hands
> and soon they will tear
> his head from his body in one burst
> of furious refusal.
> He foresees this. Yet he will go on
> singing, and in praise.
> To sing is either praise
> or defiance. Praise is defiance. (78)

The Robber Bridegroom theme of "Interlunar" reaches a climax in the published "Robber Bridegroom" poem and the manuscript drafts of "Robber Bridegroom II" and "The Girl Without
Hands" (Atwood Papers, *I* Manuscripts, Box 71). The draft
poems help us read the published volume by foregrounding mo-

tifs and subtexts either submerged or easily missed. The Grimms' Robber Bridegroom, who chops up and eats prospective brides, embodies the death he intends for his brides. Ironically he, rather than the woman who witnesses murder and tells her story, marries death. In the related English tale, "Mr. Fox," a cut-off hand lands in Lady Mary's lap, and Mr. Fox, the Robber, is cut into a thousand pieces after she tells her story (Carter, *Old Wives'* 8–10; see Chapters 3, 8). Atwood's versions in *The Edible Woman, Bodily Harm,* and *Interlunar,* deconstructive in different ways than Eudora Welty's comic romance (*The Robber Bridegroom,* 1942), also appropriate related motifs from "Fitcher's Bird," "The Girl Without Hands," and other fairy tales.

Like their kinsmen and the devil/father in "The Girl Without Hands," Fitcher and the Robber embody the literal or figurative touch of death throughout most of Atwood's work. *Interlunar's* again paradoxical "The Robber Bridegroom," however, emphasizes the Robber Bride's ironically killing touch, a "return to sender": "Her hands glimmering with [the Robber's] own approaching/ death," the Robber Bride not only "makes" (as in early drafts) but "*grops* [sic] her way towards [the Robber]" [italics my own]. Not handless like the Girl Without Hands or running without paths "under a moon that says nothing to her. / I mean it says: Nothing" (Atwood Papers, "The Robber Bridegroom II," Box 71, *Interlunar* Drafts of Poems), this Robber Bride, an artist of sorts like the Robber, is "ignorant and singing, / dreaming of him." Here, however, she dreams of him as he is. Although not part of the poem, her (true) *story* brings his death. And he, wishing he could "kill [the women] gently, / finger by finger and with great tenderness, so that / in the end they would melt into him" with pleasure, apparently needs not only the Bride's but his own illusions to live. Seeming to desire the D. H. Lawrence females Atwood describes as "melting like gelatin at the sight, thought, or touch of a good man's nicknamed appendage," the Robber has to settle for "rummaging in [the] flesh" of Mailer's bitchy wives (62, "If You Can't Say Something Nice"

16). Still, he is "despotic with self-pity" over his loss ("Robber" 62).

Like the Orpheus-Eurydice poems, *Interlunar's* "The Robber Bridegroom" presents both the male and female's—as well as the female quester's—points of view. Examination of the draft of "The Robber Bridegroom II" with which it was originally paired not only illuminates the three perspectives but also allows us to glimpse the seer of this and other volumes: the vision the snake woman of the first section and the female quester of the second section journey toward. In "The Robber Bridegroom II" draft, which is, thus, of considerable importance in understanding Atwood's evolving poems, this vision is embodied in the poem's narrator, the re-visioned old woman of the Grimms' "The Robber Bridegroom." She is the old woman "found always in forests like this one," the one who shows us the running girl (her alter ego), the man "who claims he is a lover / but smells of plunder," and "The darkness wash[ing] towards [the girl] / like an avalanche. Like falling." It is this "vacancy" the girl would like to make a "destination" in "leaving her body pulled off / and crumpled behind her like a sleeve."

Although the young girls of "The Robber Bridegroom" fail as melting Lawrencian heroines, the old woman in "The Robber Bridegroom II" is much more than Lawrence's "nasty bloodsucking old spiderwomen" (Atwood, "If You Can't Say Something Nice" 16). Related to Atwood's old woman muse, shamanic poet-personae, and once magical grandmothers (Atwood, *Once in August*; McCombs, "Fictive" 69; Mandel 63–64; *BH, THP*) and goddesses, she is reminiscent of the Susanna Moodie ghost "sitting across from you on the bus" whose "secret hatpin" vision destroys illusions ("A Bus Along St. Clair: December" *JSM* 61). In this section's first poem, "Doorway," the female quester initially finds "Nobody's blood on the floor" and only the potential "Power of the murdered girl's/ bone in the stream, not yet a flute") (29).[16] The old woman in "The Robber Bridegroom II" resembles the Hecate crone of *Double Persephone's* "Persephone

Departing": since "The dancing girl's a withered crone," "The articulate flesh, the singing bone" (n.p.) suggest the cycle also evident in *Interlunar*. In this sense, the murdered girls in "Doorway" and "The Robber Bridegroom II," the artist-persona, and the old woman are one. The old woman is the archetypal voice who will, when listened to, tell the naive girl, us, *Bodily Harm*'s Rennie, and this section's persona to "Go back": "Back is into the cellar / where the worst is, / where the others are, / where you can see / what you would look like dead / and who wants it. / Then you will be free / to choose. To make your way" (Atwood Papers, *I* drafts, Box 71).

As the title suggests, part 2's "The Robber Bridegroom" appears to focus on the Robber and his displacement of responsibility for his "red compulsion" onto the women who "fail him and die badly." However, in this and the next poems of the second part, we are still indirectly being shown what marriage to death means. Unlike the indifferent "watery moonlight" or the white stones in this poem, or their parallels in "A Massacre Before It is Heard About," "No Name," and "Reading a Political Thriller . . . ," we can choose to love and create instead of amputate or kill, either literally or figuratively. Significantly, as the woman approaches the Robber, holding his own death in her hands, he imagines killing women gently "finger by finger," robbing first their ability to touch. Like the boys who make *You Are Happy*'s Mud Woman, the Robber is a pseudo-artist who "values" women for what he can do to them. Ironically, however, he also resembles *Power Politics*'s ambiguous, drowned voice and the watercolor illustration (Plate 21) of a drowned person Atwood painted for its final poem ("He is last seen"). In *Power Politics* the persona waits for the curved death she expects the male other—apparently her (reverse) mirror image, whose "face is silver/ and flat"—to bring. In "The Robber Bridegroom," the killer-Robber waits passively for the death his victim-other brings. Although *Power Politics*'s journey ends abruptly with the puncture of "safety," "firm ground," and at least the hope of "love without mirrors" (55–56), the "Interlunar" section has not reached the point of trust and touch.

Not yet able to see the colonizing other, the characters in part 2 of "Interlunar"—including the central persona who re-creates them in her personal interlunar—have only begun facing their own disguises and the voices that say they do not belong. These disguises include conditioned roles projected onto them (for the female: the death of "curved space"; for the male: killing, muteness, and plasticity, leaving him exiled, missing something, and hungry) ("Three Denizen Songs" 66; "The Robber Bridegroom," "Letter from Persephone," "Singing to Genghis Khan," "No Name" 62–64, 68–69, 74–75). Characters still lack hands and are married to death. As the second "naturalized" voice of "Three Denizen Songs" (originally "Three Martian Songs") asks, "Is it my body or your vision / which is martian?" (66, Atwood Papers, "Interlunar" Drafts, Box 71). Despite her "pink print / dress," the female poet with a third eye (F512.2.1.1) is still subjected to "curious probes / . . . to see/ what kind of creature I am / really, and prove me alien" (66–67). This part's witch burning, torture, and massacres, only a few steps beyond colonizing probes, are variations of a marriage to death that now describes not only contemporary sexual politics, the plight of the anti-artist "living dead," and the repressive society they support but the situation of the artist unable to find hands as well as vision and voice.

In the draft poem, "The Girl Without Hands," written for but not published with this volume, the contemporary Girl embodies the dilemma of "Interlunar,"'s and other volumes,' characters. Walking through "ruins" "pushing the distance in front of [her] / like a metal cart on wheels," the persona of "The Girl Without Hands" recognizes that she is unable to hold the splendor of "the seen world": " . . . Distance surrounds you, / marked out by the ends of your arms. . . . / No one can enter that circle / you have made, that clean circle / of dead space you have made / and stay inside, / mourning because it is clean" (Atwood Papers, *I* Manuscript Drafts, Box 71). Ironically resembling the formalist stipulation to maintain distance, fear of being hurt—"amputated," "cannibalized," or married to death—can, in itself, be a "death."

Still, imagining the ancient Girl Without Hands, re-visioned here, the symbolically handless persona of "The Girl Without Hands" draft poem also envisions healing. Despite a "halo of hot sand, of no sound" that surrounds the Girl, "If she were here she would / reach out her arms towards / you now and touch you / with her absent hands / and you would feel nothing, but you would be / touched all the same" (Atwood papers, *I* manuscript drafts, Box 71). In the final poems of part 2, the poet quester owns her voice by returning to the "I"; and, unlike the Robber, she takes responsibility for her "killing." She embraces her art as Orpheus (2) does his: "I would say the stones / cry out, except they don't" and "I give you yourself, or / me" (73, 79).

Continuing this tone, part 3 opens with "The Words Continue Their Journey." This poem makes explicit not only the nature of the quester's journey but, despite individual differences such as women's veils or men's bravado, the fact that she and other poets are not really adversaries. They are "some doomed caravan / . . . travelling together" on this "pilgrimage" through "moon terrain," looking for water. No longer alienated and recognizing her relationship even to the nonpoets who are supposed to be "other," she still fears her and other poets' "vanishing out of sight" into the dunes (83), a concern echoed in "A Painting of One Location on the Plain" and in several poems centered in human mortality ("Heart Test . . . ," "The Sidewalk," "The Skeleton . . ."). Gradually, however, images of the shining visible world, light, phoenix burning, shape-changing, and touch—present in earlier poems—supplant the despair and darkness of "what there is" ("A Stone" 94). Such images prepare for the paradoxical closing of the first poem's unopened door ("Doorway") with "The final slit of the old [Hecate] moon" ("A Blazed Trail" 99). But, as

Atwood always reminds us, mother Hecate is part of a cycle: I will never deny you / or believe in you/only . . ." (94).

"A Painting of One Location on the Plain," modeled on a William Kurelek landscape,[17] makes clear that this is "a journey with no end / in sight, and no end / after all." Tomorrow the caravan of poets "will go out again / to make tracks in the sand" like the ones we are reading; "the wind will cover [them] soon enough, / along with the bones we also can't help making." As Atwood has been doing throughout her career from *Survival* through "Where is How" (8), her female poet / persona emphasizes the significance of place, in this case a symbolic one: she announces "Now you know where you are" with reference to her role as an artist, Canadian art, and the human condition ("A Painting" 85). Thereafter, the poet persona is able to speak more freely. Although "Heart Test With An Echo Chamber" can be taken for an autobiographical depiction of Atwood's own peace (Woodcock, "Metamorphosis" 283–84), the heart's "double flutter" is also a metaphor. Like many of Atwood's artists and some of their works, this heart speaks breathlessly and is a clenched fist "which goes on / shaking itself at fate." Probed, cross-sectioned, freeze-framed, and projected onto black and white television as "a softcore addiction / of the afternoon," the "hard" heart of religion, fairy tales, and reviewers' mythology becomes translucent and radiant: "A pear / made of smoke and about to rot ("Heart Test With An Echo Chamber" 86–87). Knowing where she and we are and observing how "each thing / burns over and over and we will / too" does not preclude celebration. Atwood's poet persona creates and celebrates the brightness of "just before" ("The Sidewalk" 38).

Increasingly through part 3 until the full sun phoenix rebirth in "The Burned House," the gift of art is a loving "touch" of open hands. Metamorphosing beyond a Robber—and the perception of the other as Robber—the quester gives and begins to regain vision and touch. The poems of this part now present "this quiet shining / which is a constant entering, / a going into" without period and without source beyond the person supplying whatever light and meaning exist in life ("The White Cup" 89, "The Light" 92). Although "To put a hand on another / is to touch death" ("The Skeleton, Not as an Image of Death" 90–91) in the Grimms' "Fitcher's Bird" and both the Grimms' and Atwood's "The Robber Bridegroom" and "The Girl Without Hands," the "I" now begins to recognize the other, like the self, as Proteus (Motif G311) rather than Robber or Robber Bride. She holds the "you" "as a quickening": "I hold you as I hold / water, swimming" ("The Skeleton, Not as an Image of Death" 90–91). The old layered hands are "eaten away," not by the Robber but by her own returning power signified in her finger-tips' thunder. The quester stretches her "new hands" into the "shimmer" of flames that once burned and "are still burning" ("The Burned House" 93). Now the remembered fire of "The Small Cabin," associated with "earlier / selves outlined in flame" (*Procedures for Underground* 15), is a phoenix fire. Rather than choosing between decaying or being buried by fire, as in part 1, part 3's persona experiences rebirth.

Just as Venus cycles toward Hecate and the full moon diminishes into, first, the old crescent moon and then the darkness of interlunar, dark moods return with "A Stone," "Sumacs," and "A Boat." Temporarily "wordless" like the sumacs with their "tongues of dried blood," the poet persona listens to "dark mother" Hecate and leaves food out, for Hecate, underground Persephone, a demon-lover "you," and her own dark reflection in the pond. Not yet ready to die, she waits for April and then the "chill" of winter (94–97), finally reaching "Interlunar"'s deceptively darkest point: "The blackness that keeps itself / under the surface in daytime / emerges from [the lake] like mist / or as mist" ("A Boat" 97). If moonlight and its goddesses leave her hand blessed but holding nothing, the poet still has her own hands. She has reached "the cellar" of the Robber's castle and her inner landscape with hills "familiar to me as sleep": "It is touch I go by, / the boat like a hand feeling / through shoals and among / dead trees, over the boulders / lifting unseen, layer / on layer of drowned time falling away" (97–98).

The title poem of "Interlunar" is "about light and darkness, about protecting love, enclosed within a kind of nature poem that stirs the sensations of smell and hearing that come into their own in darkness, and ends with an invocation of the lake's silence" and the poet's peace (Woodcock, "Metamorphosis" 284). This poem is also the poet persona's interlunar preparation for her and our new quest on another "edge," hand in hand with the other, her own shadow selves, and her readers. Although the stars, as in *Cat's Eye*, are "without regard," like the moon and the universe Camus's narrators and most of us would invest with meaning, we are invited to trust: "This darkness / is a place you can enter and be/ as safe in as you are anywhere / . . . . Memorize it. You will know it / again in your own time" (102–3).

As in *Murder in the Dark*,[18] the "Snake Poems" and "Interlunar" sections of *Interlunar* use deconstructed fairy-tale and mythic intertexts to depict the metamorphosis of symbolically dismembered artists who have been married to death. Although this postmodern text resists closure, mystically hearing the voice of nature through mother goddess and animal speech helps the personae recover amputated speech and uncover liquid, "multilingual" language.

As should now be evident, the untitled "Fitcher's Bird" watercolor (1970) (Plate 3), depicting a skull-faced bride carrying red flowers (see Chapter 2), expresses a central concern in all Atwood's work: the Bluebeard story. Along with *Bodily Harm, Murder in the Dark*, and *Interlunar, Bluebeard's Egg* puts into dramatic relief the "Fitcher's Bird" and "Robber Bridegroom" intertexts and related imagery in Atwood's visual art, poetry, and recent fiction. As Atwood is aware, her treatment of the Bluebeard story evolves between *Power Politics* (1971) and the title story "Bluebeard's Egg": she treats the Bluebeard image seriously in

Power Politics and comically in *Bluebeard's Egg* (Letter, September 1986). More recently, in *Good Bones'* "Alien Territory" (1992), she multiplies the possibilities for interpretation by shifting the tale's focus to the "hidden room" of the male body and his conditioning. Despite these variations of tone, genre, and meaning, however, the essential relationship between Atwood's embedded and frame stories seems fairly consistent between early and later works.[19] Numerous visual and literary images that may at first appear unconnected are centered in the fairy-tale sexual politics of Bluebeard and the sisters who are his brides.

The Grimm brothers' fairy tale "Fitcher's Bird" ("Fichters Vogel" 1812) is also called "Feather Bird" or "Fitch's Bird") (AT 311, No. 46).[20] "Fitcher's Bird" is one of many "Bluebeard" folktales, including the recently translated "Bluebeard" and "The Castle of Murder" and the anonymous English "Mr. Fox" (Zipes, *Complete* 660–63, 670–71; Yearsley 127–28), with the motif of a forbidden secret chamber (C611) containing the dismembered bodies of previous "brides." Atwood prefers the Grimms' version of "Fitcher's Bird" because it does not, like Perrault's "La barbe bleue," make the woman dependent upon brothers coming to her rescue after she has entered the forbidden room (Tape). "La barbe bleue" is from *Histoires ou contes du temps passé* (1697) by Charles Perrault but published under the name of his son, Pierre Perrault Darmancour, to mask his own identity (see Zipes, *Beauties, Beasts* 17–19, 31–35). Although Bruno Bettelheim claims that the more familiar "Bluebeard" ["La barbe bleue"], in which there is no egg or anything magical or supernatural, "is a story invented by Perrault for which there are no direct antecedents in folk tales as far as we know" (299), he admits that long before Perrault, the "Tale of the Third Calender" in *The Arabian Nights' Entertainments* and the Sixth Tale of the Fourth Day in the *Pentamerone* depict the consequences of entering a forbidden room (323 n. 120). In a Basque version of this "very widespread European folk tale," the youngest sister even kills Bluebeard with a saber (Leach and Fried 150). As mentioned in Chapter 2, sometimes the murderous husband is a troll, the devil, or death. Thackeray, Anatole France, Silvia Townsend Warner (see Zipes, *Spells of Enchantment*), John Fowles, Anne Hébert, Jay Macpherson, Vladimir Nabokov, Malcolm Lowry, Daryl Hines (Grace, "Courting Bluebeard" n. 2, 246), Angela Carter (*The Bloody Chamber's* title story), Kurt Vonnegut, and Susan Fromberg Schaeffer, among others, have all written Bluebeard stories. Atwood has mentioned the influence of Bela Bartók's opera, *Duke Bluebeard's Castle*,[21] and of the Grimms' "The Robber Bridegroom, for which she has created a privately owned watercolor depicting a bluish man holding both an axe and a blond head. The head emits light (Telephone Call, December 1985; see Chapters 3 and 8).

Significantly, despite her initial powerlessness, the woman protagonist in "Fitcher's Bird," like her counterpart in "The Robber Bridegroom," is a "clever and wily" opponent rather than a victim of the groom who punishes inquisitive brides. In "Fitcher's Bird," when the disguised wizard touches a woman, she is "forced to jump into his basket." He then carries her into the dark forest to his magnificent house. Following patriarchal tradition, as in ancient Rome, he gives the woman the keys to the house (Leach and Fried 575) and, supposedly, "everything [her] heart can wish for," but he lays down very explicit "rules" for her conduct: on pain of death, she may not enter one room, and she must "preserve" the egg he gives her "carefully for [him]," carrying it with her everywhere. The first two sisters, who "allow [themselves] to be carried away by curiosity" and thus oppose his will, are betrayed by the egg's indelible blood spots (Motif D474.4) from the bloody chamber. In each case, they are punished with death for breaking the taboo (Motif C920): their heads are cut off, they are chopped to pieces, and they are thrown in the bloody basin with all the previous interchangeable brides (Hunt and Stern 216–20). The third sister, however, not only safeguards the egg *outside* the room, but also rejoins the parts of her sisters' bodies, thereby restoring them to life (Motifs E30,

D1884). She is able to fool the groom as well as his friends by disguising herself as a marvelous bird (the Fitcher's Bird of the title, K521.1.) and setting an ornamented skull (the probable subject of Atwood's watercolor) in the window to represent herself as Fitcher's bride. While fairy tales, like Atwood's artistic expressions of them, are not reducible to rational explanation, the implicit sexual politics of both tale and watercolor merit further attention.

"Fitcher's Bird," like most fairy tales, is generally considered a story of initiation or a cautionary tale, warning women to guard their "eggs" for their prospective husbands, thereby testing their faithfulness to the man's orders "or, in a broader sense, to him," and possibly implying the destructive aspects of sex, jealousy (Bettelheim 300–1), or the animus.[22] However, such interpretations seem to disregard or minimize not only sexist violence but also the male's deceptive abduction of the woman, against her will, as in classic versions of the Demeter-Persephone myth. These interpretations also disregard women's "status" as prize or property in numerous fairy tales.[23] The disguised wizard, who specializes in pretty girls, begs for food. His unsought "touch," that causes the innocent girls' captivity and death, is not simply sexual initiation but also patriarchal exploitation. Like "The Robber Bridegroom," this tale is hardly gender neutral, as fairy tales were traditionally viewed (Bettelheim 226). It implies what "The Robber Bridegroom," "Little Red Cap," and most of the Atwood watercolors highlight: the trap or "death" possible in marriage or relationship[24] for any woman unable to use her powers of imagination, cunning, voice or art.[25]

As discussions of *The Edible Woman* and *Bodily Harm* indicate (Chapters 3 and 8), in some versions of "Fitcher's Bird" the bride is forced to eat human flesh; in "The Robber Bridegroom," she watches her predecessor not only being cut up, but eaten by her fiancé, much as little Red Cap is eaten by the disguised wolf. In each case, an innocent girl who doesn't heed warnings or follow rules opens a forbidden "door," off the prescribed "path." Her curiosity and new-found knowledge, like that of Eve and Pandora, bring immediate punishment: her *head* or other parts are cut off and/or she is swallowed. There's more to these tales than this, however, again suggesting that the images of women in fairy tales, still considered "polarized" even in re-visioned feminist archetypal theory, may not be as limiting as they are often considered (Wehr 35; Waelti-Walters 1–12).

"Fitcher's Bird" presents multiple gender roles. The male wizard, not only the abductor but also the society that fears female individuation and power, foils the bride's brothers and kinsmen, who avenge his actions. The abducted woman's role is similarly multiple: both the tricked victim (elder sisters and previous "brides") and the trickster savior of herself, other women, and a social order, she is also not only chopped-up corpse and "decked out skull" but possessor of the egg and its secrets of creation, immortality, and the generation of life (Jobes 492; Cirlot 90). Magnificent bird who "flies" from the establishment castle of death to sweep "all clean" in an act of purification and healing, and thus more than simply a "true bride,"[26] she asserts her individual and gender worth in a deadly test of sexual politics.

Thus, like "The Robber Bridegroom," "Fitcher's Bird" actually reverses initial audience-expectations of gender roles and plot with mirroring motifs that double the wizard and the third sister. Contrary to most interpretations, "Fitcher's Bird" actually critiques rather than perpetuating suppression of women. In the Grimms' version of the story, the third sister actually passes the test by violating patriarchal strictures: to the extent that the forbidden chamber represents her own body and knowledge of her sexuality (Stone, "Things" 47), she uses "the key" and opens the door alone. Once the woman passes the test, the wizard no longer has any power over her. Ultimately, he becomes his own victim: mirroring the fate of any woman whose egg is spotted in passage through the door of knowledge into the secret chamber, he, not the third sister, meets death in a patriarchal microcosm, trapped by the brothers in his own castle with his friends. As we have seen, the Robber Groom also dies when, at his urging, the bride breaks silence during the bridal feast to tell her story, as Rennie does at the end of *Bodily Harm*. Again it is someone other than the bride, in this case the wedding guests representing the whole community, who "[deliver] him over to justice" (200). In Atwood's *Interlunar* poem, "The Robber Bridegroom," the groom loses "the one thing / he needs to live," presumably flattering female illusions, as his ironically "ignorant and singing" bride gropes toward him, dreaming of him "as he is" (62). In "Little Red Cap," again the wolf, not his prey, dies, and Red Cap gains knowledge useful in her next encounter with a wolf. Significantly, Fitcher / the Robber / the wolf gain no knowledge: neither Fitcher nor his friends are able to distinguish between an ornamented skull (their apparent expectation) and the bride, whose disguise and basket mirror the groom's earlier ones; and they are carelessly overconfident. Like the wizard, the bride is clever, resourceful, and able to fool others with a disguise. But unlike him, she re-creates life rather than destroying it, suggesting the lingering presence of several Mother Goddess figures. Like Isis, she collects and buries the dismembered parts of her husband's body, and like Demeter, she is associated with fertility and life. Like Hecate, Athena, Ninib, and other gods and goddesses, she possesses and knows how to use the magic key (Leach and Fried 575). Still, the enthralling touch, mutual disguises, lack of recognition, and ornamented skull suggest a reality underlying gender and marital roles.

As we have seen, resembling the "Fitcher's Bird" and "The Robber Bridegroom" fairy tales, the landscape of Atwood's work is filled with images of mutilation and dismemberment, including amputation of hands, breasts, hearts, and limbs, as well as decapitation. In *True Stories*'s "True Romances," the main narrator gives a second-hand report of a "foreign country" where hands and heads are cut off "to prevent identification." In that continuous landscape, " . . . there / is no such thing as *inside*, there's no such thing as *I* / . . . . to make a difference they would have to kill all of us." Thus, "among those of us who still / have heads and hands there are no marriages" (Oxford 43). The narrator also mentions a man suspected of having cut up his wife and distributed parts of her body in four garbage cans and a woman who wants to kill herself because she has "nothing to live against" since her lover left her. The narrator once cut a hole in her arm with scissors to show her lover the real blood inside, and later, presumably the same voice tentatively re-creates scenes that have helped her feel safe by imagining her lover finding a severed finger, "a little signal of death" from the "country" that grows such things, in his breakfast coffee or tea (41–42, 44). As Atwood is quick to point out, however, these images "are not products of imagination." They are all "drawn from history or real life" (Atwood Letter, September 1986).

Among other images of sexist violence in *True Stories*, whose Canadian cover features Atwood's watercolor of a bleeding heart (Plate 17), we find a woman with a four-inch wooden peg jammed between her legs ("A Woman's Issue" 54), a woman whose pelvis is broken by hammers to extract a child ("Christmas Carols" 56), and a woman whose face has been sewn shut, all varying products of passion-denying power, "the knife that cuts lovers / out of your flesh like tumours, / leaving you breastless / and without a name" ("Torture" 51).

As we have seen, Atwood's texts both parody and echo fairy tales. Joan/Felicia in *Lady Oracle* fears death in Bluebeard's maze, much of Rennie's breast is cut off in *Bodily Harm*, and all women in *The Handmaid's Tale* are "cut up" into color-coded functions. In *Murder in the Dark*'s "Simmering," it is tips of women's tongues that are amputated, while in "Women's Novels," the novelist is a Bluebeard, with men leaving out women's heads and hands and women omitting "the stretch between the belly button and the knees" or the sense of humor (32, 34). Reading Atwood's work, we know that Bluebeards exist. No less certainly, we know that victims exist. In many cases, as the narrator of "A Women's Issue" concludes, "You'll notice that what [the victims] have in common / is between the legs" (*TS* 55).

Still, the menace of the room, from "Speeches of Dr. Franken-stein" (1966, in *The Animals in That Country*), *The Circle Game*, and *Power Politics* to *True Stories*, *Murder in the Dark*, *Interlunar*, *The Handmaid's Tale*, and *Good Bones*, is not only literal dismember-ment or, as Freudians would have it, fear of sex or adulthood (MacLulich 120–22), but also the mutual games of disguise and sexual politics that hack off parts of the other in creating her/him as Bluebeard or Frankenstein monster.

"Hesitations Outside the Door" in *Power Politics*, written at a time when Atwood was doing many of the watercolors (Atwood Tape), is not only one of the clearest instances of Bluebeardian sexual politics in Atwood's work, but also one of many works, including *Lady Oracle* and *Bodily Harm*, that embed "Fitcher's Bird" or "The Robber Bridegroom." As in the other poems of *Power Politics*, whose cover features the "Hanged Man" parody based on Atwood's watercolor (see Plate 8), the female narrator is aware of "telling the wrong lies," which will not serve as keys to the unopened door, and aware that they are both "robbers," both Bluebeards/victims for whom "either / way is loss." "If we make stories for each other / about what is in the room / we will never have to go in." If "thin women / hang on their hooks, dismem-bered" in his pockets, around her neck she wears "the head of the beloved, pressed / in the metal retina like a picked flower." As she says, "I should be doing something / other than you" (*Power Politics* 48–51). If, however, the personae of this and other vol-umes were able to drop their disguises, peel off both projected and defensive false skins like "melted celluloid" (3), and stop playing or casting parts like those in the watercolors, including termite-queen Venus ("She considers evading him," 4), drowned woman (41), Dracula/Superman ("They eat out," 5), police-man/angel (30), wooden general and statue concubine (7), and female or male god (43, 45), perhaps they could find "love without mirrors" (55), a relationship beyond narcissism in which both self and other truly exist. Both could, of course, flee Bluebeard's castle rather than face another possible horror, that "In the room we will find nothing": the void of self (Wilson, "Fragmented" 50–52) that narrators from *The Edible Woman* to *Cat's Eye* fear. On the other hand, it is just possible that "In the room we will find each other" ("Hesitations" 51).

Significantly, the gender roles in "Fitcher's Bird," probably Atwood's most important fairy-tale influence, are neither single nor simple. Neither are those of Atwood's texts, that both parody and resonate with fairy-tale nuance. Like the earlier *Dancing Girls* (slightly different Canadian and U.S. editions, both 1977) and the recent *Wilderness Tips* (1991),[27] Atwood's second short story collection, *Bluebeard's Egg* (1983), embeds fairy-tale intertexts. In addition to "Fitcher's Bird," *Bluebeard's Egg* uses a number of other folk, fairy-tale, mythic, and similar intertexts including "The Snow Queen," Disney's "Snow White and the Seven Dwarves," the sin eater (see Leach and Fried 1013), goddess, Frankenstein, and vampire stories. Still, "Fitcher's Bird" suggests volume themes and motifs such as amputation, sexual politics, and marriage to death in "The Salt Garden," "Betty," "Significant Moments," "The Sunrise," and "Uglypuss."

An unpublished early beginning of "Hurricane Hazel" called "Three Jokes" (1970/71), a prose poem resembling pieces in *Good Bones*, features a characteristic reversal of the Bluebeard story.[28] In the third "joke," Bluebeard pronounces the clever third sister "either too good or too clever to live. He prepares to chop off her head" as she asks about her two sisters. In this wonderful parody, Bluebeard tells the woman, "'They're in the triple feather bed in the front room,' he replies, 'eating grapes. They both went into the forbidden chamber the first chance they had, and got their eggs dirty immediately. They have passed the test, they are stupid and dishonest: I know that with them I am safe'" (Atwood Papers n.p., in a folder marked "Poems from *Power Politics* period," Box 12, with *PP* manuscripts). As in "Hurricane Hazel" and most of Atwood's work, passing the test of socialization, being a conventionally "true bride" or good date, is failing the test of being a human being. In the harsh irony of "Three Jokes," however, "either / way is loss" ("Hesitations Outside the Door," *Power Politics* 51)—Cixous's decapitation—for a female faced with a patriarchal double bind.[29]

The title story of *Bluebeard's Egg* self-reflexively discusses "Fitcher's Bird." Atwood provides a comic context for retelling the fairy tale in "Bluebeard's Egg" by giving Sally, her third-person center of consciousness, a "Forms of Narrative Fiction" assignment to write a "transposition, set in the present and cast in the realistic mode" (156). Another of Atwood's pseudo-artists, Sally excises the folktale as she rearranges the "story" of her and Ed's life: she chooses to omit all the details following the reversal of power, including the third sister's escape, the bird disguise, and the skull substitute, because she "already [knows] which details [stand] out for her" (158). Sally is the third wife of a heart specialist who ironically points out the "defects of beating hearts" (147). Despite women's conviction that Ed, like *Bodily Harm*'s Daniel, might possess mysterious inner knowledge, he apparently knows little about his wife's or other women's "heart" problems. Like Atwood's female Frankenstein creator in "Speeches for Dr. Frankenstein" and most of her narrators, Sally prefers to create an image of the sexual partner rather than to see him directly, so she pictures Ed as the egg rather than Bluebeard.

Sally is a Nancy Drew sleuth/Diana/Calypso who has successfully hunted and caught Ed. Once she becomes Penelope, she is unable, and perhaps unwilling, to make him see her, just as she is unable to see him, despite her obsession recalling the persona of "Hesitations . . . ," who "should be doing something / other than [him]." Throughout much of the story she watches Ed, framed in the kitchen window, puttering around outside among rocks while she, like the volume's other women, cooks food that fails to nourish her marital or emotional life. She thinks of him as a stupid child of luck, a fairy-tale "third son who, armed with nothing but a certain feeble-minded amiability, manages to make it through the forest with all of its witches and traps and pitfalls and end up with the princess, who is Sally, of course" (134–35.) But she is not living "happily ever after." For one thing, like most of the "brides" in this volume of Bluebeards, she is not his first princess, and some mystery exists about the first two women who were "severed" from him. For another, she is not the only current princess, either, and her curiosity, evident in "jokes" hiding rage about the other sirens surrounding this Odysseus (J672.1), may cause her to fail his Penelope test.

Willfully deceiving herself about her husband's apparent affairs and her own lack of protective layers, she casts both herself and Ed in multiple, contradictory roles drawn from the Grimms' and Andersen's fairy tales, popular culture (including calendar art and Agatha Christie murder mysteries), and the epics and ballads that she studies in her night class. She is the prince in "Little Brier-Rose" ("Sleeping Beauty") who "must hack her way through the brambles" to his wall (135, D1967.1) as well as (unconsciously) the sleeping or unaware princess. As the angel in "The Girl Without Hands" (AT 706), whose wings, in this case, are dingy gray and frayed, she is "tired of being an angel" administering meatloaf at set intervals (152–53). Unconsciously, however, she is also the Girl Without Hands, whose eyes and tongue are nearly cut out as well (T327.1; Hunt and Stern 164; Chapters 6–8). Passive before her televisionlike window, blinded and maimed by deceptions and self-deprecations, Sally may, just possibly, regrow her hands. Initially stuck like the elder brothers of "The Water of Life" in a ravine in which it is impossible to advance or turn (Hunt and Stern 450), unable to reach the magic elixir she imagines Ed holds (152), she is, ironically, not just faking a bad heart: her fairy-tale heavy, stone, or iron-banded heart (e.g., the Grimms' "The Frog King") does need repair.

Sally also plays a Snow Queen, whose palace, in this instance, may melt when she solves the "Citizen Kane" puzzle of her companion.[30] Ironically, however, she may also be a Snow

Queen foil (little Gerda, her grandmother, the old woman and her flowers, the clever princess, the Robber-Girl, the Lapp woman and the Finnish woman), a possible heroic rescuer, of herself if not her male partner. In another reversal, she plays the boy who is in love with the Snow Queen and who is plagued with an ice splinter in both heart and eye. In this case, however, the splinter from the devil's mirror makes "everything good and beautiful reflected in it disappear almost to nothing" without making the bad and ugly show up clearly.[31] For most of the story, it is Sally, rather than Ed, who needs a seeing-eye dog (162) and Sally who is almost as stupid as she feels Ed is. Sally is afraid to enter Bluebeard's secret room.

In terms of fairy-tale references, most significantly, of course, Sally again plays both Fitcher's bride and Fitcher. As the wives of Bluebeard/Fitcher/the Robber Bridegroom, she is in danger, like false brides in the Grimms' tales, of being replaced with other interchangeable women (165) or, like the Goose Girl's maid, "put into a barrel stuck full of nails and rolled downhill, endlessly" (136).[32] Like numerous wicked stepmothers, she thinks of the other sirens, her rivals, without pity, however: "Trouble with your heart? Get it removed . . . . Then you'll have no more problems" (140). As we have seen, even she recognizes her Bluebeard tendency to "flatten" and reduce Ed, leaving out or cutting off whatever doesn't fit her preconceived mold. Perhaps it is really Sally, rather than the hordes of women she imagines hiding in the forsythia, who wants to gobble Ed up, "chew [him] into tiny pieces" in the "little dark room" so "there won't be anything left" (148–49). But at the end of the story, after Sally has entered the forbidden room (Ed's ultrasound room, the alcove where he is touching Marylynn, and her own "inner world"), it is Sally's heart, now colorless, that is "torn out of her" and Sally's castle that is crumbling.

Like the other bride/wives in this volume as well as Atwood's other fairy-tale figures, however, Sally is more than severed pieces, more than robber or victim of herself or Ed. Whether or not she will flee Fitcher's castle like a bird is unclear, but the egg of possibility is alive, pulsing and likely to hatch. While we cannot answer definitively the question Sally asks in the story's final words, "What will come out of it?" Sally has already reminded us of the egg's mythological and folkloric significance as a fertility symbol, object in spells, and source of the universe (159). Described as "golden pink, resting in a nest of brambles, glowing softly as though there's something red and hot inside it," and then darkening to "rose-red, crimson" (166), the egg carries specific associations with golden, red, and nest eggs, including the golden egg of the world laid by the primeval goose, the red eggs of salvation or abundance, and the nest egg that may induce future birth (see Jobes 492–93, Leach and Fried 341). A number of fairy-tale connections also exist, most directly to the Grimms' "The Crystal Ball" (AT 302, No. 197). This type, called The Ogre's (Devil's) Heart in the Egg, can suggest the external soul (Motif E711.1) in the egg, which helps explain Sally's association of the egg with the heart in Atwood's story (165). Since Ed has been identified with the egg, if his heart or soul is in the egg, he no longer has power over Sally (the third sister). In the Grimms' version of this type, the crystal ball yolk of a "red hot egg" releases a beautiful king's daughter from the shape of ugliness given her by an enchanter, again implying positive transformation. In Andersen's "The Phoenix Bird," a phoenix symbolizing poetry rises from a red egg under the Tree of Knowledge.

Once the disguise has slipped, Sally, like other Atwood personae, again seems to fear a nothingness inside; but her search for a point of view in the Bluebeard story and her encounter with her own inner world promise, if not magic transformation, a new world of vision, possibly a reborn self. It would appear that she and Ed have little chance of going through the forbidden door together since Ed gives no indication of dropping disguise or, like the Robber Bridegroom in Atwood's poem of that name (first section of this chapter), of ceasing to expect women to "melt into him" (*I* 62). Possibly Sally can rejoin the severed pieces of herself

(Motif E30) and, like the Grimms' Robber Bride and the artist personae of *Interlunar*, break silence to tell her own story. If not "true," the story could at least be a renunciation of the wrong lies, which amputate both self and other (*PP* "Hesitations"; *TS* title poem).

Too frequently, critics misinterpret Atwood's gender images. Inextricably tied, female and male are often doubled. Just as Rennie in *Bodily Harm* must recognize that the eyes of "the man with the rope" "twin and reflect her own," we must recognize that Atwood's male power figures are sometimes dark reflections, anti-selves, or even Frankenstein creations of the female persona. Always reverberating with feminist meaning but never simple, Atwood's metaphors are, finally, not limited to gender roles.

Despite the painful and sometimes comic images of male and female locked in Bluebeardian embrace or Gothic disguise and of artists married to death, Atwood's visual and literary work continues to be full of possibility, if for no other reason because it makes us see what we, like her characters, would often rather not see. Once said and seen and said again (by her readers as well as narrators), how can it be forgotten? We have entered Bluebeard's room. Can we now rejoin the severed pieces of ourselves, our brothers, and our sisters?

Off the Path to Grandma's House in *The Handmaid's Tale*

"Little Red Cap"

"What do you think of when you see someone in red carrying a basket?" asks Atwood.[1] Although few critics have commented on the "Little Red Cap" or "Red Riding Hood" intertext in *The Handmaid's Tale* (1985, 1986),[2] Red Cap again meets the "wolf" in this text's sinister future. In addition, *The Handmaid's Tale* draws on Triple Goddess myth and the biblical story of Jacob, Rachel, Leah, and their handmaids, presenting not only a timeless vision of oppression in any form, but exploring sexual politics in a feminist's hell.[3]

Although Atwood says that *The Handmaid's Tale* is speculative rather than science fiction, in the tradition of *1984* (Atwood Visit), in a broader sense *The Handmaid's Tale* is an anti-narrative that both comments on and undercuts its varied intertexts, especially the fairy tale. In this sense it is, in part, a metafairy tale[4]:it is about "Red Cap" and other fairy tales. In addition to subverting "true romance" and utopian traditions, it self-consciously comments on, surrealistically distorts, even reverses the Grimms' tale. *The Handmaid's Tale* is also metacriticism: like *Bodily Harm*, it is about the reading process and literary criticism. The parodic scholarly epilogue tells us that Offred's tale of doubtful authorship is oral, supposedly tape-recorded, transcribed, reconstructed, arranged, and altered over time like folktales and parts of the Bible. Flippant about the tale's title and text and, like some discussions of *The Handmaid's Tale*, dangerously detached about its horrifying events,[5] these scholars undercut the value of their research and both the "truth" and fiction of the story we read. By linking the fairy tale with science fiction and satirizing those who would dismiss, redo, or overlook parts of fairy tales, myth, the Bible, and literature, Atwood projects past and present turbulence into the future, structuring a gender nightmare designed to move readers out of Rapunzel towers.

Implying a path through the nightmare, like most of Atwood's work *The Handmaid's Tale* is a distorting mirror: in order self-consciously to invert Little Red Cap's forest world and the biblical Eden, *The Handmaid's Tale* again incorporates the ancient myth of the Triple-Goddess (see preceding chapters). In addition to the usual Diana Maiden, Venus mother, and Hecate Crone (*Surv* 199, 210), Atwood draws on early versions of the Persephone and "Red Cap" stories and on the Triple Marys of the Bible (Walker, *Woman's Encyclopedia*, 602–3, 614), all based in Goddess myth. All the females of the book figure in a parodic goddess trilogy. Interlacing the fairy-tale, mythic, and biblical intertexts, Atwood's novel presents Offred as already eaten Red Cap, raped Persephone maiden and Venus (Aphrodite), and biblical Bilhah; the Commander as wolf, Hades, Jacob, and biblical patriarch; and Serena Joy as witch-mother, Hecate, and Rachel. The goal of Red Cap's quest is reunion with Mother Earth or Persephone's return from "hell."

As previous chapters show, characters of myth often parallel those of fairy tales and the Bible; thus, Atwood's intertexts closely connect. All three intertexts share themes, images, motifs, settings, character types, similar character doubling and foiling, elements of plot, and narrative patterns that Atwood uses in *The Handmaid's Tale*. Like *The Handmaid's Tale*, the mythic, biblical, and fairy-tale intertexts all dramatize sexual politics: patriarchal power threatens or dominates the female and the submerged matriarchy behind her. In addition, the intertexts and novel all oppose green world (fertility) to the sterility of the underworld or civilization and are about familial conflict and mothers' separation from children. Most use red symbolism of the Triple Goddess or one of her aspects,[6] feature journeys, and suggest literal or ritual dismemberment and cannibalism.[7]

In the book's mythic intertext, the Demeter—Persephone (Kore) story, also embedded in Atwood's first published work, *Double Persephone* (1961, see Chapter 2), in *Surfacing* (1972), and in *Lady Oracle* (1976), not only portrays the Great Goddess but the kind of patriarchal displacement (Graves, *Greek Myths I* 93) that occurred with the triple Marias and fairy tales (Dundes Introduction to Zipes, "Little" 121; Zipes, "Little" 126–27). In the matriarchal version of the Demeter—Persephone myth, the goddess sacrifices herself to the earth. Demeter-Ceres is "reaped as the grain with her own moon-shaped sickle." Similarly, North American Natives' Corn Mother, whose limbs are severed, gives her blood to the earth so that her children, humanity, can cultivate corn (Sjoo and Mor 165–66).

In the best-known, patriarchal versions of the Demeter—Persephone story, however, Persephone leaves the earth, not of her free will, but because Hades abducts and rapes her, symbolizing male usurpation of the female Mysteries (Graves, *Greek Myths I* 93). These versions are about a flower-picking daughter's rape, her abduction to the underworld, her separation from her mother (a second aspect of the fertility grain goddess), the sterility of the earth, the mother's efforts to recover her daughter, the daughter's taboo eating in the underworld, and her periodic return (Leach and Fried 858–59; see Chapter 2).

Similarly, at least in some versions, "Little Red Cap," like *The Handmaid's Tale*, is about a fertile daughter who delights in flowers, is separated from her mother (and in the case of *HT*, also her daughter) in an off-limits area or underworld, participates in taboo eating or hunger (Delarue 19), brings on her own rape by a wolf, and is eventually reborn. Whereas Demeter, the mother, is swallowed and disgorged by her father and tricked by her brother (Leach and Fried 306), the Grimms' Red Cap is swallowed and cut out of the wolf's stomach.

A "Modest Proposal" envisioning patriarchal theocracy, *The Handmaid's Tale* uses its mythical and other major intertexts as it uses Victorian and other literary or historical references: to suggest a distinctly feminist apocalyptic parody. According to Northrop Frye, Atwood's teacher at the University of Toronto, romantic, "realistic," and ironic literature suggest implicit mythical patterns. Undisplaced myth "takes the form of two contrasting worlds of total metaphorical identification, one desirable and the other undesirable. These worlds are often identified with the existential heavens and hells of the religions contemporary with such literature" (*Anatomy* 139). Although apocalyptic and demonic archetypes are universal, pastoral myth, with its "nostalgia for a world of peace and protection, with a spontaneous response to the nature around it," is, as Frye suggests, particularly evident in Canadian literature (*Bush Garden* 238–39). *The Handmaid's Tale* is no exception.[8]

Rather than the heaven-on-earth or pre-fall world the fathers of Gilead say, and perhaps believe, they are building, *The Handmaid's Tale* ironically depicts Frye's "world of the nightmare and the scapegoat, of bondage and pain and confusion" (*Anatomy* 147). As Jeremiah prophesized of its biblical namesake, it is "the desolation of the Promised Land" (Freibert 281). It is "the world also of perverted or wasted work, ruins and catacombs, instruments of torture and monuments of folly," replete with tree of death as well as tyrant-leader and sacrificed victim (pharmakos and sparagmos) in a parodic Eucharist. A Babylon rather than Jerusalem, it is an anti-apocalyptic world, with its euphemistic language, metaphoric wolf, sinister garden, urban waste land, temple prostitutes, and even technological Behemoths (Frye, *Anatomy* 147–48; *Code* 141). More ironically, Gilead fulfills traditional scholarly definitions of "hell" primarily because of its treatment of "gender traitors," nonwhite races, religious minorities, and especially women.

The Handmaid's Tale also foregrounds the sexual politics of its main biblical intertext, Genesis, chapters 29 and 30. Literalizing and therefore parodying this passage, the book also implicitly satirizes aspects of Islam, Puritanism, Mormonism, and Christianity, particularly the contemporary fundamentalism represented by Pat Robertson (Atwood Visit). One Catholic sect even calls the wives of its coordinators "handmaidens" (*Evening Telegram*, October 31, 1985; see Atwood Papers, *HT* "Background Materials" 1984–88). Atwood sets her narrative in what was once Cambridge, Massachusetts,[9] and is now called Gilead. Named for a region in ancient Palestine, Gilead is the place where Jacob and Laban "made a deal" about Laban's daughters (Atwood Visit). Jacob's two wives, Leah and Rachel, are "played off against each other in the quest for status." Since an androcentric perspective values a woman for her ability to produce offspring[10] and since the twelve sons of Jacob and his wives will represent the twelve tribes of Israel (Exum 79), Rachel and Leah are "having a baby contest to see who can have the most sons" (Atwood visit). "And when Rachel saw that she bare Jacob no children, Rachel envied her sister, and said unto Jacob, Give me children, or else I die. And Jacob's anger was kindled against Rachel; and he said, Am I in God's stead, who hath withheld from thee the fruit of the womb?" (Genesis 30.1–2). Atwood's retelling exposes and institutionalizes Rachel's envy and Jacob's power and anger. But it is Bilhah rather than Rachel who must produce children or die. Although Handmaids in Gilead could be punished with amputation of a hand for reading the Bible (or anything else), they are required to perform, literally, the "sacred" task that Bilhah fulfilled for Rachel in Genesis, 30.1–3: "she shall bear upon my knees, that I may also have children by her" (*HT* epigraph).

We know almost nothing about the powerless Bilhah except

that her story is written for her by the collusion of her mistress with the patriarch; she is one of numberless biblical handmaids, including Hagar and Zelpha. "The custom of using the hand-maid for progeny permeated Israelite history and custom," and legal documents pertaining to the practice date back to the fifteenth century B.C. (Freibert 282). But rarely has anyone looked at the passages about handmaids from handmaids' points of view. Whether or not Bilhah agreed to what a doctor recently called "genital rental" is unrecorded (*Manchester Guardian* October 2, 1985; *HT* "Background Materials", Atwood Papers): Bilhah exists as a use object and, like Persephone and Red Cap, is violated. Ironically, like Offred and the Virgin Mary, she is designated to be a surrogate mother and bear a child with one of God's representatives.[11] Resembling Offred and Demeter, she is separated from her child through patriarchal betrayal.

The sexual politics of the "Little Red Cap" intertext varies with the tale's different versions. Fairy and folk tales "have always symbolically depicted the nature of power relationships within a given society" (Zipes, *Fairy Tales and the Art of Subversion* 67). Usual views of "Little Red Cap" ("Rotkäppchen," 1812) focus on a girl who, taught to fear her sensuality, must be rescued by a "good father" devoid of sexuality. According to Zipes, however, the Grimms made substantial changes in oral folk tales. "It was the rise of authoritarian patriarchal societies that was responsible for (the) fear of sexuality and stringent sexual codes" evident in "Little Red Cap" (*Fairy Tales and the Art of Subversion* 46–47, 52, 59). "Whether the story is about initiation, warning, or both, one thing is clear: the folk tale celebrates the self-reliance of a young peasant girl" (Zipes, *The Trials* 8). The original villain in oral folk tradition, "either an ogre, ogress, man-eater, wild person, werewolf, or wolf," attacked a child, characteristically "a good girl gone wrong," in the forest or at home. Charles Perrault, "who appears to have had a low opinion of women and of the superstitious customs of the peasantry," made the girl totally helpless in his "contaminated" literary version, "Le petit chaperon rouge" (*Contes du temps passé* 1697), probably derived from French werewolf stories in which the girl escaped. The Grimm brothers, whose tale was originally based on the Perrault version, adapted it to "the *Biedermeier* or Victorian image of little girls and proper behavior" and provided a male savior, happy ending, and Christian moral (Zipes, *The Trials* 1–2, 6, 14–16).

Like Persephone (Diana), Demeter (Venus), early Christianity's Mary and Eve, and Snow White, Red Cap was part of a Virgin-Mother-Crone trinity; and she wore the same red garment the virgin Kali, British priestesses (Walker, *Woman's Encyclopedia*, 1068–70), and witches ("the flip side of the Maria cult") wore (Zipes, *Trials*, n. 64, 55). According to Walker, the first werewolf was Moeris, spouse of the trinitarian Fate-Goddess (Moera or Moira or the Moirai, also associated with Mary); and the She-Wolf was an aspect of the Triple Goddess (*Woman's Encyclopedia* 1068–70, 603). "Little Red Cap"'s wolf-clan traditions, emphasized in Angela Carter's twentieth-century retelling, "The Company of Wolves" (*Bloody* 142–53),[12] are evident in "the red garment, the offering of food to a 'grandmother' in the deep woods—a grandmother who wore a wolf skin—and the cannibalistic motif of devouring and resurrection." As in many other werewolf stories, the original victim was the hunter (the Lord of the hunt), not Red Cap (Walker, *Woman's Encyclopedia*, 1068–70). Since the grandmother, traditionally seen as morally weak, even betraying, was, like Red Cap, identified with the displaced goddess, interpretations of the tale frequently reveal misogyny.[13]

Sharing many feminists' disgust with "Red Cap" and apparently unaware of the tale's ties to matriarchal religion, Hélène Cixous ironically exposes the phallocentricism not only of popularized versions of the tale but also of its usual interpretations. According to Cixous, unlike "Sleeping Beauty," expressive of woman's place "[i]n bed and asleep—'laid (out),'" "Little Red Cap" is a story in which a woman "can be found standing up, but not for long." In Cixous's "little clitoris's" journey from one house to another (from mother to other), one "might imagine [the grandmother] as taking the place of the 'Great Mother,' because there are great men but not great women: there are Grand-Mothers instead." Although Cixous recognizes Red Riding Hood's detour "through her own forest," she feels the girl falls victim to her superego, the wolf. Unlike the disorder and laughter of a feminine "economy," this masculine "economy" generated by "the Law of the Father" silences and "decapitates" women through rigid inculcation ("Castration or Decapitation" 480–83). Continuing to read Red Cap as a brain-washed, passive victim, however, also silences and decapitates her.

Although Atwood gives no explicit indication of knowing either oral versions or goddess origins of "Red Cap," she refers to oral variations of another folktale in *Bluebeard's Egg* and in general uses the Grimms rather than Perrault because she prefers fairy tales with positive female images (Telephone Call). As we have seen, Atwood frequently alludes to the Triple Goddess (*Surv* 199–200; Atwood Papers, Drafts of *Lady Oracle*) and even draws on Mary's early association with the goddess in *Cat's Eye* (Chapter 11). *The Handmaid's Tale* not only evokes the goddess, but it revisions the best-known versions and interpretations of "Little Red Cap," finally restoring the Red Cap figure's inner resourcefulness and power. Among important features of the Grimms' tale that Atwood uses or parodies in her metafairy tale are the sexual politics, power politics, mothers' separation from children, familial conflict, quest, and initiation themes; the oppositions of house (culture) and green world (nature); the flower, fertility, sense, path, cannibalism, and dismemberment images; the red clothing, hood, and basket; the characterization (e.g., Red Cap's naiveté; the wolf's appetite, disguise, and use of deception); character doubling and foiling; aspects of the plot; and the narrative structure. By using a developing first-person, self-conscious narrator, initially with very limited vision, rather than the traditional reliable, privileged, third person, Atwood privileges Red Cap's point of view. By integrating the "Historical Notes"' commentary on the reading and writing process into *The*

Handmaid's Tale, Atwood's metafairy tale also becomes metacriticism.

Initially, Offred is a grown up but naive Red Cap, whose conditioning endorses contentment in the wolf's embrace. Her ironic "innocence" or naiveté is, like the initial blindness of Atwood's other narrators, partially willed. In the world of the fairy tale, innocence or ignorance is equivalent to evil (Atwood Telephone Call 1985; Visit): failure to know what the wolf is brings the same disaster as choosing the wolf. Having gone with her society through the looking glass, Atwood's Red Cap is now trapped in a mirror, "a distorted shadow, a parody of something, some fairy-tale figure in a red cloak, descending towards a moment of carelessness that is the same as danger. A Sister, dipped in blood" (McClelland *HT* 19).

Reflecting the bizarre custom—not confined to Gilead—of giving a woman the name of the man who "commands" her, Offred's name also suggests "Off-red" as a secret rebel, the "Offered" in a blood sacrifice (Lacombe 7), and, especially, the "red" figure who goes "off" the path to immerse herself in nature. Like Red Cap, Offred is identified by her clothing. Offred, however, is owned by the wolf. Like her feared witch foremothers, including Atwood's relative Mary Webster (to whom the book is dedicated), she wears an official tatoo or cattle brand (Dworkin, *Woman* 142–43); the later evening rental tag also proves ownership. Unlike Red Cap but ironically resembling Jacob and other biblical characters renamed by God, a Handmaid is renamed when she changes households. Thus, in her ongoing encounter with the patriarch/wolf, she may be denied not only personal identity, but even gender identification: when she fails to produce a child after three fairy-tale chances, she becomes "Unwoman."

Like other women in Gilead, Offred is not only denied identity but symbolically dismembered. When Offred's Compucard is canceled because she is female, in a marriage no longer legally recognized, she feels as if her feet, symbolically the freest part of her, have been amputated (188, Motif S162).[14] At the Red Center of indoctrination recalling *Jane Eyre*'s Red Room, women's feet and hands, considered inessential for Handmaids (102), are sometimes disfigured (Q451, Q451.0.1). The name of Offred's friend and alter-ego, Moira, ironically suggests the virginal Aphrodite, another aspect of the goddess trinity (Walker, *Woman's Encyclopedia* 666); the death aspect of the Moira, Ilithyia (Birth), and Callone (Beauty) triad (Graves, *White* 11); the first werewolf's spouse; the Triple Fates; and Mary (Walker, *Woman's Encyclopedia* 666, 1068–70). This name also recalls Moira Shearer's filmed version of Andersen's "The Red Shoes," the fairy tale about a woman whose feet are cut off because she dances in red shoes. In the film that also functions as an intertext in *Lady Oracle* (Chapter 5), a woman must choose between dancing or loving a man. In *The Handmaid's Tale*, choice no longer exists: Handmaids all wear red shoes and are forced to have sex with their Commanders. When Moira tries to assert herself against the system, like other "traitors" she receives a variety of torture practiced in Ayatollah Khomaini's Iran, in this case the bastinada (Atwood Papers, *HT* "Background Materials" 1984–88"): the soles of her feet are whipped with steel cables so that she is temporarily unable to walk.

Unable to speak out or even eat (102) (Motifs Q451.3, F513.0.3), Offred and the others steal packets of sugar for Moira, one of the few Gilead women to still possess a mouth. In the patriarchy of Gilead, the Handmaid exists as a two-legged womb (70, 104, 146). If, for practical purposes, other parts of her remain, they are, as in Afghanistan or on Old Dutch Cleanser packages of Atwood's childhood, totally concealed (Atwood Visit). Adorned in her red "habit" with white angel wings "to keep [her] from seeing, but also from being seen," Offred is already a "seen" woman, controlled by the wolf even within the "home" that can never be hers.

Atwood's subversion of the "Little Red Riding Hood" story most readers know is evident in the book's distorted mirroring of the fairy-tale narrative. Near the beginning of the book, Offred, like Red Cap, leaves a privileged house of abundance (Heuscher 74; Bettleheim 170) on a journey both internal and external. Now equipped with a shatterproof window, however, this house is no longer either safe or home: this image of female initiation has already been violated, "chopped up," and consumed. Red Cap's movement is severely limited. Thus, her dusty pink path, ironically "like a carpet for royalty," now begins *inside* the house. As in Atwood's watercolor of the crowned Termite Queen in a red dress (Plate 12, see Chapter 2), the royalty of this "Mother Goddess," and of all the Handmaids and Wives imprisoned on a "pedestal," is a sinister variant of television's old "Queen for a Day." A Persephone cut off from the green world, Offred is a Red Cap who has been captured, violated, and debased. Despite her patriarchal society's ironic "worship" of the fertility symbolized in Red Cap, the matriarchal goddess, and the biblical Madonna, she is forced to be "the eternal fucking machine" (Rich, *Of Woman Born* 285) rather than being honored as the bearer of life.[15]

Significantly, the relationship of *The Handmaid's Tale* to "Little Red Cap" is even suggested by the convex pier glass Offred passes as she begins her journey. Anticipating the pier glass of *Cat's Eye*, the mirror seems to the blinkered Offred "like the eye of a fish, and myself in it like a distorted shadow . . . [of] some fairy tale figure" (19). Red Cap's forest has become a polished hall, and all that is left of the enchanted vegetable world is Serena Joy's subversive "bleeding" garden and the Victorian banister (the remnant of trees and Great-Goddess Tree of Life) (Daly, *Gyn/ecology* 81). Authority replaces magic, and daughters are separated from both natural mothers and Great Mother (die Grossmütter). This Red Cap, like her daughter, has been entrusted to futuristic versions of wicked stepmothers in collusion with the wolf. Thus, she is headed, not alone to Grandma's house, but to shops ironically named "Lilies of the Field," "Milk and Honey," and "All Flesh," accompanied by her double, another Handmaid vessel awaiting filling. Passing a grandfather clock that "doles out time," as the terrible fathers of Gilead measure pleasures and pains and segment women's bodies by color-coded functions, Offred next passes "The motherly front sitting room, with its fleshtones and hints. A sitting room in which I never sit, but stand or kneel only" (18). Red Cap's "mother" is now represented by the black-gloved "Aunts" of the Red Centre, who hold electric cattle prods rather than "Cinderella" wands, and Serena Joy, who must participate with her in a ritualistic parody of sexual love. Thus, Red Cap is in a world of betrayed innocence. Ironically, it has been reached by a society's enforced travel *on* a narrow path, leading not to earthly heaven but to sexist "hell."

As Red Cap's stepmother in this demonic world, Serena Joy's role is as parodic as Offred's. Serena's name, reminding Offred of a feminine hair product, is, like Offred's, not her real one: it was selected for her former role as a television gospel singer. Undercutting the fate of all those who, Schlafly-style, are forced to practice what they preach,[16] she is neither serene nor joyful once she is confined to "the sanctity of the home" (55). As in the Grimms' version, it is her business to enforce the "rules" keeping Red Cap on the path, away from the flowers and any voluntary encounter with the wolf: Offred's predecessor hangs herself when Serena discovers her secret meetings with the Commander. In the Grimms' tale it is also Red Cap's mother who warns Red Cap against "prying into every nook and corner" (Magoun and Krappe 102; Hunt 139). Gilead's bad-witch mothers bear partial responsibility for Offred's conditioned unseeing, which, along with patriarchal control and willed blindness, keeps her in the wolf's belly.

Serena is also both biblical Rachel and Crone Goddess in this fallen world. Consistent with the kinds of women portrayed in *1984* and the Bible (Atwood Visit; Frye, *Code* 140–41; Walker, *Woman's Encyclopedia* 666), Serena, clad in Virgin-Mary blue, even plays Madonna to her opposite, Moira's Jezebel or Whore of Babylon, and to the intermediate figure dressed in red, Offred's

Mary Magdalene. Although *The Handmaid's Tale* takes place in the United States and comments most directly on U.S. culture, it illustrates the tendency Atwood observes in other Canadian literature for the Crone or Hecate to predominate, characteristically incorporating Diana and Venus figures (*Surv* 210; Chapters 6, 11). Framing Offred on the marital bed during official sex for procreation, as Wives frame Handmaids during birth, Serena almost literally incorporates Venus. A Madonna unable to give birth to any savior, she—along with the Commander—symbolizes her world's sterility.[17] Like Moira and Offred, Serena is trapped in her role, not only a bizarre parody of fairy-tale, Jacob/Rachel, and apocalyptic sexual union but another debasement of the Triple Goddess. She is forced to compete for the attention of her husband. Resembling the false mothers of "Hansel and Gretel" and "Little Snow White," Serena produces wool "children" and cultivates a Victorian garden, "something for them to order and maintain and care for" (22) in the absence of either societal power or familial responsibility.

Serena's garden re-visions the sensuous fairy-tale flowers that tempts Red Cap to forget her mother's instructions, the apocalyptic rose identified with Christian communion, and, by association, the Tree of Life important in myth, religion, and fairy tales: "the garden . . . is large and tidy: a lawn in the middle, a willow, weeping catkins; around the edges, the flower borders, in which the daffodils are now fading and the tulips are opening their cups, spilling out colour. The tulips are red, a darker crimson toward the stem, as if they had been cut and are beginning to heal there." This garden is the domain of the Commander's Wife. Ruling over her depleted kingdom with "her knees on a cushion, a light blue veil thrown over her wide gardening hat, a basket at her side with shears in it and pieces of string in it for tying the flowers into place, . . . the Commander's Wife directs, pointing with her stick" (22) while someone else does the digging.

Although the flowers forbidden Red Cap "are still allowed"

(17) in Gilead and even adorn the beds and sofas where Handmaids personally experience Gileadean control, they must be cut and tied into an appropriate position; sometimes tulips (*two lips*, according to Lacombe 10–12) are also symbolically silenced and crucified. When Offred, carrying a basket of lambchops suggesting imminent slaughter, sees "Saint Serena" in early summer, Serena is again "on her knees, doing penance," in the garden. The tulips are "shedding their petals one by one, like teeth." This time, however, Serena is "aiming, positioning the blades of the shears, then cutting with a convulsive jerk of the hands. [Is] it arthritis, creeping up? Or some blitzkrieg, some kamikaze, committed on the swelling genitalia of the flowers? The fruiting body." Ironically, however, "to cut off the seed pods is supposed to make the bulbs store energy" (160–61).

This divided Gileadean sensibility recalls not only "Little Red Cap" and the Bible but Tennyson's poetry, on which the gardens of *The Handmaid's Tale* are partly based (Atwood Visit), and the Victorian society behind it: in Gilead, as in Tennyson, we sense "a dialectic clash between the attraction of the deepest subjective levels and the resistance and restraint of other sectors of reality."[18] In Tennyson's early poem, "Sense and Conscience," when Conscience is drugged by Sense and awakened by Memory and Pain, he futilely stabs "the pleasurable flowers" and ivy, which bleeds on his feet with blood resembling tears (42–46). Imprisoned like Offred in a role that has literally as well as symbolically crippled her ability to touch or express erotic feeling (Motifs C500, Q451.1, S161), Serena Joy is as passive as some consider the Catholic Mary after patriarchal persecution of Mariolatry (Sjoo and Mor 350; Walker, *Woman's Encyclopedia* 603). Serena Joy may share Offred's repressed desire to emasculate the "godhead" and the phallocentric society it represents. At the same time, she reinforces the Commander-wolf's power with submission and collusion.

If Serena's garden bleeds sacrificially, as a scapegoat, it is, nevertheless, storing energy for Persephone's return. One of the few remnants of life and fertility in the sexist wasteland resembling *Double Persephone*'s "Formal Garden" (n.p.), flowers may be tied, dried, confined to straight borders, or captured in framed designs and stylized prints, as on the canopy bed used for "The Ceremony" (104); but they and the feelings they represent are not finally controlled by the Gileadean fathers. The power of Gilead, the power of patriarchy, is limited.

When the Grimms' Red Cap leaves the prescribed path to pick flowers, she is consumed by the world of the senses. Forgetting her infirm grandmother on her detour into the spontaneous and natural, she becomes vulnerable to the wolf, often considered an animalistic impulse, rapacious male, or "bad father" who hears, sees, touches, and then swallows her. Rescued by the "good-father" huntsman,[19] who carefully cuts open the wolf instead of impulsively shooting him, the reborn Red Cap learns how to deal with the next wolf, who can be fooled and trapped by his own senses.

Already consumed and inside the wolf's belly (Motif F911.3) from the beginning of the book, Atwood's "reversed" Red Cap does, finally, go off the path to the flowers, this time associated with ancient female power. Unlike the Grimms' Red Cap, Offred recovers amputated senses and is reborn in the sensory world. Seeming to radiate heat, breathe and breathe itself in, Serena's garden tempts Offred as well as Nick to journey off the patriarchal path to "distant pathways" (190, 239) of a paradoxically literal and archetypal past, goal of the future. Offred is drawn to no longer silenced flowers, to irises "like pastel water momentarily frozen in a splash" and to "the bleeding hearts, so female in shape it was a surprise they'd not long since been rooted out. There is something subversive about this garden of Serena's, a sense of buried things bursting upwards, wordlessly, into the light, as if to point, to say: Whatever is silenced will clamour to be heard, though silently." As Offred's dress "rustles against the flesh of [her] thighs and the grass grows underfoot," the willows whisper and she feels dizzy: "at the edges of [her] eyes there are movements, in the branches; feathers, flittings, grace notes, tree into bird, metamorphosis run wild" (161). Significantly, not only is Demeter's dead world awakening, as if from a suspected spell of enchantment (224); but Offred's Red Centre conditioning, that has suppressed her appetite by "feeding" her scriptures for breakfast and lunch (99) and attempted to blind, bind, gag, and obliterate a symbolically amputated body, is wearing off. Offred is no longer, like Tennyson's Conscience, repressing feeling. "Goddesses are possible now, and the air suffuses with desire." Even the mineral world, "softening, becoming tactile," begins to melt like the irises, and Offred is, like "a melon on a stem, . . . liquid ripeness" (161–62).

In the Grimms' fairy tale, Red Cap remarks on the wolf's large ears, eyes, hands, and mouth (Motif Z18.1); and the wolf does hear, see, touch, and then eat her (Motif F911.3). In *The Handmaid's Tale* it is Red Cap's "enlarged" sensory organs that save her: when Offred recovers her ability to hear, smell, taste, and, most significantly, touch, see, and speak, she begins to recover her self, her real name, and a position in time. In addition, by going off Gilead's theocratic path and experiencing the natural world, Atwood's transformed Red Cap begins to recover the Great Mother, displaced by phallocentric culture and its sanitized folklore in favor of the familiar figure of weakness or betrayal.

Offred expresses her recovered senses in her relationship with Nick, the huntsman figure who is in a sense also St. Nicholas, bestower of gifts (Motif N816) and miracles, and Old Nick or a parodic devil (Motif G303). The Grimms' Red Cap would presumably stay eaten without the assistance of the huntsman, the wolf's alter ego. In early oral versions of the tale, however, the girl never dies and saves herself without external help, sometimes by cutting her way out of the wolf's belly and in one later instance by shooting him with an automatic pistol (Zipes, *Trials* 1, 6–7). Again unnecessary to Red Cap's rebirth, Nick still assists Offred on her journey. Now an underground opponent to the patriarchy rather than a rational father or Disney prince, he doubles Offred both in becoming another patriarchal sex object, a "seedpod" to father the child the Commander can't (274), and a rebel of Gilead's monovalent "god." Although Serena selects Nick and even bribes Offred to cooperate, Offred goes back to Nick again and again. "I did not do it for him, but for myself entirely . . . , thankful, each time he would let me in. He didn't have to" (280). Paradoxically, in a situation without freedom, Offred and Nick freely choose one another, creating a real relationship that foils the Commander's with either Wife or Handmaid. Loving touch is again a means of disenchantment, restoration, and personal magic (Motif D782). Although Atwood's huntsman helps "Red Cap" leave the wolf's belly (Motif F913) as St. Nicholas sometimes saves girls from slavery (Motif R165.1), in *The Handmaid's Tale* only the narrator, who names herself again both to Nick and after the Particicution (282, 293), is responsible for her rebirth.[20]

Like her increased efforts to face painful memories of her lost mother,[21] her daughter, Luke, and Moira, Offred's sisterhood with Moira, Ofglen, and her "ancestress" double (305) are all evidence of her straying from the Gileadean path. Her visit to the Commander's forbidden room (Motif C611), however, not only dramatizes her metamorphosis but parodies "Little Red Cap" and the biblical intertext. The Commander is also Jacob, the father of Israel, the false god, the anti-Christ, Hades, a fairy-tale shoemaker, Bluebeard, and, significantly, the dispenser of the patriarchal "word." Comically, when Offred enters the door to be alone with this wolf, he wants her to play Scrabble, a word game, with him. In Gilead, as in the world of *1984*, the word is all (Motif D520), making the cruder disguise as a kindly grandmother unnecessary. Although he and his government have already swallowed Red Cap, this wolf not only hopes to make her stay more comfortable but wants her to kiss him with meaning and feel the "true love" of the now forbidden women's magazines. Like the Bluebeard figures of *Lady Oracle* and "Bluebeard's Egg" (Chapters 5, 9), the powerful Commander is revealed as lonely and pathetic: not only does he have a belly, but he seems to shrink, "like something being dried" (267). Resembling the wolf of "Little Red Cap," his attempt to fill his emptiness is unsuccessful: like the wolf filled with stones, he and his regime are sterile.[22]

As in *Surfacing*, Offred's ability to laugh signals her opening and rebirth (Motif D1773). Feeling she will burst, splashing red all over the cupboard, she rhymes "mirth" and "birth," listens to the sound of her own heart, and even breathes as in exercises "for giving birth" (156). No longer thinking of herself as a chalice and abolishing the authority of the wolf (the hobbling forceps and other "fancy claims" Broumas's Red Riding Hood evades, 119), Offred explodes like the blood-red tulips (55) with the anarchistic "laugh of the Medusa" (Cixous, "Laugh" 484, 488). Turning herself "inside out" in a metamorphosis reminiscent of *Bodily Harm*'s Rennie as well as of numerous folk characters, Offred "blow[s] up the law" ("Laugh" 490–91), exploding her conditioning and defying Gilead's repressions.

Offred's regained ability to smell, taste, hear, touch, see, and speak accompany her desire to know. No longer afraid, like Atwood's camera-eye narrators, of seeing (Wilson, "Camera" 32–33), she faces both dimpled and winged eyes and asks for knowledge when the Commander offers presents. Now keeping her eyes open, not only with Nick and the Commander but at the Salvaging and the Particicution, Offred records Gilead's attempt to displace and purge female rage. Witnessing the perversion of matriarchal ritual to Bacchic punishment of the regime's political enemies, she begins to understand phallocentric power. Nevertheless, her regained appetite at the Particicution is again symbolic: "Maybe it's because I've been emptied; or maybe it's the body's way of seeing to it that I remain alive, continue to repeat its bedrock prayer: **I am, I am.** I am, still" (293; see n. 20). Having traced the flowers' changes through the cycle of seasons from spring to fall, Offred, who is probably pregnant, prepares for a perennial return recalling the subterranean journeys of Persephone and the narrators of *Surfacing*, *The Journals of Susanna Moodie*, and *Bodily Harm*. She is still afraid of the red shoes and of the Bluebeard/wolf's power to turn her into a dancing doll or, like her double, a wingless angel. Nevertheless, the Handmaid's narration ends with Mayday and, like that of *Surfacing*'s unnamed narrator, an act of trust: she steps into "a darkness within; or else the light" (305, 307).

Both Mayday (May Day) and light symbolism signify "a new beginning" (307). In addition to being the international radiotelephonic signal for help, a labor holiday, and a feminist tatoo protesting artificial birth methods (*HT* "Background Materials"), May Day (Motif V70.1.1) symbolizes the natural, anarchistic fertility that counters the "procreation by fiat" of Gilead and Ceaucescu's Romania (Atwood Papers, *HT* "Background Materials"). May Day was originally a goddess festival for Maya (Maj, Mary, Kale, Freya, Flora), the Virgin Goddess or Virgin Mother of Spring. Later Walpurgisnacht, the witches' festival, May Day is celebrated in a communal dance around the May tree (the god's phallus planted in the earth's womb) (Walker, *Woman's Encyclopedia* 624–26) and by picking flowers and bringing them home, "the symbolic act of bringing home the May, i.e. bringing new life, the spring, into the village. . . . Carrying the May tree and garlands from door to door is the symbolic bestowing and sharing of this new creative power that is stirring in the world." Sometimes mock battles between summer and winter, with summer always winning, occur; the May Bride sings about nature's bounty and may even "wake" the bridegroom with a kiss (Motif D1978.5, D735; Leach and Fried 695–96). Contrasting to Red Cap's wolf filled only with stones, Offred resembles the May Queen in bringing the earth new life, symbolized by the body's magic—her probable pregnancy (283)—and the zest for life she earlier envied in her mother and Moira. Thus, by making the fertility Gilead tried to control symbolize Offred's freedom, *The Handmaid's Tale* is profoundly ironic.

Similarly, an archetypal light in the darkness is not only paradoxical but hopeful. Elsewhere it is associated with the possibilities of the resistance, inner resources, prayer, and the post-Gileadean world of the future (115, 204, 324). In the Grimms' "Little Red Cap," the girl leaves the darkness within the wolf when an opening for her escape (rebirth) appears. We know from the existence of Offred's taped narrative that the dark van does finally take her off Gilead's theocratic path to a new life where she has a voice. Ironically, Offred "fall[s] from innocence to knowledge" (205) and to "disgrace, which is the opposite of grace" (303), suggesting the light symbolism of Lucifer and Luke's names as well as Saul's mystical transformation into Saint Paul, the much-quoted Apostle of Gilead as well as the Bible. Along with that of Nick, her fellow "devil" (Motif G303) to Gilead's "god," Offred's fall not only parodies the biblical fall but also structures her path out of the sexist wasteland. Out of the books' fifteen regular chapters, seven of them—the fairy-tale, magic, and formulaic lucky number marking the end of a spell (D791.1.1) or period (e.g., week of creation) or the beginning of a transformation (A1103)—are named "Night"; consciously or not, readers are prepared for light and change. Offred presumably takes the "Underground Femaleroad" (Motif R211.3), a free and "true way" to counter the wolf's prescribed "demonic labyrinth of lost direction" (Frye, *Code* 160). Offred may reach at last the "safe house" of her sisters, a place where she can consume the sacramental cake and wine of healing once brought to the grandmother.

Thus, changing the direction of Little Red Cap's journey and going "underground," into uncolonized earth, Offred becomes an artist: she not only signals Persephone's cyclical return and reunion with Demeter but invents a time in our imaginations for Bilhah to recover her own lost child. Like the Robber Bride of the Grimms' "The Robber Bridegroom," she tells her story, in a sense "singing" as both artist and May Bride. Resembling *Surfacing*, however, the book endorses respect for humanity and nature rather than worship of either Father or Mother God. Offred's tape recordings do more than speak against Gilead's atrocities: even inventing us as readers, her female narrative substitutes personal dialogue—within Offred, with people she misses, with various readers—for The Word.

The fate of Offred's descendants, represented by Professors Crescent Moon and Pieixoto at the University of Denay, Nunavit, may be, like our own, questionable, particularly if they, like we, continue to function in "Deny Mostofit." Still, the "Historical Notes" further develop and dramatize dialogue: this section functions intertextually to question not only how well we read folklore, myth, the Bible, history, newspapers, and our own lives but how well we are reading Offred, this book, and the book's intertexts. Parodying scholars and scholarly conferences and the novel's own double endings, neither of which is "the end," the "Historical Notes" decry the dangerous blindness of treating horrors of history, including witch burning and other sexism, fascism, homophobia, racism, and religious persecution, "objectively." Both formally establishing and undercutting Offred's story and its commentary as cultural artifacts, the "Notes" include readers in the communal group trying to decode the text.

Despite their unreliability, Moon and Piexoto's narratives provide not only necessary information but postcolonial perspective. Atwood compares her "Historical Notes" to *1984*'s Appendix on "The Principles of Newspeak" since both futuristic postscripts prove the end of the dystopian society (Atwood Visit): the voice of the repressed woman we know only as Offred survives longer than the regime that tries to silence it. But the name and location of the University of Denay, Nunavit, where the Twelfth Symposium on Gileadean Studies occurs, is partly ironic. "Denay" recalls what Canada's historically repressed northern natives, the Dene, call themselves; and "Nunavit" refers to what Dene and Inuit would call their country if they had one (Atwood Visit), both words suggesting the fulfillment of thwarted dreams. Similarly, the chairship of Professor Maryann Crescent Moon, of the Department of Caucasian Anthropology, again dramatizes the end of the racist, patriarchal Gilead: the Caucasian race is now marginalized, an interesting subject for academic study. Maryann's name could also seem to suggest a futuristic return to matriarchal values associated with Diana, the new moon Goddess of virginity and childbirth, the three Marys, and the Triple Goddess Mari-Anna-Ishtar (Walker, *Woman's Encyclopedia* 614). Although the society of Crescent Moon, Pieixoto, Gopal Chatterjee, and Johnny Running Dog certainly appears richer in ethnic diversity and less patriarchal than Gilead, however, it, too, is characteristically undercut.

Too clearly in this book in which everything has happened or is happening somewhere around the world (Visit; see newspaper clippings in Atwood Papers, "*HT* Backgrounds"), the future once again fails to learn from the past, including the old stories that form intertexts in *The Handmaid's Tale*. Instead of replacing the Western ways of their oppressors, Denay, Nunavit, only reverses the usual hierarchies (Davidson, "Future" 119). Moon may introduce the main speaker, ironically from the "other" Cambridge, relatively untouched by Gilead; but Piexoto's racist and sexist comments about their all "enjoying" their "Arctic Char" and "Arctic Chair" marginalizes her, mirroring not only women's treatment in Gilead (Davidson, "Future" 119) but patriarchal confiscation and suppression of matriarchal myth and of the female voices in folklore and Biblical stories. Professor James Darcy Pieixoto, whose name links him to a macho character in an obscure Portuguese novel and to Darcy in *Pride and Prejudice* (Atwood Visit), cautions his audience to avoid passing moral judgment upon the Gileadeans (*HT* 314). Like male members of the Research Association, Moon finds Gilead important because it redraws the map of the world. Like some of us, Atwood's parodic traditional scholars too easily separate themselves from "the object" of their studies, ironically muting female text and voice and stories about both with all too familiar pedantic commentary. As Davidson argues, "the Biblical fundamentalism of Gilead poses crucial questions about the interpretative use of literary texts." Piexoto's pre-Foucault, pre-de Beauvoir form of historical criticism, rampantly encoded with patriarchal imperatives, trivializes and finally disregards not only the text he proposes to discuss and the woman who created it ("Future" 117–20) but also our culture's major intertexts, including especially folklore, mythology, and the Bible. As Larson notes, Atwood's two "testaments," of Offred and the "Historical Notes," foreground the patriarchal sexual politics of the Bible and theology that have silenced scriptural women (496–98). If we take off our own blinkers to read and reread, however, *The Handmaid's Tale* restores the voices of Red Cap, Persephone, and Bilhah.

Although the final words of *The Handmaid's Tale*, "Are there any questions?" constitute a humorously pat question, they formally establish textual space for our questions and speculations. Mirroring the self-consciousness of Offred's narrative, these words return us to Offred's voice and "the matrix" from which it comes (324). As textual commentary, the "Historical Notes" deconstruct or unwind the text we have just read—which we cannot have read since it is a "tape recording" from our future—and then itself and its authority, from yet a further point in our future. Like Holland's "Little Red Readinghood" (55–57), *The Handmaid's Tale* parodies both our theories and practices of reading, deconstructing the patriarchal myths of our cultural and literary texts. It also dissolves easy dichotomies such as the one some would draw between a contemporary Big Bad Wolf and a Canadian Little Red Riding Hood (Atwood, FitzGerald and Crabbe interview 138). Despite the mythic, fairy-tale, and biblical resonances, Offred is not a goddess, the book is an anti-fairy tale, and it utters words rather than The Word. But Atwood's postcolonial text does not simply catch us, like Holland's Grandma, in "a web of intertextuality" (56). Unlike Handmaids, we are not forbidden to read; thus, rather than simplistic messages or icons, *The Handmaid's Tale* leaves us with questions and challenges.

By embedding a "reversed" fairy tale in *The Handmaid's Tale*, much as she has reversed myths in *Surfacing* (Wilson, "Deconstructing" 59–65) and Gothic romance traditions in *Lady Oracle*, Margaret Atwood presents a timeless vision of sexual politics in a fallen world. Re-visioning Tennyson's poetry, history, scholarship, and current events as well as the Grimms' "Red Riding Hood," the Bible, and myth, *The Handmaid's Tale* again takes us *Through the Looking Glass* (1871) to a new *1984* (1949): through its intertexts it challenges us to stop reflecting nightmare visions of both past and present societies around the world, to stop being in the patriarchal mirror. Rather than being seen, silenced, and consumed, Atwood's Red Cap sees and speaks. If we cultivate our Mother's garden, the book implies possibility of rebirth: not a return to Eden or matriarchy, but harmony among animal, mineral, and vegetable worlds and peace within the human one.

Cat's Eye Vision

"Rapunzel" and "The Snow Queen"

Like the earlier *Life Before Man* (1979, Chapter 7), Margaret Atwood's recent novel, *Cat's Eye* (1978) initially seems to be a realistic departure from the deconstructed fantasy and romance dominant from *The Edible Woman* through *The Handmaid's Tale*.
Although *Life Before Man* and *Cat's Eye* are set in contemporary
Toronto and demonstrate comedy of manners traditions, on one
level they are the kind of Jamesian ghost story Atwood admires.
In the case of *Cat's Eye*, the protagonist's memories of her "girlfriends" and a Gothic childhood and adolescence in Toronto are
her ghosts. The city of Toronto, associated with poison, malice,
and the spirits of the dead, even seems out to kill her (*CE* 387,
375).

Like Atwood's earlier novels, however, *Cat's Eye*[1] re-visions or
transforms fantastic intertexts[2] that influence the novel's images,
characters, structure, and themes. This time drawing on Triple
Goddess myth, the Bible, *King Lear* (Motif M21), literary and
visual magical realism, and related images from movies, television, contemporary Canadian visual art,[3] and other popular arts
to focus on the child's fairy-tale journey into adulthood, Atwood
again portrays a symbolically dismembered character capable of
fairy-tale metamorphosis. In this case, the metamorphosis affects
not only vision and the self but conceptions of time and art.
Despite what many readers have mistaken for realism, acknowl-

edged or fictional autobiography, and even anti-feminist misogyny (see Leclaire 73–74, Ingersoll 18, 26; Greene, Review 448–55), *Cat's Eye* is deeply ironic and parodic. Another trapped Rapunzel, the book's unreliable narrator, Elaine Risley, enters a fabulous world of old ghosts, cruel stepsisters, deceitful witches and wizards, disappointing princes, a merciful fairy godmother, and tests to be faced alone in an alien inner landscape. Because Elaine is a visual artist, the development of her identity or "I" is even more dependent upon the development of her vision, her "eye," than in Atwood's earlier works. In *Cat's Eye* the main fairy-tale intertexts, the Grimms' "Rapunzel" and Hans Christian Andersen's "The Snow Queen," illuminate the "eye—I" imagery.

The main technique of presenting the book's intertexts is magical realism. Drawing on E. L. Doctorow's views of fiction, Atwood says that *"Cat's Eye* is a mixture of fact and imagination" (quoted in Carlin 32–M). Magic or magical realism, a term used by Franz Roh to describe German artists of the *neue Sachlichkeit* (new objectivity), portrays "the imaginary, the improbable, or the fantastic in a realistic or rational manner." Elements in the works of writers including Jorge Borges, Gabriel García Marquéz, Alejo Carpentier, Günter Grass, Italo Calvino, John Fowles, Emma Tennant, Angela Carter, and Salmon Rushdie and in painters such as Charles Sheeler, Edward Hopper (Drabble 606–7), and Alex Colville have been described as magical realism; and writers such as Robert Coover are beginning to explore the term's usefulness in North American writing (Coover, Conversation 1992). As in magical realism, images and scenes in *Cat's Eye* combine elements of dream, fairy story, or mythology with the everyday (Drabble 607). Elaine Risley's paintings, especially *Unified Field Theory, Cat's Eye, Rubber Plant: The Ascension,* and *Erbug, The Annunciation*; such images as the marble, the toaster, and the red plastic purse; Elaine's dreams, such as of her parents sinking into the earth (167); and scenes such as Elaine's burial and the vision of the Virgin, not only possess the inexhaustible magic of magical realism but are also perhaps the book's most impressive achievements. Because Elaine Risley is the book's narrator, she is revealed in what she sees.

From the beginning of her career, Atwood's narrators and personae have to overcome the mirror and camera vision, with their consequent narcissism, that stand in the way of genuine vision (Wilson, "Camera" 29, 31, 51). According to Atwood's *Murder in the Dark* (1983), genuine vision sometimes comes through a "third eye": "Try not to resist the third eye: it knows what it's doing. Leave it alone and it will show you that this truth is not the only truth. . . . You will reach out in any direction and you will touch the light itself. . . . You see. You see" ("Instructions for the Third Eye" 61–62).

Instead of enabling genuine vision, in Atwood's early, rare, *Kaleidoscopes Baroque* (1965), illustrated with Charles Pachter's woodcuts, "an eye of mirrors" functions like a kaleidoscope: "fragments of sight / reflected back, made multiple: / bouquets of hands unfolded . . . , a cannibal/ flower of mouths grew from each face, a sun / gathered from every lightbulb" (4). In *The Circle Game* (1966) the "camera man"'s "glass eye" freezes the persona and even the clouds and the sun into a "souvenir" ("Camera" 56). In this volume's title poem, although the narrator, caught in circular games, gropes toward the other through a melting mirror, "you"'s "eyes' cold blue thumbtacks" not only fix her in his "mind's continent" but also anticipate the dilemma most Atwood characters face in the "room" of relationship: like the lies of his touch and language, this kind of vision is an attempt to keep her "at a certain distance / and (at length) avoid / admitting [she is there]" (48–50).

Symbolically trapped in mirror vision, split between head and body, and afraid to see either past or present, the unnamed narrator of *Surfacing* (1972) lies to readers and to herself so extensively that her contradictions and revisions deconstruct or erase both the novel and her self as she creates them by telling her story (Wilson, "Deconstructing" 53, 59–65). Rennie of *Bodily Harm* (1982) actually carries and uses a camera that distances her from the realities (cancer, sexism, revolution, torture) she doesn't want to feel. But *Surfacing*'s narrator, Marian (*EW* 1969), Joan (*LO* 1982), Lesje, Nate, and Elizabeth (*LBM* 1979), and Offred (*HT* 1985) share with Rennie a tendency to freeze memory in photograph trophies and force experience into frames (Wilson, "Camera" 29–57).

In order to free themselves from the restricting roles of fairy tales, comics, television, the Bible, history, and myth and heal their split identities, Atwood's characters and personae must recover feeling. They must use what might be called an empathetic vision, one that does not lie or refuse to see (*Surf*), narcissistically reflect the viewer (*CG*, Duncan in *EW*) or the viewed ("Tricks with Mirrors"), diminish what is viewed (Lesje and Rennie's figurative telescopes in *LBM* and *BH*), dehumanize the subject (including the self) by treating subject as object Other (*CG,HT, CE*), or, like the hobgoblin's fragmented mirror in Andersen's "The Snow Queen," shrink the good in order to magnify the unpleasant or bad. In order to see rather than to reflect, they must stop being mirrors and using others as mirrors. They must remove the glass eyes of mirror or camera vision that alienate them from themselves, others, and the world. Paradoxically, cameras or mirrors also contribute to characters' fairy-tale metamorphoses (Wilson, "Camera" 40) by leading them to the recognition that they do live in conditioned textual "frames" (of fairy tales, advertising, comic books, true romance stories, prescribed sex roles, nationality) resembling mirrors and photographs.

Atwood's earliest work also associates art with the freezing vision of mirrors or glass. If in one sense art and the artist "with gorgon touch" can freeze and even kill the natural world by creating the immortality of "a world of glass" (Atwood, *DP* "Formal Garden," "Her Song" n.p.; Chapter 2),[4] art is also a true or distorting mirror reflecting the reader, the reader's world (*Surv* 15) and even the text (*LO*). At its best, art is a lens giving not merely a reflection but a distillation or condensation (Hammond Interview 79). As Atwood says in "An End to Audience?" the writer is a soothsayer (Motif D1712), "both an eye-witness and an I-witness, the one to whom personal experience happens and the one who makes experience personal for others. The writer *bears witness*, ... speak[s] the forbidden, . . . especially in times of political repression" (*SW* 348, 350). As a lens rather than a possibly faulty mirror,[5] art is vision and voice, responsive and responsible.

As we have seen, all the major characters of Atwood's fiction and many of her personae simultaneously develop vision and identity, but in Atwood's most recent works (*BH, HT, CE, I* and especially *TS*) empathetic vision is accompanied with both touch and voice: relationship or involvement and an obligation to speak out, often for those who are silenced. As long as Atwood's characters function as mirrors or cameras, they are symbolically frozen in fairy-tale towers (Motifs R41.2, F772.2.4) resembling Snow White's glass coffin (Motif F852.1). They are cut off from others and their vision, voice, and touch are either frozen (symbolically amputated) or freezing.[6]

As Chapter 6 indicates, Canada's version of the ancient Triple Goddess is "not just an Ice-Virgin-Hecate figure, but a Hecate with Venus and Diana trapped inside." This Hecate is an extension of the Grimms' Rapunzel ("Rapunzel" 1812, No. 12, AT 310). According to Atwood, the Rapunzel Syndrome, overwhelmingly evident in Canadian literature, normally has four elements: Rapunzel, the wicked witch who imprisons her, the tower she is imprisoned in, and the rescuer. In Canada's version, Rapunzel is mute: she walks around with a mouth "like [a] clenched fist." Thus, she and her tower are synonymous: "These heroines have internalized the values of their culture to such an extent that they have become their own prisons." In most cases, "the Rescuer is not much help" (209–10). Although Atwood's texts often foreground sexual-political encounters with failed male rescuers, in *Cat's Eye* the central conflict is female-female: "The fear that dares not speak its name, for some women these days, is a fear of other women" (Atwood, "If You Can't Say

Something Nice" 25). As we have seen, other fairy-tale and mythic figures, such as the Grimms' Girl Without Hands and Andersen's Snow Queen and Ice Maiden ("The Girl Without Hands," "The Snow Queen," "The Ice Maiden") may also present this image of an initially sinister or life-denying woman.

In *Cat's Eye*, the main Rapunzel/Snow Queen figure is the narrator, a visual artist named Elaine Risley. When she returns to Toronto for her "retrospective," where she humorously decides to wear vampire (403) and Hecate black, she experiences the same kind of "eye problems" (5–7) and transformations of vision as Atwood's other narrators and personae. She, too, makes a habit of watching herself in literal or metaphoric mirrors and framing others in mental photographs. Since she is a visual artist, she literally frames Mrs. Smeath, Cordelia, Jon, and Josef in "eye for an eye" paintings that lead to further blindness (405). Because she has repressed pain by "forgetting" and cultivating her own unfeeling glass eye, like what she imagines to be the alien vision of a cat's eye marble, she, too, is discomforted, diseased, by the literal and figurative amputations she notices around her. The "severed limbs" in Jon's apartment remind Elaine of the parts of her self that are missing: the eight-year-old "body," especially the vulnerable fingers, eyes, and heart, that first the "girlfriends" and then she buried in nothingness. Like other Canadian Hecates and, in a sense, all mature adults, she contains her Diana and Venus selves. Although the book's narration is retrospective and Elaine has remembered her burial and near freezing before the novel's present, Atwood withholds the scene where Elaine "sees her life entire" (398) almost until the end of the novel and restructures Elaine's life and memory as she self-consciously fragments conventional notions of both the novel and time. As the book's first section emphasizes, "If you can bend space you can bend time also, and if you knew enough and could move faster than light you could travel backwards in time and exist in two places at once" (3). When Elaine returns to her childhood home in Toronto, symbolically she (and with her the reader) is in two places and times at once. Elaine is unable to re-member until she re-views nothingness and her "death," this time meeting her "twin" Cordelia's gaze.[7] She must return to where she and Cordelia changed places in the past: the ravine, with its bridge and the frozen river of the dead, for the snow to leave her eyes and the ice her fingers and heart. She must not only resist the witch or Snow Queen: she must stop *being* either Rapunzel or the Snow Queen.

An "Early Version" of *Cat's Eye*, in which Elaine's obsession with time is linked to a surprising career as a military historian, makes the character's frozen development more overt. This middle-aged Elaine confesses that with women her own age, "rarely very old women, not at all with girls under eight," her "hands get cold, [her] knees tremble, [her] breathing goes shallow like a cat's in a car, [she] swallow[s] a lot." According to this Elaine, she owes this bodily discomfort and "bad thoughts" about women, including the desire to shut their mouths, to Cor-delia (Atwood Papers, n.p. Box 99 Manuscripts). As the novel's middle-aged "Hecate," Elaine must release the Diana self that's trapped inside.

Both the Grimms' "Rapunzel" (AT 310, No. 12) and An-dersen's "The Snow Queen" present central characters who em-body entrapment and alienation, and both are, at least in part, about regaining vision and relationship. The literary source of the Grimms' "Rapunzel" is a story by Friedrich Schultz in *Kleine Romane* (Leipzig, 1790), based on the tale "Persinette" in *Les Fées, Contes des Contes* (1692) by Mlle. Charlotte-Rose de la Force (Zipes, *Complete* 716). The enchantress of "Rapunzel," Dame Gothel (in Greece ironically a cannibal named Drakena) (Lüthi 111), has walled up herself and her lush garden as protection against oth-ers' hunger. When her "walls" are violated, she takes the viola-tor's child, Rapunzel, named after the herb rampion (sometimes *Fenchelchen*—fennel—or Petersilchen—parsley) (Lüthi 113) and creates a mirror image that Sexton emphasizes in her Rapunzel poem.[8] Dame Gothel separates Rapunzel "from all the world" in a tower (R41.2), with neither stairs nor door, within a forest. When Rapunzel, who spends her time singing to herself, hears a voice, she lets down her long hair and the witch climbs up. When the king's son hears her song and climbs up, Rapunzel gives no indication of loving him but thinks "he will love [her] more" than Dame Gothel and agrees to leave with him when she has woven a ladder. But the enchantress finds out, cuts off Rapunzel's hair, and exiles her again, this time in a desert. When the prince faces the witch's "wicked, venomous" gaze, he leaps from the tower and is blinded by thorns. In his aimless wanderings, he finally comes to the desert and is drawn again to Rapunzel's voice.

This time, rather than being obsessed with herself, Rapunzel feels for another: counteracting the witch's gaze, her tears "[wet] his eyes" and his vision grows "clear again" (Hunt and Stern 76, Motif F952.1). The couple and their twins, representing their no longer alienated selves, return to society and live happily. According to Bettelheim, who emphasizes fairy tales' positive role in maturation by externalizing a child's inner processes, the happy ending in "Rapunzel" is brought about by Rapunzel's body: "The power of the body is imaginatively exaggerated by the overlong tresses, on which one can climb up a tower, and by the tears, which can restore sight" (149, Motifs F848.1, F952.1). As we have seen, thinking through the body—feeling rather than distantly analyzing—is imperative to magical transformation throughout Atwood's work, most noticeably in *Surfacing*, *Lady Oracle*, *Bodily Harm*, and now *Cat's Eye*.[9]

Rather than using wall, tower, forest, and desert images, "The Snow Queen" symbolizes narcissism and amputating alienation with images of mirrors, ice, and snow. A fragment from the hobgoblin's distorting mirror pierces and almost freezes little Kay's heart. Then the glass gets into his eye, symbolically blinding him to life and nature and preparing him for the Snow Queen's abduction to her ice palace (F771.1.7). Made of ice but alive, the Snow Queen has "eyes [that sparkle] like bright stars, but there [is] neither peace nor rest in her glance." Kay fastens his sled to her sleigh and, because she looks at him "just as if they [are] acquainted," he continues to follow her, repeating "mental arithmetic" when he becomes frightened. Her kiss penetrates to Kay's heart and makes him feel as if he is going to die, "but only for a moment; he soon seem[s] quite well again, and [does] not notice the cold around him." When she kisses Kay for the second time, he forgets Gerda, his grandmother, and home (Motif D2004.2). The Snow Queen recognizes that she may "kiss [him] to death" if she continues (E217, F302.3.4.1; *Complete Andersen* 55–58).

When Kay's friend, Gerda, makes her archetypal journey to rescue Kay, she finds him shaping words from pieces of ice in the Snow Queen's frozen lake. Enclosed by the ice palace, this lake, over which she presides, is ironically called "The Mirror of Reason." Paradoxically, each piece is already "perfect as a work of art," but Kay wants to make something of them. Cut off from nature and playing "the icy game of reason," he is an impotent artist. Because of the glass still in his eye, he thinks the figures and words he makes are "of the highest importance," but he is unable to form the one word that would make him his own master. Like Rapunzel/Dame Gothel, the prince, and most of Atwood's characters, in order to free himself from internal and external "mirrors," he needs to balance reason with feeling, in this case again through another's tears and touch. Gerda, whose vision is neither narcissistic nor icy, proves her power and her love: they return to the green world, where they realize they are grown up. The Snow Queen, now without a double, remains alone, presiding over her frozen world (73–75).

Atwood draws the "ice women" of her Rapunzel syndrome from both "Rapunzel" and "The Snow Queen." To the extent that Atwood's personae and characters look through glass eyes without feeling, they are internally separated. Like Dame Gothel, Rapunzel, the Snow Queen, and Kay, they also separate themselves from the world behind symbolic walls, in towers or ice palaces. In order to resist the alien gaze or touch of the Other

(Sartre 263, 287), guard against becoming an Other (De Beauvoir xix–xxv),[10] and rescue themselves, they must remove the "glass" from their eyes: they must recognize the world and even the colonizing Other as subjects rather than objects or mirrors[11] of themselves. Like Rapunzel, they must reach out, symbolically regrowing or thawing "amputated" or frozen parts of themselves. In order to release her own Diana-maiden self, Elaine must recognize that her "twin," Cordelia, and the world are separate from her and that she is neither everything nor nothing. Then, like Rapunzel and Kay, she can go home.

Even more than Atwood's earlier novels, *Cat's Eye* focuses on vision: in the title, in character descriptions, and in cinematic memory scenes. Since Elaine retrospectively narrates the novel, the book's vision (and through it the reader's) is hers. Because she resees continuously changing past selves as she narrates, we experience at least eight kinds of subjective "reality" in *Cat's Eye*: Elaine's "back-seat" vision, her microscope vision, her perception of the vision of others (the Other), the nothingness of the "bad time" she "forgets," cat's eye vision, Virgin Mary vision, "tourist vision" (Wilson, "Camera" 31) of Toronto from British Columbia, and fairy-tale restored vision of herself, others, and the world.

Prior to the girlfriends, prior to Elaine's repression of her internal "fracture" and the accompanying experience of nothingness, Elaine presents her vision as "backseat," the innocent vision of a child being driven where her parents take her. Accompanying her family while her father does entomological fieldwork in northern Canada, she focuses on the back of her family's ears and the quickly passing side view from the car window, preparing her for later tourist vision. Because her family is transitory, she is not in school, and she plays only with her brother, she spends her time happily as a person rather than a gender-conditioned female. This back-seat vision begins to change as she acquires a camera, reads horror comic books, learns about insect infestations, and acquires an interest in cross-section drawings, in which organisms are "cut open so you can see what's inside them" (34). Visiting her father's lab when the family settles in Toronto for his new job, Elaine begins to try microscope vision, in which, since "there isn't room for a whole arm or leg," one magnifies a part. Watching a parade of "people dressed like snow-flakes . . . strangely truncated because [she's] looking down on them" from the zoology building, she ironically associates these snow figures with the lab and its dead or caged animals, including the mice who kill any mouse with an "alien" scent (36–37). Retrospectively aware of how she is already distancing and therefore alienating herself, Elaine analyzes these memory "pictures of the dead" (26) in order to recover the missing parts of her, the parts that fragment, are buried, and then freeze under the gaze of Cordelia and the girlfriends.

Others' vision includes that of God, Elaine's parents, other fathers, Mrs. Smeath, Carol and Cordelia's mothers, Toronto, the "girlfriends," Susie, Elaine's brother, other boys, Josef Hrbik, Jon, Ben, teachers, the women's group with its other women artists, hijackers and their "eye for eye" vision (388), dead animals, Elaine's daughters, and Charna and other "Sub-Versions" critics and artists. Unlike *Lady Oracle's* Joan Foster, in general Elaine feels comfortable with her immediate family, including her parents, brother, current husband, and daughters; but most other people make her feel "objectified," diminished, or unfree. To the child Elaine, the heavens are watchful and God is a faceless engine (101, 181). Mrs. Smeath is a single-breasted witch (Motif G369.6) walled up in self-righteousness, the blood-worshipped, devouring "Teeth mother" opposed by Elaine's own mother and her vision of Mary. As an evil eye that paralyzes Elaine (Motifs D2071, D2072.1), even Mrs. Smeath's "bad heart" is associated with the all-seeing eye of the cat-headed Maat and of neolithic "eye-goddesses" (McCombs, "Contrary" 17–19; Inger-soll, "Margaret" 21). Elaine would like to incinerate it with comic book "eye rays" before it sums her up and judges her with "It serves her right" (180).

Although Elaine is initially comfortable with boys whose conversations are mostly silence and whose power over her "is held through [her] eyes" (237, 240), the gaze of her later "princes" is freezing and fragmenting. Rather than rescuing her, they turn her into a "fallen" woman.[12] Instead of Elaine's healing their sight, as Rapunzel does with her prince, their gaze blurs Elaine's vision and reduces her to "fragments" (372, 316). Her art teacher Josef, whom she ironically wishes to rescue, dreams of a Rapunzel woman wrapped totally in cellophane. Seeming to have violet eyes, this "wizard" (Motif D1711) looks at women as "helpless flowers, or shapes to be arranged and contemplated" (318). As Elaine's Park Plaza Hotel mirror reflection confirms, after putting her into a perfume ad role, he changes her into a vacant Pre-Raphaelite woman (293, 298, 304–5). His touch first freezes and then erases her.[13] Later even Toronto, unlike the Seven Dwarfs' movie backdrop of British Columbia, where Elaine "vacations" in tourist reality with her travel agent husband (14–15, 41), is a mirror-hell she must reenter, with a limiting gaze she must stare down (410).

Most of all, Elaine fears the gaze of the girlfriends, this novel's "wicked stepsisters" (Motif S34). Carol takes in Elaine's unfinished house with "incredulous glee, . . . as if she's reporting on the antics of some primitive tribe" (49). Grace's "glassy eyes" register everything Elaine does in Sunday school so that she can report it to Cordelia (181, 124). As Elaine's "mirror image," Cordelia is also both the deceptive Snow Queen, whose "kisses" cause forgetfulness, betray (Motif K2021), and freeze, and the wall-erecting witch of "Rapunzel." Under the pressure of Cordelia's always "measuring" eyes, that find her "not normal" and remind her that "People are looking!" (70, 118–20), Elaine is afraid of bursting inward, of being crushed "like mud in a fist, until [she] implode[s]." If the girlfriends were enemies, Elaine could throw snowballs and feel hatred and anger. Because they are her "best friends," she wants to please. Yielding to social conditioning, trying to become "a girl" and "be for others" instead of being herself, Elaine understands the word "implode." "It has a dull final sound to it, like a lead door closing" (142).

Because Elaine uses the girlfriends (especially Cordelia) as mirrors, she sees herself as she thinks they see her. Thus, she confuses Cordelia with herself and symbolizes the eye problems of gender and cultural inculcation. Cordelia, like *King Lear*'s cursed and doomed third sister, is Cinderella's mirror image: she makes her father angry when she talks back to him and is eventually "banished" (see AT 510B, "Cap o' Rushes"). Never able to satisfy either parent and feeling she is nothing, Cordelia hides her own insecurity and possible parental abuse, including incest, by cultivating a confident "parent" image and projecting her powerlessness onto Elaine. Using "her voice for adults" and giving Elaine "a squeeze of complicity," Cordelia implies that "Everything will be all right as long as [Elaine] sit[s] still, say[s] nothing, reveal[s] nothing." Cordelia tries to do this in her family before she is silenced (evident in the rest-home slurred speech the family no longer has to hear). When asked what she has to say for herself, now and much of the time Elaine has "nothing" to say in this novel dramatizing nothingness. As Elaine explains, "Even to myself I am mute" (252, 117). Unsurprisingly, "Cordelia's voice" (the "Little Mermaid" silenced voice Elaine associates with her negative self-concept) later precipitates Elaine's suicide attempt.

Since Elaine cannot survive as a mirror of the nothingness or void of identity Cordelia actually feels, she, too, erases memory. The "bad time" Elaine does not want to remember is the winter vision of nothingness, her "burial," when the "treacherous step-sisters" (Motif K2212.1) or triple "witches"—Carol, Grace, and Cordelia—enact their own version of "Rapunzel" and "Snow Queen" entombment.[14] They dress Elaine like Mary Queen of Scots, "headless [and therefore visionless] already" (see Atwood's untitled watercolors, archive-labeled *Lady and Executioner* and *Lady and Sinister Figure*, Plates 4, 5). Then they throw Elaine into the backyard hole Cordelia digs and cover it with boards and dirt. Analogous to Marian's place of "absolute zero" or her vision of Peter the Chef's barbecue where she is missing (*EW*), Elaine's "square of darkness" is a "time-marker that separates the time before from the time after. The point at which [she loses] power." Ironically wearing a black dress and cloak, like her later vision of the Virgin Mary who saves her from freezing, Elaine has "no image of [herself] in the hole; only a black square filled with nothing, a square like a door" (253, 106–7).

This door resembles Atwood's many other fearful door images, like that in "Hesitations Outside the Door," where the female persona fears the amputations of entrapment in the Grimms' "Fitcher's Bird (see Chapter 9). When Cordelia later tries to remind Elaine of the hole and the time in which they both feel "a dark blank," Elaine first associates Cordelia's "double-cross" with poison nightshade and then again sees herself reflected in Cordelia's "mirror eyes" (her sunglasses) "in duplicate and monochrome, . . . a great deal smaller than life-size." Like Dame Gothel, Cordelia buries her alter ego in the only safe place of her own she can make, in this case a hole symbolizing void of identity and powerlessness in patriarchy. Not wanting to remember, Elaine later wonders why she relishes scaring Cordelia by pretending to be a vampire (Motif G262.1). Later still, she refuses to rescue Cordelia from the "loony bin" rest home where Cordelia is banished. Ironically imitating Narcissus and eradicating self, the Other, and the world, Elaine adopts Cordelia's narcissistic vision: confusing image with reality, she accepts the image Cordelia painfully constructs to hide her void (Motif J1793).[15] Elaine is unable even to recognize Cordelia "behind the disguise of costume" in a play (253, 302–3). Much later, Elaine shows her retrospective awareness of Cordelia's mask in her painting, *Half a Face*.

Under the gaze of others, Elaine, like other Atwood characters and the prince in "Rapunzel," goes "blind": she symbolically adopts an unseeing glass eye in order to deal with her "implosion." After Elaine loses her back-seat vision, adopts the gaze of the other as her own vision, experiences nothingness, and becomes moldable "mud," cat's eye vision temporarily helps her survive the metaphoric "snow and ice" so fatal in Canadian literature (Atwood, *Surv* 55–56, 58–59, 65–67). Ironically, to survive the Snow Queen, Elaine adopts Snow Queen vision, thereby choosing to freeze. Trying to emulate the "power" and "vision" of the beautiful cat's eye marble, she attempts to transform the lines of her implosion into such a magic eye, partly as a talisman against the "evil eyes" of Cordelia and Mrs. Smeath (see also McCombs, "Contrary" 10, 17): "The eye part of it, inside its crystal sphere, is so blue, so pure. It's like something frozen in the ice."[16]

Despite the eye's apparent "purity," however, cat's eye marbles are distinguished from the totally clear "puries," without a hidden internal pattern. When she uses cat's eye vision to see "the way it sees," she "can look at [people's] shapes and sizes, their colours, without feeling anything else about them. [She is] alive in [her] eyes only," like the dead raven that looks at her with a "shrivelled-up eye" (Motifs D2062.2.1.1, D2062.1). Also resembling the pieces of the hobgoblin's mirror that penetrate little Kay's eye and heart and distort his vision (see also McCombs, "Contrary" 10), the cold cat's eye seems to fall out of the sky. Replacing the eye of the sun (Motif A739.7), it passes right into Elaine "without hurting" (141, 144–45). Biting or peeling off skin from her lips and feet, dreaming that one of her twin selves is missing and that it is not she but her parents who are sinking through earth resembling ice (166–67), she learns to spend time outside her body: "At these times I feel blurred, as if there are two of me, one superimposed on the other, but imperfectly. There's an edge of transparency, and beside it a rim of solid flesh that's without feeling, like a scar. I can see what's happening, I can hear what's being said to me, but I don't have to pay any attention. My eyes are open but I'm not there. I'm off to the side." (173)

Learning to contain her internal fracture, Elaine even retains a clear, smooth, "intact" surface, like that of a cat's eye marble.

Inside her "protective" Rapunzel tower or Snow Queen palace, an amputated and silenced Elaine is her own prison. Looking back on this period, Elaine later does "a self-portrait of sorts" she ironically names *Cat's Eye*. Symbolically commenting on the texts Elaine and we read, the painting recalls both the cat's eye marble and the pier-glass in Van Eyck's *The Arnolfini Marriage*, studied in Elaine's art class. *Cat's Eye* depicts Elaine's "half-head" (Motif Q451.13), an ornately framed convex mirror reflecting a piece of the back of Elaine's younger head, and the three girl-friends walking "against a field of snow" (408). Elaine's mirror vision, like Van Eyck's pier glass, reflects people who "aren't in the main picture at all." In Van Eyck's painting, "These figures reflected in the mirror are slightly askew, as if a different law of gravity, a different arrangement of space exists inside, locked in, sealed up in the glass as if in a paperweight. This round mirror is like an eye, a single eye that sees more than anyone else looking" (327). Like other Atwood texts, *Cat's Eye* mirrors itself and its narrator, self-consciously drawing the reader's attention to its icy eyes and split or narcissistic I's.

When "snow angel" Cordelia becomes angry and "forces" E-laine to enter the forbidden ravine territory beneath the bridge, Elaine would possibly literally freeze without the countering sympathetic vision of her Virgin Mary (Motifs V250, G303.16.1). This novel's "fairy godmother" (Motif F311.1), the Virgin is also a Venus phase of the Triple Goddess and is sometimes cloaked in black,[17] the color of the wise hag, Hecate. Significantly, this "exposed heart" vision comes to Elaine near Easter as she is immersed in the partly frozen river of the dead, recalling not only the rivers Styx and Lethe but also the glacier pool of dissolved dead where Andersen's Ice Maiden claims Rudy ("The Ice Maiden" 412). First seeing the girlfriends' three heads, suggesting the Triple Goddess or triple witches (Motif G201) and coinciding with the book's other repeated patterns of three's,[18] and then imagining that her head is filling with black snow that gets in through her eyes, she sees the Virgin holding out her arms.

The voice tells Elaine, "You can go home now. . . . It will be all right. Go home" (185, 187–89).

Later Elaine does a painting about this experience: in *Unified Field Theory*, the Virgin of Lost Things holds a glass object, a cat's eye marble, "at the level of her heart." Below the bridge is what appears to be the universe but is "the underside of the ground" and "the land of the dead people" (408, Motif E481.1.2.1). Since ravines suggest not only sexuality but the feminine earth-womb and the door or cave (Neumann 170) to both the unconscious and art (e.g., *I*), the forbidden, usually frozen ravines of Atwood's *Lady Oracle*, *Bluebeard's Egg*, and *Cat's Eye* reinforce the Rapunzel Syndrome. Along with her burial, Elaine's experience in the ravine probably predisposes her to becoming an artist. But the snow and ice do not leave Elaine's eyes and heart, and she is not reborn after the vision. Although she is able to walk away from her shadowy alter egos, feels "free," and imagines she "can see right into them," she is "indifferent to them. There's something hard in [her], crystalline, a kernel of glass" (193–94). For years she represses her burial and freezing, the whole period in which she is subject to the gaze, and even the lost cat's eye marble.

Elaine cannot re-member herself or the Other until she sees "her life entire," significantly in a basement where she searches through a trunk. Like *The Edible Woman*'s Marian and *Surfacing*'s unnamed narrator, who have repressed the "subgrounds" of their existence (Wilson, "Camera" 48, 50), she must penetrate layers of past. Like *Bodily Harm*'s Rennie, she must bridge the distance between "here" and "there." The barrier between Elaine and her mother cannot be removed until, recovering the cat's eye marble in the trunk, Elaine symbolically removes the glass from her eye. Again Elaine's paintings are revealing. Later, "To bring her [mother] back to life" and eradicate her repressed "implosion," Elaine does her *Pressure Cooker* double triptych of her owl-wise, real earth-goddess mother, who didn't "give a hoot" about what others say a woman is supposed to be. Elaine now recognizes that her mother, unlike herself, always controlled the societal "pressure cooker," even using it for her own purposes (213–14, 150–51). In contrast, although Elaine's still lifes of Mrs. Smeath say "I see," she resembles many Atwood personae in being "blind" until, near the end of the novel, she resees with mercy or empathy. Then Elaine recognizes that the Medusa gaze of her "stepmother/ witch," Mrs. Smeath, was not self-righteous but "defeated, . . . heavy with unloved duty" (405). It is her own gaze as an artist that can freeze the Other into an unexamined past. Like "The Snow Queen" 's little Kay, who cannot find himself in the fragmented pieces of his icy art, Elaine needs heart as well as head.

Finally, Elaine reenters the world of mirrors, where she is Cordelia's reflection. Replaying her frozen memory of the scene in the ravine, Elaine rescues herself from her entrapment in reflections of the past. Revisiting the frozen underworld as a wise Hecate, the Virgin of Lost Things, Elaine becomes her own fairy godmother.[19] She releases Cordelia and her own Diana-maiden self from their internalized ice palace/tower. Transcending the "difference" or gap, merging subject and object (Davis 70), and symbolically opening a third eye,[20] Elaine puts her arms out to the Cordelia of her vision as her exposed-heart Virgin had to her and speaks against both of their silencings. No longer protecting herself with cat's eye vision, Elaine is able to give back to Cordelia the fear and insecurity that were always hers rather than Elaine's, recognize that her "twin," Cordelia, is the subject of her own story, and, send Cordelia "home," symbolically stepping out of her mirror image. When Elaine does that, "The snow in [her] eyes withdraws like smoke." Finally, when her projections cease and Toronto is cleared of witches and ghosts, she realizes that the landscape is "not empty" but "filled with whatever it is by itself when [she's] not looking" (419). No longer either Rapunzel or the Snow Queen, no longer using an ice/glass eye, Elaine can leave "frozen" Toronto for the west and home.

Now an "I" with eyes and heart, Elaine paradoxically sees with the transformed vision of myth and fairy tales.

Like other Atwood works, this postmodernist novel deconstructs and remythifies its fairy-tale intertext. Aging Elaine, a mother with two grown daughters, is not and does not wish to be a fairy-tale princess, and she is unlikely to live "happily ever after" with her aging "prince." Aware that she and Cordelia can never "play again like children, but this time without the pain," she enviously watches two giggling old women who, like her mother, "don't give a hoot." Her vision has come at a cost. Similarly, despite the unreality of its "postcard mountains," the Canadian "watery coast" she heads for is not a North American dream but where land ends in her "real life" (14). Her night is moonless and the stars, not eternal and not even where we think they are, offer "old light." "Shining out of the midst of nothing," however, now "it's enough to see by" (420–21).

Atwood's fairy-tale intertexts not only depict patriarchal victimization of females: they foreground the amputations—of the senses, of selfhood, of relationship to the natural world, and of the protagonists' national and global community—inherent in phallocentric sexual politics. In *The Edible Woman* Marian feels already digested and lives without either mouth or voice, in *Surfacing* the narrator exists as a disembodied head (Beckett's Unnamable), and in *Lady Oracle* Joan exchanges one disguise for another to compensate for cut-off feet. *You Are Happy, Life Before Man, Bodily Harm,* and *Interlunar* all portray characters without hands: Circe depends on a withered-hand amulet; Lesje, Elizabeth, and Nate wish for a wizard to turn their life-museum green; Rennie tries to be a tourist so that she will not notice how much of her is already missing; and *Interlunar*'s persona variously identifies herself with "missing" characters of myth and fairy tales, including Eurydice in the underworld, the Robber Bridegroom's eaten victims, and the Grimms' Girl Without Hands.

Like Atwood's other characters, Sally of *Bluebeard's Egg*, Offred of *The Handmaid's Tale*, and Elaine of *Cat's Eye* all try to see "reality" from Rapunzel towers: already dismembered in games of sexual politics, Sally projects her "stupidity" onto a parodic Bluebeard, her husband; Offred colludes in her own blinding, gagging, and other sensory deprivation by initially keeping to the Gileadean path; and Elaine chooses to freeze her feelings and the past by using glass eyes.

Paradoxically, although "The Robber Bridegroom," "Fitcher's Bird," and "The Girl Without Hands" convey unforgettable images of female victimization, including dismemberment and cannibalism, these tales contain previously unrecognized subtexts. In addition to seeing the female heroes of "The Robber Bridegroom" and "Fitcher's Bird" and hearing the untold stories of the silenced females in "The Girl Without Hands," we begin to see the paradoxical amputations of the amputators, what the Robber has lost, why Fitcher, not the third sister, dies trapped in his own "house" with his own kinsmen, why Atwood's snake eater ends up blind and mute ("The White Snake," *I*). Like Fitcher, we are married to cultures, institutions, and values that dismember and silence males as well as females and nature. Like the father in "The Juniper Tree," we casually consume what we think we cherish.

Atwood's work not only demonstrates the sexual-political price of phallocentric institutions and relationships; through its fairy-tale intertexts it models the kind of "magic" necessary to transform "pre-human" individuals and societies into fully human ones. Remembering the possibility of transformation and speaking against all that would silence the human voice and art, Atwood's characters re-member their own symbolically dismembered bodies and re-vision the discredited old stories.

Appendix

The appendix lists folklore types and folklore motifs of Atwood intertexts and texts, including those Atwood uses, parodies, modifies, or revisions. Folktale types in the first section are from Antti Aarne, *The Types of the Folktale: A Classification and Bibliography* (translated and enlarged Stith Thompson, 2nd rev. ed. See also Margaret Read MacDonald, *The Storyteller's Sourcebook: A Subject, Title, and Motif Index to Folklore Collections for Children*. Luc Lacourciere's *The Analytical Catalogue of French Folktales in North America* is in progress and is expected to comprise at least six volumes (123–28).

The Aarne-Thompson indexes offer comprehensive classifications of traditional tales and of the elements in all kinds of traditional narratives. In the text, tale types are indicated in parentheses following "AT" (Aarne-Thompson). Full details are given only for Atwood's major intertexts, and entries may be abbreviated to emphasize motifs Atwood uses. See index for full geographical distribution of tale types and motifs.

TALE TYPES

I. Animal Tales

Wild Animals and Domestic Animals
AT 123 *The Wolf and the Kids*. Grimm No. 5. Cf. AT 333.
AT 123B *Wolf in Sheep's Clothing Gains Admission to the Fold* [K828.1]. Aesop, *EW*.
AT 124 *Blowing the House In*. Z81 Blowing the House In. *LBM*.
AT 124A *Pigs Build Houses of Straw, Sticks and Iron*. THP, *LBM*.

II. Ordinary Folktales

300–749 A. Tales of Magic
AT 300–399 Supernatural Adversaries

AT 300 *The Dragon Slayer*. Rescue of the princess. Cf. 303 *The Twins or Blood Brothers*. B11.11 Fight with dragon. [connected to Perseus-Medusa legend. Thompson, *Folktale* 279]

AT 302 *The Ogre's (Devil's) Heart in the Egg*. Cf. AT 665, 400, 425. Grimm No. 197 "The Crystal Ball" (*BE*). E711.1 Soul in egg.

AT 306 *The Danced-out Shoes*. Grimm No. 133 "The Shoes That Were Danced to Pieces." Underworld. *LO, HT*.

AT 310 Rapunzel: *The Maiden in the Tower*. Grimm No. 12. *GB, Surv*.
 I *Promise of Child*. S222 Man promises child to save himself. G204 Girl in service of witch.
 II *The Hair Ladder*. R41.2 Captivity in tower. T381 Imprisoned virgin to prevent knowledge of men. F848.1 Girl's long hair as ladder into tower. L162 Lowly heroine marries prince (king).
 III *Abandonment and Blinding*. S144 Abandonment in desert. S165 Mutilation: putting out eyes.
 IV *Blindness cured*. F952.1 Blindness cured by tears.

AT 311 *Rescue by the Sister*. Grimm No. 46 "Fitcher's Bird" and No. 66 "The Hare's Bride" with a straw doll substitute bride. Cf. Types 312, 1132. *PP, BE*.
 I *The Forbidden Chamber*.
  G400 Person falls into ogre's power. R11.1 Maiden abducted by monster. G81 Unwitting marriage to cannibal. C611 Forbidden chamber. C913 Bloody key as sign of disobedience.
 II *Punishment*. C920 Death for breaking taboo.
 III *Rescue by Youngest Sister*. R157.1 Youngest sister rescues elder. G551.2 Rescue of sister from ogre by another sister. E30 Resuscitation by arrangement of members. EO Resuscitation.
 IV *Carrying the Sacks*. G501 Stupid ogre. G561 Ogre tricked into carrying his prisoners home in bag on own back.
 V *Disguise as Bird*. K525 Escape by use of substituted object. K521.1 Escape by dressing in animal (bird) skin.
 VI *Punishment of the Murderer*. Q211.

AT 312 *The Giant-Killer and his Dog (Bluebeard)*. Grimm Nos. 46, 66. The brother rescues his sisters. See Type 311 for introduction. The youngest sister threatened with death for disobedience asks respite for prayer. Her brother with the aid of animals kills the ogre (cf. Type 300) and rescues his sisters. S61.1 Bluebeard. G551.1 Rescue of sister from ogre by brother.

AT 313 *The Girl as Helper in the Hero's Flight*. The Forgotten Fiancée. Jason and Medea myth. C915.1 Troubles escape when forbidden casket is opened. E33 Resuscitation with missing member. D1611 Magic object left behind to impersonate fugitive. D672 Obstacle flight. D2003 Forgotten fiancée.

AT 313A Grimm No. 51 "Fundevogel," 79 "The Water-Nixie."

AT 313B The same, introduced by *The Forbidden Box*, AT 222 + 537. Grimm No. 56 "Sweetheart Roland," 113 "The Two Kings' Children," 186 "The True Bride," 193 "The Drummer."

AT 313C The same, followed by *The Forgotten Fiancee*. Grimm No. 56 113, 186, 193.

AT 313D *Magic Flight and Transformation to Bird*

AT 313H *Flight from the Witch.*

AT 327 *The Children and the Ogre.*

AT 327A. *Hansel and Gretel.* Grimm No. 15. "Fall and All," *EW, BH, GB.*

    I *Arrival at Ogre's House.* S321 Destitute parents abandon children. S301 Children abandoned. F771.1.10 Gingerbread house. G10 Cannibalism. G401 Children wander into ogre's house. G422 Ogre imprisons victim.

    II *The Ogre Deceived.* G526 Ogre deceived by feigned ignorance of hero. G512.3.2 Ogre burned in own oven.

    III *Escape.* D672 Obstacle flight.

AT 333 *Redcap: The Glutton.* Grimm No. 26. Cf. ATs. 123 *The Wolf and the Kids*, 2027 *The Fat Cat*, 2028 *The Troll (Wolf) Who Was Cut Open. HT, GB.*

    I *Wolf's Feast.* K2011. Wolf poses as grandmother and kills child. Z18.1. What makes your ears so big? F911.3. Animal swallows man (not fatally).

    II *Rescue.* F913 Victims rescued from swallower's belly. Q426 Wolf cut open and filled with stones as punishment.

AT 361. *Bearskin.* [F821.1.3.1] Grimm No. 101. *Surfacing.*

AT 363 *The Vampire.* Devours bride. *LBM.*

AT 365. *The Dead Bridegroom Carries Off His Bride (Lenore).* Child's English and Scottish Popular Ballads V 60–61. *LBM.*

400–459. Supernatural or Enchanted Husband (Wife) or Other Relatives

AT 400 *Descent to the underworld in search of a lost wife.* Orpheus and Eurydice. Grimm Nos. 92, 93, 193. F81.1 Orpheus journeys to land of dead to bring back wife (*I*). C31.6 Taboo: calling on supernatural wife. C932 Loss of husband for breaking taboo (*LBM*). H1385.3 Quest for vanished wife (mistress) (reversed in *LBM*). D1520 Magic object transports.

AT 410 *Sleeping Beauty.* Grimm "Brier Rose" ("Little Briar Rose") No. 50. Perrault "La Belle an Bois Dormant." M412.1 Curse given at birth of child. F316 Fairy lays curse on child. D735 Disenchantment by kiss. D1960.3 Magic sleep for definite period. D1962.1 Magic sleep through curse. D1364.17 Spindle causes magic sleep. D1967.1 Person in magic sleep surrounded by magic hedge. M341.2.13 Prophecy: death through spindle wound.

*The Petrified Kingdom. Russian. Afanasiev. Eris, Peleus, and Thetis. *LBM.* [See also AT 425 A or G Armor/ Cupid and Psyche type with male sleeper, The Monster (Animal) as Bridegroom.]

AT 425 *The Search for the Lost Husband. LBM.* D721.3 Disenchantment by destroying skin (covering). D735.1 Beauty and the Beast.

AT 425C *Beauty and the Beast.* Grimm No. 88 "The Singing, Springing Lark." B640.1 Marriage to beast by day and man by night. B620.1 Daughter promised to animal suitor. S222 Man promises (sells) child in order to save himself from danger or death. D721.3 Disenchantment by destroying skin (covering).

AT 440 *The Frog King or Iron Henry.* Grimm No. 1. *WT.* D195 Transformation: man to frog. F875 Iron bands around heart to keep it from breaking.

500–559. Supernatural Helpers

AT 500–501 The Spinning-Women

AT 500 *The Name of the Helper* (Titeliture, Rumpelstilzchen, Tom-Tit-Tot) The maiden learns the name of her supernatural helper. Grimm No. 55. "Rumpelstiltskin." C432.1.

I *Impossible Task.*

II *Bargain with the Helper.* S222 Man promises (sells) child in order to save himself from danger or death. S222.1 Woman promises unborn child to appease offended witch. H512 Guessing with life as wager. H521 Test: guessing unknown propounder's name.

III *The Helper Overcome.* C432.1 Guessing name of supernatural creature gives power over him.

AT 510 *Cinderella and Cap O' Rushes.*

I *Persecuted Heroine.* S31 Cruel stepmother. L55 Stepdaughter heroine. L102 Unpromising heroine. K521.1 Escape by dressing in animal (bird, human) skin. T411.1 Lecherous father. S322.1.2 Father casts daughter forth when she will not marry him. T311.1 Flight of maiden to escape marriage.

II *Magic Help.* E323.2 Dead mother returns to aid persecuted daughter. E366 Return from dead to give counsel. D815.1 Magic object received from mother. E631 Reincarnation in plant (tree) growing from grave. N810 Supernatural helpers. F311.1 Fairy godmother. B313.1 Helpful animal reincarnation of parent. B450 Helpful bird. B100.2 Magic animal supplies treasure. B100.1 Treasure found in slain helpful animal. B335 Helpful animal killed by hero's enemy. D950 Magic tree.

III *Meeting the Prince.* H151.6 Heroine in menial disguise discovered in her beautiful clothes: recognition follows.

IV *Proof of Identity.* K2212.1 Treacherous stepsisters. H36.1 Slipper test. K1911.3.3.1 False bride's mutilated feet.

V *Marriage with the Prince*

AT 510A *Cinderella* Grimm No. 21 "Ashputtle" ("*Ashenputtle*"). GB, SW.

AT 510B *The Dress of Gold, of Silver, and of Stars* (Cap o' Rushes). Grimm No. 65 "All Fur." Father wants to marry own daughter. Fur disguise. Forgotten shoe. Shakespeare's *King Lear* (Tatar, *Off* n. 17, 257), CE.

AT 516 *Faithful Johannes* ("Der treue Johannes") Grimm No. 6. B176.1 Magic serpent.

AT 517 *The Boy Who Learned Many Things.* Cf. AT 670, 671. A boy understands the language of birds. The birds prophesy that the parents shall humble thmselves before him. On repetition of the prophecy, the parents drive him away. The boy becomes great, returns unknown to his parents, and the prophecy is fulfilled. Cf. AT 725. *Surf.*

Motifs: B215.1 Bird language. B216 Knowledge of animal languages. B143 Prophetic bird. N451 Secrets overheard from animal conversation. M312.0.2 Prophecy of future greatness given by animals. S10 Cruel parents. M373 Expulsion to avoid fulfillment of prophecy. N682 Prophecy of future greatness fulfilled when hero returns home unknown (often with AT 671).

AT 530 *The Princess on the Glass Mountain.* Cf. AT 550. Russian, French, Franco-American. See also AT 313B, 313C Grimm No. 193 "The Drummer," originally titled "The Glass Mountain."

I *Reward for the Vigil.* G346 Devastating monster. H1471 Watch for monster, youngest alone successful. L10 Victorious youngest son. B315 Animal helpful after being conquered.

II *The Glass Mountain.* F751 Glass mountain. R111.2.2 Rescue of princess from glass mountain.

III *Unknown Knight.* H80 Identification by tokens.

AT 533 *The Speaking Horse Head.* Grimm No. 89 "The Goose Girl." Substitute bride.

AT 550 *The Golden Phoenix.* French-Canadian, Grimm No. 57. "The Golden Bird"): Search for the Golden Bird. *Surf.*

I *Object of the Quest.* F813.1.2 Silver Apple (F813.1.1. Golden Apple). B102.1 Golden bird. Bird with golden feathers. H1210.1 Quest assigned by father. H1213 Quest for remarkable bird caused by sight of one of the feathers. H1331.1 Quest for marvelous bird. H1213 Quest for remarkable bird caused by sight of one of its feathers. H1331.1.3 Quest for golden bird.

II *The Three Sons.*

III *Success of the Quest.* H1241 Series of quests. D961 Magic garden. N711.3 Hero finds maiden in garden. H1242 Youngest brother alone succeeds on quest.

IV *The Treacherous Brothers.*

V *Conclusion.* L10 Victorious youngest son.

AT 551 [related to 550] Grimm No. 97 *Water of Life* (Fr-Can. "The Fountain of Youth"): Sons on a Quest for a Wonderful Remedy for their Father.

I *Object of the Quest.* H1210.1 Quest assigned by father. H1324 Quest for miraculous remedy. H1321.2 Quest for healing water. D1500.1.18 Magic healing water. H1321.3 Quest for water of youth. D1338.1.2 Water of youth.

II *The Three Sons.* L13 Compassionate youngest son.

III *Success of the Quest.* H1239.3 Quest accomplished by means of objects given by helpers. H1242 Youngest brother alone succeeds on quest.

IV *The Treacherous Brothers.* W154.12.3 Ungrateful brothers plot against rescuer. K1932 Imposters claim reward earned by hero.

V *Conclusion.* L10 Victorious youngest son.

560–649 Magic Objects

AT 571 *Golden Goose.* Grimm No. 64. "The Golden Goose." N102.1 Golden bird. B172 Magic bird.

650–699. Supernatural Power or Knowledge

AT 670 *The Animal Languages.* Cf. 671 *The Three Languages.* 517 *The Boy Who Learned Many Things* (speech of birds, prophecy that parents will humble self before him). 781 *Princess Who Has Destroyed Her Child. Surf.*

I *The Gift of the Snake.* B216 Knowledge of animal languages.

II *The Curious Wife.*

III *The Speech of the Cock.*

AT 671 *The Three Languages.* Grimm No. 33. The youth learns the languages of dogs, birds, and frogs. Through this knowledge he makes his fortune. Cures sick princess and discovers treasure Cf. 613 III b,c. *Surf.* Often mixed with AT 517.

AT 673. *The White Serpent's Flesh.* "The White Snake" ["The White Serpent"] Grimm No. 17. *Surf.* Contrary to warning, Servant tastes of forbidden dish, white snake. He learns the speech of animals B217.1.1. He hears how two ravens converse: "The house will sink in the earth." Entreats his master to flee and save himself; or he learns where the queen's necklace (or lost ring) is N451. B582.2 (grateful animals). Lang (Green 305–310.) See also H1213.1K.

700–749. Other Tales of the Supernatural

AT 704 *Princess on the Pea.* Motif H41.1, Andersen's "The Princess and the Pea" ("Prindsessen paa Aerten" 1835); Grimm No. 182A "The Pea Test," published as No. 182 in 1843.

AT 705 *Born of Fish.*

N711 Tree-maiden. S163 Tongue mutilation. Q414 Female punished by being burned alive. T412 Mother-son incest.

AT 706 *The Maiden Without Hands.* Grimm No. 31. *LBM, BH, I.*

I *The Mutilated Heroine.* S322.1.2 Father casts daughter forth when she will not marry him. Q451.1 Hands cut off as punishment. T411.1 Lecherous father. T327.1 Maiden sends to lecherous lover (brother) her eyes (hands, breasts) which he has admired. S211 Child sold to the devil. (S31 Cruel Stepmother or K2212.2 treacherous sister-in-law.)

II *Marriage to the King.* F1033 Person lives without food or drink for year or more. N711.3 Hero finds maiden in (magic) garden.

III *The Calumniated Wife.* K2117 The calumniated wife: substitued letter (falsified message).

IV *The Hands Restored.* E782.1 Hands restored. H57.5 Recognition by artifical hands. S451 Outcast wife united with husband.

AT 709 *Snow-White.* Grimm "Snow-White and Seven Dwarves" ("Little Snow White") No. 53. "The Dwarf" ("Five Poems" 32), CE.

I *Snow White and her Stepmother.* L55 Stepdaughter heroine. D1311.1 Mirror answers questions. D1323.1 Magic mirror (clairvoyent).

II *Snow-White's Rescue.* S31 Cruel stepmother. S322.2 Jealous mother casts daughter forth. K512.2 Compassionate executioner: substituted heart. F451.5.1.2 Dwarfs adopt girl as sister. N831.1 Mysterious housekeeper.

III *The Poisoning.* D1364.4.1 Apple causes magic sleep. S111.4 Murder with poisoned apple.

IV *Help of the Dwarfs.* F852.1 Glass coffin.

V *Her Revival.* N711.1 King (prince) accidentally finds maiden in woods (tree) and marries her. E21.1 Resuscitation by removal of poisoned apple. Q414.4 Punishment: dancing to death in red-hot shoes.

AT 720 *My Mother Slew Me; My Father Ate Me.* "The Juniper Tree." Grimm No. 47. "The Little Sister" ("Five Poems" 29), *Surf.*

I *The Murder.* Z65.1 Red as blood, white as snow. S31 Cruel stepmother. S121 Murder by slamming down chest lid. G61 Relative's flesh eaten unwittingly. E30 Resuscitation by arrangement of members. E607.1 Bones of dead collected and buried. Return in another form directly from grave. V63 Bones of dismembered person assembled and buried. E610.1.1 Reincarnation: boy to bird to boy. E613.0.1 Reincarnation of murdered child as bird.

II *The Transformation.*

III *The Revenge.* N271 Murder will out. Q211.4 Murder punished. Q412Punishment: millstone dropped on guilty person.

IV *The Second Transformation.* E610.1.1 Reincarnation: boy to bird to boy.

Variant: "Applie and Orangie." Scotland. S31. G61. E607.1. E613.0.1. N271. Q211.4. Q412.

750–849 B. Religious Tales

AT 781. *The Princess who Murdered her child.* [Q211.4]. The hero learns the bird language [B131.1, B215]. The bird sings "The bones lie under the tree" [N271.4]. Cf. AT 517.

AT 810–814 *The Man Promised to the Devil.*

AT 810. *The Snares of the Evil One.* "The King of the Golden Mountain." Grimm No. 92. M211 Man sells soul to devil. S211 Child sold (promised to devil).

850–999. C. Novelle (Romantic tales)

870–879 The Heroine Marries the Prince

AT 870 *The Princess Confined in the Mound.* Grimm No. 198. "Maid Maleen."

I *Imprisoned Princess.* S11 Cruel father. R45 Captivity in mound (cave, hollow hill).

II *Escape and Service.* R211 Escape from prison. K1816.0.2 Girl in menial disguise at lover's court. K1843.1 Bride has maid sleep in husband's bed to conceal pregnancy.

III *The Substituted Bride.* H13 Recognition by overheard conversation (usually with animals or objects). H92 Identification by necklace.

IV *Recognition.* H15.1 Identity tested (Impostor fails). H400 Chastity test. K1911.3 Reinstatement of true bride.

AT 870A *The Little Goose Girl* (akin to AT 870). Substitute bride.

AT 870D *Magic Mirror Reflects Blemishes* of character of all women who gaze in it.

AT 879 *The Basil Maiden (The Sugar Puppet, Viola).*

IV *The Sugar Puppet.* The prince takes the princess to wife but the first night seeks to revenge himself by cutting off her head, but she saves herself by putting in her place a puppet of sugar. K525.1. *Pentamerone.*

AT 931 *Oedipus. BH.*

AT 955 *The Robber Bridegroom.* Grimm No. 40 [K1916]. The Maiden in the Den of Robbers. While hidden under the bed she sees another maiden murdered. The severed finger serves her as a token. Cf. AT 311. *EW, BH, RB.*

R145 Strews path with ashes or peas. [G81 Unwitting marriage to cannibal] [not in Aarne]. H57.2.1 Severed finger exposes bridegroom. K525 Escape by use of substituted object.

Children's Legends

Legend 5. Grimm No. 205 "God's Food." *MD.*

MOTIFS

Motif numbers are from Stith Thompson, *Motif-Index of Folk Literature*, rev. ed., 6 vols. Bloomington: Indiana University Press, 1955. Reprinted by permission. I have omitted some headings, and in some cases (*taboo* for *tabu*) I have slightly edited entries.

NOTE: My practice here differs from folklorists' treatment of oral folktales. Since identifying motifs in a literary metanarrative is a matter of interpretation, I am pointing to broad folkloric patterns Atwood uses to foreground fairy-tale intertexts in her metanarratives. In some cases particular folk motifs are identifiable; in others, Atwood's motif may be parallel to, similar to, a blend of more than one, or parodic of folk motifs. By listing fairy-tale motifs in Atwood's literary works I do not mean to imply that Atwood consciously uses these particular motifs or that her usage is the same as in oral folklore. Certainly she may give the motif symbolic rather than literal meaning, shift its tone (e.g. make it comic), and may "re-view" it. Since many similar motifs exist, when not tied to an identifiable tale type (one of Atwood's major intertexts), the motif numbers are used as examples to illustrate folkloric connections and patterns and thereby illuminate Atwood's literary techniques and meanings. Names of Atwood works following motifs are meant as illustrations, not comprehensive listings.

A. Mythological Motifs

A0-A99. Creator.
  A3 Creative mother source of everything.
  A13.2.2 Eagle as creator of man.

A13.4.1 Snake as creator. *I.*

A18.2 Creator with two horns on his head. *Surf.*

A54 Rebel angel.

A63.6 Devil in serpent form tempts first woman. *I.*

A100-A499. GODS.

A100-A199. The gods in general.

A112.1.1 Goddess of dance.

A116 Twin gods.

A123.4.1.1 Three-headed God. *LO.*

A131.6 Horned god. *Surf.*

A132.1 Snake-god. *I.*

A132.5 Bear-god (goddess). *Surf.*, *LBM.*

A132.6 Bird deity. *LBM.*

A132.6.2. Goddess in form of bird. *Surf.*

A137.9 Snakes attend goddess. *I.*

A191 Goddess rejuvenates self when old.

A192.1.2 God killed and eaten. *I.*

A200-A299. Gods of the upper world.

A240.1 Moon-goddess.

A257.1.0.2 Eve named female animals. *YAH.*

A300-A399. Gods of the underworld.

A300 God of underworld.

A300.1 Goddess of underworld.

A310 God of world of dead.

A310.1 Goddess of world of dead. Persephone. *DP, LO.*

A316 Goddess divides time between upper and lower worlds.

A400–A499. Gods of the earth.

A400.1 Goddess of earth.

A401 Mother Earth. North American native and other.

A431.1 Goddess of fertility.

A454.1 Goddess of healing. *LBM*

A463.1, A463.1.1 The Fates, The Fates weave. *HT.*

A475.1 Goddess of love.

A483.1 Goddess of mercy. *CE.*

A500-A599. Demigods and culture heroes.

A515.1.1 Twin culture heroes.

A600–A899. COSMOGONY AND COSMOLOGY.

A655 World as egg. *BE, HT.*

A700–A799. The heavens.

A739.7 Sun's eye.

A1100–A1199. Establishment of natural order.

A1103 Nature transformed after 7 years.

A1200–A1699. CREATION AND ORDERING OF HUMAN LIFE.

A1200–A1299. Creation of human.

A1217 Satan's creation of animals always lifeless.

A1300–A1399. Ordering of human life.

A1331.1 Satan's success in the Garden of Eden, Paradise lost because of forbidden fruit.

A1337.0.1.1 Disease brought to human beings in box. *BH, GB*.

A2223.4 Christ as king of fishes. *BH*.

B. Animals

B0–B99. Mythical animals.

B11.11 Fight with dragon. *BH*.

B29.1 Lamia.

B29.2.3 Snake body with woman's head. *DP* cover, Figs. 3, 4. *CE* manuscript.

B32 Phoenix. *Surf, YAH*.

B32.1 Phoenix renews youth.

B50–59 Bird-people.

B51 Sphinx. Plate 15.

B52 Harpy. Plates 10, 13, *GB* collage Plate 14, "Bad News" (*GB*).

B53 Sirens. *GB*.

B55 Man with bird's head. Plate 10, *YAH*.

B81 Mermaid. Watercolor.

B81.2 Mermaid marries man.

B100–B199. Magic animals.

B100.1 Treasure found in slain helpful animal.

B100.2 Magic animal supplies treasure.

B102.1 Golden Bird. Bird with golden feathers. AT550, *Surf*.

B109 Treasure animals.

B113.3 Treasure from bird feathers.

B123.1 Wise serpent.

B160 *Wisdom-giving animals.*

B161 Wisdom from serpent. *I.*

B161.1 Power of soothsaying from serpent's licking ears.

B161.3 Magic wisdom from eating serpent. Siegfried (Thompson, *The Folktale* 245). *I.*

B165.1 Animal languages learned from serpent.

B165.1.1 Animal languages learned by having ears licked by serpent.

B172 Magic bird. *FB.*

B176.1 Magic serpent. AT 516, Grimm No. 6. Irish myth.

B176.1.1 Serpent as deceiver in paradise. *I.*

B200–B299. Animals with human traits.

B211.6.1 Speaking snake. *I.*

B214.1.10 Singing snake. *I.*

B216 Knowledge of animal languages. Person understands them.

B217.1.1 Animal languages learned by eating serpent. *Surf, I.*

B217.2 Animal languages learned by eating plant. *Surf.*

B217.5 Bird language learned by having ears magically cleansed. Greek: Frazer. Athena and Tiresias. *Surf.*

B217.8 Language of animals learned by Adam from Eve.

B220 Animal kingdom.

B300–B599. FRIENDLY ANIMALS.

B300–B349. Helpful animals—general.

B313.1 Dead mother appears to heroine in form of animal.

B335 Helpful animal killed by hero's enemy. *Surf.*

B400–B499. Kinds of helpful animals.

B450 Helpful bird.

B454 Helpful heron. *Surf.*

B500–B599. Services of helpful animals.

B511.1 Snake heals mutilated maiden with magic herbs.

B600–B699. Marriage of person to animal.

B601.16 Marriage to wolf. *HT.*

B700–B799. Fanciful traits of animals.

B721 Cat's luminous eye.

C. Tabu (Taboo)

C0–C99. Taboo connected with supernatural beings.

C31.6 Taboo: calling on supernatural wife.

C32 Taboo: offending supernatural husband. *LBM.*

C51.1.5 Dancing in churchyard forbidden.

C300–C399. Looking taboo.

C321 Looking into box forbidden. Pandora. *BH, GB.*

C331 Looking back. Orpheus. *I.*

C400–C499. Speaking taboo.

C400 Speaking taboo. AT 451, 710, Frazer.

C432.1 Guessing name of supernatural creature gives power over him. *Surf.*

C460 Laughing taboo. *Wizard.*

C500–C549. Taboo: touching.

C500 Touching.

C533 Touching magic box taboo.

C600–C699. Unique prohibitions and compulsions.

C610 The one forbidden place. *Surf.*

C611 Forbidden chamber. *PP, BE, HT, GB.*

C621 Forbidden tree.

C621.1 Tree of knowledge forbidden. *I, GB.*

C700–C899. Miscellaneous taboos.

C721.1 Neither wash nor comb for 7 years. *Surf.*

C900–C999. Punishment for breaking taboo.

C915.1 Troubles escape when forbidden casket is opened. AT 313, *BH.*

C920. Death for breaking taboo.

C932 Loss of husband for breaking taboo. *LBM.*

C953 Person must remain in other world because of broken taboo.

D. Magic

D0–D699. TRANSFORMATION.

D100–D199. Transformation: man to animal.

D100 Transformation: person to animal. *Surf.*

D113.1.1 Werewolf. "The Witch's house" ("Fall"), *Surf, LBM.*

D150 Transformation: man (woman) to bird. *Surf.*

D150 Princess changes herself into a golden bird. *Surf.*

D151.4 Transformation: man to crow. *FB.*

D152.1 Man transformed to hawk. *YAH.*

D152.2 Man transformed to eagle. *YAH.*

D161 Transformation: person to swan. *LO.*

D191.1 Lucifer as serpent. *I.*

D195 Transformation: man to frog.

D200–D299. Transformation: man to object.

D231 Transformation: man to stone.

D283.1 Transformation: woman to pool of water. "Tricks with Mirrors" (*YAH*), *LBM.*

D300–D399. Transformation: animal to person.

D352.1 Hawk transformed to person. *YAH.*

D352.2 Eagle transformed to person. *YAH.*

D361.1 Swan Maiden. Swan transforms into maiden.

D400–D499. Other forms of transformation.

D430 Transformation: object to person.

D435.1 Transformation: statue to person. *LBM.*

D474.4. Egg bloodied through disobedience. "Fitcher's Bird," *BE.*

D500–D599. Means of transformation.

D513.1 Man transformed to woman by looking at copulating snakes. Tiresias, *BH.*

D520 Transformation through power of the word. *YAH.*

D522 Transformation through magic word (charm). *YAH.*

D529.1 Petrification when woman's voice is heard.

D531. Transformation by putting on skin (feathers).

D550. Transformation by eating or drinking.

D551.2. Transformation by eating vegetable. *Surf.*

D551.5 Transformation by eating leaf. *Surf.*

D565. Transformation by touching.

D565.5 Transformation by kiss.

D578 Transformation from stepping in footprints. *Surf.*

D579 Transformation by looking in mirror. *Surf, CE.*

D581. Petrification by glance. Perseus overcoming Medusa in spite of her glance. *Surf, CE.*

D600–D699. Miscellaneous transformation incidents.

D610 Vampire bridegroom appears in other form and devours bride. *LBM*

D619 Woman into bird. *Surf.*

9D672 Obstacle flight. AT 313, *EW.*

D683.2 Transformation by witch. "Fall and All."

D684 Transformation by helpful animals.

D700–D799. Disenchantment.

D700 Person disenchanted.

D720 Disenchantment by removing (destroying) covering of enchanted person. *Surf.*

D721 Disenchantment by removing skin (covering). *Surf.*

D721.3 Disenchantment by destroying skin (covering).

D735.1 Beauty and the Beast. *SW.*

D766.1 Disenchantment by bathing (immersing) in water. *Surf.*

D766.1.2 Disenchantment by touching water.

D771.12 Disenchantment by use of crystal ball. Grimm No. 197.

D772 Disenchantment by naming. *Surf.*

D782 Disenchantment by physical contact (touch). Grimm Nos. 49, 56, 60, 76, 96.

D782.2 Disenchantment by touching earth. *Surf.*

D789.6.1 Disenchantment by speaking proper words.

D791.1.1 Disenchantment at end of seven years. *Surf.*

D800–D1699. MAGIC OBJECTS.

D815.1 Magic object received from mother. *Surf.*

D900–D1299. Kinds of magic objects.

D950 Magic birds associated with magic tree. *Surf.*

D961 Magic garden.

D991.3 Magic ball of hair. *WT.*

D992.5 Magic tongue.

D993 Magic eye. *CE.*

D996 Magic hand. "Third-handed" (*GB*).

D1171.6 Holy Grail. *Surf.*

D1171.6.2. Magic glass.

D1171.6.4 Magic chalice. *Surf.*

D1268 Magic statue (doll). *EW.*

D1294 Magic footprints. *Surf.*

D1311.8.2 Cut-off head prophesies. *I.*

D1313.13 Magic shoe points out road. *Wizard.*

D1323.3 Magic clairvoyant windows.

D1335.1.2 Heart of enemy eaten produces magic strength. *CE* manuscript.

D1338.1.2 Water of youth.

D1364.17 Spindle causes magic sleep.

D1427.1 Irresistible music. *I.*

D1500.1.4 Magic healing plant. AT 612. *Surf.*

D1500.1.18 Magic healing water. AT 590. *Surf.*

D1500.1.18.4 Magic healing lake. *Surf.*

D1503.9 Magic healing by hand. *LBM, BH.*

D1505.5 Magic water restores sight. AT 590, 613.

D1505.5.3 Magic fountain restores sight.

D1505.9. Magic flower restores sight. *HT.*

D1520 Magic object transports. *Wizard.*

D1532.3 Magic shoes bear person aloft. *Wizard.*

D1563.1.2 Magic song makes barren land fruitful. *YAH, I.*

D1610.4 Speaking flower. *Alice, HT.*

D1610.5 Speaking head. *I.*

D1611 Magic object left behind to impersonate fugitive. AT 313, *EW.*

D1615.6 Singing head. *I.*

D1620.0.1 Automatic doll. *EW, LO.*

D1628 Magic doll, answers for fugitive. *EW, LO.*

D1635 Golem. *EW,* "Speeches for Dr. Frankenstein."

D1700–D2199. MAGIC POWERS AND MANIFESTATIONS.

D1711 Magician. *CE.*

D1712 Soothsayer. "An End to Audience" (*SW*).

D1761 Magic results produced by wishing. Grimm Nos. 50, 76. *LBM.*

D1773 Magic results from laughing. *Surf, HT.*

D1778 Magic results from contact with earth.

D1793 Magic results from eating or drinking.

D1799.4 Magic powers from touching.

D1800–D2199. Manifestations of magic power.

D1800–D1949. LASTING MAGIC QUALITIES

D1810.0.11 Magic knowledge of poet. *I.*

D1810.8.1 Truth given in vision.

D1812 Magic power of prophecy. *I.*

D1815.2 Magic knowledge of language of animals. *Surf.*

D1815.4 Magic knowledge of language of trees.

D1820 Magic sight by hearing.

D1827 Magic hearing.

D1880. Magic rejuvenation.

D1881 Magic self-rejuvenation.

D1884 Rejuvenation by dismemberment. Goddess.

D1886 Rejuvenation by burning. AT 753, Grimm No. 147. *Surf.*

D1887 Rejuvenation by bathing. *Surf.*

D1900 Love induced by magic. AT 580.

D1920 Other permanent magic characteristics

D1905.2 Apple divided and eaten as love charm.

D1923 Magic power of hearing. *Surf.*

D1950–2049. Temporary magic characteristics

D1960 Magic sleep.

D1960.3 Sleeping Beauty. AT 410.

D1961 Sleepless watcher has magic watchful eye. *Apollodorus*, Argus. *CE.*

D1967.1 Person in magic sleep surrounded by magic hedge. AT410.

D1971. Magic sleep. Husband (lover) put to sleep by false bride. "BE."

D1978.4 Hero wakened from magic sleep by wife who has purchased place in his bed from false bride.

D1980 Magic invisibility. AT 306. *LBM, BH.*

D2000 Magic forgetfulness.

D2000 Forgotten Fiancée. Grimm Nos. 56, 67, 113, 186, 193, 198.

D2003 Forgotten Fiancée. *GB*, "BE."

D2004.2 Kiss of forgetfulness. "Snow Queen," *CE.*

D2006.1.6 Forgotten Fiancée remembered by means of doll. *EW.*

D2061.1.2. Persons magically caused to dance selves to death. *LO.*

D2061.2.1 Death-giving glance. *Surf, YAH.*

D2062 Maiming by magic.

D2062.1 Heart removed by magic. *LBM, YAH, BE, CE.*

D2062.2.1.1 "Crookedness" in eye from curse. *CE.*

D2070.1 Magic hair-ball used for bewitching. *WT.*

D2071 Evil eye. *CE.*

D2072 Magic paralysis. AT 952. "Fall and All," "The Witch's House" ("Fall"), "The Dwarf" ("Five Poems").

D2072.1 Magic paralysis by evil eye. *CE.*

D2072.2.1 Charm used by witch to cause paralysis.

D2121.7.2 Magic journey in snow. *CE.*

D2131 Magic underground journey.

D2161.3.2 Magic restoration of severed hand. *BH.*

D2161.3.5 Deafness magically cured.

D2161.3.6.1 Cut-out tongue magically restored.

D2161.4.16 Magic cure by touch. "The Girl Without Hands" (*I* manuscripts), *YAH, LBM, CE.*

D2161.5.5 Ministering angel. *LBM, BE.*

D2161.6.1 Diseases cured at Christ's birth.

D2174 Magic dancing until released. *LO.*

D2185 Magician carries woman in glass coffin. AT 709. Grimm "The Glass Coffin" No. 163. "The Dwarf" ("Five Poems").

E. The Dead

E0–E199. Resuscitation.

E11.3 Resuscitation by touching body.

E12.1 Red thread on neck of person who has been decapitated and resuscitated. *BE, EW.*

E30 Resuscitation by arrangement of members. *EW, BE.*

E33 Resuscitation with missing member. AT 313, *Surf.*

E63.2 Resuscitation by nine-day dance. *LO.*

E71 Resuscitation by wishing. *LBM.*

E80 Water of life. *Surf.*

E90 Tree of life. *Surf.*

E105 Resuscitation by herbs (leaves). *Surf.*

E149.2 Hero resuscitates decapitated princess. *Surf.*

E121.1.2 Resuscitation by power of goddess. *CE.*

E121.3 Resuscitation by Virgin Mary. *CE.*

E200–E599. GHOSTS AND OTHER REVENANTS.

E200–E299. Malevolent return from the dead.

E200 Malevolent return from dead. "The Revenant" ("Fall and All")

E210 Dead lover's malevolent return. *LBM.*

E215 Bride pulled into grave by dead bridegroom. Poe, *LBM.*

E217 Fatal kiss from dead. "Snow Queen."

E251 Vampire. AT 307, 363. "My Life as a Bat" (*GB*), *FB.*

E251.3.3 Vampire sucks blood. *FB, GB, CE.*

E323 Helpful magic birds associated with dead mother. *Surf.*

E323.2 Dead mother returns to aid persecuted daughter.

E366 Return from dead to give counsel.

E422.1.11.2 Ghost as head. *LBM.*

E443.3 Ghosts exorcized by name. *Surf.*

E481.1.2.1 Bridge to land of the dead. *CE.*

E600–E699. Reincarnation.

E607.1 Bones of dead collected and buried

E610 Reincarnation as animal. *Surf.*

E610.1.1 Reincarnation (boy) to bird from buried bones

E613.0.1 Reincarnation of murdered child as bird *Juniper Tree* in *Surf.*

E614.1 Reincarnation as snake. *I.*

E631 Reincarnation in plant (tree) growing on the site of the first mother's grave.

E700–E799. The soul.

E711.1 Soul in egg. Grimm No. 197, *BE.*

E722.2.11 Soul leaves body through eye.

E732 Soul in form of bird. *Surf, FB.*

E781.2 Eyes brought back and replaced.

E782.1. Hands restored. *YAH, LBM, BH.*

E783.2 Severed head regrows. *Surf.*

E783.2.1 Origin of Pegasus, from slain Medusa.

F. Marvels

F0–F199. Otherworld journeys.

F10–F79 The Upper World.

F34 Temptress sent from upper world by deity (Pandora).

F80–F109 The Lower World.

F80. Journey to the lower world. AT301.

F81 Descent to lower world of dead. *Surf., CE.*

F81.1 Orpheus. Journey to land of dead to bring back person from dead. *I.*

F85 Ishtar unveiled. *LBM*

F96 Rope to lower world. *BH.*

F93 Water entrance to lower world. *Surf, LO.*

F101 Return from lower world. Rescue.

F127 Journey to underground animal kingdom. *AC.*

F153 Other world reached by diving into water. *Surf.*

F162.4.1 Sea of ice in underworld. *CE.*

F200–F699. MARVELOUS CREATURES.

F302.3.4.1 Fairy's kiss fatal. "Snow Queen."

F302.4.2 Fairy comes into man's power when he steals her wings. *LO.*

F311.1 Fairy godmother. *CE.*

F316 Fairy lays curse on child. *EW.*

F321.1 Changeling. *EW.*

F401.3.8 Spirit as snake. *I.*

F402.6.7 Spirits dwell on island. *Surf.*

F406 Spirits propitiated.

F406.2 Food left out for spirits at night.

F407 Departure of spirits. *Surf.*

F422.1.11.2 Ghost as head. *LBM.*

F451 Dwarf (underground spirit).

F451.5.1.2 Dwarves adopt girl as sister. AT 709 "Snow White." "Loulou . . ." (*BE*), *CE.*

F451.5.2 Malevolent dwarf. AT 301. "The Dwarf" ("Five Poems" 32).

F465 Mountain and storm spirit. *LBM.*

F473.6.4 Spirit eats food. *Surf.*

F482.1.1 Brownie with red hair dances. *LO.*

F482.5.1 Brownies dance. *LO.*

F501 Person consisting only of head. *Surf, LBM.*

F511.0.1 Headless person. *LBM, GB.*

F511.0.2 Person with more than one head. *EW, THP.*

F511.0.2.1 Two-headed person. *THP*, Plate 2.

F511.1.0.1 Person without features (with flat face). Plate 6.

F511.2.4 Person without ears.

F512.1 Person with one eye. *Wizard.*

F512.1.1 Person with one eye in center of forehead. *LBM*, Greek myth.

F512.2.1.1 Three-eyed person. "Three-Eyes," *I, MD.*

F512.2.1.2 Eight-eyed person. *EW*

F512.5 Person without eyes.

F513.0.3 Person without mouth. *EW, HT*, Plate 5.

F513.2 Person without tongue. *EW.*

F514.1 Noseless person.

F515.0.1 Person without hands.

F516.1 Armless people. Plate 6.

F517.1.1 Person without feet. *EW, LO.*

F521.1 Man covered with hair like animal. *Surf.*

F521.1.1 Woman with animal hair, transformed through taking off animal skin. *Surf.*

F521.3 Men of metal. *PP, YAH,* "Scarlet Ibis" (*BE*).

F523 Two persons with bodies joined. "The Siamese Twins" ("Fall and All."

F525 Person with half a body. *Surf.*

F525.2 Man splits into two parts. *Surf.*

F526.3 Gorgon. "Fall and All."

F546.2 Woman with three breasts. *GB.*

F547.1 North American native devouring and toothed vagina legends.

F547.1.1 *Vagina dentata.*

F555.1 Golden hair.

F642.5 Celestial nymphs dance. *LO.*

F700–F899. Extraordinary places and things.

    F751 Glass mountain. *FB.*

    F771.1.7 Palace of ice. Andersen's "The Snow Queen." *CE.*

    F771.1.10 Gingerbread house. "Hansel and Gretel."

    F772.2.4 Glass tower. French Canadian. *FB.*

    F813.1.2 Silver apple. *Surf.*

    F821.1.3.1 Bear-skin. *Surf.*

    F823.4 Silver shoes. *Wizard.*

    F848.1 Girl's long hair as ladder into tower. AT 310 "Rapunzel." "Towered Woman."

    F852.1 Glass coffin. AT 709. Grimm "Snow-White and Seven Dwarves" ("Little Snow White") No. 53, Grimm "The Glass Coffin" No. 163. "The Dwarf" ("Five Poems" 32), *Surf, CE.*

    F875 Iron bands around heart to keep it from breaking. Grimm No. 1.

F900–F1099. Extraordinary occurrences.

    F911.3 Animal swallows man (not fatally). AT 311. *HT.*

    F913 Victims rescued from swallowers' belly. *HT.*

    F952.1 Blindness cured by tears.

    F952.7 Eyes restored by bathing in spring.

    F966 Voices from heaven (or from the air). *LBM.*

    F979.5.1 Burning Bush.

    F991.3.1 Bleeding bread. Grimm No. 205. "God's Food," *MD.*

F1015.1.1 Dancing shoes danced to pieces daily. *LO.*

F1021.1 Daedalus flies on artificial wings. *LO, YAH.*

F1021.2.1 Icarus's wings melt. *CE.*

F1033 Person without food or drink for a year (or more). AT 706, *EW* (parody).

F1035 Disintegration: eating or dismemberment of self.

F1041.1.1 Death from broken heart. *TS.*

F1041.1.1.1 Heart bursts when drinking third glass of liquid. "Robber Bridegroom."

F1041.1.1.2 Heart breaks when girl hears lover kiss another.

F1096.1 Person lives on after having heart cut free. *CE.*

G. Ogres

G10–G399. KINDS OF OGRES.

G10–G99. Cannibals and cannibalism.

G10 Cannibalism. AT 327A, *GB.*

G11.3 Cannibal witch. "The Revelation" ("Fall and All"), *LBM.*

G60 Human flesh eaten unwittingly.

G61 Relative's flesh eaten unwittingly. AT 720.

G81 Unwitting marriage to cannibal. AT311. *LBM.*

G200–G299. Witches.

G201 Three witch sisters. *CE.*

G204 Girl in service of witch. AT 310, *EW.*

G205 Witch stepmother. *LBM, CE, GB.*

G211.8.1 Witch as snake.

G224.12 Word-charm gives witch power. *YAH*

G247 Witches dance.

G262.0.1.1 Vampire (Lamia) devouring her lover.

G262.1 Vampire. *CE.*

G262.2 Witch eats person's heart. *BH, LBM, CE.*

G263.1 Witch transforms person into animal. Grimm Nos. 11, 49, 69, 123, 141, 197

G263.1.0.1 Witch transforms lovers into animals. Circe transforms Odysseus's men. *YAH.*

G263.4.3 Witch cripples or lames through illness.

G263.4.4 Witch makes person dumb.

G264. *La belle dame sans meri.*

G269.11.2 Witch causes person's arm to wither.

G283.3 Witch produces snow. *CE.*

G291 Witch executed for witchcraft.

G303 Devil. Old Nick. "The Interior Decorator" ("Five Poems"), *HT.*

G303.3.1.18 Devil as shoemaker. *Red Shoes* film.

G303.3.3.6.1 Devil in form of snake. *I.*

G303.4.1.3.1 Devil has red beard. "The Red Shoes."

G303.10.4.1 Devil dances with a maid until she dies. *LO.*

G303.16.1 The Virgin Mary's intervention cheats the devil. *CE.*

G307 Jinn (Genie). "The Bottled Woman" ("Three Poems" 21).

G311 Successive transformations of Proteus. *LO, I.*

G312. Cannibal ogre.

G335. Decapitation of princess by ogre. Plate 5, *Surf.*

G369.6 One-breasted ogress. *CE.*

G400–G499. Falling into ogre's power.

G440. Ogre abducts person.

G500–G599. Ogre defeated.

G512.3.2 Cannibal ogre falls into own trap.

G530.2 Defeat of minotaur in labyrinth.

G551.1 Rescue of sister from ogre by brother.

H. Tests

Ho–H199. Identity tests: recognition.

H15.1 Identity tested (Impostor fails).

H36.1 Slipper test.

H41.1 Princess who can't sleep on a pea.

H57.2.1 Severed finger as sign of crime.

H57.5. Recognition by artifical hands.

H151.6 Heroine in menial disguise discovered in her beautiful clothes: recognition follows.

H200–H299. Tests of truth.

H233.1 Chalice used in guilt test. *Surf.*

H300–H499. Marriage tests.

H310 Suitor tests.

H331 Suitor contests: bride offered as prize. *EW.*

H331.1.1 Suitor test to win princess (AT 425 and 530).

H331.2.1 Suitor contest: success in battle.

H331.4.1 Suitor contest with bride's father in shooting. Frazer's Apollodorus.

H383 Bride test: domestic skill. *EW.*

H383.1 Bride test: bread-making. *EW.*

H400 Chastity test.

H421 Tests for true lover.

H500–H899. TESTS OF CLEVERNESS.

H512 Guessing with life as wager. Test: guessing unknown propounder's name.

H530–H899. Riddles.

H541.1.1 Sphinx propounds riddle on pain of death. Plate 15. Frazer.

H761 Riddle of Sphinx: what is it that goes on four legs . . . . Plate 15, *BH.*

H900–H1199. TESTS OF PROWESS: TASKS.

H914 Mother willing to sell children. *LBM.*

H982 Animals help man perform task.

H1114 Task: climbing glass mountain. AT 425.

H1174.2 Overcoming dragon as task. *BH*, Medusa.

H1200–H1399. TESTS OF PROWESS: QUESTS.

H1213 Quest for remarkable bird caused by sight of one of its feathers. AT 550.

H1242 Youngest brother alone succeeds on quest. AT 402, 471, 550, 551, 577. *Surf.*

H1321.2 Quest for healing water. *Surf.*

H1332.3 Perseus seeks the Gorgon's head.

H1385.3 Quest for vanished wife (mistress) (reversed in *LBM*).

H1400–H1599. OTHER TESTS.

H1531.1 Dancing on sharp instruments as a test. "The Little Mermaid." *LO.*

H1557.4 Pope tests women's obedience: not to look into box.

J. The Wise and the Foolish

J0–J199. Aquisition and possession of wisdom (knowledge).

J130 Wisdom acquired from animals.

J133.6 Big fish eat little. Plate 1.

J200–J1099. WISE AND UNWISE CONDUCT.

J672.1 Sirens and Odysseus. "BE" (*BE*).

J1100–J1699. CLEVERNESS.

J1185.1 Sheherezade (Scheherezade). *I, LBM, HT.*

J1700–J2749. FOOLS (AND OTHER UNWISE PERSONS).

J1793 Mask mistaken for face. *CE.*

J2131.3.1 Girl hacks off heel to get shoe on. *GB.*

J2337 Dupe persuaded that he is invisible. *BH.*

J2412.2 Pulling out eye so pain will cease. Oedipus.

K. Deceptions

K210 Shoemaker makes shoes for devil, saves himself when he does not take all the money he was promised. AT 515. *Red Shoes* film.

K500–K699. Escape by deception.

K512.2 Compassionate executioner: substituted heart. AT 709.

K521.1 Escape by dressing in animal (bird) skin. "Fitcher's Bird," *Surf.*

K522.6 Escape by shammed drowning. *LO.*

K525 Escape by use of substituted object. AT 160, 311, 955. *EW.*

K525.1 Substituted object, including sugar puppet, left in bed while intended victim escapes. AT 879. *EW.*

K527 Escape by substituting another person in place of intended victim. AT 953. *EW.*

K532 Escape under mantle of invisibility.

K533 Escape by successive disguises. *LO.*

K571.1 Escape by dancing. *LO.*

K700–K799. Capture by deception.

K772 Victim enticed into dancing, captured. *LO.*

K800–K999. Fatal deception.

K815.2 Spider invites fly (wasp) to rest. "Fall and All," "The Witch's House" ("Fall"), *LBM.*

K826 Hoodwinked dancers. *LO.*

K828.1 Wolf in sheep's clothing gains admission to the fold. Aesop, *EW.*

K891.1 Wolf falls down chimney and dies.

K1700–K2099. DECEPTION THROUGH SHAMS.

K1815.1 Ulysses (Odysseus) returns home in humble disguise.

K1816.0.2 Girl in menial disguise at lover's court.

K1822 Red Riding Hood and wolf. *HT.*

K1828 Disguise as angel. *BE, HT.*

K1828.1. Disguise as angel of death. *HT.*

K1839.1 Wolf disguises himself with flour.

K1840 Deception by substitution. *EW.*

K1843.1 Bride has maid sleep in husband's bed to conceal pregnancy.

K1883.7 Mirror-reflection makes dupe think he is captive. *CE, Surf, CE.*

K1911 The false bride (substituted bride).

K1911.1.1 False bride takes true bride's place on way to wedding.

K1911.3 Reinstatement of true bride.

K1911.3.3.1 False bride's mutilated feet. "Cinderella," *LO, GB.*

K1916 Robber Bridegroom. *EW, BH, LBM,* watercolor.

K1992 The devil tries to pass for Christ.

K2011 Wolf poses as Grandmother and kills child.

K2021 Betrayal by a kiss.

K2111 Potiphar's wife.

K2117 The Calumniated wife: substituted letter (falsified message). AT 706.

K2200–K2299. Villains and traitors.

K2212.1 Treacherous stepsisters. *CE, GB.*

L. Reversal of fortune

L0–L99. Victorious youngest child.

L10 Victorious youngest son.

L50 Victorious youngest daughter.

L55 Stepdaughter heroine.

L55.1 Abused stepdaughter. *LBM.*

L100–L199. Unpromising hero (heroine).

L101 Unpromising hero. Male Cinderella.

L102 Unpromising heroine. Cinderella.

L112 Heroine of unpromising appearance. *LO.*

L140 The unpromising surpasses the promising. "The Ugly Duckling," *LO.*

L160 Success of the unpromising heroine.

M. Ordaining the future.

M21 King Lear. *CE.*

M200–M299. Bargains and promises.

M211 Selling of soul to devil. *LO, BH, I.*

M300–M399. Prophecies.

M301.0.1 Cassandra. Destined never to be believed. *I.*

M301.21 Sibyll as prophet. "The Acid Sibyl" ("Fall and All").

M341.2.13 Prophecy: death through spindle wound. AT 410.

M371.0.2 Twins drowned.

M400–M499. Curses.

M431 Curse: bodily injury. *BH.*

N. Chance and Faith

N300–N399. Unlucky accidents.

N339.10 Youth drowned gazing at own image. Narcissus. *EW, PP, LO, CE.*

N400–N699. LUCKY ACCIDENTS.

N700–N799. Accidental encounters.

N711 Tree-maiden. *LBM.*

N711.1 King (prince) accidentally finds maiden in woods (tree) and marries her.

N711.3 Hero finds maiden in (magic) garden. ATs 550, 551, 706.

N800–N899. Helpers.

N810 Supernatural helpers.

N816 St. Nicholas as bestower of gifts. *HT.*

P. Society

P200–P299. The family.

P272.1 Witch foster mother

P500–599. Government.

P512.1 Release from execution by marrying (woman). "Marrying the Hangman."

Q. Rewards and Punishments

Q200–Q399. Deeds punished.

Q211 Murder punished. *EW.*

Q385 Captured animals avenge themselves. *Surf.*

Q386 Dancing punished. *LO.*

Q386.1 Devil punishes girl who loves to dance. "Red Shoes," *LO.*

Q400–Q599. Kinds of punishment.

Q412 Punishment: millstone dropped on guilty person.

Q414 Female punished by being burned alive.

Q414.0.10. Burning for witchcraft. "The Revelation" ("Fall and All").

Q414.4 Dancing to death in red-hot shoes. "Snow White," *LO, GB.*

Q426 Wolf cut open and filled with stones as punishment.

Q451 Mutilation as punishment.

Q451.0.1 Hands and feet cut off.

Q451.1 Hands cut off as punishment. *BH, LBM,* "The Girl Without Hands."

Q451.1.1 Hands and feet cut off. AT 706.

Q451.2.4 Legs cut off as punishment. *GB.*

Q451.3 Loss of speech. AT 710.

Q451.4 Tongue cut off as punishment. *TS.*

Q451.9 Breasts cut off as punishment. *BH.*

Q451.10 Genitals cut off. *LBM, MD.*

Q451.10.1 Castration. *LBM, MD.*

Q451.13 Head split as punishment. *CE.*

Q456 Burial alive as punishment. *I, CE.*

Q463. Spiked Cask Punishment. AT 533, *BE, GB.*

Q478.1 Adulteress caused unwittingly to eat her lover's heart. Eating heart gives one owner's qualities. *EW*

Q551.3.4 Transformation to stone as punishment. *CE.*

Q551.6 Magic sickness as punishment. *Surf.*

Q552.2.3.1 Girl sinks into earth for dancing in church.

R. Captives and Fugitives

R0–R99. Captivity.

R11.1 Maiden abducted by monster (ogre). *EW.*

R41.2 Captivity in tower. *Surv.*

R45 Captivity in mound (cave, hollow hill).

R100–R199. Rescues.

R111.2.1 Princess(es) rescued from lower world.

R138.1 Mermaid rescues hero from shipwreck. "Little Mermaid."

R145 Marks path with peas and lentils. "Robber Bridegroom."

R165.1 Rescue of poor girl by St. Nicholas.

R168 Angels as rescuers.

R200–R299. Escapes and pursuits.

R211 Escape from prison.

R211.3 Escape through underground passage. *EW.*

S. Unnatural Cruelty

S0–S99. Cruel relatives.

S11 Cruel father.

S12 Cruel mother. AT 511.

S31 Cruel stepmothers. *LBM, HT, GB.*

S34 Cruel stepsister.

S61.6 Bluebeard.

S62.1 Girl marries Bluebeard. "The Dwarf" ("Five Poems"), *GB.*

S72 Cruel aunt. *LBM.*

S100–S199. Revolting murders or mutilations.

S123 Burial alive. *CE.*

S139.6 Murder by tearing out heart. *YAH.*

S160.1 Self-mutilation.

S161 Mutilation: cutting off hands. AT 706, *LBM, BH*, Plate 4.

S162 Mutilation: cutting off legs (feet). AT 519. *LBM, LO, GB.*

S163 Mutilation: cutting (tearing) out tongue. AT 705, *TS, SW.*

S165 Mutilation: putting out eyes. AT 310.

S168 Tearing off ears.

S172 Nose cut off.

S176 Sex organs cut off. *LBM.*

S200–S299. Cruel sacrifices.

S211 Child sold (promised) to devil.

S215.1 Girl promises herself to animal suitor.

S222. Man promises (sells) child in order to save himself from danger or death. "Beauty and the Beast."

S222.1. Woman promises unborn child to appease offended witch.

S300–S399. Abandoned or murdered children.

S301 Child abandoned (exposed). *LBM,BH.*

S314 Twins exposed.

S321 Destitute parents abandon children.

S322.1.2 Father casts daughter forth when she will not marry him.

S451 Outcast wife united with husband. AT 706.

T. Sex

T0–T99. Love.

T11.8 Falling in love with voice. "Marrying the Hangman."

T68 Princess offered as prize. AT 306. *Surf., LBM.*

T81 Death from love. *TS.*

T100–T199. Marriage.

T117.8 Marriage to doll. *EW, LO.*

T118 Girl (man) married to (enamored of) monster.

T172.1 Culture hero banishes snake.

T300–T399. Chastity and celebacy.

T311.1 Flight of maiden to escape marriage. AT 510. *EW, LO.*

T327.1 Maiden sends to lecherous lover (brother) her eyes (hands, breasts) which he has admired. *BE.*

T336 Sight or touch of woman as source of sin. Bible, Koran.

T381 Virgin imprisoned in tower to prevent knowledge of men.

T400–T499. Illicit sexual relations.

T411.1 Lecherous father. AT 706.

T412 Mother-son incest.

T500–T599. Conception and birth.

T551.2 Child born with two heads. *THP.*

T685 Twins. *CE.*

V. Religion

V0–V99. Religious services.

V30.1 The eaten god. *I.*

V70.1.1 May Day. *HT.*

V250 Virgin Mary. *CE.*

W. Traits of Character.

W0–W99. Favorable traits of character.

W100–W199. Unfavorable traits of character.

W155 Hardness of heart.

X. Humor.

X900–X1899. HUMOR OF LIES AND EXAGGERATION.

X1124.2. Hunter turns animal inside out.

X1154.1.1 Fish with larger fish inside. Reverse of Plate 1.

X1321 Lies about snakes. *I.*

Z. Miscellaneous Groups of motifs.

Z0–Z99. Formulas.

Z18.1. What makes your ears so big? "Red Cap," *HT.*

Z33.1 Gingerbread man. "Fall and All," *EW, GB.*

Z81 Blowing the house in. "The Three Pigs," *LBM,* "The Puppet of the Wolf" *(THP).*

Z200–Z299. Heroes.

Z252 Hero at first nameless. *Surf.*

Z300–Z399. Unique exceptions.

Z311 Achilles heel. *LBM.*

Notes

INTRODUCTION

1. Atwood discussed fairy tales in the University of Delaware's Humanities Forum, Newark, Delaware, November 1985 (1986 Atwood letter). In the video film interview with Hermione Lee ("Writers in Conversation"), Atwood refers to Bettelheim.

2. Throughout this study, *archetype* and *archetypal* refer to broad pre-existing patterns or types rather than narrowly Jungian ones.

3. When, for brevity, I later use the word *Canadian* to refer to the peoples or literatures of Canada regardless of region or of cultural or ethnic background, I do not mean to suggest that any group of distinct culture within Canada can or should be subsumed in "Canadian."

4. *Gyn/ecology* 44, 90–91, 151–52, 266, 351–52. As provocative as Daly's comments are, she overgeneralizes. Waelti-Walters, again referring only to popular versions of popular tales, unjustly damns all fairy tales (1–12). Wehr feels fairy tales polarize images of women (35). The folklorist Kay Stone suggests that, rather than being problem solving, fairy tales are often problem creating for females. While "not inherently sexist, many readers perceive them as such." Readers can, however, learn to reinterpret or recreate fairy tales ("Misuses" 128, 142–44. Also see Zipes's *Fairy-Tales and the Art of Subversion* 46, 59.)

5. "Interpreting 'Little Red'" 193–96 n. 228). Agreeing that fellow folklorists rarely pursue possible relationships between folklore and literature, Kathleen Manley offers an interesting brief discussion of how Anne Sexton's *Transformations*, Olga Broumas's "Little Red Riding Hood," and Margaret Atwood's "Bluebeard's Egg" and *The Handmaid's Tale*, all using *Märchen*, "embody a previously unrecognized relationship between folklore and literature." She suggests that "The writers deconstruct the original tale, finding one or more subtexts therein; they then reconstruct the tale in order to make the subtext obvious" (unpublished article).

6. Throughout this book, *Robber Bride* refers to the female protagonist of the Grimms' "The Robber Bridegroom." As I write this, Atwood's novel, *The Robber Bride* (1993), has not yet been published.

CHAPTER 1

1. Toni Morrison has recently admitted that she uses "Sleeping Beauty" in *Beloved*. Morrison says she avoids literary references "unless oblique and based on written folklore," and she briefly discusses how, in *Beloved*, *The Third Life of Grange Copeland*, and *Tar Baby*, she tailors the tale ("Hansel and Gretel," "Goldilocks and the Three Bears," "Tar Baby") to characters' thoughts and actions "in a way that flags him or her and provides irony, sometimes humor" ("Memory" 387). See Waelti-Walters on Isabelle-Marie as Cinderella in Blais's *Mad Shadows* and on "Beauty and the Beast" in *The Silent Rooms*. Patrice in *Mad Shadows* also seems to be an ironic Sleeping Beauty. Arnold Davidson suggests that Hébert's *The Silent Rooms* inverts fairy tales, including "Cinderella," "Rapunzel," and "The Princess and the Pea" ("Rapunzel" 29–30, 32).

2. In a very broad sense, if the novel's stylistics are distinguished by "dialogism" of "heteroglossia" (interaction between meanings of different discourses or languages, including "alien" speech and incorporated genres) as Bakhtin suggests (277, 320), any text might be considered an intertext. O'Donnell and Davis admit that, "at an extreme," their definition of intertext "projects all texts as further divisible into other texts, and these into yet other texts (or signifiers), ad infinitum" (ix–x). Studies of intertextuality in contemporary narrative are numerous, and theories of the intertext occur in hermeneutics, narrative theory, cultural anthropology, psychoanalysis, and political theory (Jenkins 295).

3. All references to tale-type numbers, indicated in parentheses in the text following "AT" (Aarne-Thompson), are from Aarne and Thompson. Motif numbers, in parentheses after *Motif*, are from Stith Thompson, *Motif-Index of Folk-Literature*. Both sets of references are listed in the appendix to this book.

4. See, for example, rewritten *Red Cap* stories such as some Goldenbook versions, where the wolf does not eat Red Cap. The hunter or even Red Cap's father chases the wolf away rather than killing him or filling his stomach with stones. In Ideals' *Storybook Favorites*, Grandma safely hides in a clothes closet. When Red Riding Hood's father happens to hear his daughter scream, he chops off the wolf's head and carries her home on his shoulders. This version not only omits the red wine Red Cap carries but even the concluding communal eating (66–67). Unfortunately, such fiddling with tales amputates meaning, in both cases removing the rebirth or resurrection theme. Similarly, based on extensive study of the Osbourne Collection of Early Children's Books at the University of Toronto, Paul notes that fairy-tale illustrations often highlight either barely noticeable features of tales, such as the Little Mermaid "worshipping" the statue of a boy, or what she sees as images of female passivity, such as the popular wake-up kiss. See also Zipes (*Don't* 232–59) on Red Cap illustrations.

5. See Daly (*Gyn/ecology* 44, 90–91, 151–52, 266, 351–52) and Waelti-Walters (1–12). Although Kolbenschlag also sometimes oversimplifies, especially in book and chapter titles suggesting that we must "kiss Sleeping Beauty [and the Frog Prince] good-bye," she recognizes fairy tales as "the bedtime stories of the collective unconsciousness" (3). Among recent works perpetuating fairy-tale stereotypes are those by Wehr (1985, 35), Cranny-Francis (1990; 85, 94; see n. 16), and, by implication, DuPlessis (1985). DuPlessis begins *Writing Beyond the Ending* with words reminding every reader of fairy tales: "Once upon a time, the end, the rightful end, of women in novels was social—successful courtship, marriage—or judgmental of her sexual and social failure—death. These are both resolutions of romance" (1). Although she does not directly address fairy tales, she implies a common, reductionist view of fairy tales: that their endings express little more than message, the need for social acceptance and conformity.

6. For verification of the long tradition of matriarchal fairy tales and of Grimms' tales that contradict usual feminist stereotypes concerning female passivity, ageism, and classism, see Zipes, a Marxist folklorist who voices some of these same concerns (*Don't* 6, 13). Stone states the case even more strongly, faulting even Zipes. Finding his anthology of North American "feminist fairy tales," including Atwood's "Bluebeard's Egg," flat because it fails to recognize "the move of feminism (and particularly folklore feminism) beyond victimization and toward self-realization," she feels that his confusion of popularized (the Grimms and Perrault) and traditional *Märchen* "leads him into misconceptions" about *Märchen* heroines. She details a repressed English and American folk tradition portraying women as "aggressive, active, clever, and adventurous" (Review of *Don't* 110; "Things" 42–45).

7. Even Jack Zipes, who has translated and edited Grimm tales, devoted a whole book (*Brothers*) and parts of several others to the study of the Grimms, and has probably done more than any other scholar to stimulate popular interest in them and their work, sometimes implies that tales so damaging to society should be forgotten, suppressed, or rewritten (*Don't* 259; *Fairy Tales and the Art of Subversion* 67).

8. Uncovering, recovering, or discovering what I am calling an empowering "goddess" voice inside an individual is not the same as following any party line, in this case what Atwood perceives as a "feminist" one. Atwood makes her suspicion of current critical theory very clear in "If You Can't Say Something Nice" by defending art against "those who want a neatly ordered universe," "prescriptionists" (21) who seem to resemble formalists or structuralists more than contemporary theorists. She even tells a story about kicking deconstructionists rather than a stone to demonstrate, after Dr. Johnson, that authors of both criticism and what she considers literature exist (Conversation 1991). Like Doris Lessing, Atwood dislikes labels. Still, her literary practice, including

genre bending, intertextuality, self-conscious play with "truth" and "story," "ironies and loose ends" ("If You Can't Say Something Nice" 21), and especially deconstruction of old stories—often the story she is telling—seems clearly poststructuralist. Sometimes subjected to uninformed reviews or questions, Atwood feels the need to explain that she doesn't write on prescription or favor "silenc[ing] women in the name of Woman": "I view with some alarm the attempts being made to dictate to women writers, on ideological grounds, various "acceptable" modes of approach, style, form, language, subject or voice. . . . In fiction, those who write from the abstract theory on down instead of from the specific earth up all too often end by producing work that resembles a filled-in colouring book. . . . I think I am a writer, not a sort of tabula rasa for the Zeitgeist or a non-existent generator of 'texts'" ("If You Can't Say Something Nice" 22–23).

9. This 1958 pattern applies to Classic, British, and American poetry. In Canadian poetry, however, "nature rather than culture takes the foreground," and an unnamed Medusa is likely to be merged with the landscape (Pratt, "Medusa" 6).

10. The male version of Rapunzel is symbolized in James Joyce's Stephen Daedalus (*A Portrait of the Artist as a Young Man* and *Ulysses*) and the Martello tower in Sandycove he (and Joyce) chose as home. Attempting to fly by the nets of nation, family, religion, and love, Stephen turns on his heroic refrigeration apparatus when he sees E. C. (Eileen) in *Portrait*.

11. Some versions of the closely related tale, "Cap o' Rushes" (AT 510B), which has influenced "Cinderella," have an independent female protagonist who cures the prince. This tale significantly resembles two other stories important to Atwood: "The Girl Without Hands" (AT 706) and "The Juniper Tree" (AT 720). Both "Cap" and "Girl" begin with "the flight of the female protagonist from home, or with her banishment, because the father wishes to marry her. . . . Or it may be that, like Cordelia in *King Lear* [an intertext in *CE*], she does not reply as her father wishes when he asks her how much she loves him" (Thompson, *Folktale* 128; see Chapter 7). "Cinderella" also shares motifs with "The Juniper Tree," another tale significant to Atwood (see Chapter 4). Both tale cycles feature cruel stepmothers (Motif S31), and in both cases, females visit trees growing on the site of the first mother's grave (E631) and are helped by magic birds associated with the dead mother (E323) and the magic tree (D950).

12. For further discussion of "Cinderella"'s matriarchal elements, see Dundes, ed., *Cinderella*; Zipes, *Don't* 6.

13. See Rubenstein, *Novelistic*; Piercy 63–64; Rich, "When We Dead Awaken" 2045.

14. Godard borrowed the title of her book, *Gynocritics*, which may undergo

national "border blur" while moving north, from Elaine Showalter, and she thanks Sandra Gilbert for her comments. Drawing on Daphne Marlatt's Kristeva-inspired "Musing with Mothertongue," she states that "feminist critics are by definition bilingual—equally at ease in academic discourse and in their 'Mothertongue' in which we a-muse ourselves" (*Gynocritics* ii–iii, "Acknowledgements," 223–26).

15. By referring to Atwood's *You Are Happy* and *Survival*, DuPlessis equivocates her definition of *displacement*. She seems to equate the narrative displacement she initially defines with the psychological displacement or repression Atwood discusses in *Survival*'s first and second "victim positions": denying victimhood and naming fate or nature as its cause (112). Seeing *You Are Happy* as an illustration of displacement more than delegitimation because Circe abandons her "nonhegemonic speech" when Odysseus arrives, allowing the old romantic story to dominate, DuPlessis still recognizes narrative debating within the text.

16. Unfortunately, Cranny-Francis fails to question the usual sweeping generalizations about fairy tales. She assumes that "the good women, the heroines, are invariably beautiful, passive, and powerless," that Perrault's or Disney's Cinderella typifies fairy-tale females, and that traditional fairy tales necessarily encode an anti-woman ideology (85, 94).

17. We speak of American anti-novels even though most North American "novels" are more accurately described as fusions of romance and the novel. In *Life Before Man* Atwood pushes features of the money-manners-marriage-morals tradition of the English novel into parody, but many scholars recognize that her long narratives are closer to romance than to the novel genre (e.g. McLay 123–38; Carrington, "Demons" 229–45).

18. According to Cranny-Francis, feminist fairy-tale metanarratives present two authoritative narratives: "the revised version of the traditional narrative and its discursive referent, the traditional narrative" (89). In practice, of course, intertextual art is not always this simple, particularly in reference to fairy and folktales, which exist in numerous variants and change with the teller. In using intertexts, artists do more than graft narratives onto unchanging, monolithic material, and, as in Byatt's *Possession*, may interweave a number of intertexts. The interwoven narrative strands are also not easily separable.

19. "True Trash" (9–37). Atwood's unfinished doctoral dissertation for Harvard, "Nature and Power in the English Metaphysical Romance of the Nineteenth and Twentieth Centuries" (Atwood Papers), her study with Northrop Frye at the University of Toronto, and her frequent mention of the genres she uses suggest considerable knowledge of romance forms.

20. Eugene Vinaver contrasts interlaced narratives with stories "which fell apart, clearly and dramatically marked off at each end" (*Form* 22). In Vinaver's

seminars at the University of Wisconsin, he frequently compared medieval and twentieth-century texts and encouraged my own comparative discussion focusing on E. R. Eddison ("Doctrine of Organic Unity"), one of the writers covered in Atwood's uncompleted doctoral dissertation (Atwood Papers; see n. 19).

21. Written fairy tales are commonly considered omniscient, "neutral, impersonalized, set apart from the reader," making the reader "a passive receiver of events" (Jackson 154), and few studies discuss narration. The Grimms' tales Atwood uses have third-person, reliable, privileged narration. Still, there is no reason to believe that fairy tales, any more than other third-person narratives, are necessarily reliable or privileged. Oral storytellers may spontaneously modify the tale for particular audiences and social contexts, and they commonly use gestures and even grimaces (Bolton 137, Kirschenblatt-Gimblett 292), which could undercut the tale. Some fairy and folktale narrators even in written versions use unreliable and first-person narration.

CHAPTER 2

Sections of Chapter 2, including color plates of eight watercolors (1–6, 13, 14), appeared under the title, "Several Politics in Margaret Atwood's Visual Art," in *Margaret Atwood: Vision and Forms*, ed. Kathryn Van Spanckeren and Jan Garden Castro (Carbondale: S. Illinois Univ. Press, 1988), 205–14. Two reproductions with brief commentary were previously published in black and white in *Antipodes: A North American Journal of Australian Literature* 4:2 (Winter 1990), 111, 113, 115–16.

Part of the Goddess section was first presented in a Modern Language Association paper, "The Goddess in Atwood's Visual Art: Debased, Dismembered, and Reborn," New Orleans, December 1988.

1. Box 58 and Mapcase. Box numbers in the Atwood Papers are subject to updating as the Fisher Library receives more material. Consult the most current finding guide to locate materials.

2. See Margaret Atwood Correspondence, 1961–1967, Charles Pachter file, letter from Atwood to Pachter, Dec. 3 (year omitted, but presumably 1965). Pachter, a well-known Canadian artist and Atwood's friend, "whose visual imagination is quite different from [hers]" (Tape), did the original covers of *The Circle Game*, *The Edible Woman*, and *Second Words* as well as the art work for the rare editions of *Speeches for Doctor Frankenstein*, *Expeditions*, *Kaleidoscope Baroque*, *What Was in the Garden?*, and *The Journals of Susanna Moodie*. Despite Pachter's suggestion that she use his last illustration, a "sort of cameo-womb-circle-what have you" (Pachter to Atwood, "close to Hallowe'en," 1965), Atwood did her own Contact edition cover for *Circle Game*. The correspondence includes background and discussion of *The Circle Game*, *KB*, and other matters, including

Pachter's thesis project of making and illustrating the first edition of *The Circle Game*, including only that one poem. Several of the rare, early poetry volumes accompanied with Charles Pachter's lithographs, silkscreens, or wood or linoleum block prints are available in the Atwood Papers. Pachter's stunning *The Journals of Susanna Moodie* may be seen at the Art Gallery of Ontario in Toronto. Atwood is quite aware that many of her images, in *The Circle Game* and other works, are visual. See, for example, her February 3, 1965, letter to Pachter. I am grateful to Alan J. Horne, whose "Checklist of Writings By and About Margaret Atwood" brought both Atwood and Pachter's visual art to my attention, and to Judith McCombs, whose conversational references to the art and the Atwood Papers caught my interest.

3. The Alcorn cover shows a baroque frame of a nude woman in a spoon (Boston: Little, Brown, 1969).

4. Atwood is among many well-known Canadian writers, including Dennis Lee, Mordecai Richler, Margaret Laurence, Roch Carrier, and Joy Kogawa, to do children's books. Atwood first thought of Pachter to illustrate *Up in the Tree* (Papers); Ann Blades illustrated *Anna's Pet* (1980) and John Bianchi, *For the Birds* (1990). The *Confederation Incantation* holograph booklet and *Confederation Capers* by "Mabel Macfarlane McQuinney," illustrated by "Charlatan Botchter," are both unpublished illustrations for children's books in the Atwood Papers. Atwood has done quite a few other pictures that are not, as of this writing, in the archive, including a mermaid with eggs (Letter 1986), the "Robber Bridegroom" owned by Jay Macpherson (Telephone call 1985), and the original art for *The Journals of Susanna Moodie, Murder in the Dark, Interlunar, The CanLit Foodbook, Good Bones,* and *Two-Headed Poems.* The other works mentioned, as well as most of Charles Pachter's illustrations of Atwood texts, are available in the Atwood Papers. In addition, the archive includes two landscapes (1980) that are prototypes for *Interlunar's* cover (Tape) and these untitled and undated watercolors: one of a red oval or egg shape surrounded by purple, two similar shapes with white centers, one of a girl or woman looking at two figures in the background, and two of figures (one red, one blue) with outstretched arms. Other media include three early oil paintings and an early charcoal sketch.

In addition, archive art includes cover designs for "Epicoene; or, The Silent Woman" and other Victoria College dramatic production programs and *Acta Victoriana* magazine (1959–61); comic strip drawings, including "The Glamour and Fashion Page" and "Kanadian Kulture Komix" (see Fig. 12); and greeting card designs. While not directly related, Atwood's screenplays for (Blais) *Mad Shadow, Memoirs of a Great Detective, Snowbirds, Lady Oracle, Surfacing, The Edible Woman, Heaven on Earth, The Festival of Missed Crass (Forbidden Christmas),* and *Cat's Eye* also indicate a strong visual sense (see Atwood Papers, Screenplays).

5. Paradoxically, in "Siamese Twins": "Now Love cannot sever / Their too-single heart / Though they must tear themselves apart / To ever come together." "Fall and All: A Sequence" also includes three other doubled personae: a person aware of a revenant's hand "Too close within my own" ("The Revenant"), a staid spinster whose bone bears "some hidden cannibal name" ("The Revelation"), and a "double nun" ("The Double Nun") (58–62).

6. In the Jungian archetype of the Great Mother, the key is not only "the phallic opening power of the male" that the Gorgon, mistress of the night road, of fate, and of the world of the dead, can use, but also the emblem of the Goddess (Neumann 170).

7. Atwood says the color is red-orange (Letter 1986).

8. Even Circe (*YAH*) is the death-bird *kirkos*, or falcon, and the name of her isle, Aeaea, means "Wailing" (Walker, *Woman's Encyclopedia* 168).

9. Lewenstein bought out John Kemeny's share of the film rights and selected Tony Richardson as director but was unable to make the film of *The Edible Woman*. As of 1990, Alan Cooke, a British television director, has written a screen play and is planning to film *The Edible Woman*. *Surfacing* and *The Handmaid's Tale* have already been made into films, directed by Claude Jutra and Volker Schlondorff, respectively; and film projects are planned or underway for *Life Before Man*, *Bodily Harm*, and *Cat's Eye*, the last possibly using Atwood's script and starring Meryl Streep. *Heaven on Earth*, a television script, was broadcast in 1987, and "Forbidden Christmas" (earlier "The Festival of Missed Crass"), based on a story published in *Chatelaine*, was performed by the Canadian Stage Company fall, 1991 (Knelman 33–34, Atwood Papers), and later appeared on television. Margot Kidder's plan to produce and star in *Lady Oracle* didn't work out (see correspondence in Atwood papers), but Atwood and her agent Phoebe Larmore are (as of this writing) looking for "someone who would be loyal to the book" (Knelman 34), which certainly was not the case in *Surfacing* and debatably so in *The Handmaid's Tale*.

10. See also Grace, *Violent* 5–6. From another angle, these writers, like Atwood, question the roles their characters play and the society that conditions or expects such role-playing. See Munro's "The Peace of Utrecht," Hébert's "The House on the Esplanade," Page's "The Green Bird," Marshall's "The Old Woman," Laurence's *The Stone Angel* (1961), and Watson's *The Double Hook* (1959). Although Del in Munro's *Lives of Girls and Women* (1971) could become a Hagar Shipley (*The Stone Angel*) if she stayed in Jubilee, she becomes an artist. Even Hagar, a Medusa who has turned herself to stone, regains her feelings.

11. Atwood's ideas for visual art—Elaine Risley's paintings in *Cat's Eye*—are similarly revealing. Elaine's painting of the black-robed Mary again suggests the Great Goddess, whose role Elaine eventually plays when she recovers compas-

sionate vision. As in *Surfacing* and "New Poems" (*SP II*), gods dwindle as human beings and human values gain importance (see Chapters 4 and 11).

12. Because early drafts include poems titled "Street Singer" and "Boston Incident" and the name on the manuscript is "Annabel Ulaluna 6 Appian Way, Cambridge, Mass.," a derivation from Poe, Barbara Godard suggests that *Double Persephone* is a parody ("Telling" 9, 28–29).

13. As of December 1992, a combined *Good Bones/ Murder in the Dark* with illustrations (Plates 14, 16) is targeted for U.S. publication in Nan Talese's Doubleday imprint after Atwood's forthcoming novel appears (December 8, 1992, Atwood letter).

14. See Atwood's "Afterword" (*JSM* 62–64) and Lorraine Weir's "Meridians of Perception," which discusses the collages as part of the text (69–80).

15. "God's Food," one of the Grimms' Children's Legends, ends with a religious moral: although the husband hurries to offer the widow food, three of her children are already dead. After she says, "For earthly food have we no longer any desire," she and her remaining children die (Hunt and Sterne 822).

16. Free-living, one-celled algae whose cell walls consist of two boxlike parts or valves, diatoms demonstrate one of the four basic categories of cells in their tendency "to cluster together in casual, nondependent associations of primitive colonies." With the protozoa that feed on them, diatoms "stay near the surface" and form plankton, which feed the larger animals of the seas (Pfeiffer 18–19). Although the cover was not used for *Bodily Harm*, the dust jacket for the McClelland and Stewart edition does feature a metastasizing cancer cell. As *Bodily Harm* indicates, cancer cells "show up hot orange under one kind of light, hot blue under another" (Simon and Schuster 93).

17. Judith McCombs suggests that a 1980s poisonous black cloud "would also refer to air pollution, the mushroom clouds of atomic bombs, and bomb testing" (25 November 1992 Letter).

18. Three chapters of the unfinished novel, "Destroying Angels," became short stories: "Walking on Water," "The Whirlpool Rapids" (both published in *BE*), and "The Bog Man" (*WT*).

19. Atwood says that she does not remember whether the figure is male or female but that it is more likely to be male (Letter to Sharon Wilson, December 1992), as the poem suggests.

CHAPTER 3

1. Chapter 3, on *The Edible Woman*, is based on "Fairy-Tale Cannibalism in *The Edible Woman*," *Cooking By the Book: Food in Literature and Culture*, ed. Mary Ann Schofield (Bowling Green: Popular Press, 1989) and on a paper delivered

in the Literature and Culinary Arts section of the Popular Culture Association, Montreal, Canada, 28 March 1987. All page references to *The Edible Woman* are to the Popular Library edition.

2. Atwood received her A.M. from Radcliffe in 1962. When she received a Canada Council grant to return to Harvard, she moved to Cambridge in 1965 (Atwood Papers Chronology). McCombs dates the thirteen-page manuscript called "The Edible Woman," the earliest surviving version of what became the published novel, between spring 1964 and spring 1965 ("Narrator, Dark Self, and Dolls").

3. The title of Atwood's novel, *The Robber Bride*, forthcoming in 1993, promises another re-visioning of "The Robber Bridegroom." "Hansel and Gretel" (No. 15, AT 327A), "Cinderella" (No. 21, AT 510A), "Sleeping Beauty" ("Brier Rose") (No. 50, AT 410), and "Rapunzel" (No. 12, AT 310) are Grimms' tales. Perrault's "Sleeping Beauty" is also suggested. "The Gingerbread Boy," also an intertext in Atwood's "Fall and All" and *Good Bones*, is based on folk motif Z33.1. For "Peter Peter, Pumpkin-Eater" see *Best Loved* (52). The predecessor of "Goldilocks and the Three Bears" was Robert Southey's "Three Bears" (*The Doctor*, 1834–47). Other sources of the tale include the Grimms' "Little Snow White" (No. 53, AT 709), Horace Scudder's retelling of Southey's tale with Silverhair as the trespasser, and possibly an oral Norwegian tale (Leach and Fried 1110). Charles Dodgson's *Alice's Adventures in Wonderland* (1865) is also an intertext in *Life Before Man*. See n. 6.

4. Goddard c.f. offers a useful discussion of a few Atwood "tales within tales," but she does not discuss *The Edible Woman*; MacLulich c.f. compares *The Edible Woman* to "The Gingerbread Man" and "Little-Red-Cap" (111–19) but misses *The Edible Woman*'s parody (120–22). He agrees with Ainsley that Marian rejects her femininity.

5. The manuscript draft of *The Edible Woman* labeled "The Edible Woman" and, in handwriting, "First Try?" begins: "Yesterday I made up my mind to destroy her; or at least to put her where she can do no harm. She's been in the way too much lately and it's making me nervous: I can never tell in advance what she will do next" (1). The narrator, more radically split between an "I" and "she" than the narrator of the published novel, dramatizes her split through description of the two dolls on her dresser, "on either side of the mirror." To protect "her" territory from the other she knows "doesn't really exist" (3), the "I" steals the smaller, older doll with glass eyes and amputated (chewed off) fingers and toes. In order to diminish its "power," she tapes the eyes shut, takes the stuffing out, ties the arms into a knot, wraps the doll in a pillowcase, and hides it in the bottom drawer under underwear and sanitary napkins. Now, "The space on the other side of the mirror was empty for the first time since I can remember." The "I" remembers setting food before the doll, as Marian did,

and recognizes that "she" is "a private talisman, a fetish . . . the watcher, presider over certain portions of my time" (2–3). Of course, it is the "she" rather than the "I" who is responsible for behavior Robert (later Peter) finds unsatisfactory (Atwood Papers, Box 18).

This manuscript makes overt several related folk patterns important in the published book and in Atwood's drawings: the transformation of a woman into a doll or a doll as a replacement for a woman (Motifs D1620.0.1, D2006.1.6, D1268, T117.8). Marian's socialization, especially to become a desirable, marriageable object, makes her feel like a doll. This manuscript, like other material in the Atwood Papers, needs further exploration. See Judith McCombs's paper, at this writing not yet published: "Narrator, Dark Self, and Dolls: From an Early Version to Atwood's *The Edible Woman.*"

6. A number of articles investigate *Alice in Wonderland*'s relationship to *The Edible Woman.* See Harkness 103–11; Stow 90–95, 100–101; Lorsch 471–74.

7. Van Spanckeren ("Magic" 4) and I ("'The Juniper Tree'") independently reached this conclusion the same year (1987). Van Spanckeren sees fairy tales as one of several western magic sources in Atwood's early fiction and feels that *Life Before Man, Bodily Harm,* and *Two-Headed Poems* turn away from "an overt use of magical and folk material in favor of greater realism." She also notes fairy tales' binary structures (1–2).

C H A P T E R 4

1. This chapter is based on two papers, "'The Juniper Tree' and Other Fairy-Tale Elements in *Surfacing,*" The Association for Canadian Studies in the United States, Montreal, Canada, October 8, 1987; and "'The Golden Phoenix' and Other Fairy-Tale Intertext in Margaret Atwood's *Surfacing,*" XI Annual Commonwealth Literature and Language Conference in German-Speaking Countries, Aachen, West Germany, and Liege, Belgium, June 16–19, 1988. All page references are to the Popular Library edition.

2. According to Carole Carpenter, "If at all familiar with folklore, Canadians associate the term with Dr. Barbeau" (220). Barbeau and Hornyansky's edition of French-Canadian folktales continues to be the best known. This edition does not, however, contain the story *Surfacing*'s narrator mentions about a king able to speak with animals. Atwood says that the tale, called either "The Magic Snake" or "The Magic Leaf," possibly "The Magic Mushroom," is an old translation in a book published, like Barbeau's, by Oxford University Press (Telephone Call 1987; Letter 1987). William Toye, editor of the press, does not recall it (Telephone Call 1988); and I have been unable to locate either tale or book.

Numerous ordinary folktales contain the motif of talking animals (Fowke, *Canadian Folklore* 27), including AT 517 "The Boy Who Learned Many

Things," 670 "The Animal Languages," 671 "The Three Languages," 671*
"The Father Sends His Son into the Woods to Learn Animal Languages," 671B
"The Host Puts the Frog into His Spring," 672 "The Serpent's Crown," 673
"The White Serpent's Flesh," and 516 "Faithful John," including Grimms' No.
6. Motif B217.1.1, used in the Grimms' "The White Snake" (No. 17, AT 673),
is about learning animals' languages by eating serpent, and B217.2 deals specifically with learning animals' languages from eating a plant. Although there is a
motif (B176.1) called the magic serpent, present in the Melanesian story "The
Myth of Fuusai" (in Dorson) and often associated with AT 516, I have not
found a French-Canadian version of this type. Even though the Grimms' Johannes in "Faithful Johannes" does understand the language of animals, the tale
offers no explanation for his powers and he possesses no magic snake or leaf.
The Grimms' "The Three Snake Leaves" and "The Three Languages" possess
some of the elements of the posited "The Magic Snake": magic leaves and
snake, restoration of senses ("The Three Snake Leaves"), understanding of the
language of animals, and animals' revelation of a treasure ("The Three Languages"). Motifs B161 wisdom from a serpent, B161.3 magic wisdom from
eating a serpent [including the Siegfried story] (Thompson, *Folktale* 245),
B165.1 animal languages learned from serpent, B217.5 bird language learned
by having ears magically cleansed, and B217.8 Adam learning animal language
from Eve are also relevant.

3. Using Propp's *Morphology* as a basis, Granovsky does a useful structural
analysis of *Surfacing* to show that Atwood critiques and parodies fairy-tale
structure in this work. He mentions only "Snow White" and "The Golden
Phoenix" and states that, rather than individual intertexts, Atwood uses the
"structure of the fairy-tale form as a subtext." Again assuming that "the traditional fairy tale portrays women as passive victims" (59–60), Granovsky discusses how Propp's absentation, interdiction, violations, villainy, mediation,
departure, unrecognized arrival, transfiguration, punishment, and wedding are
inverted in *Surfacing* (51–65).

4. Wendigo (windigo) stories are about people who are crazed by hunger and
turn cannibal (Fowke, *Canadian Folklore* 29; also see McCombs, "Crossing" 107–
17). Literally "man-wolf," the loup garou is "a human being transformed into a
wolf or able to assume wolf form." In Canada the loup garou became confused
with the wendigo of the Algonquian Indians and is usually considered to be
controlled by Satan and "transformed because of a curse or as a punishment for
not going to mass or confession, usually over a period of seven years. He is
reputed to eat human flesh, and to return to human form at daybreak" (Fowke,
Folktales of French Canada 78–79).

5. "Beautiful Joe" is parodically named after Marshall Saunders's *Beautiful Joe*
(1894), an autobiographical children's story sometimes compared to *Black Beauty*.

6. In the Greek myth, Melampus is the first person with prophetic powers, the first mortal doctor, and the first Greek to worship Dionysus. Known to be kind to animals, Melampus, cousin of Bellerophon, gives a dead mother snake (or two snakes) a funeral and rears the little snakes. They lick his ears so clean that he can understand the languages of all animals, crawling and flying. By understanding a fierce dog, termites (or worms), and vultures, he is able to steal the cattle of Iphiclus, is saved from prison, and either cures Iphiclus' sick son or assists the childless Iphiclus in having sons. Melampus and his brother marry princesses of Tiryns after Melampus heals them (D'Aulaire 130–31; Leach and Fried 701, 527).

7. Before and after the narrator has her werewolf vision, she sees what she thinks are her father's footprints. In North America as well as Australia, Africa, India, and Burma, folk belief suggests that body impressions, including the mark of the foot in the earth, offer a means by which magic can be worked on a person or supernaturals might be compelled to perform a particular action. Folktales often feature magic footprints (Motif D1294) and even transformations from stepping in footprints (Motif D578) (Leach and Fried 410–11). Thus, by stepping into her own prints (*Surf* 219), the narrator effectively works magic on herself and transforms herself. Throughout *Surfacing* the narrator is, in a sense, following footprints, of her father's search for pictographs, her mother's closeness to nature, her own past, and the meaning of the rock paintings themselves, widely held, like petroglyphs and other marks on rocks, cliffs, and mountains, to be "footprints of gods, demons, and other supernaturals" (Leach and Fried 410–11).

8. Atwood Papers, Box 55. Also see Atwood's untitled 1968 watercolor, an illustration for the poem, "Dream: Blue Jay or Archeopteryx" (*Procedures for Underground*), depicting a blue jay metamorphosing into a bird-god-man (Plate 9), and the poem "Bluejays" (*True Stories*).

9. The Anglo-Scots dialect variant, "Applie and Orangie," ending with revenge on the cruel stepmother, has these motifs: S31 Cruel stepmother; G61 Relative's flesh eaten unwittingly; E607.1 Bones of dead collected and buried, Return in another form directly from grave; E613.0.1 Reincarnation of murdered child as bird; N271 Murder will out; Q211.4 Murder of children punished; and Q412 Punishment: millstone (axe) dropped on guilty person (Dorson, *Folktales* 37–40).

10. Like the worm, the frog, and the dead fish the narrator hooks while fishing (70–75), Joe and her father are "hooked" (101, 183). Fishers in this wasteland catch nothingness and death.

11. Leach and Fried 60. According to Graves, the nectar and ambrosia of the gods and of the Elysian Mysteries celebrating Demeter were really intoxicant mushrooms, including the *amanita muscaria* that induces hallucinations, prophetic sight, and erotic energy (*Greek Myths I* 9–10, 94).

12. As Guédon notes, "Whether slowly eaten, dismembered, drowned, or cooked by the spirits, the shaman is dehumanized, only the skeleton of his or her former self remaining. The shaman is then put back together and returns to the human world, having acquired the powers of gifts inherent in his or her experience of the non-human world" (105). Although Van Spanckeren makes a convincing argument for seeing Atwood's use of shamanic images (especially magic sight), journey structures, and supernatural themes as shamanistic, she recognizes that Atwood sometimes uses shamanic material "to enforce an antimythic meaning" ("Shamanism" 193, 197, 200). As Guédon demonstrates, in *Surfacing* "the essence of the shamanic world is absent" (109). In *Surfacing* (Wilson, "Deconstructing" 59) as in most of her work, Atwood often subverts or parodies fairy-tale, mythic, and shamanic patterns to emphasize her characters' humanity.

CHAPTER 5

An early version of Chapter 5 was presented at the Fourth International Canadian Studies Conference, Laval University, Quebec, 5 June 1989.

1. Produced in Great Britain, the 1948 film features Powell and Pressburger as directors, producers, and scriptwriters and Jack Cardill as cameraman. Brian Easdale and the Royal Philharmonic Orchestra, conducted by Sir Thomas Beecham, supply music, and art director is Hein Heckroth. Page references to *Lady Oracle* are to the Avon edition.

2. See Charles Pachter's 1968 painting, *It Was Fascination I Know*, of a winged Atwood as a butterfly offering both artist and viewer a caterpillar (Welsh-Ovcharov 31). Atwood's butterfly images are undoubtedly linked to the experience and knowledge she gained as a child accompanying her entomologist father in his field research. Still, as "one of the many insectomorphic manifestations of the Goddess in whose hands was the magic transformation from death to life," the butterfly is also an image of mythic becoming. Although in folklore the butterfly is often feared and associated with the witch, "the demonized Prehistoric Goddess," butterfly designs occur with goddess whirls and double-axes in Catal Hüyük and Minoan art (Gimbutas, *Language* 270–75).

3. The count tells Joan that she has the body of a goddess, and her first "sexual experience" is a parody supplication to the great breast associated with Diana of Ephesus (*LO* manuscripts, Atwood Papers). Later, Arthur and Joan visit Tivoli Gardens and see Diana of Ephesus "draped in breasts from neck to ankle, as though afflicted with a case of yaws" (282). However, the "power" of this ironic image of both earth goddess and female body is linked to powerlessness in society. Apparently missing the irony and unreliable narration in Joan Foster's description of Mother Nature, Patton seems to find the body, rather than Joan's internalized patriarchal assumptions about the goddess and female

bodies, "incredibly grotesque" ("Lady Oracle" 33–34). Joan needs to stop trying to match any external image, but she also needs to stop seeing her own breasts and body as "other."

4. In *Lady Oracle* Atwood parodies Joan's association of "The Red Shoes" and "The Little Mermaid" with the popular films, *With a Song in My Heart* and *Interrupted Melody*, both about crippled opera singers. Then she refers to "The Whale Who Wanted to Sing at the Met," about an ambitious harpooned whale; Mr. Peanut, a parking lot attraction who puts on a blind dance; and *Dumbo the Flying Elephant*. Carroll's *Through the Looking Glass*, Tennyson's "The Lady of Shalott" (Givner 140–41), and various popular romances also function as intertexts. Atwood once considered imitating true-confession magazine stories to make money ("Where" 9–10).

5. Lederer's further association of red with stoplights seems strained, but the blood in the shoe "is a sign of impurity. . . . The wicked sisters are no longer virgins, whereas Cinderella is untouched—in her glass slipper there is nothing to hide" (35–37).

6. Like Andersen's Karen and Gerda—both doubles and foils of the Snow Queen and Kay—the Girl Without Hands, Fitcher's Bride, and Red Cap are also either explicitly or implicitly associated with "impure" blood (see Chapters 6–11). That witches and "bad mothers" ("The Juniper Tree") also dance in red (hot) shoes (Motif Q414.4) is further evidence of punished female sexuality or "potency" in fairy tales (See Gilbert and Gubar, *The Madwoman* 36–44 on the queen in "Snow White"). On the other hand, however, the "appetites" of the Grimms' Fitcher, wolf, and Robber Bridegroom are also punished.

7. When Victoria Paige leaps in front of the train in the film, *The Red Shoes*, the ballet is danced without a Karen, dramatizing her loss of identity and ultimate invisibility in the war of sexual politics. Like many women, the young Joan in *Lady Oracle* eats partly in order to claim space for herself, to insist that she exists (*LO* 82). According to Orbach, fat may be a woman's way of saying "no" to inadequate mothering, the powerlessness of her mother, and society's tendency to treat her as a product (31–34). In addition to being a means of desexualization, compulsive eating may be protection against emotional hunger and a means of disguising anger, a way of saying, "Fuck you" (43, 68, 54–55). As I argue in a 1982 article citing the work of psychoanalysts Heinz Kohut and Otto Kernberg, Joan resembles characters in texts by Joyce, Woolf, Beckett, Sartre, and Camus: she exhibits "narcissistic qualities characteristic of Western culture" ("Fragmented Self" 52–53, 61–62, 65–67). Later, Bouson also uses Kohut's work on narcissism to discuss *Lady Oracle*, including Joan's obesity (154–66), and Hite refers to Orbach (149).

8. Wilson, "Fragmented" 50–85; "Self-Conscious," e.g., 13–14, 146–273. Also see Lecker 177, 203; Hutcheon, *Narcissistic* 1, 6–7.

9. Using several images central to Atwood's portrayal of sexual politics, Rennie and Lora of *Bodily Harm* are also aware of the dangers of cut or crippled "feet." According to Rennie, "Being in love was like running barefoot along a street covered with broken bottles. It was foolhardy, and if you got through it without damage it was only by sheer luck. . . . It gave [people] power over you. It made you visible, soft, penetrable." Although Lora, who is "quick on [her] feet," prides herself in being able to outrun her stepfather Bob, her mother ironically tells her to pretend that Bob is "a closed door" (94–95, 102–3).

10. In the difficulty of retracing steps to the underworld, Joan's maze also resembles those of Theseus and other Greek mythological figures, and of Macpherson, Borges, and, metaphorically, Cortazar. See Macpherson's *The Boatman and Other Poems*, Borges's *Labyrinths*, and Cortazar's *Hopscotch*. The maze also suggests Aeneas's escape from Hades. See Macpherson's translation of Virgil's *Aeneid* (*Four Ages of Man*, qtd. in Bennett and Brown, and their comments on it 289 n. 2).

11. Jane Rule even states that Joan may be in love again (49), and Lecker says that the novel "returns us to its beginning." Although I agree that Atwood parodies a closed archetypal "return" and that "all of Atwood's fiction may be read as an expression of the need to see truth as a shifting construct," her characters are not, therefore, static (177, 202–3).

CHAPTER 6

1. Although females may suffer further deprivations in a fairy-tale tower, at least they will not be burned as witches, which frequently happens when they are entrapped in a forest (Bottigheimer, *Grimms' Bad* 101–2). Towers may, of course, symbolize the alienation of the artist, including male artists (Yeats, Joyce), and in Keri Hulme's *The Bone People* (1989) its symbolism can include alienation from one's family and ethnic identity.

2. Most of Atwood's narrators and personae are female, but in *Life Before Man*'s multiple third-person centers of consciousness, we see double love triangles from three main points of view, including Nate's. Thus, like Joel in "Uglypuss" (*Bluebeard's Egg*), he is more sympathetic, more human if not more egalitarian, than *Power Politics*'s male or *The Edible Woman*'s Peter.

3. As Tatar points out, cutting off the breasts desexualizes the girl and suggests the martyrdom of Saint Agnes, more explicitly evoked in *Bodily Harm*'s twin islands, and of Saint Barbara. Cutting out the tongue recalls Tereus's rape and mutilation of his sister-in-law Philomela in Ovid's *Metamorphoses* (*Off With Their Heads* 122). Like clitoridectomy, infibulation (Motif S176), footbinding, and other forms of female dismemberment or mutilation, these actions bear witness to historic and cultural misogyny and sexual colonization. As Dworkin argues, "incest, too, is genital mutilation—with the penis doing the cutting. . . . In the United States,

incest is frequently the sadism of choice, the intercourse wounding the female child and socializing her to her female status—early (*Intercourse* 192–94).

4. See, for example, Ellis, 77–78; Tatar, *Hard Facts* 30, 152. In *Off With Their Heads* Tatar does offer a perceptive interpretation of "The Girl Without Hands" motif, including the Grimms' version and a Mecklenburg variant, where the girl must choose between being burned or having both arms and feet cut off. She compares AT 706 tales to the Cinderella variants Cox, and later Rooth with some modification, identify: "Catskin" tales of "unnatural fathers" who force their daughters to flee—Perrault's ("Donkey-Skin"), Straparola's (*The Facetious Nights*), and Jacobs's (*English Fairy Tales*)—and Cap o' Rushes tales of "King Lear judgment" that make the heroine an outcast (AT 510B The Dress of Gold, of Silver, and of Stars), such as the Grimms' "All Fur" (No. 65) (120–39, 257).

5. The Russian tale, "The Armless Maiden" (Carter, *Old Wives'* 135–39), has no explicit brother-sister incest, but after the bother's jealous wife, a sorceress, cuts off the heads of her baby and her husband's favorite horse and blames these actions on the sister, the brother cuts off the sister's arms and leaves her in the woods. The maiden's child has partially gold arms, and her arms regrow when she stretches them out to rescue her baby from a well. Like the Robber Bride, she tells her story: as a result, the jealous wife is punished. Similarly, a French version, "The Woman with Her Hands Cut Off," blames women for the girl's amputation although the brother again cuts off his sister's hands. The tale features a "spiteful" sister-in-law (eventually burned) and a wicked mother-in-law. Unlike the Grimms' version, in which the father is punished only indirectly (through his double, the king), the brother is confined to bed for seven years awaiting his sister's healing touch (Massignon 116–20).

6. "The Falcon's Daughter," an Egyptian tale combining AT 705 Born of Fish and 706, features a tree-maiden (N711), tongue mutilation (S163), and a female punished by being burned alive (Q414) as well as T412, mother-son incest. The girl, a moon goddess in a tree, is born from a man who, like Persephone, eats a pomegranate; he leaves the girl next to a tree and a falcon raises her. In this case, after her love-sick son marries "the falcon's daughter," the incestuous mother cuts off all of the girl's appendages, reducing her to "a lump of flesh," becomes pregnant with her son's child, and is burned alive when the restored woman tells her story. Episodes of AT 705 also suggest the myths of the falcon-formed God Horus and goddess Hathor, who lived in a sun tree, and of Horus and Seth, a mother who cuts off her incestuous son's "contaminated" hand and replaces it with a "pure" one (Dorson, *Folktales* 159–63).

7. In Anne Sexton's "The Maiden Without Hands" the hands "were polished daily and kept in place, / like tin mittens" (83).

8. Marie-Louise von Franz's "feminine" rather than feminist reading suggests that the king, usually "the dominant content of collective consciousness" and a

symbol of the self, is probably "the ruling principle of collective life" to which the woman must adapt. The son Sorrowful ("Schmerzensreich," "rich in sorrow") "is the fruit of the woman's life that has passed through the whole experience of suffering and thus acquired serenity and wisdom." The woman, representing the miller's anima, must find a connection with the positive animus. The angel is the woman's spiritual experience (*Feminine* 80, 89, 76, 84, 86).

9. Assuming that masturbatory activity substitutes for sexual involvement with the father, Otto Rank suggests that an adolescent girl's hands might be cut off for masturbation on the rationale that the punishment fits the crime (*Das Inzest-Motiv in Dichtung und Sage*, cited in Dundes, "Psychoanalytic" 141). Under the Hammurabi code, hands might also be cut off for stealing.

10. Jean Mallinson comments on the pervasive influence of Macpherson throughout Atwood's work, including *YAH*, and suggests that Macpherson, P. K. Page, Yeats, Anne Wilkinson, and Wilfred Watson influence Atwood's use of ballad and folksong as models or allusions in early poems. Mallinson also mentions the poetry of Anne Hébert, Phyllis Webb, Gwendolyn MacEwen, James Reaney, T. S. Eliot, Donne, Keats, Hardy, Hopkins, Auden, Henry Reed, Thomas, Plath, and Rich as possible influences (4–6, 53).

11. From its first drafts, "Newsreel: Man and Firing Squad," which becomes *YAH*'s first poem, depicts what seems to be a male counterpart of Medusa in the second section. The "green and lethal" eye gun of the "you" parallels the firing squad's "bullets." Atwood ironically inverts the snake image by associating it with the victim of what is usually considered Medusa vision: "serpents of blood" (at one point "snakes") "jerked" from the victim's *wrists*. In contrast, "Variation on the Word Need," dropped from the published volume, has a proud female Medusa who seems to be Circe, with a "charm, skin of interlocked letters" as well as "snakes in the hair." Although this poem's "I" wants to "unclose, be naked," voice and syllables hit and force her to spell out her feelings (Atwood Papers, Box 13, *YAH* Manuscripts). See the Medusa discussion in Chapter 1.

12. In addition to the Circe poems and the separately published "Marsh/Hawk," *You Are Happy*'s projected contents included twenty-nine poems rather than the published thirty-two, some never published. A structural development is already evident in the movement from I *War Movies*, II *Other Bodies*, III *Circe/Mud Poems*, to IV [initially unlabeled, later "Is\Not"] beginning with "Is\Not" and ending with "Late August." "First Prayer" began and "Tricks With Mirrors" ended the second section, which included "Songs of the Transformed" (Atwood Papers, Box 13, *YAH* Manuscripts).

13. Many of the poems cut from *You Are Happy* explicitly depict the sterility of handlessness and the importance of touch. An untitled poem beginning "How light it feels" and the draft of "Ancestor" even recall the amputation of the Grimms' "The Girl Without Hands." In "Ancestor" only the detached doll

arm remains. Maimed and shrunken, the white china arm of the I's "limited" predecessor lifts as if warning or "drowning" in the garden. The arm is "a sad word spoken from the earth." In "Diurnal Motions: Traditional," "you," the Odysseus figure in boots, touches the surface of the earth only with [his] shadow and the objects, including buttons and bombs, [he] drops on it. "I," the Circe / Mud Woman "buried waist deep in red mud," wallows "like a sentient radish or a moon waterlogged in warm quicksand." "To speak with the hands is better" in drafts of "Theatre of the Deaf." An untitled poem beginning "If you sleep in the sun" features a bird transforming into a human being as in "Dream: Bluejay or Archeopteryx" (*PU* 8–9) and its watercolor (Plate 9): finally, wings grow fingers (Atwood Papers, Box 13, *YAH* Manuscripts).

14. Lauter states that Circe is a Venus rather than a Diana or Hecate and that she symbolizes the release from Rapunzel difficulties: "She has *not* become her own tower" (73). The images of dismemberment at the beginning of Circe's section, however, suggest that, like most Atwood personae, she transforms.

15. Van Spanckeren says that, like other Atwood characters, Circe is a shaman with affinities to the Inuit Lady of Beasts, including the power to grant wishes ("Shamanism" 194–95).

16. Davey says that Odysseus changes and gives up his expectation that Circe continue to be "a gorgonesque statue" (*Margaret* 46–47), but he supplies no proof. We see Odysseus only through Circe's eyes and Circe's art, which Davey, like Robert Graves, does not include in his definition of female space.

17. Circe's doubling/foiling connection to Penelope, evident also in Homer, was more explicit in an early draft of an untitled prose poem labeled only "Circe Poems" and not included in the final *YAH*. As a transforming artist, both Circes resemble Homer's Penelope, an archetypal deconstructionist predating Beckett's Malone by several centuries: to avoid remarrying, Penelope unweaves at night everything she weaves during the day. The early Circe also has "spent a lot of time weaving." She weaves people, walls, and, goddess that she is, controls the moon, but her weaving has "gone all to hell" since Odysseus came, with holes appearing in walls and animals turning back to men (*YAH* Manuscripts, Atwood Papers Box 13).

18. See "Web," "Webster," and "Weaving" in Daly, *Wickedary* xv, 99–100.

19. In a draft of this poem, the fist "demands" Circe's transformation (Atwood Papers, Box 13, *YAH* Manuscripts).

20. I disagree with Johnston that the mud woman is intuition, the power of the earth ("powerful because she is silent" and passive), or as might be extrapolated from what he says, a genuine earth goddess simply because she is made of mud, particularly when this mud, hardly "unformed earth," has been shaped by male hands (169, 171–72, 174). Drafts of poems not used in *YAH* include parallel parodic images, such as the woman planted "feet up, head in the earth"

(untitled), the coin-operated female Oracle who "does not exist below the waist" and is kept in a glass jar so she can be seen but not heard ("Oracle Poem One"), a Termite Queen who stands on the brow of a ship in a dress wired to keep her upright ("Variations for the Termite Queen," published in *Kayak*; Plate 12), and the Miraculous Mother (Leda, Mary, Hera-Europa-Io) who is tired of gods coming down in the form of rabid animals ("Song of the Miraculous Mother") (Atwood Papers, Box 13, *YAH* Manuscripts).

21. A draft of the first "Circe / Mud" poem, beginning "through this forest," is even titled with a palindrome suggesting the name of Circe's island, Aeaea: "Island/dnalsI," with the letters also written backwards. Conversely, a draft of Circe's last poem reads "nothing is finished, nothing is reversible" instead of "this land is not finished, this body is not reversible" (Atwood Papers, Box 13, *YAH* Manuscripts; *YAH* 69).

22. Additional support for this idea, and for the couple's unending struggle toward transformation into the fully human, may be found in *YAH*'s manuscripts. In "Last Prayer," one of the poems cut from the volume's final draft but later published unchanged in *Unmuzzled Ox*, the you is "fully human / at last, no feathers or scales of the god." However, in the poem's second section, the flesh and the room of the "you" dissolve: "the words / claim you and enclose you," and his head sinks into an "oracular lake of fire" (Atwood Papers; 57). A final shape cannot hold because the Protean striving cannot end.

23. More clearly than the volume's ambiguous final poem, "He is Last Seen" (Chapter 2), the persona of "Hesitations Outside the Door" reaches a consciousness beyond mirror tricks ("Tricks with Mirrors") and circle games. "Hesitations'" "ends" without ending, without closing off possibilities, even by the use of a period. Although the final two lines are contradictory statements, the tone is peaceful and positive: "In the room we will find nothing / In the room we will find each other" (*PP* 51).

CHAPTER 7

1. Elsewhere Atwood mediates her position by saying: "Depression or pessimism are relative to what you think is really out there in the world. If you think the world is Disneyland, my book is depressing; if you think it's Buchenwald, it's Anne of Green Gables. I think I'm a realist. I give many more rays of hope than people deserve" (Freedman E1).

2. The Russian tale "Alyonushka" ("Alyonushka and her Brother"), which *Life Before Man* evokes in reference to Elizabeth and her sister, is about two orphans wandering the world. Suggesting the failure of self-object mirroring that *Lady Oracle*'s Joan (see Wilson, "Fragmented" 72), Elizabeth, and her sister also demonstrate, Ivanushka's thirst and inappropriate drinking cause him to

turn into a goat. Suggesting Auntie Muriel's effect on Elizabeth in *Life Before Man*, an evil witch in the tale ties a heavy stone around Alyonushka's neck and takes her shape. The flowers stop blooming. As Alyonushka is able to disentangle herself to save her brother and make the flowers bloom again, Elizabeth begins to bring back her own green world when she is moved by the magic flowers of the Chinese art show (in Maxym 48–50). Other Russian fairy tales such as "Snegurochka" ("The Snowmaiden"), "The Stone Flower," and "The Firebird" are relevant to *Life Before Man* and other Atwood texts. *Life Before Man*'s Elizabeth initially resembles the malachite woman incapable of returning love in Pavel Petrovich Bazov's version of "The Stone Flower" (in Maxym 63). As in *Surfacing*, the image of the phoenixlike firebird in "The Tale of the Firebird, Tsarevich Ivan and the Gray Wolf" (in Maxym 32–36) and in Stravinsky's ballet also suggests the metamorphosis of *Life Before Man*'s Elizabeth and other "walking-dead" characters.

Ukrainian Canadians have identifiable versions of European fairy tales, "have the most widespread and flourishing folk music and folklore in western Canada," and constitute the fifth-largest ethnic group in the country (Kenneth Peacock qtd. in Fowke; Fowke, *Folklore of Canada* 279). Since Atwood also arranged interviews with people having either Ukrainian or Lithuanian Jewish grandmothers (Atwood Papers, Research Materials and Correspondence, *LBM* Manuscripts), she is likely to be familiar not only with the Caravan Festival dancers and the Ukrainian summer camp song (*LBM* 93) but also with other folklore of these groups.

3. The popular Chinese nursery rhyme "Lady-Bug," associated with "Lady-Bird," emphasizes escape: "Lady-bug, lady-bug, / Fly away, do" (*Best* 149). Despite various efforts to assign authors, "Mother Goose" nursery rhymes are anonymous, traditional oral rhymes, known at least as early as sixteenth- and seventeenth-century French and Italian collections: Perrault's *Histoires ou contes du temps passé*, Basile's *Pentamerone*, Straparola's *Tredici piacevoli notti* (Leach and Fried 751–52).

4. Like her Aunt Muriel, Elizabeth comically plays both the apparently proper Miss Muffet, denying and escaping from her "spider self," and the double fly / spider of the folktale: "Come into my parlour / Said the spider to the fly" (Motif K815.2). In Elizabeth's view, Muriel has a parlor rather than a living room because she "cannot be said to live." Nate feels uncomfortable in Elizabeth's "parlour," however, and Elizabeth is bothered by Nate's reflecting and distorting "fly-eyes." If Auntie Muriel "is both the spider and the fly, the vampire sucker of life juice and the empty husk" (119, 206), so are Elizabeth, Chris, and to some extent Nate. According to Elizabeth, who thinks of sex in terms of cannibalism (often spiderlike) and amputation (178–79, 229), Nate moves onto Lesje when he has "used up" Martha. Lesje feels that she, at least, is "not a web-spinner" (139, 127). But if she is no calculating husband stealer, she

still succeeds in stealing Nate. In *Life Before Man*, spider-fly cannibalism is one variety of "power politics." Since "The Spider and the Fly" suggests "the once widespread belief that flies are souls in search of a female entity to eat them and give them rebirth" (Walker, *Woman's Encyclopedia* 958), however, Atwood's folktale intertext again implies the possibility of transformation.

5. "The Legend of Sleepy Hollow," from Washington Irving's *The Sketch Book*, is, like his "Rip Van Winkle," probably an Americanized version of a European folktale, in this case based on Burger's Der wilde Jager and one of the Rübezahl folktales about a mountain and storm spirit (Motif F465). Traditionally acknowledged as the United States' first classic writer, Irving's "all-pervasive theme" is mutation (Hart 410, 467; Spiller et al. 242–43, 247; Thompson 249), also one of Atwood's central concerns.

6. The Gothic atmosphere of numerous Poe works is comically evoked in this and other Atwood texts. In the first part of *Life Before Man*, numerous characters live in houses of death, seem buried alive ("Ligeia," "The Premature Burial"), and have walled-up or covered-over repressions that give them away or must be dealt with (e.g., Elizabeth, *CE*'s Elaine). Nate has a telltale heart in his "crime" of desiring Lesje, and Elizabeth can be said to wall up part of herself as she exiles Chris ("The Cask of Amontillado"). The major adult characters who do not die do contemplate suicide and death and do age appreciably throughout the book. By creating "houses" over the abyss and structuring futures, Nate, Elizabeth, and Lesje all avoid the likely literal and symbolic deaths of Canada, Western culture (the Canadian-born McCrae's "In Flanders Fields" about World War I), and the planet, including the extinction William predicts.

7. Although Charles's conversation in Flaubert's *Madame Bovary* seems as flat as the sidewalk, suddenly he transforms into a passionate person. Similarly, William, whom Lesje has trusted "like a sidewalk" (196), unexpectedly tries to rape her. Because "The big show is inside [his] head," and by extension, everyone's, the parodic creator Philboyd Studge in Kurt Vonnegut's *Breakfast of Champions* can (with some flaws) shrink, explode, and re-create his universe. Like the "you" in Kafka's "An Imperial Message," who decides to dream to himself "a message from a dead man" that can never arrive (Kafka 13, 15), a small part of Nate "still expects, longs for a message, a messenger" as he proclaims "a message he suspects is a joke" (a petition opposing corruption among the Mounties, which he expects the prime minister to disregard). Despite the German Catholic theologian's expected hand grip for "a kindred spirit," Nate "refuses to be defined" either as his mother's son or as one of "the apathetic, the fatalistic, the uncommitted" (*LBM* 306). No longer believing in an absolute truth and recognizing the existential absurd, he authentically commits himself to action without deceiving himself (Sartrean bad faith) that these actions have absolute or ultimate meaning (see Camus, *The Myth of Sisyphus*;

Sartre, *Being and Nothingness*). Beran suggests that Nate's feeling like a huge white insect is an echo of Kafka's *Metamorphosis* (208).

8. Like other Atwood intertexts and allusions, of more significance than it may seem, "Mary Had a Little Lamb," "the best-known four-line verse in the English language" (E. V. Lucas cited in *Annotated Mother Goose* 121), symbolizes the innocence and purity of Nate's earlier decision to act on a dream: to make toys with his hands and to live an honest life. Nate often feels like a wolf, but the fleece of Mary's lamb is "white as snow." Unlike Little Bo-Peep's sheep, Mary's lamb is whole and always with her (*Best* 24–25). In the system in which everything has a price (like the world of *The Edible Woman* where everyone is both consumer and consumed), the lamb Nate makes is no longer Mary's: it, too, is sold, "His share ten bucks." At this point in the novel Nate "can't [does not wish to] connect any act . . . with any consequence" and, thus, is "segmented," "dismembered" (243–44). Nate's initial vision of Lesje is similarly pure and divorced from his civilization. While some of us may laugh at his mythologizing Lesje as Diana Goddess (the Davidson's say Madonna, "Prospects" 213) and Elizabeth as a Canadian version of Hecate (morally neutral like a snowstorm, *LBM* 245), he is not to be faulted for having dreams in this wasteland. He does finally see and listen to Lesje when she stops hiding herself.

9. Using another metaphor, one could say that *Life Before Man*'s characters are in an icy "hell," an underworld drawing on Greek mythology (Persephone, Eurydice), Ovid's *Metamorphoses*, Virgil's *The Aenead*, Dante's *Inferno*, Coleridge's "Kubla Khan," Andersen's "The Snow Queen," the Russian fairy tale "Snegurochka," and folklore of Canada as frozen North. "Snegurochka" ("The Snowmaiden") (in Maxym 51–54), also the subject and title of Rimsky-Korsakov's opera (1882), is about winter transforming into spring, a movement also apparent in the novel.

10. Motifs K1916, D610, D113.1.1, G11.3, AT 363. Sublimated or symbolic cannibalism, important in all Atwood's work (see Chapters 3 and 8), is a major motif in folklore, including several of *Life Before Man*'s intertexts: "The Robber Bridegroom," "The Juniper Tree," "Little Red Cap," *Dracula*, "The Spider and the Fly," *Jaws*, and "Trees." Cannibalism is still practiced in many parts of the world, often as a social event with its own etiquette. In addition to supplying a source of food, it is thought to be a means of assimilating the strength or qualities of a person (as of an animal), guaranteeing power over the person and the person's clan, or of attaining Eucharist unity with the eaten god (Leach and Fried 186–89). In *Life Before Man* it is also a means of mutilation, one dimension of the themes of struggle for survival and power politics. Martha and Elizabeth, rivals for Nate, are "being civilized" by going out to lunch to discuss their "taste" in men, and, of course, Elizabeth invites Lesje to dinner when she suspects Nate is interested in her (145–47). William, discussing the inevitability

of human extinction while eating noodles Romanoff, has a taste for *Jaws* and needs extra food (comically blood smeared) when Lesje fails to meet his needs (142–45). In the dinner-party game of Lifeboat the characters play, the CBC woman even suggests saving people to eat (156). "Food is always part of" the sex and marriage trap (178), which is baited with flesh. Obsession with having or being sexual food occurs in all three characters' narratives. Nate and Lesje begin to fall in love as they eat, Nate is drawn into Elizabeth's parlor (258–59), the salesman's hand moves like a spider on Elizabeth's thigh (229), William and Chris bite Lesje and Elizabeth (25, 28), and Martha is abandoned when "used up" (139). If Nate is Elizabeth's cake, she is his cheese (33). As in *The Edible Woman*, everything, even trees or children, feeds on something else.

11. For a surreal French-Canadian example of another fatal attraction, see Anne Hébert's *Héloïse*. Bernard is finally united with Héloïse, the beautiful vampire of the Paris metro, in "a savage pieta" within the crowd of the dead (101).

12. The whole membership of the "Kanadian Film Directors' Guild" marches barefoot on "Parliament Hole" singing, "We're off to see the Wizard . . . the wonderful Wizard of Ooze."

13. Motifs A132.6, A132.5, D610. As Isis, Elizabeth searches for her lost "husband" (AT 425, similar to the Orpheus pattern, AT 400, Motifs F81.1, H1385.3), not only breaking a taboo by calling on him but fearing that she offends him (Motifs C31.6, C32). To Elizabeth it may seem that she loses Chris for breaking a personal taboo (Motif C932)—caring.

14. *LBM* 306; *Being and Nothingness* 617. According to Atwood, "Philosophically, Nate has 'fallen' from an optimistic 18th C. view of man as a *tabula rasa* and therefore improvable to a pessimistic view which incorporates something like Original Sin (or you could say a Hobbesian one). . . . Elizabeth has the personal past uppermost, Nate the historical-political" (Atwood Papers, Box 32, "Nan's Minor Points," *LBM* Correspondence Re. Revisions, Publication, etc.).

15. Among the Grimms' "immured, incarcerated, or sequestered heroines" is a sister who spends seven years isolated in a tree, without speaking or laughing, in order to save her twelve brothers ("The Twelve Brothers," No. 9). The Grimms' "The Six Swans" (No. 49), "All Fur" (No. 65), and "Our Lady's Child" ["The Virgin Mary's Child"] (No. 3), in which a girl is mute and naked year after year until a king "forces his way into her thorny enclosure" (Bottigheimer, *Grimms'* 101, 104), are related examples. In the Egyptian story, "The Falcon's Daughter" (AT 705 and 706), however, the woman in the tree has goddess powers. She looks "just like the moon" to a love-sick Sultan's son. He grabs her when she reduces the tree to the size of her little finger in order to get down (Dorson, *Folktales* 160–61).

16. Motifs Q451.10, S176. With "exotic" Lesje he plays Dracula when he makes love, but to Elizabeth, a woman he believes to be of "his own kind," he is like a fairly active slab of "cream cheese" (29, 213).

CHAPTER 8

1. Fowke recounts a group of riddles "of great antiquity, coming perhaps from an age when talking in riddles was one of the characteristics of magicians or priests." One Newfoundland riddle is about a man, "the fox," who dug a grave for his sweetheart, but she was up in a tree and saw him (*Canadian Folklore* 141).

2. *Interlunar* uses "Fitcher's Bird" (AT 311), "The Robber Bridegroom" (AT 955), "The Girl Without Hands" (AT 706), "The White Snake" ("Die weisse Schlange" 1812, AT 673), and variant or similar European and native folktales (the search for the wife AT 400).

In addition, myths (Persephone, Orpheus and Eurydice, the Norse Mimir, Athena and Tiresius, Motif B217.5), legends (the fisher king), and biblical stories (Adam and Eve) are all important. The main intertext in *Bluebeard's Egg*, also discussed in Chapter 9, is the Grimms' "Fitcher's Bird." In addition to "Fitcher's Bird" and "The Robber Bridegroom," *MD* uses the Grimms' "God's Food" (No. 205).

3. In early drafts of the novel, Miss Wilson (not Wilford until the revised *BH* proofs, Atwood Papers, Box 37) opens her clothing to show the policemen in her Toronto apartment her fake breast and suggests they take it home with them. In one version she tosses it in the air like a rubber ball (Atwood Papers, Box 33). In the published novel, Rennie has had a partial mastectomy.

4. AT 300 and Motif H1174.2 are about the dragon-slayer; D1171.6 refers to the holy grail. See also Motifs A2223.4 (Christ as king of fishes), K1992 (the devil tries to pass for Christ), and D2161.6.1 (diseases cured at Christ's birth). Implausibly, Rigney asserts that Minnow may be a quasi-religious "minor Christ embattled against 'Prince,' the Prince of Darkness," or, alternatively, that Prince might represent the Prince of Peace if Minnow's role is reversed (110). Irvine sees Minnow as a "shrunken Fisher King" (*Sub/version* 42).

5. As author of "The Wasteland," T. S. Eliot is an important influence in Atwood's early poetry. Later works tend to redefine his vision and deconstruct his style. Drafts of *Bodily Harm* contain this deleted Eliot epigraph: "Every man wants to, needs to, has to, some time, somewhere, do a girl in" (Atwood Papers, Box 33).

6. For an alternative view, see Annette Kolodny, who asserts that "After *Life Before Man*, Atwood turned away from her previous concentration on the power politics of intimate relations and looked, instead, at the abuse of power in the public arena" (97). Kolodny seems to overlook the multileveled symbolism of *Surfacing* and other volumes.

7. In addition to this version, "The Robber Bridegroom" manuscript draft, dated May 21, 1980, 10:22 P.M., indicates two other beginnings, equally open

to interpretation: "[This] was the beginning of it" and ["This] is why I left." "The Rope Quartet" typescript offers another: "This was the second thing, says Rennie" replaces the published beginning (Atwood, Papers, Boxes 33-34).

8. Friedman argues convincingly that reinstitution of the author and agency is a component of current intertextual reformation. American intertextual criticism has tended to ignore or refuse the "death of the author" "as a precondition of intertextual reading": "We have come full circle, back to the fabric of the text, this time an intertextual web of critical discourses that are endlessly woven and re-woven. Central to this (intertextual) reweaving of the critical discourses of intertextuality is the reinsertion of the author, along with some of the biographical and historical methodologies of influence studies, back into the pattern of the fabric" (161, 155, 173).

9. As with *Lady Oracle*, life even imitates art: following Fraser Bucchanan's pilfering in a writer's underwear drawer in *Lady Oracle*, *Toronto Life* went through Atwood's garbage. She joked that no one should tell the Atwood Society (Woodward B3). When Atwood wore one of *Bodily Harms*'s drain-chain necklaces to the 1984 MLA convention, where Atwood scholars failed to recognize it, she again parodied trends and critics, calling into question traditional lines between fiction and reality as her literature does.

10. In correspondence with Dan Green of Simon and Schuster regarding revisions are notes listing Fort Industry with Fort Inniskillin, after the Inniskillin Fusiliers, and mentioning that forts in the West Indies are named after kings, queens, and admirals (Atwood Papers, "Bodily Harm" Revised Proofs and Correspondence 1981, Box 37).

11. Although I do not agree with McCombs, who finds two kinds of artists in Atwood's fiction through 1983, "either . . . the maimed, the sold-out, and the parodied; or else . . . the mythically distanced, curiously faceless opening through which art speaks" ("Fictive" 86), see her informed discussion of Atwood's artist characters, particularly those in *Dancing Girls*. McCombs's chronological division of Atwood's fiction into two stages, Stage I, the Closed, Divided, Mirroring World through "Giving Birth" (1977), and Stage II, the realistic Open World (1978–83) (69), doesn't seem useful for the surrealist or magical realist *Bodily Harm* and other works using the same intertexts and motifs as in the earlier period. Still, such division indirectly invites readers to find continuing, sometimes submerged, Stage I mirror and paralyzed Canadian artist patterns in recent fiction.

12. Symbolically, the Robber has marked the path with ashes. The Robber Bride inscribes the way back with images of life and the goddess: peas and lentils, which have already "sprouted and unfurled (Motif R145), pointing the way in the moonlight" by the time she escapes (Zipes, *Complete* 153, 155). Similarly, both Rennie and *The Handmaid's Tale*'s Offred (Chapter 10) must leave patriarchy's narrow path.

13. Typical of Atwood's double-voiced intertextuality and her taste for irony is her ability to relish a form or genre as she undercuts it. Atwood apparently reads popular mystery stories, including those of John LeCarré (Vitale), with enjoyment. *Good Bones* includes "In Love with Raymond Chandler" (47–48), praising not "the mangled bodies and the marinated cops" but Chandler's interest in furniture. Atwood has allowed "Murder in the Dark" to be reprinted in *Great Canadian Murder and Mystery Stories*, ed. Don Bailey and Daile Unruh (14–15). Even more remarkable is the selection from *The Handmaid's Tale* in a recent collection of erotic literature.

14. Among reading errors have been varied resolutions to the unresolved future-tense "conclusion" and, because of the narrator's initial detachment and the book's painful detailing of sexist abuses, feminist confusion of Atwood's book with the pornography it indicts. Rigney (111) apparently overlooks the delayed intercourse with Daniel that Rennie compares to a rape (*BH* 211).

15. In the "Rope Quartet" drafts Atwood added a new self-reflexive section after Rennie touches Lora. Lora is telling about a gentle man who tells her he loves her: "He must've pushed a button or something, but it doesn't say, maybe it's a rope he pulls. . . . That's my favourite ending" (Atwood Papers, Box 34).

16. The policeman introduces the film clip of the rat emerging from a black woman's vagina as "our grand finale" (188). Another "amputation" showing only part of a woman's body, the film clip significantly omits her probably dead face and possibly the ropes or chains forcing her to suffer this ultimate invasion. In patting Rennie on the back "as if she's passed a test of some sort" and flippantly saying, "Look at it this way, at least it's not for queers," after Rennie throws up, the policeman implies that the killing and abuse of women is a normal part of sexual behavior, or at least more normal than lesbianism or homosexuality. Another sinister implication is that many women not only enjoy viewing such slides but also enjoy being killed or tortured during sex.

17. Atwood, *Two-Headed Poems* 37; Irvine, "One Woman Leads to Another" 95–106.

18. "According to the Waspishiana and Taruma Indians the first woman had a carnivorous fish inside her vagina" (Leach and Fried 1152; see Dworkin, *Intercourse* 122). In the rites of the Melanesian "Terrible Goddess," Malekula, "the monster Le-hev-hev, as negative power of the feminine," is associated with "the underworld animal, the rat," in addition to the spider, the clawed-crab woman, and a giant bivalve (the female genital organ) (Neumann 177).

19. Although she discusses cultural limitations and women's alienation from their own bodies, Patton misses the irony in Joan Foster's description of Mother Nature, Artemis (Diana) of Ephesus, as "draped in breasts from neck to ankle, as though afflicted with a case of yaws." Patton still seems to accept Graves's White Goddess, like the patriarchal version of Medusa—one of the monsters we have all internalized—as *The* Goddess: "What stands out is the difference

between the 'serene' head and the incredibly grotesque body. Unlike the statues in the Gardens, with normal human bodies attached to normal human heads, this monstrosity encapsulates the complete lack of fit between mind and body. This contrast emphasizes 'Mother Nature's' (and woman's) alienation from her own body, as if the female function of the body (childbearing and breast-feeding) had gone completely out of control, usurping every other function" ("Lady Oracle" 33–34). For ground-breaking scholarship about the Goddess and for instruction in re-visioning history and historical artifacts, see the works of Marija Gimbutas, including *The Civilization of the Goddess* (223).

20. See the discussion of the Daedalus myth and *Lady Oracle*'s butterfly image in Chapter 5; also see Cirlot 104 on flight. In "Lives of the Poets" (*DG*, 1977), the poet Julia believes that "language could seize [her] by the hair and draw [her] straight up, out into the free air[.] But if you stop believing, you can't do it any longer, you can't fly" (207). In *The Handmaid's Tale* the woman who inhabits Offred's room before her is "a bird stopped in flight, a woman made into an angel" (305).

Chapter 9

Part of Chapter 9, "Bluebeard's Forbidden Room," appeared in "Bluebeard's Forbidden Room: Gender Images in Margaret Atwood's Visual and Literary Art," *American Review of Canadian Studies* 16:4 (Winter 1986), 385–97.

1. See Letters to Bill [Toye], 7 August 1983, December 16, 1983, Atwood Papers, Correspondence, Box 71.

2. Motif B217.1.1, used in the Grimms' "The White Snake" (No. 17, AT 673), is about learning animal languages by eating serpent; but B217.2, dealing specifically with learning animal languages from eating a plant, and D551.5, depicting transformation by eating a leaf, are both apparently used in *Surfacing*. The Grimms' "The Three Snake Leaves" and "The Three Languages" possess some similar elements, and other "Ordinary Folktales" contain the motif of talking animals (Fowke, *Canadian Folklore* 27).

3. Snakes, including the great horned underwater serpent, the rattlesnake, and the horned or plumed serpent, "enter into the myths or religious obser-vances of nearly all American Indian tribes" and ordinarily symbolize "the fertility inherent in the earth and rain." Songs usually figure in a healing ritual, and dancers may invoke the snake's magical powers with serpentine motion (Leach and Fried 1029–30). One snake goddess, Coatlicue, the "Lady of the Serpent Skirt" invoked in Sandra Cisneros's *Woman Hollering Creek* (1991, 128–29), was mother of all the Aztec deities and of sun, moon, and stars (Walker, *Woman's Encyclopedia* 172).

4. Graves, *Greek I* 80; Walker, *Woman's Encyclopedia* 907, 218). Even when

Apollo took over not only Mother Earth's temple, situated at the omphalos or navel of the earth, but also her uterine "cave" of inspiration, ceremonies continued. A priestess, the Pythia or Pythoness, seated on a tripod, was said to become intoxicated by vapors from an opening in the earth and to deliver the oracle to priests who wrote them down in hexameter verses ("Delphic Oracle," Leach and Fried 305).

5. In *Popol Vuh*, the Mayan sacred book, the plumed serpent "produces life and humanity out of immobility and silence" (Leach and Fried 1029–30).

6. According to Ronald Hatch, in order to make the point that the snake possesses "a fundamental importance in its own right," Atwood employs "a recording 'I,' a straw man 'You,' and the snake as the third party" ("Towards" 51). Although this diagram of Atwood's method works initially, Atwood deliberately blurs the divisions, as I suggest, implying, as in *Bodily Harm*, that "I" can't be "I" without "you," "it," and by implication here, "her" and "him." *Bodily Harm* and the "Interlunar" section further develop the necessity of "them." Although critics have said little about Atwood's snakes and gender, Irvine, who does see gender issues in *Interlunar*, assumes the snake's androgyny and its representation of pure body, the union of body and spirit, amoral nature, and poetic inspiration (Review 3).

7. This mother-child relationship also suggests the Great Mother's nursing of her serpent children (Motif Q452), including the serpent god Quetzalcoatl (Walker, *Woman's Dictionary* 489).

8. Although Atwood's editor found the title poem's position at the end of the volume "jarring" and suggested that it end part 2, Atwood was characteristically firm about the sequence of her poems and sections, including the placement of the "Interlunar" section after "Snake Poems" (Letters from Bill [Toye] to Peggy [Atwood], August 17, 1983, and to Bill [Toye] from Peggy [Atwood], August 7, 1983, Atwood Papers, Correspondence, Box 71).

9. Motif M301.0.1. "Precognition" was earlier called, "A Letter from Saint Dimorphia, Afflicted with the Disease of Precognition."

10. Although the order of peoms in draft tables of contents is similar to that of the published book, a William Toye letter to Atwood suggests that "A Sunday Drive" and "Anchorage" be moved from part 2 to end part 1 (August 17, 1983). "Mothers," eventually published in the "New Poems" section of both U.S. and Canadian editions of *Selected Poems II: Poems Selected and New 1976–1986*, also appears in drafts of *Interlunar* and its table of contents between "Nomads" and "Valediction, Intergalactic." It was not withdrawn from the finished volume until November 5, 1983, along with "The Rest" (Letter to Bill [Toye] from Peggy, Correspondence, *I* Drafts). "The Standing Stones," listed after "Letter from Persephone," and "The Signer," after "The Words Continue Their Journey," were removed from the second and third sections, respectively.

Other poems considered for *Interlunar* include "An Enemy," "The Boom," "A Colour Print of a Man Who Is Not My Lover and a Dog Which Does Not Bite People," and an untitled poem beginning "Here is the future" (Atwood Papers, *I* Drafts and Typescripts, Box 71). "Keep," "An Enemy," "The Signer," and "A Colour Print" all have hand imagery; and "The Boom" and "The Rest" are about victims. "Colour Print" and the untitled poem use light images that seem linked to the shining of "The White Cup," "The Skeleton, Not as an Image of Death," and "The Light."

11. Either this painting, possibly a disputed work or no longer attributed to Bosch, is not in most collections reproducing Bosch paintings or Atwood is blending details of two paintings. Almost certainly based on Bosch's ascetic works in which a single figure dominates the foreground, the painting referred to in "One Species of Love" resembles *St. John of Patmos*, which has no "plush-furred and blunted" lion (55) and whose lady stands on ground. *St. Jerome in Prayer* has a lion, but not in the position Atwood indicates (see Tolnay 257, 265).

12. Sometimes this cycle uses a glass mountain, Motif F751, as in *Surfacing*'s intertext, "The Golden Phoenix." "Orpheus (1)" was earlier titled "O. and E., E. Speaking" and then "Euredice, [*or her* crossed out] Returning," Atwood Papers, Box 71.

13. Not only is "Orpheus (2)" based on the political repression of the Pinochet regime in Chile, but also Atwood confirms that "A Massacre Before It Is Heard About" (72–73) is about Cambodia and Sri Lanka and that "Letter from the House of Questions," originally "Letter from the Inside to the Out" (Atwood Papers, *I* Drafts and Typescripts, Box 71), is about Argentina (Letter, December 7, 1992). "The Boom" poem of *Interlunar* drafts is about a man who carried unwanted words from island to island (*I* Drafts).

14. Motif J1185.1. One of the epigraphs Atwood considered using for *The Handmaid's Tale*, from Paulette Jiles's "Horror Stories," suggests that "All women believe they are Scheherazade" (Atwood Papers, *HT* Manuscripts).

15. Thanks to Judith McCombs for calling Jara's story to my attention.

16. Although hardly proof of a connection, my thoughts are influenced by Atwood's handwritten word, *door*, next to the manuscript of "The Robber Bridegroom II"'s second, third, and fourth stanzas.

17. The manuscript of "A Painting of One Location on the Plain" indicates in Atwood's handwriting that the poem, dated "9/1/82," is "after Kurelek" (Atwood Papers, *I* Drafts, Box 71), referring to the self-taught painter William Kurelek (1927–77), whose monumental, panoramic landscapes of limitless expanse sometimes threaten human engulfment (Murray 13). Kurelek, the only recent Canadian artist who believed his artistic ability was a gift from God (Murray 11), also celebrated the experiences of Eastern European immigrants.

18. Some of the short fiction and prose poems in *Murder in the Dark* (1983) are fairy tales of sorts. "Bread" alludes to the Grimms' "God's Food" (No. 205),

including its bleeding bread motif (F991.3.1). Atwood sent "Simmering" to *Anthology of Contemporary Fairy Tales*, whose editor, Naomi Rachel, returned it, saying she didn't feel it was a fairy tale and would have used the piece if she were including the folktale (Atwood Papers, Correspondence 1981, Box 71).

19. Godard, whose comments are sometimes perceptive and intriguing, states that this relationship alters between *Surfacing* and *Bluebeard's Egg* and that, with *Bluebeard's Egg*, Atwood experiences a "breakthrough" in technique and in the type of folk narrative embedded (57–58, 60, 82). But her distinction between Atwood's earlier and "later" narratives is misleading, sometimes inconsistent, and seemingly invalidated by *WT* and *GB*.

20. The word *Fichter* is taken from an Icelandic word referring to a web-footed bird (Zipes, *Complete* 717–18).

21. Sherrill Grace says the conversation (unpublished) with her occurred in the spring of 1978 ("Courting Bluebeard" 246). Grace's article is a useful introduction to the Bluebeard motif in Perrault's "barbe bleue," in nineteenth- and twentieth-century literature, and in Atwood's *Lady Oracle*. I do not agree, however, that Atwood's treatment refuses the affirmation of the fairy tale or of Maeterlinck's play or that the wife in "Bluebeard's Egg," "like the other women in the collection, is shattered by knowledge yet helpless to change or improve anything" (261).

22. Grace, drawing on Marie-Louise von Franz, says that the Bluebeard of the Bartók opera "destroys his real women in favor of his anima. Or, if one were to interpret the work from the female point of view, Judith is destroyed by her animus." The Castle, a third "character,"

> represents Bluebeard's world, our world, reduced to silence and darkness by our brutal acquisitive-ness. . . . the 'happy ending' of the fairy tale . . . has gone; knowing and having are equally destructive; male and female, man [*sic*] and nature are doomed (254). . . . [In Atwood's *Lady Oracle*,] we are Bluebeard, wife, and castle, repeating the story of our destruction, continuing to think in terms of hostile dualities, reducing our relationships with ourselves, each other, and the natural world to castles, to rooms with metal doors, to spaces separated from their context, exclusive and closed. (261; see also Von Franz, *Introduction* 25)

23. See, for example, Motif T68, AT 306 "The Shoes That Were Danced to Pieces" on women as prizes and AT 706 "The Girl Without Hands" on women as property.

24. Although *The Handmaid's Tale* gives little detail about lesbian/homosexual relationships, *Cat's Eye* dramatizes the submerged violence of "girlfriends." Rich blames the perils of "power politics" inherent in Bluebeard folklore on institutionalized heterosexuality rather than on patriarchy ("Compulsory Heterosexuality and Lesbian Existence," 125–28), but in Atwood's work there is no reason to suppose that same-sex relationship is easier or less fraught with game-playing superficialities than heterosexual relationship.

25. In "Little Red Cap," it is the wolf who uses his art (involving both voice and disguise) to deceive both the grandmother and the inexperienced and innocent young girl, but "it is also related" that Red Cap (having been cut out of the wolf's stomach) fools and traps another wolf (Hunt and Sterne, 143; see Chapter 10).

26. In some versions of "Cinderella" (AT 510, 510A), Cinderella also escapes by dressing in an animal (bird, human) skin (Motif K521.1). Although the Grimms' "true" bride ("The True Bride," No. 186, AT 510) faithfully waits and waits for her betrothed, even though he cannot recognize her and is engaged to another woman, he first touches and then pierces her heart (Hunt and Stern 752–60.) Another way of recognizing a real bride or princess is by her inability to sleep on a pea under piles of mattresses (Motif H41.1), as in Andersen's "The Princess and the Pea" ("Prindsessen paa Aerten," 1835) (AT 704) (Kingsland 24–25). See also Grimm No. 182A "The Pea Test," published as No. 182 in 1843 and omitted in 1850 because of the similarity to the Andersen tale.

27. Wilson, quoted in Ross C11 on *WT*. Among fairy-tale intertexts in *WT* are "The Frog King" (AT 440, Grimms No. 1), "Fitcher's Bird," "The Girl Without Hands," and "The Red Shoes." Folklore motifs include D991.3 Magic ball of hair, D1761 Magic results produced by wishing, D2070.1 Magic hairball used for bewitching, E71 Resuscitation by wishing, Q451 Mutilation as punishment, and S169.1 Self-mutilation.

28. "Three Jokes" originally had five sections, and each reverses a story we all know: I on Tarzan and Jane, II on the False Bride, III on Bluebeard and the third sister, IV on Hugh Heffner abducted by bunny girls, and V on a princess who kisses the frog prince. Although the Fisher Papers Container List enumerates "Three Jokes" with Box 80's Short Stories 1969–74, it was in a folder labeled "Prose Poem." A note from K[atharine] M[artyn] says the short story "The Dreg" 1970/71 was found in the file with "Three Jokes." "Three Jokes" does not constitute any part of the handwritten manuscripts for either "The Dreg" or "Hurricane Hazel," is not found in the manuscript table of contents for either *Power Politics* or *Bluebeard's Egg*, and does not seem to bear any direct relationship to either "The Dreg" or "Hurricane Hazel." Still, the Container List quotes Atwood saying "Three Jokes" is "the beginning of a short story called 'The Dreg' which is the precursor of 'Hurricane Hazel' from *Bluebeard's Egg*" (Fisher Paper Container List for Short Stories 1969–74, Box 80).

29. In Cixous's "masculine economy," "an order that works by inculcation, by education," women live under the sentence Atwood visually depicts in her second untitled watercolor of Mary Queen of Scots or Anne Boleyn (archive-labeled "Lady and Executioner with Axe," 1969, Atwood Papers); (see Plate 5 and Chapter 2). "Women have no choice other than to be decapitated, and in

any case the moral is that if they don't actually lose their heads by the sword, they only keep them on condition that they lose them—lose them, that is, to complete silence, turned into automatons (Cixous, "Castration or Decapitation" 480–81).

30. See AT 410, Grimm No. 50, Motif D1967.1, for "Little Brier-Rose" ("Sleeping Beauty"); AT 706, Grimm No. 31, Motif T327.1, "The Girl Without Hands"; AT 551, Grimm No. 97, Motif D1500.1.18 for "The Water of Life"; AT 440, Grimm No. 1 Motif F875 for "The Frog Prince" ("The Frog King"); and Motifs F771.1.7, D2062 for Andersen's "The Snow Queen."

31. Kingsland 153. The Snow Queen is explicitly mentioned in *Bluebeard's Egg's* "The Salt Garden." See Chapter 11 for summary.

32. "The Goose Girl," Grimm No. 89, AT 533, Motif Q463. In Atwood's manuscript of the unpublished "Three Jokes," originally beginning the story that became "Hurricane Hazel," the False Bride of the second section sulks as she enters "the cask studded with nails." Thinking her sentence is unjust, she could be speaking for the Grimms' ugly bride in "Maid Maleen" (No. 198, AT 870): "Of course she used magic to deceive the Handsome Prince, but so did the True Bride. . . . Morally there is little to choose between them: she knows she is being disposed of because she is uglier" (Atwood Papers, "Power Politics" manuscripts, Box 12). See n. 28. In contrast, the "low-born" real bride in Shakespeare's *All's Well That Ends Well* must trick her husband by pretending to be a mistress in order to be accepted as his bride. See n. 26. Substitute brides also occur in AT 870, Grimm No. 198, "Maid Maleen," and AT 870A "The Little Goose Girl."

CHAPTER 10

1. Telephone Call 1985. The 1986 American cover for *The Handmaid's Tale* helps readers recognize the fairy-tale intertext. The Fred Marcellino design, that Atwood calls "a knock-out!" (Atwood Tape), features two red-robed Handmaids carrying baskets and walking away from one another beside an immense wall. The first Canadian cover is just as appropriate. Gail Geltner's puzzlelike collage, with mismatching pieces of bodies and art periods, shows a large man holding a nude, infant-bodied Madonna. As Chapter 2 indicates, Atwood frequently designs her own covers, sometimes used in Canadian editions, and she saw both American and Canadian *HT* covers before publication (Atwood Tape).

2. No. 26, AT 333, Motif K1822. An exception is David Cowart, who sees the state as the wolf, Serena Joy as "granny," and Nick as the huntsman in his brief discussion of the fairy tale. Although he says that *HT*, like the fairy tale, can be read as "a study in Oedipal ambiguities," Cowart recognizes that *HT*'s fairy-tale subtext is mythic, contributing to the novel's historic significance,

affecting its structure, and suggesting that "women at the end of the twentieth century risk losing all that their mothers gained for them by treating too casually the freedoms they have inherited, taking them for granted or—worse—consolidating them irresponsibly by flirting with the fascist ideology of censorship" (112–14). See also Cowart's discussion of Chaucer's *Canterbury Tales* and Eliot's "The Waste Land" as intertexts (114–16).

3. This chapter draws on two papers. The first, substantially different but with the same title, was presented at the Ninth Commonwealth and Third-World Literature Conference on Sex and Power, June 1986, Laufen, West Germany. "Fairy-Tale, Biblical, and Mythic Intertexts in Margaret Atwood's *The Handmaid's Tale*" was presented at the International Association for the Fantastic in the Arts Tenth Anniversary Conference, March 17, 1989, Dania, Florida.

4. By definition, since anti-narratives parody traditional ones, and since parody is self-reflexive, anti-narratives are metanarratives.

5. For example, Lacombe makes a number of perceptive observations about the book's "palimpsest" of semiotic layering and its allusions to Woolf and Plath, but she concludes that the Commander's "desire to shape and possess [Offred's] being and her art" is "innocent and all too human." Like the sexist Pieixoto, the Commander is supposedly well intentioned (19). Good intentions can in no way explain or justify the torture and mutilations of the Gileadean regime (see Rubenstein 104–5, Davidson, "Future" 113, and even Lacombe 8–10).

6. Red is the color of love, battle (Graves, *White* 70), and resurrection (Gimbutas, *Goddesses* 159) connected to the full-moon Goddess and Mary Magdalen. See also discussions of visual art (Chapter 2) and *The Edible Woman* (Chapter 3).

7. Chapter 2 discusses goddess devotees' participation in ritual dismemberment and cannibalism, an attempt to partake of eternal rebirth in the Great Mother, whose womb wound heals itself (Sjoo and Mor 81–82). Some of these rites linger symbolically in Christian communion (Walker, *Woman's Encyclopedia*, 135–39) and many fairy tales, including "The Juniper Tree" (Chapter 4) and some oral versions of "Red Cap," where Little Red Cap drinks the grandmother's blood and eats her flesh (Delarue 15, 19). With different motives, phallocentric culture dismembers the Goddess (Daly, *Gyn/ecology* 85). Patriarchal heroes (St. George, St. Patrick, Perseus) kill the moon mother, associated with Eve, the Catholic Church's Mary, and Hinduism's Kali, in the shape of a great serpent, dragon, or sea monster (Sjoo and Mor 155; Chapter 2).

8. Frye says that he borrowed the title of his *The Bush Garden: Essays on the Canadian Imagination* from Atwood's *The Journals of Susanna Moodie*, "a book unusually rich in suggestive phrases defining a Canadian sensibility" (x). Like

all of Atwood's texts, *The Handmaid's Tale* is a characteristically Canadian vision, in part because of the way it uses pastoral myth.

9. Atwood worked on a Ph.D. in Victorian literature at Harvard University 1965–67, where she studied the Puritans under Perry Miller and abandoned a dissertation on English metaphysical romance in 1977. She has joked in conversation that *The Handmaid's Tale* is an exposé of the Harvard English Department (Visit). Like *The Edible Woman* (written 1965; Chapter 3), *The Handmaid's Tale* parodies scholars and scholarly procedures. The epigraph also parodies scholarly conferences such as the 'Modern Language Association, where Atwood spoke in 1984. Following the 1984 special session on Margaret Atwood, she presented the Margaret Atwood Society with a hand-printed "Message From Your Mascot" offering "a unique one-of-a-kind Atwood Fetish! suitable for framing!"—"a special T-shirt . . . In nouveau punk style, large size for Big Dressing," reading (your choice): "1. Atwood Lives (perhaps), 2. Atwood Lives (more or less), or 3. Atwood Lives (nevertheless)" (Received by Founding Co-President Sharon Wilson, December 1984).

10. Exum suggests that the biblical narrative invites both sympathy and laughter for Leah. However, "while there is something ludicrous in the preoccupation with producing sons, the real butt of our laughter is none other than the patriarch himself, whose sexual services are traded for some aphrodisiacs" (77).

11. See n. 13 and n. 22 on the wolf and grandmother as possible surrogate mothers. After Jacob wrestles with an angel, is renamed Israel, and is given "power with God and with men," he says he has seen the face of God (Genesis 32: 24–30). Like the God Zeus and twentieth-century polygamists, he has more than one wife and countless children. Like the Commander Fred, he is designated to hear and repeat the voice of God (Genesis 35.1–2). Demeter is herself a goddess who visits and then leaves the earth (Leach and Fried 306–7). Other biblical characters, such as Lazarus and Saul, experience quests or rebirth similar to Red Cap's or, in Adam's case, engage in taboo eating resembling Red Cap's and Persephone's.

12. Like Atwood and Carter, both Olga Broumas and Lola Lemire Tostevin re-vision phallocentric interpretations by reading Red Cap's story "through the body," in their case in terms of Red Cap's willed sexuality. For Broumas, Red Cap's hood is secret blood, and what it sheaths, more "secret still. / I opened / it only at night, and with other women" ("Little Red Riding Hood" 120). The "little/red little red riding hood" of Tostevin's persona is playfully and joyfully "ridden" in marriage ("Song of Songs," *'Sophie* 72). By contrast, Anne Sexton's "Red Riding Hood" is presented as a tale of deception analogous to contemporary stories of hypocrisy, larceny, suicide, and facade among "respectable" suburbanites. The transvestite wolf gobbles Red Riding Hood down "like a

gumdrop," appears to be in his ninth month of pregnancy, and delivers grandma and Red after a kind of caesarian surgery (77–78).

13. In a Yiddish-Canadian tale similar to "Little Red Cap" the grandmother tricks the bear who has eaten the children and slices him open ("A Granny Who Had Many Children," AT 123) (Fowke, *Canadian Folklore* 291–93). Psychoanalytic scholars frequently interpret "Little Red Cap" through Oedipal myth. Heuscher and others double grandmother and wolf: both are graycaps and the wolf pretends to be the grandmother; thus, the "grandmother" or witch-mother betrays and devours Red Cap. Heuscher asserts that the maternal principle (the wolf-grandmother) yields to the strong father (the huntsman) and the successful solution of the Oedipal conflict (76–79). According to Fromm, however, this tale, "in which the main figures are three generations of women, . . . is a story of the triumph by man-hating women . . . exactly the opposite of the Oedipus myth" (240–41). He feels the story is also antagonistic of male sexual desire by describing sexual intercourse "as a cannibalistic act in which the male devours the female. This view is not held by women who like men and enjoy sex." Since Heuscher and Fromm seem to recognize the grandmother as "the Great Mother," these interpretations are ominous, supporting patriarchal displacement of female power.

14. Like most of the novel's events, their precursors, and their consequences, the Compucard has a basis in reality. *HT*'s background materials include newspaper clippings about religious cults, acid rain, toxic wastes, AIDS, infertility, fetal and infant deaths, sexual inequality, surrogate motherhood, the Nazi "lebensborn" project, the American religious right, Romania's policy of compulsory pregnancy, Phillipine "salvaging," Iranian torture, German "identity cards," and a Canadian drug addict whose foetus was seized in a Caesarian section she refused. In addition, one clipping discusses the "Smart Card," a plastic bank card electronically encoded with a cash value. Although Canadians have resisted such cards (Atwood Papers, *HT* "Background Materials" 1984–88, they are widely used in the United States and Japan.

15. Compared to "a queen ant with eggs," Offred must produce a child soon in order to justify her food and keep, and it must be a "keeper" rather than a "shredder" (145). Alluding to creation myth, Offred thinks of both God and moon as she prepares to eat an egg glowing like the one in *Bluebeard's Egg* (120; see Chapter 9). A glowing egg also suggests the folk belief of an external soul residing in an egg, box, or animal (Frazer 779). In addition, a conceiving Handmaid also resembles the Catholic Mary, who, "without ever seeing or touching the man," is in one view the object of "Yahweh's divinely disembodied attention" (Sjoo and Mor 350).

16. Phyllis (Stewart) Schlafly is an ultraconservative Republican who headed the Stop-ERA movement and helped prevent ratification of the Equal Rights

Amendment. In 1972 she began her crusade against the ERA, charging it would destroy the American family. Atwood's Serena Joy appears to be based in part on Schlafly, who did extensive traveling, made speeches, and frequently appeared on television while saying that women's place is in the home.

17. As Atwood notes, the Rapunzel syndrome transcends national boundaries and is a pattern even in "realistic" novels about "normal women" (*Surv* 209). Birthing in Gilead also portrays Hecate's incorporation of Venus. Held by a Commander's Wife behind and above her while giving birth, Janine "glows like a moon in cloud" (135). Serena Joy may also recall Spenser's Serena, who is stripped and prepared for a demonic Eucharist in *The Faerie Queene*.

18. Carr 315. Gilead shares a number of what are usually considered "typical" Victorian features, such as dogmatism, rigidity, reliance on authority, moral pretension, hypocrisy, anti-intellectual and anti-aesthetic biases, censorship, and enforced respectability, including body covering and forbidden words. See, for example, chapter and subheadings in Houghton. Kim Hicks, a former student, identifies the many angel references in *The Handmaid's Tale* with Coventry Patmore's poem, "The Angel in the House." Virginia Woolf says the woman writer must kill this negative heritage and self-image (*Professions* 285).

19. Bettelheim states that the hunter represents rationality and ego against the wolf's id: "Little Red Cap" "deals with the child's ambivalence about whether to live by the pleasure principle or the reality principle" (170–72). In Atwood's reversed fairy tale, this dichotomy becomes suspect.

20. Atwood's "wolf" is cut open (Motif Q426) (stabbed) only in Volker Schlondorff's 1990 film, *The Handmaid's Tale* (Harold Pinter script). Like the God speaking from the burning bush in the Bible (Exodus 3.14, Motif F979.5.1) and in Cecil B. De Mille's *The Ten Commandments* (1923, 1956), Offred announces her identity as "*I Am*" (293) (in the Bible and film, "I Am That I Am"). Thanks to my colleague Edward Kearns for initially suggesting this similarity.

21. Unlike the Bolshevik-occupied village of Saratoff, Russia, where an edict abolished private ownership of women and made them state property (*The Times*, London, February 11, 1919; Atwood Papers, *HT* "Background Materials"), Gilead offers no benefits to women who are beyond the age of child bearing. In *The Handmaid's Tale* the Demeter character, Offred's real mother, cannot, phoenixlike, rise from the colonies' toxic ashes where she, other crones outliving their usefulness as egg bearers, and gender traitors are exposed to radiation that amputates before it kills (260–64). On the symbolic level, however, Offred is not only reunited with her earth mother but, in conceiving, is carrying on the life cycle and restoring the dead earth.

22. See Heuscher (77–78) and Fromm on the wolf's "pregnancy envy" in swallowing both grandmother and girl. In Fromm's view, "Little Red Cap"

ridicules the wolf because he attempts to play the role of a pregnant woman. The belly full of stones symbolizes sterility (240–41).

C H A P T E R 11

Chapter 11, on *Cat's Eye*, is based on "Eyes and I's," *International Literature in English: Essays on the Major Writers*, ed. Robert Ross (New York and London: Garland, 1991).

1. Atwood says she actually "made notes for *Cat's Eye* in 1964, but other novels kept intruding" (cited in Carlin 32–M); the seven boxes of *Cat's Eye* material in the Atwood Papers contain notes, drafts, and stories dated 1964–65. In notes marked "The Edible Woman," a character with a double personality suffers emotional vampirism: her husband and children break open her head and drink the contents of her skull. Afterward, she gets up and goes to a bridge club meeting. Two other drafts directly relate to *Cat's Eye*: in "Cut-Outs," three girls are cutting stoves, chairs, dresses, and "Ladies" out of a catalogue; and in "Scribblers" girls are tracing a woman's face from a magazine. See also "The Ravine" and "Suffer the Little Children" (1964–65).

2. Early drafts of *Cat's Eye* contain fairy-tale, mythic, folk, and Gothic references that are often more explicit than in the published work, which still retains a real princess (Elizabeth II). Perhaps partly because she used word processing, Atwood's drafts of *CE* are more numerous than usual, revealing major changes in conception as well as her usual preference for artful indirection. The narrator and her mother are both referred to or compared to the Witch of Endor, and the narrator seems to worry that she is Dracula. Manuscripts also mention the "Alice Through the Looking-Glass universe" associated with the brother's games, woman-headed snakes in art (Motif B29.2.3), and native peoples who eat the hearts of their enemies (D1335.1.2). Atwood also sometimes internalizes or symbolizes action that was once part of a scene. Before leaving for the gallery, the symbolically amputated Elaine character of one draft thinks about wearing a burnt half-a-face mask: *Cat's Eye* has a painting of Cordelia titled *Half a Face* and a section of this name. In this section, Elaine doesn't want her horror comics in her room at night because she is afraid she will see such a half face in the mirror (212). In the manuscript, however, the mask has "one peeled blood-shot eye," and Elaine also thinks about strapping a plastic arm to her arm and coming in like a Hindu goddess, or slipping her feet into hollow cast feet.

Images in the manuscript often illuminate Atwood's fairy-tale intertexts. In one early version, the girls play the game of statues and must stay the way they land. Cordelia plays Elizabeth I and Mary Queen of Scots about to get her head chopped off, and the Elaine character sees an image of herself "frozen in place," tongue out, hand behind her for a jail. When Cordelia mentions the hole in the ground, the Elaine of a word-processed draft remembers being in the hole and actually confronts Cordelia. Alluding to the severed finger of "The Robber Bridegroom" and the punished feet of "The Little Mermaid," this Elaine finds the knowledge of what Cordelia has done to her "like the return of some object. . . . At the same time it's like a cut-off finger lying on the doorstep. Somebody else's, somebody I know. I look at it and feel a numb, sickening recognition." In one version, she even accuses Cordelia of eating her heart (G262.2, Box 100). In a cut scene with Ben before he becomes her husband, the narrator thinks about dressing up a store mannequin as herself. She compares her refusal to discuss what is bothering her to the Hardy Boys' reticence (48). While walking on Queen Street toward "Sub-Versions," she ironically refers to Disney's "Snow White," which she didn't see until she had grown up, as "a gap in my childhood": "Hi ho, hi ho It's off to work we go." Earlier chapter titles are also sometimes revealing. "The Tomb of the Biscuit Queen" became "Half a Face," and "The Garden of Earthly Delights" [also "Angels of Darkness"], the former referring to the famous Bosch painting became, "One Wing" (Atwood Papers, Boxes 99–100, Early Holograph Drafts, Early Version, Early Word-Processed Drafts).

3. In 1943 the term *magical realism* was adopted for the U.S. exhibition of Charles Sheeler and Edward Hopper's works, entitled "American Realists and Magical Realists" (Drabble 606–7). The Nova Scotian Alex Colville founded the Magic Realist school of painting identified in Canada with the Maritimes and Newfoundland since the late fifties (Brown C.S.6). In the acknowledgments of *Cat's Eye*, Atwood says that the paintings and other modern art works of the book do not exist but have been influenced by the first Isaacs Gallery and these artists: Joyce Wieland (see McCombs, "Contrary" 13–14), Jack Chambers, Charles Pachter (see designs for early Atwood poetry volumes in the Atwood Papers and Atwood's introduction to Welsh-Ovcharov's *Charles Pachter*), Erica Heron, Gail Geltner (see Canadian *HT* cover), Denis Burton, Louis de Niverville, Heather Cooper (see *BH*'s references), William Kurelek (see *I* discussion), Greg Curnoe, and Lenore M. Atwood (Atwood's sister-in-law).

4. See Sherrill Grace's early discussion of the way Atwood shows "the controlling power of art" in her poetry through images of snow, ice, eyes, circles, and mirrors. *You Are Happy*'s "Tricks With Mirrors" shows that "In order to be a mirror, a perfect lover, the woman must repress her own identity. . . . In addition, the man loses a chance for love and freedom." Grace connects "the life of mirrors" to "the life of vision": "The exclusive reliance upon the visual sense separates objects in space, splits things off from their contexts, isolates the viewer from the thing viewed. By simply looking *at* something, we are able to keep ourselves at a distance, uninvolved" (*Violent* 51–52, 10, 66–68). Hutcheon

also discusses "that recurring motif in Atwood's verse that links the stasis of ice to that of art" ("From Poetic" 20).

5. According to Atwood:

The reader looks at the mirror and sees not the writer but himself; and behind his own image in the foreground, a reflection of the world he lives in. If a country or culture lacks such mirrors, it has no way of knowing what it looks like; it must travel blind. If, as has long been the case in this country [Canada], the viewer is given a mirror that reflects not him but someone else, and told at the same time that the reflection he sees is himself, he will get a very distorted idea of what he is really like. He will also get a distorted idea of what other people are like: it's hard to find out who anyone else is until you have found out who *you* are. . . . [T]he extent to which Canadian literature has been neglected in its home territory suggests, among other things, a fear on the part of Canadians of knowing who they are: while the large number of mirror and reflection images contained within that literature suggest a society engaged in a vain search for an image, a reflection that will answer it. (*Surv* 15–16)

6. In "Snow White" (AT 709, Grimm No. 53), the evil, "heartless" queen wants to eat Snow White's heart (or lungs and liver, Motif G262.2); instead, the huntsman substitutes a heart (Motif K512.2) for hers. In *CE* Elaine lives on even though her heart seems to have been magically removed (D2062.1, F1096.1). In addition to "The Snow Queen" and "Snow White," *CE* also suggests native Canadian tales such as "The Cold Princess," about the Princess of Freezeland who learns that warm hearts make summer and sunshine, and "The Snow-Man's Bride," about a woman who marries Snow-Man; by the end, ice leaves the river (Kennedy, *The Canadian Fairy Book* 329–54). Russian tales about summer replacing winter are also relevant (see Chapter 7, ns. 2, 9).

7. The book is filled with Elaine's twin or split identities: her imagined vampire twin, "split-pumpkin" body, and missing twin (233, 155, 166); her brother Stephen, Susie, and especially Cordelia as twins: "We are like the twins in old fables, each of whom has been given half a key" (411). Her painting of Cordelia is titled, *Half a Face*. There are also twin sweater sets, twins in a lab jar, both "good" and "bad" hearts, and comic books about one twin in a rocket ship and one with a burned face (50–51, 169, 219, 211). In folklore, twins (Motif T685) can be either fortuitous, as in twin culture heroes or gods (A515.1.1, A116), or disastrous. Sometimes one or both twins are exposed or drowned (S314, M371.0.2).

8. Rapunzel can be considered Dame Gothel's mirror image (double) in the same way that Snow White might be viewed as the queen's in "Snow White" (AT 709). In Sexton's "Rapunzel," the girl and the woman are "two birds / washing in the same mirror," one a copy of the other and both "fair game," exposed to the same "rain" and in danger of falling into the same "cesspool." If "stone-cold" and locked, the tower is also a museum against time: "A woman / who loves a woman / is forever young" (35, 38–40). As in "Snow White,"

Rapunzel and Dame Gothel are two phases in both maturation and goddess cycles. In phallocentric politics, as in Atwood's use of goddess imagery and initially polarized characterization, neither Dame Gothel nor the queen is evil in herself. If we listen to the submerged stories of Dame Gothel, the nameless mother in "The Girl Without Hands," the Queen in "Snow White" (see Barzilai 260–72), and other "good" or "bad" mothers, we will begin to hear their pain or loneliness as we read that of Atwood's Auntie Muriel and Mrs. Smeath. In *CE*, Elaine transforms by replacing her "an eye for an eye" philosophy with empathetic vision.

9. Several of the Grimms' tales, including "Rapunzel" and "Hansel and Gretel," include magic formulae, "vestiges of primitive ways" featuring early Germanic verse style: "Rapunzel, Rapunzel, / Lass dein Haar herunter" (J. Campbell, "Folkloristic Commentary" 847). See also Van Spanckeren ("Magic" 1) on "Magic as transformational theme and structural 'figure'" in Atwood's three early novels.

10. Consider Marian (*EW*) and Anna (*Surf*) in the camera's eye, Joan in her "monster" mother's gaze (*LO*), Rennie in the eyes of the rope man, Jake, and Daniel (*BH*; Wilson, "Camera Images," "Fragmented Self"), and Offred under the official Eyes of Gilead (*HT*).

11. Even the nickname of Cordelia's sister, "Mirrie" for the Shakespeare-named Miranda, suggests being trapped in a mirror, a fate the woman who is queen and mother in "Snow White" also partly chooses. Through deception a mirror reflection may make a dupe think he or she is captive (Motif K1883.7). Like Alice in Carroll's *Through the Looking Glass*, many of Atwood's characters feel trapped behind glass, on the wrong side of the mirror. Characters in folklore as well as in Atwood's work also transform by looking in a mirror (D579).

12. See her later painting *Falling Women*. "[M]en, the kind who caused women to fall. . . . were like the weather. They didn't have a mind. They merely drenched you or struck you like lightning and moved on, mindless as blizzards. Or they were like rocks, a line of sharp slippery rocks with jagged edges. . . . Fallen women were women who had fallen onto men and hurt themselves" (268). By changing *fallen* to *falling* for her painting's title, and, as McCombs mentions, reversing the gender of the image from Lorelei legend ("Contrary" 12), Elaine (and behind her, Atwood) reopens the closure of so many real and fictional women's stories and causes the reader to resee images of both women and men.

13. Although Jon seems less threatening, he also fails to rescue her. The *absence* of his "gaze" contributes to Elaine's attempted suicide. Jon seems to be an escape from the world of grownups. He creates "eye-damaging" art, smashed constructions, and then "hacked-up body-part stuff" for the movies,

art which mirrors his and the world's fragmentation. Since, "Like one of a pair of bookends, he is incomplete by himself" (324), Elaine first becomes Snow White to the many painters who surround him (Motif F451.5.1.2) and then another child. With him, Elaine's eyes become "disused" (335, 18, 342).

14. Being buried alive (e.g., Motifs S123, Q456), either by walling in or actual burial in earth, was an ancient punishment, generally for the powerless. Girls of noble blood [Antigone], nuns, and wives of knights were walled in to save them the shame of public execution. In Rome vestal virgins found guilty of immorality and in Peru unfaithful wives of the sun were buried alive. In Central America, fifteenth-century Germany, and even contemporary China, wives and servants of "great" men were buried with them (Leach and Fried, "Buried Alive" 174). See Sexton's poem, "The Moss of His Skin" (Gilbert and Gubar 1993–94), about a daughter buried with her father. A fairy tale about being walled in or buried, in this case in a mound, cave, or hollow hill (Motif R45) because a cruel father doesn't approve his daughter's choice of husbands, is Maid Maleen" (AT 870 Grimm No. 198). Folklore and legends also cluster around those buried while in a cataleptic trance: the "living dead" (Leach and Fried 174) of Poe and others' stories.

15. See my discussion of narcissism and ego theory in "Fragmented Self" (50–85).

16. Motifs D993, D1961, and B721 pertain to a magic eye; and Motifs F405.5 and B501 to a talisman. In early, crossed-out draft passages of *Cat's Eye*, the main character kept two eyes from a doll, whose head she had opened, in her red plastic purse. The marble, substituted for the doll eyes, was "like my own secret eye, that I could use to see through walls and in the dark." In another early holograph draft, Cordelia throws the cat's eye off the bridge into the creek and "I stand on the bridge, mouth slack, hands dangling. I feel blinded" (Atwood Papers, *CE* Manuscripts).

17. Atwood recalls seeing about six Virgin Marys, "one for every occasion," while visiting a church in Mexico. One was dressed in white, one in blue, and one in black "and you prayed to her when all the others had failed" (Hammond Interview, "Articulating" 115).

18. Elaine has three friends and three men, she uses three main shapes in her paintings *Three Muses* and *Life Drawing*, and she paints a triptych and a double triptych. Cordelia is one of three daughters. The novel also has three main settings.

19. In a less effective, more "explained," earlier version of this scene, Elaine gathers Cordelia in "like a daughter, and my arms pass through her as if both of us are air. She blends into me and the ravine is empty." In thinking about what happened then and when she was a child, Elaine thinks: "It was my own face though, the face I used to see as a child, in the mirror. . . . an image I once

despised. I accept it back now, it is mine also." She recognizes that Cordelia "did to me what was being done to her. Cruelty is the inside of fear, where the teeth are. We turn ourselves inside out, for protection; whoever's close gets bitten" (*CE* Manuscripts, Box 100).

20. Atwood's image of the third eye, also important in showing the narrator's transformed vision in *Surfacing* (24), seems to build intertextually not only on the mystical vision with which it is traditionally associated but also on Jay Macpherson's poem, "The Third Eye" (*The Boatman*, Bennett and Brown 290) and even James Reaney's review of it suggesting that readers use their own "third eyes" (*Can. Lit.* 30). Located in the center of the forehead (F512.1.1), the third eye is a real vestigial organ. For Atwood, it suggests artistic vision more than a portal to the soul.

Works Cited

Aarne, Antti, and Stith Thompson. *The Types of the Folktale: A Classification and Bibliography.* Trans. and enlarged Stith Thompson, 2nd rev. Folklore Fellows Communications 184. Ed. Walter Anderson et al. Helsinki: Academia Scientiarum Fennica, 1961.

Adam, Ian, and Helen Tiffin, eds. *Past the Last Post: Theorizing Post-Colonialism and Post-Modernism.* Calgary: U of Calgary P, 1990.

Annotated Mother Goose. William Baring-Gould and Cecil Baring-Gould. New York: Branhall House, [c. 1962].

Atwood, Margaret. *The Animals in That Country.* Toronto: Oxford UP, 1968.

———. Art Work. 1958–1980. Margaret Atwood Papers, Thomas Fisher Rare Book Library, University of Toronto, Toronto, Canada.

———. *Bluebeard's Egg.* Toronto: McClelland and Stewart, 1983.

———. *Bodily Harm.* New York: Simon and Schuster, 1982.

———. *Bodily Harm.* Toronto: McClelland and Stewart, 1981.

———. "Canadian-American Relations: Surviving the Eighties." *Second Words.* 371–92.

———. "Canadian Monsters: Some Aspects of the Supernatural in Canadian Fiction." *Second Words.* 229–53.

———. *The CanLit Foodbook: From Pen To Palate—A Collection of Tasty Literary Fare.* Toronto: Totem, 1987.

———. *Cat's Eye.* Toronto: McClelland and Stewart, 1988.

———. *The Circle Game.* Toronto: Anansi, 1966.

———. *The Circle Game.* Toronto: Anansi, 1978.

———, with illustrations by Charles Pachter. *The Circle Game.* Bloomfield Hills, MI: Cranbrook Academy of Art, 1964.

———. Conversation. Charles Pachter art exhibition, Canada Trust Bank, June 5, 1991.

———. Conversation. University of Northern Colorado, April 30, 1986.

———. Correspondence. Margaret Atwood Papers.

———. *Dancing Girls and Other Stories.* McClelland and Stewart-Bantam: Toronto, 1977.

——— [M.E.]. *Double Persephone.* 1, Market Book Series. Toronto: Hawkshead Press, 1961. See Atwood Papers in Thomas Fisher Library.

———. *The Edible Woman.* Boston: Little, Brown, 1969.

————. *The Edible Woman*. New York: Popular Library, 1976.

———— [M.E]. "Fall and All: a Sequence." *The Fiddlehead* No. 59 (Winter 1963): 58–63.

————. "Five Poems." *Tamarack Review* 27 (Spring 1963): 29–33.

————. Foreword. *Charles Pachter*, by Bogomila Welsh-Ovcharov. 1–5.

————. *For the Birds*. Boxes and sidebars by Shelley Tanaka. Illus. John Bianchi. Earth Care Books. Toronto: Douglas and McIntyre, 1990.

————. "From *Cave Series*." Vision and Forms. *River Styx* 13: 31.

————. *Good Bones*. Toronto: Coach House, 1992.

————. "Great Unexpectations." *Margaret Atwood: Vision and Forms*. Ed. Kathryn Van Spanckeren and Jan Garden Castro. Carbondale: S. Illinois UP, Spring 1988. viii–xvi.

————. *The Handmaid's Tale*. Toronto: McClelland and Stewart, 1985.

————. *The Handmaid's Tale*. Boston: Houghton Mifflin, 1986.

————. "If You Can't Say Something Nice, Don't Say Anything At All." *Language in Her Eye: Views on Writing and Gender by Canadian Women Writing in English*. Ed. Libby Scheier, Sarah Sheard and Eleanor Wachtel. Toronto: Coach House, 1990. 15–25.

————. *Interlunar*. Toronto: Oxford UP, 1984.

————. Introduction. *The New Oxford Book of Canadian Verse*. Ed. Margaret Atwood. Toronto: Oxford UP, 1982. xxvii–xxx.

————. *The Journals of Susanna Moodie: Poems by Margaret Atwood*. Toronto: Oxford UP, 1970.

————, with illustrations by Charles Pachter. *The Journals of Susanna Moodie*. Toronto: Manuel and Abel Bello-Sanchez, 1980. Limited edition.

————. *Lady Oracle*. New York: Avon, 1976.

————. "Last Prayer." *Unmuzzled Ox* 1. 3 (Summer 1972): 57.

————. Lecture. University of Delaware Humanities Forum, Newark, Delaware, November 1985 (1986 Atwood letter).

————. Letter to Sharon Wilson. September 29, 1986.

————. Letter to Sharon Wilson. December 30, 1987.

————. Letter to Sharon Wilson. August 27, 1991.

————. Letter to Sharon Wilson. December 8, 1992.

————. Letter to Sharon Wilson. July 6, 1993.

————. *Life Before Man*. New York: Simon and Schuster, 1979.

————. *Murder in the Dark*. Toronto: Coach House, 1983.

————. "Murder in the Dark." Rpt. *Great Canadian Murder and Mystery Stories*. Ed. Don Bailey and Daile Unruh. Kingston, Ont. and Clayton, NY: Quarry Press, 1991. 14–15.

————. Papers, Manuscript Collection 200. Thomas Fisher Rare Book Library, University of Toronto. Toronto, Canada.

————. *Power Politics*. Toronto: Anansi, 1971.

————. *Procedures for Underground*. Toronto: Oxford UP, 1970.

————. *Second Words: Selected Critical Prose*. Toronto: Anansi, 1982.

————. *Selected Poems*. New York: Simon and Schuster, 1976.

————. *Selected Poems II: Poems Selected and New 1976–1986*. Toronto: Oxford UP, 1986.

————. *Surfacing*. New York: Popular Library, 1976.

————. *Survival: A Thematic Guide to Canadian Literature*. Toronto: Anansi, 1972.

————. Tape-recording for Sharon R. Wilson. August 1985.

————. Telephone call. Placed by Sharon Wilson. December 1985.

————. Telephone call. Placed by Sharon Wilson. September 29, 1987.

————. "Three Chronicles: Epaulettes, Coldblooded, Hardball." *This Magazine* 24.3 (September 1990): 38–41.

————. "Three-Eyes." *West Coast Line* 25.3 (Winter 1991/92): 142–43.

————. "Three Poems." *The Tamarack Review* 21 (Autumn 1961): 20–21.

————. "Through the One-Way Mirror." *The Nation*, March 22, 1986: 332–34.

———— [M.E.]. "Towered Woman." *The Canadian Forum* 40 (June 1960): 60.

————. "The Triple Goddess: A Poem for Voices." *Acta Victoriana* 85.3 (1960): 8–13. Cited in Godard, "Telling" 29.

————. *True Stories*. Toronto: Oxford UP, 1981.

————. *True Stories*. New York: Simon and Schuster, 1981.

————. *Two-Headed Poems*. Toronto: Oxford UP, 1978.

————. "Two Stories: An Angel and Theology." Rpt. from *Malahat Review* and *Now. Translation*. Canadian Feature Issue: English Literature and Literature du Quebec. 20 (Spring 1988): 43–45. Also in *Selected Poems II*.

————. "Variations for the Termite Queen." *Kayak* No. 32 (1973): 3–6.

————. Visit. University of Northern Colorado, Greeley. April 30–May 2, 1986.

————. "Where Is How: A Celebrated Novelist Lightheartedly Links the Mysteries of Location and Creativity." *Publishers Weekly* 238.35 (August 8, 1991): 8.

————. *Wilderness Tips*. Toronto: McClelland and Stewart, 1991.

————. *You Are Happy*. Toronto: Oxford UP, 1974.

————, ed. *The New Oxford Book of Canadian Verse in English*. Toronto: Oxford UP, 1982.

"Atwood, Margarets" [pseudonym]. "Review of *Second Words*." *Critical Essays on Margaret Atwood*. Ed. Judith McCombs. G. K. Hall, 1988.

Baer, Elizabeth. "Pilgrimage Inward: Quest and Fairy Tale Motifs in *Surfacing*." *Margaret Atwood: Vision and Form*. Ed. Kathryn Van Spanckeren and Jan Garden Castro. Carbondale: S Illinois UP, 1988. 24–34.

Bakhtin, M. M. *The Dialogic Imagination: Four Essays*. Trans. Caryl Emerson and Michael Holquist. Ed. Michael Holquist. Slavic Series No. 1. Austin: U of Texas P, 1981.

Barbeau, Marius. "About the Stories." *The Golden Phoenix and Other French-Canadian Fairy Tales*. New York: Henry Z. Walck, 1967. 140–44.

Barbeau, Marius, and Michael Hornyansky. *The Golden Phoenix and Other French-Canadian Fairy Tales*. New York: Henry Z. Walck, 1967.

Barzilai, Shuli. "Reading 'Snow White': The Mother's Story." *Ties That Bind: Essays on Mothering and Patriarchy*. Ed. Jean F. O'Barr, Deborah Pope, and Mary Wyer. Chicago: U of Chicago P, 1990. 253–72.

Baum, L. Frank. *The Wizard of Oz* [Called "The New Wizard of Oz" on the title page and "The Wonderful Wizard of Oz" in the "Introduction"]. Indianapolis and New York: Bobbs-Merrill, 1944.

Beckett, Samuel. *Waiting for Godot*. New York: Grove, 1954.

Bennett, Donna, and Russell Brown. *An Anthology of Canadian Literature in English*. Vol. 2. Toronto: Oxford UP, 1983. 289–93.

Beran, Carol L. "Intertexts of Margaret Atwood's *Life Before Man*." *American Review of Canadian Studies* 22.2 (Summer 1992): 199–214.

Best Loved Nursery Rhymes and Songs. Including Mother Goose Selections. Ed. Augusta Baker. New York: Parents' Magazine Enterprises for Playmore, 1974.

Bettelheim, Bruno. *The Uses of Enchantment: The Meaning and Importance of Fairy Tales*. New York: Knopf, 1976.

The Holy Bible. King James Version. Cleveland and New York: World, n.d.

Bogan, Louise. "Medusa." Ed. Gilbert and Gubar. *Norton Anthology of Literature by Women*. 1611.

Bolton, Laura. "In Search of Inuit Music." Fowke, *Explorations*. 137–43.

Booth, Wayne. *The Rhetoric of Fiction*. Chicago: U Chicago, 1961.

Bottigheimer, Ruth B. *Grimms' Bad Girls and Bold Boys: The Moral and Social Vision of the Tales*. New Haven: Yale UP, 1987.

———. "Tale Spinners: Submerged Voices in Grimms' Fairy Tales." *New German Critique* 27 (Fall 1982): 141–50.

Bouson, J. Brooks. *The Empathic Reader: A Study of the Narcissistic Character and the Drama of the Self*. Amherst: U of Massachusetts P, 1989.

Bowering, George. "Margaret Atwood's Hands." *Studies in Canadian Literature* 6.1 (1981): 39–52.

Broumas, Olga. "Little Red Riding Hood." Zipes. *Don't*. 119–20.

Brown, Craig, ed. *The Illustrated History of Canada*. Toronto: Lester and Orpen Dennys, 1987.

Brydon, Diana. "Caribbean Revolution and Literary Convention." *Canadian Literature* 95 (1982): 181–85.

Cameron, Elspeth. "Famininity, or Parody of Autonomy: Anorexia Nervosa and *The Edible Woman*." *Journal of Canadian Studies* 20.2 (Summer 1985): 45–69.

———. "Margaret Atwood: A Patchwork Self." *Book Forum* 4 (1978): 42–43.

Campbell, Elizabeth A. "The Woman Artist as Sibyl: Sappho, George Eliot, and Margaret Atwood." *The Nassau Review* 5.5 (1989): 6–14.

Campbell, Joseph. *The Flight of the Wild Gander: Explorations in the Mythological Dimensions of Fairy Tales, Legends, and Symbols.* New York: Harper Perennial, 1990.

———. "Folkloristic Commentary." Hunt and Stern. 833–64.

———. *The Masks of God: Creative Mythology.* New York: Penguin, 1976.

Camus, Albert. *The Myth of Sisyphus and Other Essays.* New York: Vintage, 1955.

Carlin, Margaret. "Nobody Said Writing Was Easy." Rev. of *Cat's Eye. Rocky Mountain News Sunday Magazine/Books*, March 19, 1989, 32M.

Carpenter, Carole Henderson. *Many Voices: A Study of Folklore Activities in Canada and Their Role in Canadian Culture.* Ottawa: National Museums of Canada Mercury Series, 1979.

Carr, Arthur J. "Tennyson as a Modern Poet." *Victorian Literature: Essays in Literature.* Ed. Austin Wright. New York: Oxford UP, 1961. 311–333.

Carrington, Ildiko de Papp. "Another Symbolic Descent." *Essays on Canadian Writing* 26 (1983): 45–63.

———. "Demons, Doubles, and Dinosaurs: *Life Before Man, The Origin of Consciousness*, and 'The Icicle.'" *Essays on Canadian Writing* 33 (1986) 68–88.

———. "Margaret Atwood and Her Works." *Canadian Writers and Their Works, Fiction Series.* Vol. 9. Ed. Robert Lecker, Jack David, and Ellen Quigley, intro. George Woodcock. Toronto: ECW Press, 1987. 23–116.

Carroll, Lewis [Dodgson]. *Alice in Wonderland and Through the Looking Glass.* Illus. John Tenniel. Grosset and Dunlap, 1985.

Carter, Angela. *The Bloody Chamber and Other Adult Tales.* New York: Harper Colophon, 1981.

Carter, Angela, ed. *The Old Wives' Fairy Tale Book.* Illus. Corinna Sargood. New York: Pantheon, 1990.

Castro, Jan Garden. "Interview with Margaret Atwood." *River Styx* 15 (Women's Issues): 6–21.

Chadwick, Whitney. *Women, Art, and Society.* London: Thames and Hudson, 1990.

Chavkin, Samuel. *The Murder of Chile: Eyewitness Accounts of the Coup, the Terror, and the Resistance Today.* New York: Everest House, 1982.

Cirlot, J. E. *A Dictionary of Symbols.* Trans. Jack Sage. New York: Philosophical Library, 1962.

Cisneros, Sandra. *Woman Hollering Creek and Other Stories.* New York: Random House, 1991.

Cixous, Hélène. "Castration or Decapitation?" *Contemporary Literary Criticism: Literary and Cultural Studies.* Ed. Robert Con Davis and Ronald Schliefer. 2nd ed. Trans. Annette Kuhn. New York: Longman, 1989. 479–91.

———. "The Laugh of the Medusa." Trans. Keith Cohen and Paula Cohen. *Women's Voices: Visions and Perspectives*. Ed. Pat C. Hoy II, Esther H. Schor, and Robert DiYanni. New York: McGraw-Hill, 1990. 481–96.

The Complete Hans Christian Andersen Fairy Tales. Ed. Lily Owens. New York: Avenel, 1981.

Clayton, Jay, and Eric Rothstein, ed. *Influence and Intertextuality in Literary History*. Madison: U of Wisconsin P, 1991.

Coleridge, Samuel Taylor. "Kubla Khan." *An Oxford Anthology of English Poetry*, ed. Howard Foster Lowry and Willard Thorp with Howard C. Horsford. 2d ed. New York: Oxford UP, 1956. 683–84.

Columbo, John Robert. "Margaret Atwood." *Contemporary Poets*. Ed. James Vinson. New York: St. Martin's Press, 1975.

Conlogue, Ray. "How Atwood Creates Novels That Are Really Mortuaries." *Globe and Mail*, August 8, 1990: C1.

Coover, Robert. Conversation. University of Northern Colorado, October 22, 1992.

Cowart, David. *History and the Contemporary Novel*. Carbondale and Edwardsville: S Illinois UP, 1989.

Cranny-Francis, Anne. *Feminist Fiction: Feminist Uses of Generic Fiction*. New York: St. Martin's Press, 1990.

Daly, Mary. *Gyn/ecology: The Metaethics of Radical Feminism*. Boston: Beacon Press, 1978.

———, with Jane Caputi. *Webster's First New Intergalactic Wickedary of the English Language*. Boston: Beacon, 1987.

D'Aulaire, Ingri, and Edgar Parin. *D'Aulaires' Book of Greek Myths*. Garden City: Doubleday, 1962.

Davey, Frank. "Atwood's Gorgon Touch." Rpt. *Critical Essays on Margaret Atwood*. Ed. Judith McCombs. 134–52.

———. "Life After Man." Rev. of *Bodily Harm*, by Margaret Atwood. *Canadian Literature* 95 (1982): 29–30.

———. *Margaret Atwood: A Feminist Poetics*. Vancouver: Talonbooks, 1984.

Davidson, Arnold E. "Future Tense: Making History in *The Handmaid's Tale*." *Margaret Atwood: Vision and Forms*. Ed. Kathryn Van Spanckeren and Jan Garden Castro. Carbondale: S. Illinois UP, 1988. 113–21.

———. "Rapunzel in The Silent Rooms: Inverted Fairy Tales in Anne Hébert's First Novel." *The Colby Library Quarterly* 17.1 (March 1983): 29–36.

Davidson, Arnold E., and Cathy N. Davidson, eds. *The Art of Margaret Atwood: Essays in Criticism*. Toronto: Anansi, 1981.

———. "Prospects and Retrospect in *Life Before Man*." Davidson and Davidson. 205–21.

Davis, Robert Con, and Ronald Schliefer. "Julia Kristeva." *Contemporary Literary Criticism: Literary and Cultural Studies*. Ed. Robert Con Davis and Ronald Schliefer. 2nd ed. Trans. Annette Kuhn. New York: Longman, 1989. 185–86.

De Beauvoir, Simone. *The Second Sex*. Trans. H. M. Parshley. New York: Random, 1952.

Degh, Linda. "What Did the Grimm Brothers Give to and Take from the Folk?" *The Brothers Grimm and Folktale*. Ed. James M. McGlathery with Larry W. Danielson, Ruth E. Lorbe, Selma K. Richardson. Urbana: U of Illinois P, 1988. 66–90.

Delarue, Paul. "The Story of Grandmother." Ed. Dundes. *Little Red Riding Hood*. 13–20.

De Tolnay, Charles. *Hieronymous Bosch*. New York: Reynal, 1966.

Dorson, Richard M. "Folklore and Fake Lore." *American Mercury* 70 (1950): 335–43.

Dorson, Richard M., ed. *Folktales Told Around the World*. Chicago: U of Chicago P, 1975.

Drabble, Margaret, ed. *The Oxford Companion to English Literature*. Fifth Edition. Oxford, New York, Tokyo, Melbourne: Oxford UP, 1985.

Draine, Betsy. "An Interview with Margaret Atwood." *Interviews with Contemporary Writers: Second Series, 1972–1982*. Ed. L. S. Dembo. Madison: U of Wisconsin P, 1983. 366–81.

Dundes, Alan. "Interpreting 'Little Red Riding Hood' Psychoanalytically." Dundes. *Little Red*. 192–236.

———. "Introduction to the Second Edition." Propp. xi–xvii.

———. Introduction to Zipes's "'Little Red.'" Dundes. *Little Red*. 121.

———. "The Psychoanalytic Study of the Grimms' Tales": 'The Maiden Without Hands (AT 706).'" *Folklore Matters*. Ed. Dundes. Knoxville: U of Tennessee P, 1989. 112–50.

Dundes, Alan, ed. *Cinderella: A Casebook*. New York: Wildman Press, 1983.

———. *Little Red Riding Hood: A Casebook*. Madison: U of Wisconsin P, 1989.

DuPlessis, Rachel Blau. *Writing Beyond the Ending: Narrative Strategies of Twentieth-Century Women Writers*. Bloomington: Indiana UP, 1985.

Dworkin, Andrea. *Intercourse*. London: Secker and Warburg, 1987.

———. *Woman Hating*. New York: Dutton, 1974.

Eisler, Riane. *The Chalice and the Blade: Our History, Our Future*. New York: Harper, 1987.

Eliot, T. S. *Selected Poems*. New York: Harcourt, 1964.

Ellis, John M. *One Fairy Story Too Many: The Brothers Grimm and Their Tales*. Chicago: U of Chicago P, 1985.

Exum, J. Cheryl. "'Mother in Israel': A Familiar Figure Reconsidered." *Feminist Interpretation of the Bible*. Ed. Letty M. Russell. Philadelphia: Westminster Press, 1985. 73–85.

Fitz Gerald, Gregory and Kathryn Crabbe. "Evading the Pigeonholers." Ingersoll 131–39.

Fleming, Victor, Dir. *The Wizard of Oz*. MGM, 1939.

Fowke, Edith. *Canadian Folklore: Perspectives on Canadian Culture*. Toronto: Oxford UP, 1988.

———. *Folklore of Canada*. Toronto: mcCleeland and Steward, 1990.

———. *Folktales of French Canada*. Toronto: NC Press, 1982.

Fowke, Edith, and Carole Carpenter. *Explorations in Canadian Folklore*. Toronto: McClelland and Steward, 1985.

Frazer, Sir James George. *The Golden Bough: A Study in Magic and Religion*. New York: Macmillan, 1963.

Freedman, Adele. "Happy Heroine and 'Freak' of Can Lit." *Globe and Mail*, October 25, 1980: E1.

Freibert, Lucy M. "Control and Creativity: The Politics of Risk in Margaret Atwood's *The Handmaid's Tale*." *Critical Essays on Margaret Atwood*. Ed. McCombs. 280–91.

Friedman, Susan Stanford. "Weavings: Intertextuality and the (Re)Birth of the Author." Clayton and Rothstein. 146–80.

Fromm, Erich. *The Forgotten Language*. New York: Grove, 1951.

Frye. Northrop. *Anatomy of Criticism: Four Essays*. New York: Atheneum, 1966.

———. *The Bush Garden: Essays on the Canadian Imagination*. Toronto: Anansi, 1971.

———. *The Great Code: The Bible and Literature*. San Diego: Harcourt Brace Jovanovich, 1982.

Garza, Hedda. *Salvadore Allende*. World Leaders Past and Present. New York: Chelsea House, 1989.

Gibson, Graeme. Interview with Margaret Atwood. *Eleven Canadian Novelists*. Toronto: Anansi, 1973.

Gilbert, Sandra M., and Susan Gubar. *The Madwoman in the Attic: The Woman Writer and the Nineteenth-Century Literary Imagination*. New Haven: Yale, 1979.

Gilbert, Sandra M., and Susan Gubar, eds. *The Norton Anthology of Literature by Women: The Tradition in English*. New York: W. W. Norton, 1985.

Gimbutas, Marija. *The Civilization of the Goddess: The World of Old Europe*. Ed. Joan Marler. San Francisco: Harper, 1991.

———. *The Goddesses and Gods of Old Europe: Myths and Cult Images*. Berkeley and Los Angeles: U of California P, 1982.

———. *The Language of the Goddess*. San Francisco: Harper and Row, 1989.

Givner, Jessie. "Mirror Images in Margaret Atwood's *Lady Oracle. Studies in Canadian Literature* 14 (1989): 139–46.

Godard, Barbara. "Tales Within Tales: Margaret Atwood's Folk Narratives." *Canadian Literature* 109 (1986): 57–84.

———. "Telling it Over Again: Atwood's Art of Parody." *Canadian Poetry* 21 (Fall/ Winter 1987): 1–30.

Godard, Barbara, ed. *Gynocritics: Feminist Approaches to Writing by Canadian and Quebecoise Women.* Toronto: ECW Press, 1987.

Goldie, Terry. "Folklore; Popular Culture and Individuation in 'Surfacing' and 'The Diviners.'" *Canadian Literature* 104 (Spring 1985): 95–108.

Goodwin, Ken. "Revolution as Bodily fiction—Thea Astley and Margaret Atwood." *Antipodes* 4.2 (Winter 1990): 109–15.

Grace, Sherrill. "Courting Bluebeard with Bartók, Atwood, and Fowles: Modern Treatment of the Bluebeard Theme," *Journal of Modern Literature* 11.2 (1984): 245–62.

———. *Violent Duality: A Study of Margaret Atwood.* Ed. Ken Norris. Montreal: Vehicle Press, 1980.

Grace, Sherrill E., and Lorraine Weir, eds. *Margaret Atwood: Language, Text and System.* Vancouver: U of British Columbia, 1983.

Granofsky, Ronald. "Fairy-Tale Morphology in Margaret Atwood's *Surfacing.*" *Mosaic* 23/24: 51–65.

Graves, Robert. *The Greek Myths: I, II.* Baltimore: Penguin, 1968, 1969.

———. *The White Goddess: A Historic Grammar of Poetic Mythology.* Amended and enlarged edition. New York: Farrar, Straus and Giroux, 1966.

Greene, Gayle. *Changing the Story: Feminist Fiction and the Tradition.* Bloomington and Indianapolis: Indiana UP, 1991.

———. "Life Before Man: 'Can Anything be Saved?'." Van Spanckeren and Castro. 65–84.

———. Rev. of *Cat's Eye. Women's Studies* 18.4 (1991): 445–55.

Greer, Germaine. *The Female Eunuch.* New York: McGraw-Hill, 1971.

Griffiths, Gareth. "Being there, being There: Kosinsky and Malouf." *Past the Last Post.* Ed. Adam and Tiffin. 153–66.

Guédon, Marie-Francoise. "*Surfacing*: Amerindian Themes and Shamanism." Grace and Weir. 91–111.

Hammond, Karla. "A Margaret Atwood Interview with Karla Hammond." *Concerning Poetry* 12.11 (1979): 73–81.

———. Interview. "Articulating the Mute." Rpt. Ingersoll 109–20.

Harkness, David L. "Alice in Toronto: The Carrollian Intertext in *The Edible Woman.*" *Essays on Canadian Writing* 37 (Spring 1989): 103–11.

Hart, James D. *The Oxford Companion to American Literature.* 4th ed. New York: Oxford UP, 1965.

Hay, Sara Henderson. "Rapunzel." Zipes. *Don't*. 121.

Hébert, Anne. *Héloise*. Trans. Sheila Fischman. Toronto: General Publishing Co., 1983.

Heuscher, Julius E. *A Psychiatric Study of Fairy Tales: Their Origin, Meaning and Usefulness*. Springfield, IL: Charles C. Thomas, 1963.

Hite, Molly. "Other Side, Other Woman: *Lady Oracle*." *The Other Side of the Story: Structures and Strategies of Contemporary Feminist Narrative*. Ithaca: Cornell UP, 1989. 127–67.

Holland, Norman N. "The I and the Nay: A Fable." *Profession 89*. 55–57.

Horne, Alan J. "Margaret Atwood: A Checklist of Writings By and About Margaret Atwood." Davidson and Davidson. 243–85.

Houghton, Walter. *The Victorian Frame of Mind*. New Haven: Yale, 1957.

Hunt, Margaret, and James Stern. Trans. *The Complete Grimm's Fairy Tales*. New York: Pantheon, 1972.

Hutcheon, Linda. *The Canadian Postmodern: A Study of Contemporary English-Canadian Fiction*. Toronto: Oxford UP, 1988.

———. "'Circling the Downspout of Empire.'" *Past the Last Post*. Ed. Adam and Tiffin. 167–89.

———. "From Poetic to Narrative Structures: The Novels of Margaret Atwood." Ed. Grace and Weir. 17–31.

———. "Historiographic Metafiction: Parody and the Intertextuality of History." Ed. O'Donnell and Davis. 3–32.

———. *Narcissistic Narrative: The Metafictional Paradox*. New York and London: Methuen, 1980.

———. *The Politics of Post-Modernism*. London and New York: Routledge, 1990.

Ingersoll, Earl G., ed. *Margaret Atwood Conversations*. Princeton, NJ: Ontario Review Press, 1990.

———. "Margaret Atwood's 'Cat's Eye': Re-Viewing Women in a Postmodern World." *Ariel* 22:4 (October 1991): 17–27.

Irvine, Lorna. "One Woman Leads to Another." Davidson and Davidson. 95–106.

———. Review of *Interlunar*. *Journal of Canadian Poetry* 1 (1986): 2–6.

———. *Sub/version*. Toronto: ECW, 1986.

Jackson, Rosemary. *Fantasy: The Literature of Subversion*. London and New York: Methuen, 1981.

Jacoby, Mario. "C. G. Jung's View of Fairy Tale Interpretation: General Reflections on Hermeneutics in Depth Psychology." Ed. Jacoby, Kast and Riedel. 3–15.

Jacoby, Mario, Verena Kast, and Ingrid Riedel. *Witches, Ogres, and the Devil's Daughter: Encounters with Evil in Fairy Tales*. Trans. Michael H. Kohn. Boston and London: Shambhala, 1992.

Jenkins, Jennifer. "A Selected Bibliography of Intertextual, Postmodern, and Contemporary American Studies." Ed. O'Donnell and Davis. 295–313.

Jensen, Emily. "Margaret Atwood's *Lady Oracle*: A Modern Parable." *Essays in Canadian Writing* 33 (Fall 1986): 29–49.

Jobes, Gertrude. *Dictionary of Mythology Folklore and Symbols.* 3 vols. New York: Scarecrow Press, 1962.

Johnston, Gordon. "'The Ruthless Story and the Future Tense' in Margaret Atwood's 'Circe/Mud Poems.'" *Studies in Canadian Literature* 5 (1980). 167–76.

Juhasz, Suzanne. *Naked and Fiery Forms: Modern American Poetry by Women.* New York: Farrar, Straus, and Giroux, 1978.

Jung, Carl G. *Psychology and Alchemy.* Trans. R.F.C. Hull. 2nd ed. Bollingen Series. Princeton: Princeton UP, 1980.

Jung, Carl G., ed. with M.-L. von Franz, Joseph L. Henderson, Jolande Jacobi, Aniela Jaffe. *Man and His Symbols.* New York: Dell, 1964.

Kafka, Franz. *Parables and Paradoxes* (Bilingual Edition). New York: Schocken Books, 1974.

Kaster, Joseph. *Putnam's Concise Mythological Dictionary.* New York: Putnam, [1963].

Katz-Stoker, Fraya. "The Other Criticism: Feminism vs. Formalism." *Images of Women in Fiction: Feminist Perspectives.* Ed. Susan Koppelman Cornillon. Bowling Green: Bowling Green U Popular Press, 1972. 315–27.

Kennedy, Howard Angus, illus. H. R. Miller. *The Canadian Fairy Book.* Toronto and London: J. J. Dent and Sons, 1927.

Kingsland, L. W., trans. *Hans's Andersen's Fairy Tales.* Oxford: Oxford UP, 1985.

Kirshenblatt-Gimblett, Barbara. "A Parable in Context: A Social Interactional Analysis of Storytelling Performance." Fowke, *Explorations.* 289–319.

Knelman, Martin. "Lights! Camera! Atwood!" *Toronto Life* 24.6 (April 1990): 33–34.

Kolbenschlag, Madonna. *Kiss Sleeping Beauty Good-Bye: Breaking the Spell of Feminine Myths and Models.* New York: Harper and Row, 1979.

Kolodny, Annette. "Margaret Atwood and the Politics of Narrative." *Studies on Canadian Literature: Introductory and Critical Essays.* Ed. Arnold E. Davidson. New York: Modern Language Association, 1990. 90–109.

Konrad, Victor. "President's Corner." *Canadian Studies Update* 10. 3: 1.

Kristeva, Julia. *Desire in Language: A Semiotic Approach to Literature and Art.* Ed. Leon S. Roudiez, trans. Thomas Gora, Alice Jardine, and Leon S. Roudiez. New York: Columbia UP, 1980.

———. "Stabat Mater." Rpt. Davis and Schliefer. 186–203.

Kurelek, William. *Kurelek's Canada.* Toronto: Pagurian Press, 1978.

Lacombe, Michele. "The Writing on the Wall: Amputated Speech in Margaret Atwood's *The Handmaid's Tale*." *Wascana Review* 21.2 (Fall 1986): 3–20.

Lacourciere, Luc. "The Analytical Catalogue of French Folktales in North America." *Laurentian University Review. Revue de l'Université Laurentienne* 8 (February 1976): 123–28.

Larson, Janet Karsten. "Margaret Atwood's Testaments: Resisting the Gilead Within." *Christian Century* 104 (May 20–27): 496–98.

Laurence, Margaret. *The Stone Angel.* New York: Bantam Windstone, 1978.

Lauter, Estella. *Women as Mythmakers: Poetry and Visual Art by Twentieth-Century Women.* Bloomington: Indiana UP, 1984.

Leach, Maria. ed., and Jerome Fried, asst. ed. *Funk and Wagnalls Standard Dictionary of Folklore, Mythology, and Legend.* San Francisco: Harper and Row, 1984.

Lecker, Robert. "Janus Through the looking Glass: Atwood's First Three Novels." Davidson and Davidson. 177–203.

Leclaire, Jacques. "Margaret Atwood's *Cat's Eye* as a Portrait of the Artist." *Commonwealth.* 13.1 (1990): 73–80.

Lederer, Wolfgang. *The Kiss of the Snow Queen: Hans Christian Andersen and Man's Redemption by Woman.* Berkeley: U California P, 1986.

Lee, Hermione. "Writers in Conversation: Margaret Atwood." Interview. VHS Video film. Roland Collection No. 43, 52 minutes, Color. Northbrook, Illinois.

Lieberman, Marcia K. "'Some Day My Prince Will Come': Female Acculturation through the Fairy Tale." *College English* 34 (1972): 383–95. Rpt. Zipes, *Don't.* 185–200.

Lilienfeld, Jane. "Circe's Emergence: Transforming Traditional Love in Margaret Atwood's *You Are Happy*." *Critical Essays on Margaret Atwood.* Ed. McCombs. 123–30.

Liszka, James Jakób. *The Semiotic of Myth: A critical Study of the Symbol.* Bloomington: Indiana UP, 1989.

"Little Red Riding Hood." *Storybook Favorites: Best-Loved Stories for Children.* Ed. Maryjane Hooper Tonn. Milwaukee: Ideals Publishing Corp., n.d. 64–67. Rpt. *Famous Fairy Tales.* Ed. Watty Piper. n.p.: Platt and Munk, n.d.

Lorsch, Susan E. "Androgyny and the Idea of the Double: Margaret Atwood's *The Edible Woman*." *Dalhousie Review* 63.3 (Autumn 1983): 464–74.

Lucking, David. "In Pursuit of the Faceless Stranger: Depths and Surfaces in Margaret Atwood's *Bodily Harm*." *Studies in Canadian Literature* 15.1 (1990): 76–93.

Lüthi, Max. *The European Folktale: Form and Nature.* Trans. John D. Niles. Bloomington and Indianapolis: Indiana UP, 1982.

Lyons, Bonnie. "Using Other People's Dreadful Childhoods." Ingersoll. 221–33.

McCombs, Judith. "Atwood's Fictive Portraits of the Artist: from Victim to Surfacer, From Oracle to Birth." *Women's Studies* 12.1 (1986). 69–88.

———. "Contrary Re-memberings: the Creating Self and Feminism in *Cat's Eye*." *Canadian Literature* 129 (Summer 1991): 9–23.

———. "Crossing Over: Atwood's Wilderness *Journals* and *Surfacing*." Ed. Armand E. Singer. *Essays on the Literature of Mountaineering*. Morgantown: West Virginia UP, 1982. 106–17.

———. Introduction. *Critical Essays on Margaret Atwood*. Ed. Judith McCombs. Boston: G. K. Hall, 1988. 1–28.

———. Letter. November 25, 1992.

———. "Narrator, Dark Self, and Dolls: From an Early Version to Atwood's *The Edible Woman*." Unpublished article.

———. "Politics, Structure, and Poetic Development in Atwood's Canadian-American Sequences: From an Apprentice Pair to 'The Circle Game' to 'Two-Headed Poems.'" Van Spanckeren and Castro. 142–62.

———. Review of *Power Politics*, by Margaret Atwood. *Moving Out* 3.2 (Spring 1973): 54–69.

McCombs, Judith, and Carole L. Palmer. *Margaret Atwood: A Reference Guide*. Boston: G. K. Hall, 1991.

MacDonald, Margaret Read. *The Storyteller's Sourcebook: A Subject, Title, and Motif Index to Folklore Collections for Children*. 1st ed. Detroit: Neal-Schuman, 1979.

McLay, Catherine. "The Dark Voyage: *The Edible Woman* as Romance." Davidson and Davidson. 123–38.

MacLulich, T. D. "Atwood's Adult Fairy Tale: Levi-Strauss, Bettelheim, and *The Edible Woman*." *Essays on Canadian Writing* 11 (Summer 1978): 111–29.

Macpherson, Jay. "From *The Boatman*." *An Anthology of Canadian Literature in English*. Ed. Donna Bennett and Russell Brown. Vol. 2. Toronto: Oxford UP 1983. 289–93.

Magoun, Francis P., Jr., and Alexander H. Krappe, trans. *Grimms' German Folk Tales*. Carbondale: S Illinois UP, 1960.

Mallinson, Jean. *Margaret Atwood and Her Works*. Toronto: ECW Press, n.d. [1984?]

Mandel, Eli. "Atwood's Poetic Politics." Grace and Weir. 53–66.

Manley, Kathleen E. B. "Folklore and Literature: Another Expansion." Unpublished article.

Margaret Atwood: Once in August. Dir. Michael Rubbo. National Film Board of Canada, 1984.

Massignon, Genevieve, ed. *Folktales of France*. Trans. Jacqueline Hyland. Chicago: U of Chicago P, 1968.

Mathews, Robin. "Opening Address." XI Annual Commonwealth Literature and Language Conference in German-Speaking Countries. Aachen, Germany. June 16, 1988.

Maxym, Lucy. *Russian Lacquer, Legends and Fairy Tales*. Manhasset, NY: Siamese Imports, 1981.

Mendez-Egle, Beatrice, ed. *Margaret Atwood: Reflection and Reality*. Edinburg, TX: Pan American U, 1987.

Metcalfe, William. *International Journal of Canadian Studies/ Revue Internationale D'Etudes Canadiennes*. Research on Canada. 1–2 (Spring–Fall 1990). 203–16.

Mieder, Wolfgang. *Tradition and Innovation in Folk Literature*. Hanover and London: UP of New England, 1987.

Millett, Kate. *Sexual Politics*. New York: Avon, 1971.

Morrison, Toni. "Memory, Creation, and Writing." *Thought* 59.235 (December 1984): 385–90.

Murray, Joan. *Kurelek's Vision of Canada: The Robert McLaughlin Gallery Oshawa*. Exhibition Catalogue. 1982?

Neuman, Shirley, and Smaro Kamboureli, ed. *Amazing Space: Writing Canadian Women Writing*. Edmonton: Longspoon / Newest, 1986.

Neumann, Erich. *The Great Mother*. Trans. Ralph Manheim. New York: Bollingen Foundation, 1955.

Nicholson, Linda J., ed. "Introduction." *Feminism/Postmodernism*. New York and London: Routledge, 1990.

Nicholson, Mervyn. "Food and Power: Homer, Carroll, Atwood and Others." *Mosaic* 20.3 (Summer 1987): 37–55.

Oates, Joyce Carol. "My Mother Would Rather Skate Than Scrub Floors." Ingersoll 69–85.

Onley, Gloria. "Power Politics in Bluebeard's Castle." *Poets and Critics: Essays from Canadian Literature 1966–1974*. Ed. George Woodcock. Toronto: Oxford UP, 1974. 191–214.

O'Donnell, Patrick and Robert Con Davis, ed. *Intertextuality and Contemporary American Fiction*. Baltimore: Johns Hopkins, 1989. 3–32.

———. "Introduction." O'Donnell and Davis. ix–xxii.

Orbach, Susie. *Fat is a Feminist Issue*. Feltham, England: Hamlyn, 1978.

Orenstein, Gloria Feman. "The Reemergence of the Archetype of the Great Goddess in Art by Contemporary Women." *Visibly Female: Feminism and Art Today*. Ed. Hilary Robinson. New York: Universe. 1988. 158–170.

Pachter, Charles. Conversation. September 1992, Toronto.

Page, P. K. "The Permanent Tourists." Atwood. *The New Oxford Book of Canadian Verse in English*. 186–87.

Page, Sheila. "Supermarket Survival: A Critical Analysis of Margaret Atwood's *The Edible Woman*." *Sphinx* 1 (1974): 9–19.

Patton, Marilyn. "'Lady Oracle': The Politics of the Body." *Ariel* 22.4 (October 1991): 29–48.

———. "Tourists and Terrorists: The Creation of Bodily Harm." *Papers on Language and Literature* 28.2 (Spring 1992): 150–73.

Paul, Lissa. "Changing Faces: Pictures of Women in Fairy Tales." The Family as Fictional Construct in Children's Literature, Division on Children's Literature. Modern Language Association Convention paper. Chicago, December 29, 1990.

Petersen, Nancy J. "'Bluebeard's Egg': Not Entirely a 'Grimm' Tale." Mendez-Egle. 131–38.

———. "Fairy Tale Elements in Margaret Atwood's Novels: Breaking the Magic Spell." M.A. Thesis, North Texas State University. University Microfilms, 1985.

Pfeiffer, John and *Life* editors. *The Cell*. Life Science Library. New York: Time, 1964.

Phelps, Ethel Johnston, ed. *Tatterhood and Other Tales*. Illus. by Pamela Baldwin Ford. New York: Feminist Press, 1978.

Piercy, Marge. "'Dear Frontiers': Letters from Women Fantasy and Science Fiction Writers." *Frontiers* 2 (1977), 62–65.

Plath, Sylvia. "Medusa." Gilbert and Gubar. *Norton Anthology.* 2209–10.

Powell, Michael, and Emeric Pressburger. Directors, producers, and scriptwriters. *The Red Shoes*. Great Britain, 1948.

Pratt, Annis. "Medusa in Canada." *Centennial Review* 31.1 (Winter 1987) 1–32.

———. "*Surfacing* and the Rebirth Journey." Davidson and Davidson. 139–57.

Propp, V. *Morphology of the Folktale*, rev. and ed. Louis A. Wagner. American Folklore Society Bibliographical and Special Series. Vol. 9. Austin: U of Texas P, 1968.

The Real Mother Goose. Chicago: Rand McNally, 1978.

Reaney, James. "The Third Eye: Jay Macpherson's *The Boatman*." *Canadian Literature* 3 (Winter 1960). 23–34.

Rich, Adrienne. "Compulsory Heterosexuality and Lesbian Existence." *Woman-Identified Women*. Ed. Trudy Darty and Sandee Potter. Palo Alto, CA: Mayfield, 1984.

———. *Of Woman Born: Motherhood as Experience and Institution*. New York: Norton, 1976.

———. "When We Dead Awaken: Writing as Re-Vision." Gilbert and Gubar. *Norton.* 2044–56.

Riedel, Ingrid. "Preface." Jacoby, Kast, and Riedel. vii–xi.

Rigney, Barbara Hill. *Margaret Atwood*. Totowa, NJ: Barnes and Noble, 1987.

Robbe-Grillet, Alain. *For a New Novel: Essays on Fiction*. New York: Grove, 1965.

Rooke, Constance. *Fear of the Open Heart: Essays on Contemporary Canadian Writing*. Toronto: Coach House, 1989.

Rooth, Anna Birgitta. *The Cinderella Cycle*. Folklore of the World Series. New York: Arno, 1980.

Rosenberg, Bruce. *Folklore and Literature: Rival Siblings*. Knoxville: U of Tennessee P, 1991.

Rosenberg, Jerome H. *Margaret Atwood*. Boston: Twayne, 1984.

Ross, Val. "I've Always Been Funny." *Daily Globe and Mail*, August 24, 1991. C1, C5.

Rubenstein, Roberta. "Nature and Nurture in Dystopia: *The Handmaid's Tale*." Van Spanckeren and Castro. 101–12.

———. *The Novelistic Vision of Doris Lessing: Breaking the Forms of Consciousness*. Urbana: U of Chicago P, 1979.

———. "Pandora's Box and Female Survival: Margaret Atwood's *Bodily Harm*." Rpt. McCombs 259–75.

Sandler, Linda. "Interview with Margaret Atwood." "Margaret Atwood: A Symposium," *The Malahat Review* 41 (January 1977): 7–27.

Sarton, May. "The Muse as Medusa." Gilbert and Gubar. *Norton* 1777.

Sartre, Jean-Paul. *Being and Nothingness*. Trans. Hazel E. Barnes. New York: Philosophical Library, 1956.

Scholes, Robert. *Semiotics and Interpretation*. New Haven: Yale UP, 1982.

Sciff-Zamaro, Roberta. "The Re/membering of the Female Power in 'Lady Oracle.'" *Canadian Literature* 112 (Spring 1987): 32–38.

Sexton, Anne. *Transformations*. Boston: Houghton Mifflin, 1971.

Shklovsky, Victor. "Art as Technique" and "Sterne's *Tristram Shandy*: Stylistic Commentary." *Russian Formalist Criticism: Four Essays*. Trans. Lee T. Lemon and Marion J. Reis. Lincoln: U of Nebraska P, 1965. 3–24, 25–60.

Sjoo, Monica, and Barbara Mor. *The Great Cosmic Mother: Rediscovering the Religion of the Earth*. San Francisco: Harper and Row, 1987.

Smith, Rowland. "Margaret Atwood and the City: Style and Substance in *Bodily Harm* and *Bluebeard's Egg*." *World Literature Written in English* 25.2 (1985): 252–64.

Spiller, Robert E., et al. *Literary History of the United States: History*. 4th ed. rev. New York: Macmillan, 1974.

Stewart, Grace. *A New Mythos: The Novel of the Artist as Heroine 1877–1977*. St. Albans, VT: Eden Press, 1979.

Stewart, Susan. *Nonsense: Aspects of Intertextuality in Folklore and Literature*. Baltimore and London: Johns Hopkins, 1978, 1979.

Stone, Kay. "The Misuses of Enchantment." *Women's Folklore, Women's Culture*. Ed. Rosan A. Jordan and Susan J. Kalcik. Philadelphia: U Pennsylvania P, 1985.

————. Rev. of *Don't Bet on the Prince: Contemporary Feminist Fairy Tales in North America and England. Journal of American Folklore* 101 (1988). 110–11.

————. "Things Walt Disney Never Told Us." *Women and Folklore*. Ed. Claire R. Farrer. Austin: U of Texas P, 1975. 42–50.

Stow, Glenys. "Nonsense as Social Commentary in *The Edible Woman*." *Journal of Canadian Studies. Revue d'etudes canadiennes* 23.3 (Fall 1988): 90–101.

Symons, Scott. "Atwood as Icon: A Meditation on the Public Persona of Our Lady of Control and Bondage." *Idler* No. 28 (May 1990): 36–39.

Tatar, Maria. *The Hard Facts of the Grimms' Fairy Tales*. Princeton: Princeton UP, 1987.

————. *Off With Their Heads: Fairy Tales and the Culture of Childhood*. Princeton: Princeton UP, 1992.

Tennyson, Alfred. *The Devil and the Lady and Unpublished Early Poems*. Ed. Charles Tennyson. Bloomington: Indiana U, 1964. 42–46.

Thompson, Stith. *The Folktale*. Berkeley, Los Angeles, London: U of California P, 1977.

————. *Motif-Index of Folk-Literature: A Classification of Narrative Elements in Folktales, Ballads, Myths, Fables, Mediaeval Romances, Exempla, Fabliaux, Jest-Books, and Local Legends*. 6 volumes. Revised and Enlarged Edition. Bloomington and Indianapolis: Indiana UP, 1955.

Tindall, W. Y. *James Joyce: His Way of Interpreting the Modern World*. New York: Scribner's, 1950.

Toronto Star. August 1, 1992.

Tostevin, Lola Lemire. *'Sophie*. Toronto: Coach House, 1988.

Toye, William. Spring 1988, Telephone Call.

Trinh, T. Minh-ha. *Woman, Native, Other: Writing Postcoloniality and Feminism*. Bloomington and Indianapolis: Indiana UP, 1989.

Van Spanckeren, Kathryn. "Magic in the Novels of Margaret Atwood." Mendez-Egle. 1–13.

————. "Shamanism in the Works of Margaret Atwood." Van Spanckeren and Castro. 183–204.

Van Spanckeren, Kathryn, and Jan Garden Castro, eds. *Margaret Atwood: Vision and Forms*. Carbondale: S Illinois UP, Spring 1988.

Vinaver, Eugéne. *Form and Meaning in Medieval Romance*. Cambridge, England: Modern Humanities Research Assn., 1966.

————. *The Rise of Romance*. New York: Oxford UP, 1971.

Vitale, Tom. "Margaret Atwood Reads Excerpt from *Bodily Harm* and Talks about Politics and the Writer and Why She Writes." *A Moveable Feast*. No. 1. Tape recording. 30 minutes. n.d.

Von Franz, Marie Louise. *An Introduction to the Interpretation of Fairytales*. Dallas, TX: Spring Publications, 1970.

————. *Problems of the Feminine in Fairy Tales*. Irving, TX: Spring Publications, 1972.

————. *Shadow and Evil in Fairy Tales*. Dallas, TX: Spring Publications, 1987.

Vonnegut, Kurt, Jr. *Breakfast of Champions*. New York: Delta, 1973.

Waelti-Walters, Jennifer. "On Princesses: Fairy Tales, Sex Roles and Loss of Self." *Fairy Tales and the Female Imagination*. Montreal: Eden, 1982.

Walker, Barbara G. *The Woman's Dictionary of Symbols and Sacred Objects*. San Francisco: Harper and Row, 1988.

————. *The Woman's Encyclopedia of Myths and Secrets*. San Francisco: Harper and Row, 1983.

Wall, Kathleen. *The Callisto Myth from Ovid to Atwood: Initiation and Rape in Literature*. Kingston: McGill-Queen's UP, 1988.

————. "Healing the Divisions: Goddess Figures in Two Works of Twentieth-Century Literature." *Goddesses in Religions and Modern Debate*. Ed. Larry W. Hurtado. Atlanta: Scholars Press, 1990. 205–26.

Waller, Margaret. "An Interview with Julia Kristeva." Trans. Richard Macksay. O'Donnell and Davis. 280–93.

Wehr, Demaris S. "Religious and Social Dimensions of Jung's Concept of the Archetype: A Feminist Perspective." *Feminist Archetypal Theory: Interdisciplinary Re-Visions of Jungian Thought*. Ed. Estella Lauter and Carol Schreier Rupprecht. Knoxville: U of Tennessee, 1985.

Weir, Lorraine. "Meridians of Perception: A Reading of *The Journals of Susanna Moodie*." Davidson and Davidson. 69–80.

Welsh-Ovcharov, Bogomila. *Charles Pachter*. Toronto: McClelland and Stewart, 1992.

Wilson, Sharon R. "Bluebeard's Forbidden Room: Gender Images in Margaret Atwood's Visual and Literary Art." *American Review of Canadian Studies* 16.4 (Winter 1986) 385–97.

————. "Camera Images in Margaret Atwood's Novels." *Margaret Atwood: Reflection and Reality*. Mendez-Egle. 29–57.

————. "Deconstructing Text and Self: Mirroring in Atwood's *Surfacing* and Beckett's *Molloy*." *Journal of Popular Literature* 3 (Spring/Summer 1987): 53–69.

————. "The Doctrine of Organic Unity: E. R. Eddison and the Romance Tradition." *Extrapolation* 25.1 (Spring 1984): 12–19.

————. "Eyes and I's." *International Literature in English: The Major Writers*. Ed. Robert Ross. New York: Garland, 1991.

————. "Fairy-Tale Cannibalism in *The Edible Woman*." *Cooking by the Book: Food in Literature and Culture*. Ed. Mary Ann Schofield. Bowling Green: Popular Press, 1989. 78–88.

———. "The Fragmented Self in *Lady Oracle.*" *Commonwealth Novel in English* 1.1 (1982): 50–85.

———. "'The Golden Phoenix' and Other Fairy-Tale Intertext in Margaret Atwood's *Surfacing.*" XI Annual Commonwealth Literature and Language Conference in German-Speaking Countries. Aachen, West Germany and Liege, Belgium, June 16–19, 1988.

———. "'The Juniper Tree' and Other Fairy-Tale Elements in *Surfacing.*" The Association for Canadian Studies in the United States. Montreal, Canada, October 8, 1987.

———. "A Note on Margaret Atwood's Visual Art and *Bodily Harm.*" *Antipodes: A North American Journal of Australian Literature* 4.2 (Winter 1990): 111–16.

———. "Off the Path to Grandma's House: Offred and the Wolf in *The Handmaid's Tale.*" Ninth Commonwealth Literature Conference. Laufen, West Germany, June 1986.

———. *The Self-Conscious Narrator and His Twentieth-Century Faces.* PhD Diss., University of Wisconsin, 1976. Ann Arbor, MI: UMI, 1976.

———. "Sexual Politics in Margaret Atwood's Visual Art." Van Spanckeren and Castro. 205–14 and eight unnumbered pages.

———. "*Turning Life Into Art: Bodily Harm's* Life-Tourist." *Studies in Canadian Literature* 10.1 and 2 (1985):136–45.

Wilson, Sharon R., Thomas Friedman, and Shannon Hengen, ed. *Approaches to Teaching Atwood's The Handmaid's Tale and Other Works.* New York: Modern Language Association, 1994.

Woodcock, George. "Margaret Atwood: Poet as Novelist." *The Canadian Novel in the Twentieth-Century.* Ed. George Woodcock. Toronto: McClelland and Stewart, 1975. 312–27.

———. "Metamorphosis and Survival: Notes on the Recent Poetry of Margaret Atwood." *Northern Spring: The Flowering of Canadian Literature.* Vancouver/Toronto: Douglas and McIntyre, 1987. 266–84.

Woodward, Calvin. "Margaret Atwood a Very Lively 'Bug on a Pin.'" *The Toronto Star.* August 15, 1990. B3.

Woolf, Virginia. "Professions for Women." *Collected Essays.* 4 vols. New York: Harcourt, Brace, and World, 1967.

———. *A Room of One's Own.* New York: Harcourt, Brace and Company, 1929.

Yearsley, Macleod. *The Folklore of the Fairy-Tale.* London: Watts, 1924.

York, Lorrane M. "The Habits of Language: Uniform(ity), Transgression and Margaret Atwood." *Canadian Literature* 126 (Autumn 1990): 6–19.

Zipes, Jack. *The Brothers Grimm: From Enchanted Forests to the Modern World.* New York: Routledge, 1988.

————. *Don't Bet on the Prince: Contemporary Feminist Fairy Tales in North America and England.* New York: Methuen, 1986.

————. *Fairy Tales and the Art of Subversion: The Classical Genre for Children and the Process of Civilization.* New York: Methuen, 1988.

————. "'Little Red Riding Hood' as Male Creation and Projection." Dundes, *Little Red.* 122–28.

————. *The Trials and Tribulations of Little Red Riding Hood.* South Hadley, MA: Bergin and Garvey, 1983.

————, trans. and ed. *Beauties, Beasts and Enchantment: Classic French Fairy Tales.* New York: New American Library, 1989.

————, trans. *The Complete Tales of the Brothers Grimm.* New York: Bantam, 1987.

————, ed. *Spells of Enchantment: The Wondrous Fairy Tales of Western Culture.* New York: Viking, 1991.

Index